Dear John

with best wishes

Dave

THE FAILURE OF MARXISM

For my parents, Ian and Vera Campbell

In apology for the time it took me to realise that their disregard for the theories discussed in this book represents the theories' failure, not theirs

The Failure of Marxism

The Concept of Inversion in Marx's Critique of Capitalism

DAVID CAMPBELL

Dartmouth

Aldershot • Brookfield USA • Singapore • Sydney

Published by
Dartmouth Publishing Company Limited
Gower House
Croft Road
Aldershot
Hants GU11 3HR
England

Dartmouth Publishing Company
Old Post Road
Brookfield
Vermont 05036
USA

British Library Cataloguing in Publication Data
Campbell, David
    Failure of Marxism:Concept of Inversion
in Marx's Critique of Capitalism
    I. Title
    335.4

Library of Congress Cataloging-in-Publication Data
Campbell, David, 1958-
    The failure of Marxism : the concept of inversion in Marx's
critique of capitalism / David Campbell.
        p.   cm.
    "Socio-legal series".
    Includes bibliographical references and index.
    ISBN 1-85521-692-2
    1. Socialism. 2. Hegal, Georg Wilhelm Friedrich, 1770-1831.
3. Immanence (Philosophy). 4. Marx, Karl, 1818-1883. 5. Saving and
investment. 6. Capitalism. 7. Corporate reorganizations.
I. Title.
HX36.C28   1995
335.4'12–dc20   95-20532
                                                                          CIP

ISBN 1 85521 692 2
Printed in Great Britain by Ipswich Book Co. Ltd., Ipswich, Suffolk.

Liberation from capitalism is liberation from the rule of the economy. When the autonomy of the economy has ended, "political economy" as an independent science also disappears.
Gyorgy Lukács

It is also true that Marxist theory contains the notion of inexorable laws of society - although here it is precisely the *abolition* of these *oppressive* laws that is the aim.
Herbert Marcuse

Contents

Acknowledgments

This book is composed of three principal sections: one on Hegel's views on immanent critique, one on Marx's views on capital accumulation and one on the corporate restructuring of the capitalist economy. The majority of the work on the first two of these sections was carried out principally in the Department of Sociology of the University of Edinburgh. Work on the third section, and the overall revision of the book, has been carried out principally at the Centre for Socio-legal Studies of the University of Oxford. I should like to thank all the past and present staff and students of both of these institutions who have helped me and commented upon this work. I have also worked on this book at the Department of Law, University of Central Lancashire; the Department of Law, Leeds Metropolitan University; the Department of Law, City University of Hong Kong and the School of Financial Studies and Law, Sheffield Hallam University, and I should like to thank those members of the administrative staffs of those Universities who have assisted me with this work. I should also like to thank Stephen Woerner for checking the manuscript and Tim Moore, Andrew Thomas and Paul Watson for their invaluable help in making accessible sources in languages other than English.

I should like to take this opportunity to acknowledge a wider debt to three people in particular. It is particularly fit that this book appear in a series edited by Phil Thomas, for without Phil's friendship and support over almost twenty years it is unlikely that I would have been in the position to write this book. Don Harris has done a great deal to provide me with an environment in which I could write over the past seven years. John Holmwood has read and reread all of the script of this book many times and his comments have been invaluable. If I may adopt an acknowledgment which I have seen elsewhere but upon which I cannot improve: Holmwood is the godfather of this book.

Parts of this work have earlier appeared in another form. The first two sections of the book are based on *On Inverting Hegel*, Phd thesis, University of Edinburgh,

1985. Chapters 1 and 2 in part draw on "Rationality, Democracy and Freedom in Marxist Critiques of Hegel's Philosophy of Right" (1985) vol 28 *Inquiry*, pp 59-74. Chapters 10 and 11 draw on 'Why Regulate the Modern Corporation? The Failure of Market Failure', in J McCahery *et al*, eds, *Corporate Accountability and Control*, Oxford, Oxford University Press, 1993, pp 103-31. I should like to thank those who hold the copyright in this material for their permission to use it here.

Abbreviations

The following abbreviations are used in the footnotes and bibliography. Full references are given in the bibliography.

AD
Engels, Anti-Dühring

BP
Hegel, *Phenomenology of Mind* (Baillie Edition)

C
Marx, 'The Commodity'

C1
Marx, *Capital*, vol 1

C2
Marx, *Capital*, vol 2 (Penguin edn)

C2(LW)
Marx, *Capital*, vol 2 (Lawrence and Wishart edn)

C3
Marx, *Capital*, vol 3

CHPL
Marx, 'Contribution to the Critique of Hegel's Philosophy of Law'

CHPLI
Marx, 'Contribution to the Critique of Hegel's Philosophy of Law. Introduction'

CMNABP
Marx, 'Critical Marginal Notes on the Article "The King of Prussia and Social Reform", by a Prussian'

COGP
Marx, 'Critique of the Gotha Programme'

CPE
Marx, 'A Contribution to the Critique of Political Economy'

CW
Marx and Engels, *Collected Works*

DBFS
Hegel, *The Distinction Between Fichte's and Schelling's System of Philosophy*

DN
Engels, 'Dialectics of Nature'

EB
Marx, 'The Eighteenth Brumaire of Louis Bonaparte'

EM
Marx, 'Economic Manuscripts of 1857-8' (*Grundrisse*)

EPM
Marx, 'Economic and Philosophical Manuscripts' (*Paris Manuscripts*)

EN
Marx, *Ethnological Notebooks*

FK
Hegel, *Faith and Knowledge*

GI
Mary and Engels, 'The German Ideology'

HF
Mary and Engels, 'The Holy Family'

L
Hegel, *Logic*

LF
Engels, 'Ludwig Feuerbach and the End of Classical German Philosophy'

LHP1
Hegel, *Lectures on the History of Philosophy*, vol 1

LHP3
Hegel, *Lectures on the History of Philosophy*, vol 3

LPEG
Hegel, 'Lectures on the Proofs of the Existence of God'

MCP
Marx and Engels, 'Manifesto of the Communist Party'

NW
Marx, 'Notes on Adolph Wagner'

PH
Hegel, *Philosophy of History*

PM
Hegel, *Philosophy of Mind*

PN
Hegel, *Philosophy of Nature*

PP
Marx, 'The Poverty of Philosophy'

PPE
Ricardo, 'On the Principles of Political Economy and Taxation'

PR
Hegel, *Philosophy of Right*

PS
Hegel, *Phenomenology of Spirit*

RIPP
Marx, 'Results of the Intermediate Process of Production'

SL
Hegel, *Science of Logic*

SUS
Engels, 'Socialism: Utopia n of Scientific?'

SW
Marx and Engels, *Selected Works in One Volume*

TF
Marx, 'Theses on Feuerbach'

TSV1
Marx, *Theories of Surplus Value*, vol 1

TSV2
Marx, *Theories of Surplus Value*, vol 2

TSV3
Marx, *Theories of Surplus Value*, vol 3

VF
Marx, 'The Value-form'

W
Marx, 'Wages'

WLC
Marx, 'Wage-labour and Capital'

WN
Smith, *The Wealth of Nations*

WPP
Marx, 'Wages, Price and Profit'

1 The Failure of Marxism and the Problem of Inverting Hegel

The fundamental issue faced by all intellectual histories of marxism has been the role to give, or to deny, Hegel in the formation of Marx's views. The assessment of Hegel's influence has been a theme of commentaries upon Marx's writings traceable to Marx's own brief efforts of self-exposition and to Engels' attempts systematically to state historical materialism. Indeed, it is the key to the character of interpretations of Marx's work. The reasons for this are clear. When looking at Marx's texts we are immediately presented with a great number of hegelian motifs. Determining how far these extend into the substance of those texts is an obvious task, and one which both Engels and Marx suggested must be undertaken.

Marx is the author of *Capital* and there is, as far as we now know, *no* possibility of correctly understanding the modern world that does not accept the core argument of that book. This is a remarkable thing to say, but nevertheless Hegel's stature can hardly be said to be determined merely by the use Marx made of him. Hegel's encyclopaedic thought has made a lasting impression on virtually every area it has touched, and in fact the closer one moves towards Marx's concerns, the deeper is that impression. It will be the argument of this work that the interpretation of Marx must begin by recognising that Marx's significance is more determined by the way he took up Hegel than is Hegel's by the way he was taken up by Marx. It should be able to go without saying that this is not to disparage Marx. It is to ask for the adoption of a correct attitude to his work.

Marx's status of course lies in his being the principal source of the theory of socialism as the analysis and solution of the social problems of bourgeois society. This status rests on the development of hegelian themes in socialism's intended resolution of the contradiction of the individual and the social that distinguishes bourgeois society and is the source of its problems. Hegel is to the forefront of the criticism of alienation that faces social theory, and indeed bourgeois society, as its principal task, for he shows that the solution of the difficulties of establishing rational political life in that society turns on carrying through that criticism. Let me briefly expand this link between the political philosophies of Hegel and Marx.

Arising out of the development of the capitalist economy which generalises the commercial exchange of commodities by individual parties,[1] bourgeois society has as its central feature a paradoxical denial of its own social character. The principle of individuality is paramount in a social order which is atomistic in that the individuals within it aim their conduct at the satisfaction of their own narrowly personal desires.[2] The social contract as the political order of bourgeois society is established to prevent the generalised competitive pursuit of desire leading to chaos akin to a state of nature.[3] However, necessary common functions such as the basic maintenance of order are relegated to a state which is outside of the main body of civil society, and whose confinement to these bounds is jealously maintained[4] in order to preserve a freedom identified with as large as possible a margin of individual licence.[5] For though the social contract implies conscious political life, generating a basic impulse towards the recognition of the rights of others, including the right to participate in the political life set up by the contract, this is set against a civil society which remains predicated upon selfish individual desire. In this situation, of the opposition of individuality and sociality,[6] neither personal morality[7] nor general political participation[8] can be secured.

Though it may be sought to make duty[9] and respect for others[10] central to bourgeois ethics, the argument for this on an individualistic basis can refer only to the necessity for the individual to perform as obliged by the social contract in order to secure her or his well-being.[11] Limits to essentially selfish actions have to be set, lest the pursuit of desire have disastrously undesirable consequences, but the motive of acting whilst acknowledging this in civil society remains just the same as if in a state of nature, narrow self-interest. This sets the principle of those ethics on a self-interestedly prudential - indeed explicitly utilitarian[12] - basis rather than on a moral ground. Consequently, in bourgeois society the observation of essential duties is overwhelmingly a matter of coercion[13] by a system of justice rather than a question of virtue.[14]

Equally, though democratic aspiration is central to bourgeois political thought, commitment to the general will is beset with reservations over whether it can ever mean the will of all or the will of all only when they adopt socially responsible positions.[15] This restriction on the possibility of mass democracy is set out by bourgeois society as part of its political positing of that possibility. It is not that human beings are not the angels they would have to be were this political arrangement to work.[16] It is that in acting under the selfish ethics of commercial society, they eschew the responsibilities of citizenship.[17] With democracy limited in this way, the state and the mass remain divorced. What is at issue in these profound difficulties of modern political philosophy, in the separation of state and civil society, is the alienation of the individual from social concerns. Hegel shows this separation not to be the character of human life as such but the product of the alienation of social self-consciousness.

The possibility of non-alienated life figures in Hegel's developed political views as his concept of the state. The state appears as the third of a set of forms of "ethical life" (we should take this term to mean general patterns of social relationships). Hegel intends this triadic arrangement to be representative of the substance of his discussion of the state, which is conceived of as an, as it were, syllogistic resolution of two valuable and yet at first glance opposed components of non-alienated life contained in the first two types of ethical life he distinguishes - the family and civil society.[18]

Hegel identifies in the family, which we may take as representing broadly traditional social relationships,[19] an immediate unity of the members expressed in a feeling of love and mutual concern based on sexual relationships.[20] Though characterised by unity, the family is an inadequate form of ethical life because this unity is one of immediate feeling. In not being consciously established but in being an unquestioned given, the unity of the family intrinsically is restrictive of freedom. In the immediacy of their unity, the members of the family do not develop their individualities but can figure only as, precisely, members of the family. In imposing its unity through roles which prevent the development of individuality, the family's ties are repressive.[21]

In reference to the individualism of bourgeois society, Hegel calls the second form of ethical life he distinguishes civil society.[22] Hegel recognises the satisfaction of personal desires as the principle of this society.[23] A social order predicated upon this type of narrow selfishness obviously is imbued with very profound contradictions, and of course there must be some paradoxical cohesion of the atomistic components of this society for the society to exist.[24] However, Hegel rejected as radically insufficient the idea, central to apologies for bourgeois society since at least[25] the *Fable of the Bees*,[26] that it is individually selfish actions that best guarantee the common good. It is not that, in what would be merely a return to Hobbes, Hegel insists on the intrinsically destructive qualities of selfish acts. Rather he finds the mysterious way in which the transmutation of individual selfishness into common good is to take place, summed up in Smith's image of the invisible hand,[27] to be an inadequate form of ethical life. Restricted by the state, the pursuit of desire which would lead to chaos in a state of nature is to lead to an unprecedented accumulation of wealth in civil society.[28] But the invisible hand's transformation of potentially destructive competition into the provision of general welfare is done, precisely, invisibly. Classical political economy, the laws of which seem of a piece with natural laws,[29] and its corollary in liberal political theory, describe processes which are regular only by virtue of being mysterious,[30] that is to say, alienated.

Classical political economy and its underpinnings in the emergent social theory show social influences on individuals' conduct inevitably to exist, even in civil society, but these influences gain their power in civil society precisely by not being generally recognised. The individuals in civil society in fact labour under unacknowledged restraints on their freedom. It is not that if they could be purely selfish they would be free. In the first place, there is no reason to suppose unmediated pursuit of desire, with its surrender of self-imposed morality to naturalistic impulse, to be freedom.[31] Furthermore, envisaging this impossible asocial condition involves a distorted idea of freedom stemming from the inadequacies of civil society's form of the relationship of the individual and the social.[32] In having it only mysteriously represented to them that they cannot be wholly selfish, members of civil society lack self-consciousness of what they actually are, social beings, and are thereby unfree. Whilst social influences are mysterious, their supposed absence is taken to be freedom. Society, represented in bourgeois society by the state, can be felt to be only a constraint, because the mistaken notion of individuality at work here posits society not as the condition of individuality but as its negation.[33]

In his more formal fashion, Hegel presents all this by saying that civil society contains a valuable moment of particularity as the family contains one of unity. Both moments are expressed only tendentiously, indeed antithetically, as they stand, and are thereby inadequate. This formal way of speaking tends rather to obscure the indispensable social content which gives concrete meaning to Hegel's thought. However, bearing this in mind, we can see the way that the state is to take its place amongst all that is rational by having a syllogistic form.[34]

The state is the rational form of ethical life because in it individuals consciously recognise their sociality, or to put this the other way around, mutually recognise the free individualities of each other.[35] Individual selfishness, with its implicit treating of others only as objects to be manipulated for the satisfaction of one's desires, involves the negation of other individuals' status as equally significant. This may be morally distasteful,[36] but more than this, as it is only in social relationships that we may develop our own individualities, atomistic individualism is flatly mistaken in its representation of what individuality may be.[37] The mistake is based in the alienation of the social basis of individuality. In the state, the truth of sociality is formalised in obedience to laws that are rational in that they take a universal rather than a narrowly particular perspective, and thus express the non-alienated social conditions of individuality. Freedom is thereby achieved, not as the self-contradictory goal of generalised selfishness, but as the proper understanding and consequent acceptance of socialised individuality or individualised sociality.[38]

As we have seen, Hegel's analysis of bourgeois society is in terms of the division of civil society and state,[39] which for him quite bluntly represents a division between the pursuit of narrowly individual desires and the conscious development of universal perspectives. Though civil society generates certain tendencies towards universality,[40] it is in the state that these are actualised. Hegel takes the perspective of a state which he regards as essentially rational[41] in order to criticise civil society. The character of Marx's own views was founded by a rejection of Hegel's expectations for the state as unfoundedly speculative, and a conclusion that the empirically extant bourgeois state, rather than Hegel's ideal statement, is itself subject to particular interests to such a degree as to prevent it from being concerned with the general social interest.[42] Marx's developed explanation of alienation is put forward not from the perspective of a state beyond civil society but as an expansion of his awareness of particularistic influences on the state into a general location of legal relations and forms of state within civil society - the anatomy of which is to be sought through political economy.[43] This is to be a materialism, but in a social sense defined by its polemical context. Marx comes to the conclusion that it is because in the capitalist economy production is carried out on an unplanned, seemingly independent basis that civil society posits individualism in opposition to sociality,[44] and the state therefore has to be the distinct seat of the necessary and yet alienated social concerns in bourgeois society.[45]

However, in *Capital* Marx does not see capitalistic economic forces as only disruptive of political rationality but goes on to claim that they also - and ultimately more powerfully - foster it through the inner socialisation of capitalist production. The fundamentally economic restrictions on social self-consciousness and the ethics and democracy it would make possible are undercut by a development of civil society itself as the capitalist economy generates its own obsolescence. It is this idea of the criticism of alienation that is the import of the notion of socialisation. For Marx, socialism is a resource, a development grounded in tendencies of extant civil society that will make non-alienated freedom possible.

The crucial feature of this freedom is that it should possess no utopian quality. What, for example, is absolute freedom for Hegel? When, looking for the secret, one opens Hegel's books at their ends and begins with chapters such as "Absolute Knowing", one is very disappointed. For what one finds is no more than the histories discussed in the earlier parts of the books but now understood for what they truly were, historical creations. Absolute knowing is self-consciousness of social determination, and absolute freedom is doing what we will in the non-alienated condition of possession of such knowledge. Marx's typical refusal to attempt any detailed account of the nature of communist society, and his consequent poor opinion of Comte,[46] follows from his own similarly anti-utopian idea of socialism as a present resource.

Such criticism of present alienated conditions immediately raises the problem of justifying the distance one takes from those conditions when claiming to be able to make that criticism. This problem can be addressed at the level of political and social analysis, and it was at this level that Marx himself principally took up this issue in Hegel.[47] It will be argued that Marx's economics are entirely formed, and have a defensible meaning, within this project of the criticism of alienation. This is so not least because, as Marx himself knew,[48] Hegel is addressing social theory's principal task of settling with the ethical legacy of political economy, a task which Marx himself thought essential. Now, almost every claim made for Hegel and Marx in the above account would be fundamentally contested at the moment. However, I shall not directly attempt to defend the basic necessity of the critique of alienation, although I will make very serious reservations about the way Hegel and Marx carry it out. I will accept this necessity in broad outline and principally address the acceptability of the epistemology of social scientific explanation that could generate such a necessity.

Hegel explicitly takes up the justification of the criticism of alienation at the level of epistemologically securing a distance from alienated beliefs upon which any discussion of the institutional character of alienated and non-alienated conditions turns. The securing of a non-alienated perspective and using it to address and correct, or as he puts it "invert", alienated beliefs is the task of Hegel's first major work, the *Phenomenology of Spirit*, which he regarded as a necessary introduction to his philosophical system. The whole point of "phenomenology" as Hegel renders it is that immersion in given phenomenal beliefs and describing an immanent dialectic between them and their essential non-alienated truth will accomplish the inversion of those beliefs in a way rationally convincing to those who earlier held them.

There is no similarly powerful or even concerted effort epistemologically to secure critique in Marx. However, the present work will examine the intellectual relationship of Marx and Hegel at both the political and particularly epistemological levels of their criticism of alienation and will argue that Marx substantially assimilated the thrust of the hegelian phenomenological dialectic. The work will be conducted through a detailed comparison of the 'Introduction' to the *Phenomenology of Spirit* and Marx's *Capital*. The 'Introduction' is one of Hegel's most important programmatic statements of his dialectical method; *Capital* is the culmination of Marx's attempt to produce substantive results by the use of that method as he understood it. In the similarities and dissimilarities of these works there lies the key to the comprehension of Marx's work.

In so doing, I will take up the most prominent line of inquiry hitherto adopted in the interpretation of Marx's relationship to Hegel. This is the line of evaluating Marx's own idea, though utilising Hegel's locution, of his having "inverted" Hegel as an account of their relationship. This is a recurrent theme not only in the exegetical writings of Engels and Marx but also throughout those interpretations of Marx's work, amongst which we must again count the later Engels' writings, which have in fact been marxism's knowledge of this part of its intellectual history up to well into the latter half of this century.[49] These interpretations have pictured that history as Marx's taking over valuable elements of Hegel's philosophical method, but "inverting" its unacceptable content of commitment to an ideal state in order to give the materialist - or sociological, or humanist, or historical, or economic, etc. - construction of the class struggle.

One might peremptorily single out, apart from *Anti-Dühring* (and works to which this and other of Engels' later writings rather directly gave rise such as Plekhanov's *The Development of the Monist View of History*), Lenin's *Philosophical Notebooks*, Lukács' *History and Class Consciousness* and Korsch's *Marxism and Philosophy*, Gramsci's *Prison Notebooks*, Stalin's *Dialectical and Historical Materialism*, Marcuse's *Reason and Revolution* and Lefebvre's *Dialectical Materialism* as perhaps, after their different fashions, particularly significant expositions of these interpretations. Despite its length, this list certainly is not exhaustive, but it does serve to illustrate a point crucially at issue here. These are obviously diverse and divergent, indeed in many respects explicitly opposed, interpretations, containing readings of Marx's work as the bases of such a wide variety of historical marxisms that it seems illegitimate to join them even in this clearly collective noun. Nevertheless, when taken, as I think it legitimate to do on these matters of intellectual history, as a whole, they represent a common crisis in the understanding of Marx's work and its relationship to Hegel. For, as we can now recognise, if Hegel's thought was unacceptably determinist, then a Hegel inverted or a Hegel with the rational kernel of materialist method extracted from within the mystical shell of idealist system would nonetheless still unacceptably be Hegel, though now to be called by another name - Marx.[50] If I may again be allowed a merely illustrative list, I would link Della Volpe's *Logic as a Positive (Historical) Science*, Althusser's *For Marx*, Zeleny's *The Method of Marx*, and the second part of Colletti's *Marxism and Hegel* with the successful criticism of the representation of Marx's relationship to Hegel as a mere inversion or change of subject, from, say, spirit to class struggle or growth of productive forces. Indeed these writings and others have firmly established the necessity of a radical discontinuity of method between Hegel and Marx were the latter to have laid the foundations of an adequate science of history and of a politics which is informed by that science. We clearly are faced with a conflict of interpretations around the notion of " inverting" Hegel, and a conflict which involves a special hermeneutic difficulty.[51] For if we accept, as I think we must, the criticisms of the adequacy of the metaphor of "inversion", then this conflict amounts to a paradox in respect of the two main figures who put forward this metaphor - Engels and Marx themselves.

First, consider the position of the later Engels. The difficulty in assessing the significance of Engels' later contributions has already been registered above by these writings being, as it were, counted twice. There are immediate obstacles[52] to any attempt[53] to deny or severely to restrict Engels' authority to speak for Marx, which certainly is necessary if Marx is to be separated from the metaphor of inversion, since the later Engels' attempts to systematise Marxist philosophy revolve around the idea of Marx and himself having inverted Hegel. There are explicit textual cross-references, spanning more than fifty years, between the preface to the *Critique of Political Economy*, the foreword to *Ludwig Feuerbach* and *The German Ideology*[54] and between *Socialism: Utopian and Scientific* and *The Holy Family*.[55] These should bring to mind the extent to which Engels' efforts were the explication of work of the period up to 1847 upon which, after Marx, he (Engels) was uniquely privileged to comment. Furthermore, there is Marx's continued support for the later Engels' work, which is exemplified by the former's encouragement of, assistance with and approval of *Anti-Dühring*.[56]

This leads by a circular route to the second figure who presents especial difficulty for the rejection of the metaphor of inversion; the figure of Marx himself. Not only did Marx unto his death repeatedly affirm his debt to Hegel, but furthermore he did so in the very terms which have made the inversion metaphor of central importance. He famously expressed this debt in this way in the afterword to the second German edition of the first volume of *Capital*.[57] He also saw fit to reproduce this rare published methodological explication of his principal achievement as an explicit commentary, though allowing the omission of the interesting metaphor of kernel and shell, in the last edition of volume one he saw in print, the French edition of 1873.[58]

I do not believe that these hermeneutic difficulties will allow of resolution if treated in a basically negative fashion, as largely a problem of determining when Marx was able to free himself from hegelian influence. In so far as their interpretations involve a Marx at his best when wholly opposed to Hegel, this is the problem for both Althusser and Colletti. The former has devoted most attention to this. It is not merely that if posed in this way these difficulties must, as we have seen, on the direct testimony of Marx himself flatly be denied a resolution before the mid- to late-1870s. This has compelled Althusser nonsensically to withdraw his claim of an epistemological break with Hegel not merely from 1845 but behind *Capital* itself to the *Critique of the Gotha Programme* and the *Notes on Wagner*.[59] It is that such a break leaves substantially unanswered the vital question of how did Marx accomplish his own development in work earlier than that which is approved?.[60] Althusser's fetishistic pursuit of internal "coherence" or "rigour"[61] as the mark of adequacy in Marx's writings necessarily cuts off any such question. The break in fact presumes, on the basis of Althusser's own rejection of Hegel, that Hegel's presence in Marx's later writings can be treated as an incidental survival.[62]

After his achievement of the preliminary indication of the necessary existence in Marx of a fundamental departure in method from Hegel, particularly in 'Contradiction and Overdetermination', Althusser seems to have proceeded to evaluate Marx's works to determine how far they measure up to the conclusions of that essay. It is in this vein that those who follow Althusser have extended what recognisably is his research programme in social philosophy. Nevertheless, it is wholly incorrect to treat this sort of effort as an investigation of how Marx himself accomplished the indicated departure, and in fact to do so necessarily involves misunderstanding the character of Marx's own intellectual development. Hence Althusser's interpretations of, and even detailed commentaries on, Marx's writings contain perhaps the most fantastic infelicities that can be found in any reading at all sympathetic to Marx.[63] Discussion of whether these are even remotely plausible interpretations is so absurd that it can be conducted only in an exasperated or outraged tone.[64]

Althusser's contributions do, I believe, cast light on certain of the basic thrusts of Marx's work in an interesting way,[65] but by no means explain the genesis or fully describe the significance of these within Marx himself, and thus in the end are inadequate even to what is approved within those writings. That is to say, as has now often enough been said,[66] that Althusser's substantive accounts of ideology and of capitalist institutions fall far beneath the positions won by Marx himself. As Althusser would be the first to insist, it is only within an entire body of thought that any particular aspect of it may be fully understood, and this tells us a great deal about the replacement of the metaphor of "inversion" with that of "break". It is clearly the case that Althusser's marxism requires that hegelian influence be eradicated. But it is only if this is quite falsely presented as Marx's own thought that the *Critique of the Gotha Programme*, one of the principal sources of Marx's developed political formulations of alienation and its transcendence,[67] and the *Notes on Wagner*, the most extensive of Marx's defences of the method of volume one of *Capital* especially in respect of its debt to Hegel,[68] can be said to be totally free of hegelian influence. Equally, it is only upon this basis that the section on 'The Fetishism of Commodities and Its Secret', which is the key to Marx's political economy in its summary of the critique of value as the critique of the alienation of capitalist production,[69] can be regarded as a flagrant and harmful hegelian survival.[70] But this is to seriously violate the boundary between critical exposition and independent criticism, and Althusser can, I think, be severely censured for not paying sufficient attention to this.

Much the same could be said of Colletti's wholly arbitrary, from the point of view of interpretation, attempt to link Marx and Kant directly, to the exclusion of Hegel. Having suppressed the Hegel in Marx, Althusser was driven to seek the philosophical sources of Marx's thought in other antecedents, and alighted upon Spinoza.[71] Colletti's recasting of Marx's intellectual ancestry is more explicit, though the evidence of Marx's direct indebtedness to the figure chosen - Kant - is even more slight than in the case of Spinoza. It seems as if, at whatever cost of violence to Marx's own clear testimony with respect to his evaluation of German idealism and the English and French sources of his materialism, Colletti felt compelled to press on with the challenge to the heuristic value of the metaphor of inversion until he had completely bridged Hegel. He thereby directly connects Marx to the materialist intent in Kant's defence of phenomenal knowledge. The epistemological result[72] is indeed hardly an advance upon the unsatisfactory ontological status of the to-be-known in Kant, and it certainly cannot represent Marx.[73]

There is a further paradox here, though I think a more instructive one than the earlier. I can find but little trace of Marx's ever complex conjunctural analyses in the simple functionalism[74] of Althusser's analysis of ideology,[75] nor of Marx's materialism in the idealist relativism[76] set out in Colletti's introduction to Bernstein or in his essay on 'Marxism: Science or Revolution?'.[77] One is lead back to Marx because there is a clear gap between the departure from Hegel in Marx which has been indicated and the explicitly anti-hegelian marxisms which have been put forward as rigorous marxism fully cognisant of this departure. This is particularly important because the gap shows to the detriment of the latter.

However, in recognising this, it is vital to retain the positive contributions which have been made. We must now begin with the recognition that it is fruitless to regard Marx's relationship to Hegel as that of a simple inversion. In so far as it fails to do this, Timpanaro's valuable defence of, and building upon, the significance of the philosophy of the later Engels[78] tends to merge with complete acceptance of or even accentuation of the mechanistic tone of that philosophy,[79] and is thus in severe danger of returning to certain of the positions of the Second International which least merit revival. For marxist philosophy to have to free itself from these positions once again would indeed be a farce.

Althusser continues to have a remarkable status in the present situation. There is much in his work that is gimmickry, but I believe it unarguable that he gives formalised marxism after the dialectical materialist fashion its best, and, it would thankfully seem, final expression. The rejection of Althusser's work implies the rejection of all marxism of this type. This is no bad thing at all, but the possibility that such a root and branch cutting away of a very strong line of the interpretation of Marx's work must cut away at the plausibility of that work itself must be considered.[80] It would be wrong were such fundamental reconsideration not pursued and "marxism" must now be called into question as any sort of clear research programme in the social sciences at all. This work is written in the belief that rejection of marxism in this sense would be a mistake. To argue this one must be clear about one's attitude to Marx, and such clarity, even after the discrediting of Althusser's canons of interpretation, still is lacking.

Leaving aside the vulgar liberal propagandising which seems to have been vitalised by the collapse of the international political legacy of Stalinism,[81] two lines seem to have been pursued. One is effectively to give up the claim to be interpreting Marx to search for a broadly workable social philosophy and draw from his work only those elements which one wants in order to develop an original position. This is an entirely defensible line which has been taken over the analysis of particular phenomena on innumerable occasions. Habermas and Giddens give contemporary examples of this line even when the effort is the development of a general social philosophy. In Habermas, an attitude which came to be described as the "reconstruction of historical materialism"[82] has more or less always been explicit and his latest statement of that social philosophy pays less attention to Marx than to Weber or even Parsons.[83] In Giddens, the ability to give fine work of exposition of Marx and other important figures[84] has been clearly distinguished from the adoption of elements of Marx[85] into his own position.[86] This perfectly acceptable way of using Marx develops a clear attitude which one wishes was more widely displayed, whatever one's opinion about the actual merits of the works put forward. Nevertheless, though I have no wish to argue it here, it is my opinion that resources in Marx still far outweigh the productivity of the novel elements in Habermas, Giddens and others, which indeed seem to be offering rapidly diminishing returns to their consideration.[87]

Such clarity about one's eclecticism in approaching Marx obviously was not present in Althusser or Colletti. Nor is it present in the recent "analytical marxism" of particularly Cohen, Elster and Roemer who, rather like less insistent[88] Althussers, put forward substantially novel social philosophies in Marx's own name[89] or in avowed attempts to "introduce"[90] or to "make sense"[91] of Marx. These writings have rather striking Althusserian echoes. They pursue abstract coherence in Marx's work[92] and are so disappointed in what they find in this respect that they feel free to consign this work as a whole to a pre-scientific state[93] and to slough off elements of it that they do not like.[94] They also feel free to make good these deficiencies by importing methods that can only anachronistically be attributed to Marx. In Elster's case this is a thoroughgoing methodological individualism, the individual involved, in Elster and Roemer, being the rational utility maximiser of neo-classical economics. Cohen's innovation is an overt functionalism.

Nothing could read more differently from the analytic vocabulary[95] of these authors than Althusser's jargon; nothing could be more distanced from the cool way in which they reopen issues such as the justice of exploitation[96] than Althusser's impassioned and interminable avowals of commitment.[97] But Althusser clearly has given shape to what they think it is permissible to do with Marx's texts and we must be clear about this. When inevitably their work decays into its unproductive phases, it should not follow that their problems implicate Marx. For, as one might expect from the outset, when Elster and Cohen have made public their mutually cancelling disagreements,[98] they have done so in ways which call to mind perennial debates over (methodological) individualism and holism[99] rather than any particular issue in the interpretation of Marx.[100] When their work runs out of productive power in this way, we should be free to choose, as I do now, to return to what one finds to be Marx's still lively research programme in order to explore new possibilities of development.

There is some degree to which the work of these authors can, properly, be called revisionist in that, with the advantage of being able to assess developments in socialism more than one hundred years after Marx's death, they attempt to recast that work in the form which they feel will make it seem apposite to those developments.[101] Thus, Roemer's introduction to Marxist economics[102] is actually a work of similar intent to that of the worst, because most opportunistically "relevant", aspects of Bernstein.[103] Distortion in pursuit of this sort of relevance is hardly defensible. However, although Elster to a degree and Cohen to a very large degree put forward notions of historical materialism that do not distort their starting points in Marx in the way that Althusser and Colletti did, paradoxically they do not hit on similarly significant points in the interpretation of Marx. The reason is clear: for them Hegel is no issue. Roemer does not write about Hegel's influence on Marx in any substantial way. Cohen's account of Marx's relationship to Hegel, being that of the simple metaphor of changed content within a similar form, adds nothing to Engels.[104] Elster has studied Hegel and so sets about his influence in Marx with the avowed intention of expunging it. But as even the elements of Marx he retains are all methodologically individualist, it is rather hard to see what for him is the difference between rejecting and retaining Marx's own thought. A great deal of work has been done on the plausibility of methodological individualism and functionalism in the wake of this episode. This does not lack its own interest. Cohen is a particularly clear writer whose work provokes debate about the detail of positions in a way which is highly uncommon in social philosophy. Elster is a popular reworker of even well known examples of social explanation.[105] But it is not Marx and there is no *hermeneutic* interest in it. If one believes that *the interpretation* of Marx retains productive potential, then one simply cannot go about the task in this way. Very strangely, one is thrown back to Althusser, who imports as much functionalism into Marx as Cohen and as alien a view of human nature to Marx's own as that of Elster and Roemer, but who, in the question of inversion, actually sets up a problem in, rather than possibly a problem for, Marx.

One rightly is apprehensive when one says, as I now am obliged to do, that I have something entirely novel to say in the interpretation of Marx and that grasping it extends our knowledge of why marxism is a failure as a political programme and what the contemporary significance of that failure is. Claims like this are now so tired that it is with considerable reluctance that one makes one. All I can do is state my case, argue it in detail and leave it to the reader. I think I know why *Capital* could not be an adequate account of capitalism and I believe that this failure is expressive of a major weakness in Marx's thought and in subsequent marxism.

The best way to begin the brief statement of my case is to say that, even after all the effort spent on it, there still seems to me to be a necessity for further consideration of what it exactly meant to "invert" Hegel. There stand as the conclusions of earlier investigations that this metaphor cannot be discounted as merely a figure of speech, but nor can it be accepted at face value. But it may be investigated again, drawing upon the instructive successes and failures of these earlier contributions in order to move towards a resolution of their opposing insights. This is indeed something of a necessity. For on the one hand, Althusser's and Colletti's discovery of shortcomings bound up in the metaphor of inversion led them unacceptably to distance Marx from Hegel and to consequent weaknesses in their own interpretative and substantive positions. But equally, if criticism of the metaphor of inversion threatens our lines of theoretical supply from Hegel and Marx,[106] the threat arises principally because the criticism exposes serious existing weaknesses. The idea of inversion in Marx's work should lead us to an appreciation of the unevenness of that work's contribution, and thus the problem now must be, for all responses other than the unproductively dogmatic defence of established positions, the reassessment of fundamental issues in the interpretation of Hegel and Marx.

My argument is the following. Hegel compellingly posits the project of the overcoming of existing alienated conditions, and he does much to formulate the method of addressing this project. He sets out both the epistemological possibility of achieving *any* non-alienated apprehension of the world, and, in the phenomenological dialectic, a way of obtaining such an apprehension which strenuously seeks to avoid dogmatic assertion by pursuing progressive internal criticism of extant beliefs. However, it must be concluded that Hegel's dialectic itself is extremely unsuccessful when it comes to securing its own overall argument. It is shaped by a basic aim of representing non-alienated conditions as an end of history which cannot be demonstrated in accord with the test of winning rational conviction which Hegel himself establishes as the condition of truth. Hegel certainly seeks to invert alienated beliefs, but, as detailed examination of the 'Introduction' will show, the inversion set out in the *Phenomenology* is ultimately indefensible.

The hegelian method of progressive immanent criticism of existing conditions will be shown to be central to the way Marx describes capitalism. It is, of course, a common criticism of Marx's work that it is dogmatic. Detailed textual comparisons, however, will reveal hegelian dialectical themes which are utterly opposed to dogmatism to be not merely an influence upon Marx's work, but indeed to be at the core of *Capital*. I will conclude that Marx is substantially more rigorous when carrying out the criticism of alienation than is Hegel. Though I will say this with important reservations, core elements of Marx's criticism of political economy and the capitalist mode of production are of a form which is in principle able to win social scientific conviction.

I will argue that for Marx, as well as for Hegel, inversion describes the way the criticism of alienation is undertaken, for Marx seeks to invert the laws of political economy to show that they produce not ineluctable capitalism but socialism. When turning to inversion understood in this way, criticisms of Marx of a rather basic character must be made. Marx's contribution must, as he would have insisted, ultimately be assessed on the ground of its practical effectiveness, and, I will argue, the idea of inverting alienated beliefs cannot express what Marx wants to say of the immanent movement from capitalism to socialism.

The form of the description of capitalism which Marx gives is ineluctably law-like, even on occasion on a parallel with the natural sciences. One not wholly invalid reason for this is that it *is* the character of alienated social life to appear outside of human creation, seemingly after the fashion of natural structures. However, socialism, a statement of (increasingly) non-alienated conditions, should not be described in this manner, but rather in a way which registers the self-consciousness specifically absent from capitalism. To invert the type of account suited to capitalism in order to describe socialism is contradictory, and the consequences are disruptive of Marx's account of the establishment of socialism.

One consequence is that Marx sometimes lapses into speaking of the inevitability of socialism, doing so because he carries over to the establishment of socialism the way in which it is not incorrect to speak of alienated developments in the capitalist economy as apparently inevitable. Socialism indeed must have a basis in capitalist economic development, but equally it must represent the diminution of alienation and thus of the adequacy of the language of inevitability to explain historical events. This mistake, though a great deal has been made of it, can relatively readily be seen to be a misdescription of what Marx himself, in the predominantly better parts of his work, insists is the creation of social self-consciousness. But to recognise that Marx was not entirely committed to a wrong position does not, as it often has been taken to, mean that he developed a right one. The substantial, indeed disastrous, consequence of the idea of inversion lies in Marx's failure properly to distinguish, and then run together as linked but distinct, the accounts of capitalist and socialist development. The *political* movements that will establish socialism are given no integrated place in *Capital*, for they work towards an overcoming of alienation which runs entirely counter to the necessary form of an account of capitalist *economic* processes and concomitant alienated life in bourgeois society.

This dissonance must be stated in a very strong way indeed, for it created a space in Marx's work which has been filled in by errors the importance of which it is impossible to overestimate. The element of economic determination in Marx's view of socialism is a weakness in itself, though not a terminal one. It is an intellectual disaster, and a foundation of much political tragedy, because the substance of the economics Marx used in the determination was seriously obsolete in many main parts in 1867. Marx analyses capitalism as an alienated and inefficient form of economic life and this is right. He also saw it as an economic system tending to self-abolition and this is wrong. Marx's account of capitalism's development turns on free market assumptions of competition which the emergent joint stock form made redundant before *Capital* volume one was published. *Capital* as a whole could never entirely work because the consideration of capitalism outside of the immediate process of production did not confirm to the competitive assumption on which it was based.

If this criticism of Marx's economics is a criticism, then it is in a sense a slight one when set alongside what he accomplished. By the end of volume one, probably even by the end of chapter one of that volume, Marx had taken social theory to a position it never before had occupied by securing the hegelian critique of alienation in a social scientifically corrigible way, indeed in a way that has not been superceded in a century and a quarter. One tries to steer clear of such expressions, but there really is no other way to capture what Marx, following Hegel, did than to say that he significantly expanded the sum of all human knowledge. That *Capital* then contains a serious flaw is just what one expects in science.

Nevertheless, if the joint stock form undercut *Capital's* economics, it was inevitable that, when Marx threw himself into a politics which was informed by those economics, the consequences were regrettable in a very important sense. After the publication of volume one, Marx committed the majority of his efforts to the formation of the First International. This has been viewed as a splendid commitment to the practical actualisation of theoretical conclusions. But if one accepts, as I do, what Marx says about locating the nature of future developments in present resources, this was *bound* to be a failure for it was in complete contradiction of all that is best in Hegel's and Marx's ideas of critique. Many of the unsatisfactory elements of the character of marxism since Marx have, I will go on to suggest, been given by a failure to come to terms with the rather basic limitations of *Capital*, crippling the effectiveness of Marx's thought just where he sought to find it ultimately vindicated, in political practice.

In sum, then, I would like to use the idea of Marx's "inversion" of Hegel as the guiding thread of a commentary upon both of these figures and their relationship. This will be a fruitful tack, even more so than has been hitherto imagined, because of the strong and strongly self-conscious way in which both Hegel and Marx did wish, as the central aim of both of their works, to actually invert contemporaneous social consciousness. The whole issue remains vital in that both Hegel and Marx demonstrate the inestimable importance of the project of inversion they set out; but marxism is a failure and the project remains to be realised.

First, then, as Althusser has suggested in calling for further work on the idea of inversion,[107] a little more light on Hegel himself; which obliges us to return to the 'Introduction' to the *Phenomenology*.

Notes

1   *Vide* WN, bk 1, ch 2.

2   *Vide* Gossen, *The Laws of Human Relations*, pt 1.

3   *Vide* Hobbes, *Leviathan*, ch 13.

4   *Vide* Montesquieu, *The Spirit of the Laws*, bk 1, ch 3.

5   *Vide* Mill, 'On Liberty', ch 4.

6   *Vide* Kant, 'Idea for a Universal History with a Cosmopolitan Intent', pp 31-2.

7   I have tried to argue this in 'Individualism, Equality and the Possibility of Rights'.

8   I have tried to argue this in 'Rationality, Democracy and Freedom in Marxist Critiques of Hegel's Philosophy of Right'.

9   *Vide Kant*, 'Grounding for the Metaphysic of Morals', pp 9-16.

10 *Vide idem*, 'The Metapysical Principles of Virtue', pp 127-9.

11 *Vide idem, The Metaphysical Elements of Justice*, pp 36-9.

12 *Vide* Bentham, *An Introduction to the Principles of Morals and Legislation*, ch 1.

13 *Vide* Austin, *The Province of Jurisprudence Determined*, lec 1.

14 *Vide* Kant, *The Metaphysical Elements of Justice*, pp 35-6.

15 *Vide* Rousseau, 'The Social Contract', bk 2, ch 3.

16 Pace ibid, p 218

17 *Vide* Ferguson, *An Essay on the History of Civil Society*, pt 4 sec 3.

18 PM, sec 517 and PR, sec 157.

19 PS, pp 268-89.

20 PM, sec 518 and PR, sec 159.

21 *Ibid*, sec 158.

22 PS, pp 296-328.

23 PM, sec 523.

24 *Ibid*, secs 524-8 and PR, secs 182-208.

25 *Vide* Keynes, 'General Theory of Employment, Interest and Money', ch 23, sec 7.

26 Mandeville, *The Fable of the Bees*, pp 230, 327-71.

27 WN, vol 1, pp 26-7, 456. Modern versions of this metaphor, following Walras, *Elements of Pure Economics*, p 44 (where tâtonnement is translated as "groping") are no less mysterious. Arrow, 'Limited Knowledge and Economic Analysis', p 157 and *idem*, 'Economic Equilibrium', pp 110-3.

28 Locke, *Two Treatises of Government*, bk 2 ch 5.

29 Petty, 'Political Arithmetick', p 244.

30 PR, sec 189 addn.

31 *Vide* Kant, *Critique of Practical Reason*, pp 22-4.

32 *Vide* L, sec 175 addn.

33 PR, sec 199.

34 SL, pp 664-5 and L, sec 198.

35 PM, sec 535 and PR, sec 257.

36 Kant, 'Grounding for the Metaphysic of Morals', pp 35-6.

37 PS, pp 11-9 and PM, secs 430-5.

38 *Ibid*, sec 538 and PR, secs 209-56.

39 *Ibid*, secs 267, 273, 276.

40   PM, secs 529-34 and PR, secs 260-6.

41   *Ibid*, pp 1-13.

42   Marx, 'Proceedings of the Sixth Rhine Province Assembly: Third Article', p 262.

43   CPE, p 262.

44   EPM, pp 290-4.

45   CHPL, pp 31-2 and CHPLI, pp 175-6

46   *Idem*, 'First Draft of The Civil War in France', p 267.

47   CPE, p 262. Cf CHPL and CHPLI.

48   EPM, p 332.

49   *Vide* Colletti,'From Hegel to Marcuse' and *idem, Marxism and Hegel*, ch 3.

50   *Vide* Therborn, *Science, Class and Society*, ch 1, sec 2.

51   *Vide* Timpanaro, *On Materialism*, ch 3.

52   *Vide* Carver, *Engels*, p 76.

53   Eg Jordan, *The Evolution of Dealectical Materalism* and Levine, *The Tragic Deception*. The problems disappear, of course, when approached with sufficient insensitivity. In Guerin, 'Marxism and Anarchism', p 110 we are told that "What I mean by 'Marxism' is all of the writings of Karl Marx and Freidrich Engels themselves". The point of this is to allow Guerin to disparage "the works of their more or less faithless successors, who have usurped the label of 'Marxists'". Guerin is particularly interested in pursuing the anarchistic mileage that can be got from discussion of the reformism of Bernstein, but he has, of course, a problem with Engels' 1895 preface to *The Class Struggles in France*. So on the very page in which the above definition of marxism is given we are also told that in 1895 "Engels himself was no longer 'Marxist' in the sense that I understand it."

54   CPE, p 264; LF, pp 584-5 and GI.

55   SUS pp 377-9 and HF, pp 127-9.

56   AD, pref 2nd edn. In *Engels*, Carver questions Engels' account of Marx's interest in *Anti-Dühring* because it is uncorroborated . This is to accuse Engels of lying, whilst Carver surely was right when earlier, p 63, he said: "In his glosses on Marx, Engels' intentions, so far as I can tell, were wholly honest and honourable...he kept his claims and ambitions within the bounds of discipleship". Furthermore, there is such corroboration, not only in comparison between the section of *Anti-Dühring* Marx allegedly drafted and Marx's own notes on Quesnay (cf AD, pt 2, ch 10 and TSV1, ch 6), but also in correspondence between Engels and Marx (Engels, 'To Marx, 24 May 1876'; Marx, 'To Engels, 25 May 1876'; Engels, 'To Marx, 28 May 1876' and *idem,* To Marx, 6 March 1877). When Carver pursues this to exhaustion in *Marx and Engels*, pp 119-30, it is to similar effect. The corroboration afforded by the notes on Quesnay is passed over without detailed comment. The tendency of this type of interpretation is displayed in Carver's most recent, full-scale, effort to interpret Engels' work.

Engels later works, surely the most significant political writings of modern times, occupy a very minor part indeed of the text of Carver's *Friedrich Engels*. Surely the divergence between Carver's line and what Marx himself thought about the value of Engels' political writings must be serious on a first blush. After the 'Preface' to *On the Critique of Political Economy*, Marx published nothing on his background philosophy, and, in effect, Carver asks us to believe he just watched Engels distort his work between 1859 and 1883. The implausibility of this becomes acutely manifest after one notes that Marx was entirely prepared to write an 'Introduction to the French Edition of *Socialism: Utopian and Scientific*' declaring it to be "an introduction of scientific socialism" (p 339).

57   C1, pp 102-3.

58   *Idem, Le Capital*, vol 1, pp 347-51.

59   Althusser, 'Introduction: Today', pp 33-8 and *idem*, 'Preface to *Capital* Volume One', pp 89-92.

60   *Vide* Walton and Gamble, *From Alienation to Surplus Value*, p 142.

61   Althusser, 'Philosophy as a Revolutionary Weapon', sec 7.

62   *Vide* Lewis, 'The Althusser Case', pp 23-8, 35, 43-8.

63   *Vide* Kolakowski, 'Althusser's Marx', pp 112-3,117-8, 125-7,

64   Eg Thompson, 'The Poverty of Theory', p 196; Anderson, *Arguments Within English Marxism*, pp 125-6 and Hirst, *Marxism and Historical Writing*, chs 1, 4. Hirst's replies evidence hurt at the tone taken and then, incredibly enough, shift the interpretative claims being made yet again.

65   This is most true in respect of the ideas on structure and determination which Althusser intimately bound to his essential criticism of Hegel. *Vide* Giddens, *Central Problems in Social Theory*, pp 155-60 and McLennan *et al*, 'Althusser's Theory of Ideology', pp 77-105.

66   *Vide* Benton, *The Rise and Fall of Structural Marxism*; Clarke, 'Althusserian Marxism' and Collier, *Scientific Realism and Socialist Thought*.

67   *Vide* Geras, 'Proletarian Self-emancipation', pp 131-2.

68   *Vide* Pilling, *Marx's 'Capital'*, pp 131-2.

69   *Vide* Geras, 'Marx and the Critique of Political Economy', pp 288-91, 301-5.

70   Althusser, 'Preface to *Capital* Volume One', pp 91-2.

71   *Idem*, 'Elements of Self-criticism', sec 4 and *idem*, 'Is it Simple to be a Marxist in Philosophy?', pp 187-93. Althusser here draws attention to Spinozist themes developed *passim* throughout his earlier writings. *Vide* Anderson, *Considerations on Western Marxism*, pp 64-6 and Norris, *Spinoza and the Origins of Modern Critical Theory*, ch 1.

72   Hardly superior is the attempt to in some way "return to Kant" (p 285) as representing a sensible politics set out at length in Howard, *From Marx to Kant*. It surely is the case, indeed I have argued it myself in 'Individualism, Equality and the Possibility of Rights', that we have failed to realise central elements of

the enlightenment political aspiration which Kant, amongst others, expressed. But to argue that this realisation should be pursued now in the guise of a return to Kant (bridging Hegel and many others) is absurd, for it asks us to forego learning from subsequent experience why this task has proven so hard. Such an attitude is possible only if post-Kantian political philosophy can be viewed as unrelieved error, but this, absurdly enough, is just what Howard is pushed to argue (p 46).

73 *Vide* Edgely, 'Dialectic: The Contradictions of Colletti', pp 47-52.

74 *Vide* Hirst, 'Althusser and the Theory of Ideology', pp 43-5.

75 Althusser, 'Ideology and Ideological State Apparatuses', pp 127-49.

76 *Vide* Ruben, 'Materialsim and Professor Colletti', pp 70-1 and *idem*, *Marxism and Materialism*, pp 147-54.

77 Colletti, 'Bernstein and the Marxism of the Second International', pp 72-6 and *idem*, 'Marxism: Science or Revolution?'.

78 Timpanaro, *On Materialism*, and *idem*, 'The Pessimistic Materialism of Giacomo Leopardi'.

79 *Vide* Williams, 'Problems of Materialism', pp 103-16.

80 Rejection is the conclusion poigantly drawn by Kolakowski, *Main Currents of Marxism*, vol 3, pref and epilogue.

81 For an evaluation of marxism's explantory power today much more addressed to the political influences on such an evaluation than the one I advance here *vide* Callinicos, *Is There a Future for Marxism?*

82 Habermas, 'Towards a Reconstruction of Historical Materialism'. The word "reconstuction" carries no guarantee of the adoption of a correct interpretative attitude, however, and so Larrain's A *Reconstruction of Historical Materialism* is simply a diatribe against the errors of "diamat" in an attempt to put forward an adequate marxism which "can solve the tension existent in Marx and Engels' thought in a sense different from the orthodox solutions" (p xii). This reconstruction has a particularly breathtaking form. In order to purge marxism of its mistakes, Larrain ends by reducing it to 32 helpful mottoes about social theory (pp 121-67), seemingly taking us back to the innocence of the theses on Feuerbach before their unfortunate subsequent interpretation. The word Larrain uses for these mottoes is "tenets" and one wonders how long he thought about using "theses". The effect of a returning to an innocent past is spoiled, however, by the way that Larrain's tenets are highly reminiscent of the conclusion of Giddens' *New Rules of Sociological Method*, to which, unfortunately, Marx had no access.

83 Habermas, *The Theory of Communicative Action*.

84 Giddens, *Capitalism and Modern Social Theory*, pt 1.

85 *Idem*, *A Contemporary Critique of Historical Materialism*.

86 *Idem*, *The Constitution of Society*.

87   *Vide* Holmwood and Stewart, *Explanation and Social Theory*.

88   Roemer, 'Introduction', pp 2, 4 and Cohen, *History, Labour and Freedom*, p xi.

89   Cohen, *Karl Marx's Philosophy of History*.

90   Roemer, *Free To Lose*, which is subtitled *An Introduction to Marxist Economic Philoslphy*.

91   Elster, *Making Sense of Marx*, chs 2-8.

92   Roemer, 'Introduction'.

93   Cohen, 'Reply to Elster on 'Marxism, Functionalism and Game Theory'', p 491.

94   Elster, *Making Sense of Marx*, p 4.

95   Roemer, 'Introduction' and *idem, Free to Lose*, p vii.

96   Cohen, 'The Labour Theory of Value and the Concept of Exploitation'. One can hardly entirely be blamed for the writings of one's critics, but surely there is something going wrong in this type of examination when it invites responses such as Gordon, *Resurrecting Marx*, ch 5. This attack on analytic marxist accounts of injustice is so utterly abstract that it represents the worst type of neo-classical economic theorising in the bad sense. Marxist discussions of justice previously have not been at a level which encouraged this type of sterile formalism as a serious reply.

97   Althusser, 'Is it Simple To Be a Marxist in Philosophy?'.

98   Elster, 'Cohen on Marx's Theory of History'; Cohen, 'Functional Explanation; Reply to Elster'; *idem*, 'Functional Explanation, Consequence Explanation and Marxism'; Elster, 'Marxism, Functionalism and Game Theory'; Cohen, 'Reply to Elster on 'Marxism, Functionalism and Game Theory'' and Elster, 'Further Thoughts on Marxism, Functionalism and Game Theory'.

99   Particularly that centring on the contrbutions of JWN Watkin. Watkins, 'Ideal Types and Historical Explanation'; *idem*, 'The Principle of Methodological Individualism'; *idem*, 'Historical Explanation in the Social Sciences'; *idem*, 'Third Reply to Mr Goldstein'; *idem*, 'Methodological Individualism: A Reply'; and *idem*, The Alleged Inadequacy of Methodological Individualism'.

100 *Vide* Giddens, 'Commentary on the Debate', p 527.

101 Elster, 'Introduction'.

102 Roemer, *Analytical Foundations of Marxist Economic Theory*.

103 Bernstein, *Evolutionary Socialism*, ch 2.

104 Cohen, *Karl Marx's Theory of History*, ch 1 nb pp 26-7. Cohen's conclusion that Hegel has no theory of history is hardly suprising when he earlier, p 3, has said that "the strictly philosophical derivation of the concept of the world spirit will not be given here". This is to say that the *Phenomenology* will be ignored, which, indeed, it is, save for certain sentences in the 'Preface' which, like many others throughout the *Phenomenology*, are so close to Marx that they cannot be dealt with in this fashion. Cohen feels at liberty to recast Hegel's argument in a way

that simply is appallingly unfair and then dismiss it as so weak as not to " deserve" to be called a theory.

105 His most stiking work still appears to be Elster, *Logic and Society*, ch 6.

106 *Vide* Thompson, 'The Poverty of Theory', p 194.

107 Althusser, 'Contradiction and Overdetermination', p 116.

2 Hegel on the Unity of Subject and Object

When in 1842-4 Marx began to develop what are recognisably his own views, his principal task was to come to terms with those of Hegel's views on the state which he himself shared up to October 1842.[1] From this, the criticism of the philosophical background of those views was an obvious step which Marx took to the furthest extent in what are now known as the *Economic and Philosophical Manuscripts* of 1844. Marx's proposed "critical discussion of Hegelian dialectic and philosophy as a whole" was based on a discussion of the *Phenomenology of Spirit* "and of its final outcome, the dialectic of negativity as the moving and generating principle". Marx turned to this book as the "the true point and origin and the secret of the hegelian philosophy".[2]

This concentration on the *Phenomenology* has typically not been reproduced in the key interpretations of Marx. With exceptions of which the first really substantial one was *History and Class Consciousness*,[3] the pattern has been that of the concentration on the later works taken by Lenin in the *Philosophical Notebooks*.[4] This really is something of a substantial handicap for the interpretation of Marx as the *Phenomenology* is the principal source of what is valuable in Hegel's philosophical method and of what Marx found to be valuable in it. This valuable content is far less clearly derived from Hegel's later writings. In particular for our purposes, the *Phenomenology* centrally shows that the attribution of any formal dialectic method to Hegel is in direct contrast to his aims in his work.[5] (On this basis one can begin to understand the *necessity* for the communist suppression of *History and Class Consciousness*).[6] It is obviously helpful if one wishes to disparage Marx to find Hegel's influence upon him to consist in a ludicrous method.[7] It is an intellectual shortcoming, which has played its part in producing some overwhelmingly tragic events, that this has also been an unintentional consequence of the efforts authoritatively to systematise Marx's thought as dialectical materialism,[8] to turn that system into a state imposed canon and to extend that canon[9] by a sort of litany posing as argument.[10] Dialectical materialism as such is now an object of ridicule to those - thankfully now a very large number - who dare laugh at it.

Now, the discussion of Hegel's philosophy by those who freely approach it with an interest in Marx does not display the jargon of this philosophy and indeed has contained some of the principal philosophical achievements of this century, not least in extending the understanding of Hegel himself.[11] Nevertheless, it is typically true that such discussion is dominated by a superficial formalism, not of dialectical materialism but of a bowdlerised version of Hegel culled from isolated lines of the *Science of Logic* and passages of the lectures on the philosophy of history.[12] It goes without saying that in these circumstances the possibility of remedying the problems indicated particularly by Althusser seems remote. If we are to make progress in this direction, it is as well actually to read Hegel to see to what the dialectic actually does amount.[13] Let us do so by turning to the *Phenomenology*.

In the opening paragraphs[14] of what is now known[15] as the 'Introduction' to the *Phenomenology of Spirit*, Hegel distinguishes his aims in the *Phenomenology* from what he quite properly regards as the classical project of modern European epistemologies.[16] In its modern form begun by Descartes,[17] this project seeks to establish the foundations of potential knowledge prior to the achievement of any substantial knowledge as such. Taking the aim of cognition to be the subject's unmediated knowledge of a distinct object, this project sceptically asks how this aim might be realised?[18]

Hegel identifies in the classical epistemological project two conceptions of cognition, as either the instrument by which knowledge is produced or the medium through which it is perceived. Though Hegel wants these metaphors to stand as characteristics of classical epistemology as such, it is particularly Kant which he has in mind here.[19] This is so not least in that Hegel does not think it necessary initially to consider the plausibility of epistemologies of direct perception.[20] He accepts Kant's drawing out of the fundamental implication of the classical epistemological project, that cognition is a creative process. Not only can knowing be predicated *only* of a subject,[21] but further the subject contributes an active interpretation to the formation of knowledge.[22] For Kant, the value of empirical knowing lies in its being informative about a distinct thing-in-itself. But the grasp of this thing-in-itself[23] can be achieved only through categories inherent in the faculty of cognition.[24]

Given that cognition involves such a moment of interpretation, Hegel does not deny the scepticism which classical epistemology directs at the effectiveness of the cognitive instrument or the transparency of the cognitive medium. Rather he argues that the cognitive use of an instrument or medium indeed necessarily must in some way affect the object, or cognition itself would be redundant. However, this means that the positive intentions of rigorously pursued scepticism ultimately must collapse into a total rejection of the possibility of gaining knowledge, at least of the properly true kind of unmediated acquaintance with the object initially envisaged.

Following this line of argument, Hegel notes that the paradox of completely eschewing considered epistemology in the name of the achievement of true knowledge, such as his contemporary Jacobi's intuitionist criticism of conceptual thinking as an obstruction to belief in the truth of God's existence,[25] is immanent in Kantian epistemology.[26] For if the employment of the instrument or the medium prevents the achievement of the desired result, why bother with it at all? Is it not better just intuitively to grasp the result? But of course the beliefs adopted through such hasty manoeuvres unfortunately are open to the scepticism of classical epistemology, which the anti-philosophy of those intuitive beliefs denies but cannot answer.[27]

Hegel next considers a possible solution to this impasse, which may lie in examining the qualities of the instrument or medium of cognition and then in subtracting these from the products of cognition to leave unmediated knowledge. He would seem to have in mind here his contemporary Reinhold's attempt to neutralise the seemingly unfortunate consequences of the subjectivity of thinking.[28] Reinhold proposed to come to terms with the acknowledgment of ineradicable presuppositions in cognition by successively holding to each different one in order to lay every one potentially open to inquiry from varying standpoints.[29] However, rather than consider Reinhold's proposal in what would be unrewarding detail for the purpose of evaluating basic epistemological positions, it will be more fruitful to develop the implications of Hegel's argument for the analogous case of the constructive aims of empiricism.

Locke's account of the simple ideas of the human understanding[30] aims to provide a sure foundation of unmediated knowledge on which the creative contributions of the understanding to more complex ideas may be based. Simple ideas are the direct products of the physical sensation of primary qualities of objects such as their extension and mobility.[31] The knowledge constituted by this small number of primary qualities is itself limited, but it is to provide a sound empirical basis for the complex ideas of secondary qualities which may be built up from it.[32] Against such an approach, Hegel stresses that if the results of cognition are subtracted from knowledge, then, given the recognition of creativity in cognition which motivates the epistemological effort, this amounts to a return to a position prior to knowledge. The isolation of the subject's contribution can never leave a residue not affected by that contribution, because we must know what that residue is. That is to say, the residue must be subjected to the cognitive effort. Even within its own terms, the greatest contribution which Locke's approach can make is a reduction of certain aspects of cognition to other perhaps more fundamental ones. With regard to these latter, basic epistemological inquiry cannot be pursued with any result other than a complete scepticism.[33] Indeed, immanent within this procedure is a thoroughgoing agnosticism with regard to true knowledge and a concession of the redundancy of epistemology. When Hume followed Berkeley's exposure of the wholly arbitrary nature of Locke's distinction between primary and secondary qualities,[34] rigorously cutting away such restraining inconsistencies, he moved the basic destructive potentialities of Lockean empiricism on to a completely nihilistic conclusion for philosophy.[35]

Having consistently pushed classical epistemological doubt through to ineradicable scepticism about its inability to demonstrate a valid cognitive approach to gaining any knowledge, Hegel extends his questioning to the formulation of its basic project. He argues that in depicting subjective cognition and the object to-be-known as radically separate and in assuming that the former is an instrument or medium through which the latter is to be grasped or perceived, this project itself is making a presumptive knowledge claim about the character of cognition. Furthermore, the project must make such a claim. Whilst it may be possible to test other instruments or media by means other than setting them to their intended tasks, this is not so in the case of cognition. One cannot search for truth with spears and staves; the very examination of cognition must itself necessarily be conducted through an act of cognition. One cannot hope to learn to swim before one ever enters the water. Any possible epistemological scrutiny of cognition's adequacy to provide true knowledge itself involves established knowledge of cognition.[36]

For example, let us return[37] to the attempt to subtract from the results of cognition the qualities of the cognitive instrument or medium. This attempt could proceed only from an initial possession of unmediated knowledge of the character of cognition. This immediately involves a circular argument from indefensible assumptions, as Berkeley and Hume observed with regard to Locke's primary qualities. Or if an attempt is made to provide a defence of the knowledge of cognition, it will decay into an infinite regression of argument, since it is necessary to inquire into the cognitive distortions of earlier knowledge of the cognitive distortions of earlier knowledge and so on.

It is, Hegel concludes, as a consequence of its own particular characterisation of potential knowledge that the classical epistemological project yields only scepticism. Proceeding as an inquiry into what cognition does, this project, in setting the object apart from any possible cognition, from the outset ensures that true knowledge is rendered unavailable. For as cognition must accomplish something if it is necessary for the attainment of knowledge, and yet the object is wholly separate from this act of knowing, then nonsensically any true knowledge can be only knowledge not arrived at through cognition.

Hegel acknowledges the possibility that after reaching this sceptical conclusion of classical doubt one may regard true knowledge as unreachable and then, for practical purposes, accept some sort of knowledge, if this is the correct word, which has eschewed claims to being true. Indeed, the common-sense necessity of this is at the root of Hume's distinction between the philosophical and the vulgar standpoints, the latter necessarily embracing the natural beliefs which are the practical content of our knowledge.[38] Hegel remarks, however, that this position again posits the necessity of epistemological investigation renewed at this new level if other than an ultimately unsupportable total relativism is to be professed. Thus, in the first *Critique*[39] Kant accepts Hume's destruction of a philosophical basis for causality but nevertheless tries to bring natural scientific explanation, which turns on the reality of cause, and not merely natural beliefs into the realm of possible knowledge.[40]

This position is a compound of absurdities. If the essential characteristic of knowledge is that it strives to be true, then what can be the status of this other knowledge which does not do so? The vocabulary of epistemology - knowledge, truth, adequacy, etc. - cannot be simply duplicated for this new level but must take on new meanings expressive of untruth. The attempt to answer scepticism with regard to, as Kant has it, noumenal knowledge of things-in-themselves by claiming possible phenomenal knowledge of objects known through categories[41] must fail, because it proceeds from an acknowledgement that there cannot really be a sure foundation for this knowledge. Acceptance of the unknowability of the thing-in-itself destroys the truth of even phenomenal knowledge.[42]

I want now to turn to a further observation which Hegel makes on the classical epistemological project in his particular formulation of the most common theme of immediately post-Kantian epistemology - the rejection of the thing-in-itself.[43] If the separation of the object from cognition vitiates the possibility of true knowledge, what then, Hegel demands, is it possible to know of that object? Clearly the answer is nothing. If knowledge is rendered always flawed by the assumptions of the classical epistemological project, then equally the object is rendered unimportant. If it is inaccessible to cognition, then it is also purely abstract in the bad sense, as it is impossible to have knowledge of it. Playing on Kant's terminology, Hegel points out that the thing-in-itself, as it cannot be available for knowledge, is indeed merely in-itself.

There is a contradiction in the concept of the thing-in-itself which underlies the shortcomings of the characterisation of cognition in classical epistemology. In claiming that it is impossible to know the thing-in-itself one is in fact claiming to know something about it; certainly that it exists and probably that it delimits the respective areas of true knowledge and of other "knowledges".[44] It is these assumptions of the classical epistemological project itself that disrupt the project.[45] The ruse of classical epistemology is to picture a sundered subject and to-be-known. This is only a ruse, and displacing it leaves, the then quite effortless *possibility* of knowing.

Hegel's argument does not merely point out the frustrations which follow from the idea of the thing-in-itself, but destroys the very quality of given being in-itself which shields that idea from criticism. The argument succeeds by uncovering an alienation. Accepting that the thing-in-itself is actually given, one must accept the frustrations to which it leads as the frustrations of philosophy or even of human life as such. But the thing-in-itself actually arises from a specific philosophical position. *Rather than the in-itself being an existential given with which we must come to terms, it is given by the alienation of the power to know within a specific epistemology.*

Once a belief has been shown to be inadequate by philosophical scepticism, it is the way of classical epistemology to consign it to a bottomless abyss of untruths.[46] The contribution to knowledge of this indiscriminate scepticism is to pronounce a blanket condemnation upon whatever conception is put forward. This situation is obviously unsatisfactory, and it is avoidable because the classical epistemological project does not, as it has been taken to do, establish the total emptiness of all claims to truth. The full comprehension of its bleak results turns on seeing these results as the results of that very project and not as the results of epistemology as such. The emptiness left by classical epistemology is fully understood only when understood as being left by it.

Hegel disparages the authenticity with which such an emptiness can be professed. He concedes the value of doubt and its stress that all beliefs must pass the test of reasoned personal conviction. However, in classical epistemology doubt is not identified with inquiry into the validity of any particular conception but with scepticism about the fruitfulness of cognition as such. Epistemology is reduced to gnoseology since cognition and the object to-be-known are rendered wholly separate and the possibility of truth is identified with that of absolute, unmediated knowledge. After setting the to-be-known apart from cognition in this way, the very admission that knowledge is a project of active cognition is enough to debar it from being true. Thus the gnoseological inquiry might well be continued forever without it in the least contributing to knowledge. Discussions about the character of such a delimited cognition do not say anything about the relationship to the to-be-known which is the crux of the epistemological problem.

If the basic scepticism of classical epistemology is made irremediable in this way, what can be the result of the initially valuable resolve to examine everything? The result is nothing. What is being criticised is not a particular conception, about the merits or otherwise of which it would be rewarding to know, but rather the faculty of cognition as such, in an empty, abstract fashion without concrete content. No specific conception is examined on its merits; all are condemned simply because they are acts of cognition. The consequences of this can amount to little more than a mere display of criticism made in rather bad faith. Such criticism, Hegel argues, perforce lapses into a mere preliminary which is gone through before coming back to the beliefs initially held. This fate of classical epistemology could be seen from the outset in the fate of Descartes' aim to submit all beliefs to personal test. It is indeed to do more than follow received opinion to make that opinion genuinely one's own.[47] However, it is not in itself a great deal more in so far as gaining truth is concerned, for the truth of an opinion does not reside in the fashion in which that opinion is held.[48] Descartes in fact examined only his own capacity to believe as such, his ability to believe irrespective of content, and furthermore did so with the express intention of rebuilding the beliefs with which he started after satisfying himself that he might believe in them.[49]

The endemic shortcomings of the narrowed conception of cognition involved in this sort of doubt mean that this renewed belief can never convincingly be demonstrated from the sceptical position adopted.[50] More fundamentally, this sort of effort does not improve, because it does not even consider, the *substance* of the belief at all. It is as if Descartes begins with truth and has only to convince himself of this. It is difficult to drop the unwarranted assumption of the truth of initial beliefs, for the method of doubt does not contribute to the substantive evaluation of any specific beliefs.[51]

In Hume, classical epistemological doubt does not stop short of complete philosophical scepticism, and this is so because Hume's attitude to philosophy is not fundamentally different from that of Descartes. It is inconsistent to demand of true knowing that it be other than an act of cognition, for after doing so one then necessarily proceeds to commit just such acts and to evaluate them after the fashion which motivated the initial epistemological effort. Hume of course allows that knowing involves confidence in statements about the real, but does so in defiance of philosophy.[52] Philosophy, then, is rejected as ridiculous, but the philosophy thus rejected is not Hume's specific idea of philosophy but philosophy as such. Hume himself moves on to natural beliefs. However, as even his contrast of the ridiculous errors of philosophy and the dangerous ones of religion[53] involves just the sort of causal claim he thinks he has demolished, it is difficult to see what the point was of the demolition if the substance of a belief castigated as philosophical is restored in the domain of natural belief.[54] Equally, to the extent that Kant's attempt to dispel Humean scepticism becomes entirely confined to the elaboration of the subjective categories, it is quite powerless to achieve its goal. As such an attempt is concerned with a narrowed cognition and not the relation of cognition to the to-be-known, it cannot provide a foundation for natural science nor provide a ground for evaluating particular beliefs in respect of their relation to the to-be-known.[55]

Paradoxically, if every belief in truth must be criticised, then none can be. The evaluation of the potential fruitfulness of any particular belief is paralysed by a rejection of the possibility of truth at all, for on what grounds could such evaluation be carried out if any alternative is just as bad? The adoption of a truly critical attitude thus becomes impossible. The very intelligibility of epistemological criticism, Hegel is arguing, turns on recognising the determinate significance of any such criticism. The negation, as he puts it, of any inadequate belief must not be conceived as a completely negative procedure but rather as an effort to learn from the specific contributions and shortcomings of what has earlier been done. Though one form of what we can now recognise as an inadequate belief, the classical epistemological project, reduced all cognition to nothing by an, as it were, empty negation, we should learn from this result of this epistemology that we must regard criticism of this and other inadequate beliefs as a determinate negation. This stress upon the determinateness of criticism follows from showing the two positions - the identification of truth with unmediated truth and the reduction of epistemology to gnoseology - which characterise classical epistemology to be untenable, and by then showing them to be the products of that epistemology.

The first position is shown to be not only inevitably frustrating and indeed unsupportable, but in itself contradictory. We have seen Hegel argue that it is nonsensical to presume an object to-be-known wholly unconnected to the procedure by which it might be known. Not only are such presumptions completely indefensible according to the criteria of the epistemological project in which they are made, but from the outset they further involve this project in an inevitable failure to achieve its goals and ultimately ridicule these very presumptions themselves. The positive moments of epistemology are undermined in its classical formulation. The eradication of possibly recognisable deficiencies in knowledge is clearly a valuable undertaking which is of the essence of cognition. However when flatly posed in terms of an empty cognition and a separate but equally empty to-be-known, this undertaking becomes that of the eradication of some unspecifiable inadequacy between knowledge without content and an unknowable. It is thus a hopeless and absurd task.

The second position is shown to follow from the first and to constitute a complete misdirection of the epistemological effort, for pushed into an examination of a narrow cognition separated from the to-be-known, this particular effort cannot contribute anything. In showing that the only plausible evaluation of a particular belief must be one which assesses its adequacy to a truth which potentially can be established, Hegel makes epistemology fully aware of what it must do, and thus efforts are able consciously to be directed towards this. In this criticism of epistemological alienation, *the power to know is not created, it is made apparent by being recovered from the obfuscated form in which it had been exercised.* Conscious reflection on knowing and knowing itself are to be united in a way which does not accept but rejects the separation of philosophical scepticism and practical belief. The valid use of "truth" and associated terms in discourse about our beliefs is to be established not by altering in some way the meaning of those terms but indeed by insisting on their natural meanings. Hegel has shown that their use in classical epistemology, which makes them completely redundant, or rather an absurd meta-language outside of possible discourse on confident knowing, is a self-defeating position which itself alienates our power to know.

Having carried out this (still) essential preliminary work, Hegel might have been expected to go on to construct his idea of knowing in order to fashion a non-alienated epistemology.[56] This would be, to draw on the terms of a later phenomenology, an epistemology of knowing being-in-the world,[57] rather than an epistemology which seeks to establish knowing being-in-the world and necessarily fails.[58] However, as we shall see in the next chapter, hegelian phenomenology cannot run too far ahead of any belief it examines, and this includes classical epistemology. When Hegel seeks to establish a superior position to that of classical epistemology it is really by way of summing up the obvious lesson of what we have so far seen: that the dissociation of subject and object is untenable.

The abiding interest of the classical epistemological project lies in that, as Hegel later claims, it represents the sophisticated development of the very common understanding which equates knowledge with a subject's immediate grasp of given facts.[59] So common is this understanding that he calls it "natural consciousness"[60] or even simply "consciousness" when turning, later in the 'Introduction',[61] to the dissociation of subject and object. This consciousness envisages a knowledge of objects distinct from the subject who is aware of the act of cognition. This consciousness distinguishes itself from objects by simultaneous attempts to relate itself to them in order to make the objects available for itself. However, an object's being-for-consciousness in this way is distinguished from an object's being-in-itself, and an object's being related to a subject in knowing also is distinguished from the object's being outside of this relationship. It is this being-in-itself that is the essential to-be-known and it is knowledge of this that is the truth. It is clear enough that what Hegel does here is give an account of natural consciousness which identifies it with the positions of the classical epistemological project, in which he already has exposed an untenable identification of truth with knowledge uncontaminated by cognition.

If we inquire into the truth of a particular knowledge in the ways made possible by this consciousness, the inquiry becomes the determining of what that knowledge is in-itself. From what we have already seen, we can hardly expect such a project to be practicable. All that can be discussed is the subject's cognition of this knowledge, and this cognition is, of course, thereby vulnerable to the scepticism which this consciousness levels at any cognition whatsoever. Hegel insists that any unfavourable evaluation of a particular knowledge can be seriously doubted by those holding to the criticised knowledge as itself not capturing the truth.

Hegel claims that the problem, or as he says the semblance of the problem, of the dissociation of subjective knowing and objective truth is overcome by virtue of the object of the inquiry we are considering, an inquiry into particular forms of knowledge. This dissociation seems to render impossible the reaching of an acceptable criterion of truth because the subject is apparently restricted to only one side of the epistemological relation of subject and object, that of the former. However, in this inquiry consciousness can be pushed to the point of recognising that it provides its own criterion, for it is necessarily within consciousness that both particular cognitions and the object to-be-known are available for knowledge.

Hegel here is attempting to turn what appears to be the pernicious consequences of the dissociation of subject and object to his own advantage. He stresses, on the basis of his earlier discussion of classical epistemology, that there is no simple grasp of objects but they are available for knowledge only in active cognition. Consciousness must be the site not only of every subjective cognition but also of every possible grasp of the object.

Putting the argument this way, it seems that the object is still only an object for-consciousness and there still is left the difficulty of knowing the object-in-itself. The solution of this difficulty is to be found in that consciousness may never know an object at all. Given the criticism of an in-itself which is in principle unknowable, the only meaningful in-itself must be one which is for-consciousness. It is the evaluations of particular knowledges that arise in consciousness that are the only plausible criteria for truth, for a criterion based on knowing the in-itself is absurd. It is true that we measure what we know against an object, but that object must itself be for-consciousness. Knowledge and the improvement of knowledge take place within consciousness. This is, as Hegel puts it in a typically paradoxical fashion, in knowing, something is for-consciousness the in-itself. Thus, in consciousness there is a particular cognition and also the criterion of truth by which the cognition can be evaluated, the criterion which takes over the role of being-in-itself.

As we shall see in the next chapter, Hegel gives a substantial account of the way this *unity* of subject and object within consciousness nevertheless has the form of subject and object. However, it is best to stop at this point to evaluate Hegel's attitude to representations of their *dissociation*. The stress on unity as opposed to dissociation is presented as the solution of the problems set by natural consciousness and its theoretical expression in classical epistemology. If one rushes ahead in Hegel's argument, one can see in what Hegel has said so far a sort of utter collapse of objectivity within which dissociation disappears as the subject and object are united in the strong sense of an ontological idealism.[62] Now, as shall be discussed in chapter four, Hegel did hold to an ontological idealism and I believe that this ontology is in error. Nevertheless, two essential points must be made. First, it is only after Hegel's critique of empty negation that we are able to claim in a useful sense that *any* belief actually is in error. Second, there is nothing in what has been said so far to commit any reader to any specific ontology. What has been established is a rationalistic defence of our power to know. In those terms of Bhaskar's which now figure largely in the discussion of these issues,[63] this is a realism.[64] The power to know is recovered from its alienated denial and epistemology is placed in the situation of knowing what it can and must achieve: a confidence that statements about the world could possibly be true.

That classical epistemology has ridiculous consequences has been undeniable since Hume. But the Humean attack upon it has to take the form of ridicule because it cannot actually refute those consequences, which then may stand as a form of existential conundrum. Hegel accomplishes this refutation by showing that the argument which would identify an existential paradox is the source of that paradox. It shows not the antinomical character of existence but the antinomical character of itself. The strength of the position Hegel develops can clearly be seen by reference to both his contemporaries and to the most modern contributions.

In order to sustain his transcendental deduction that empirical knowledge involves being informative about an object distinct from the subject[65] against empiricist scepticism, Kant of course argues that there are two sources of knowledge united in synthetic judgments. These are, of course, the *a priori* forms contributed by reason and the material substance contributed by the object.[66] The immense development of this position by Kant notwithstanding, this position represents rather than solves the problem of dissociation. For although we seem to be given both sides of consciousness, we are not because the object remains a brute object, external in the sense of being in-itself. Kant in fact accepts the, in a proper sense, epitomically empiricist identification of objectivity which he sought to refute. The ways forward from this position must be limited and led Kant to distinguish phenomena and noumena. The emphatic criticism of direct perception leaves one with a truth subjective in the bad sense, for the real truth is still identified with direct perception.

One can go back to a claim to have direct perception, but classical epistemology has done its work and, as we have seen, no such claim can stand. In the period at the end of Kant's life and subsequent to his death when the unsatisfactoriness of phenomena and noumena was becoming manifest, Fichte took substantially the opposite tack to direct perception. Fichte's epistemology is subjective in the strong sense that it moves from accepting that unmediated knowledge of an object is impossible to the position that the subject, ego as Fichte has it, is self-positing.[67] Objectivity is explained as an unconscious representation of the subjective will.[68] Ego posits otherness in an apparent non-ego and, although the otherness of non-ego is held to be immutable as it is a condition of consciousness,[69] this epistemology is quite dismissive of the sense of material substance sought by Kant.

Fichte had to welcome this outcome[70] as it was the only one left to him but it is just as much a withdrawal from the epistemological problem as Kant left it as any claim to have unmediated knowledge of the absolute.[71] Though beliefs may be evaluated in Fichte, the evaluation is carried out by a subjective tendency towards reflection and really is just an assessment of the strength with which ego strove to put those beliefs forward.[72] This is an irrational consequence forced upon Fichte at the very point Hegel rationalistically denies that there may be unknowable truths.[73]

In some comments about what I believe to be a set of fundamentally mistaken attitudes to Kant's epistemology in the way this issue has been taken up in marxism, I would now like to make more clear my claim that there is in Hegel a more sound foundation for empirical knowing than is to be found in the certainly more empirically minded Kant.

Let us first turn to Lenin's famous location of a profound ambivalence between idealism and materialism in Kant's epistemology.[74] Lenin's admittedly brief remarks set up a metaphor of Kant's thought being poised on a knife-edge between idealism and materialism, with the possibility of its being tipped over to either side. Hence in addressing himself to Kant's ambivalence, Lenin simply criticises him for not being enough of a consistent materialist.[75] But in reaching this conclusion Lenin's interpretation seems to take over the understandings which motivated the oppositional, because equally tendentious, responses to Kant which Lenin himself identifies as "idealism" and "mechanical materialism" and identifying both in Kant. In mentioning both there is the immediate benefit of pointing out a tension in Kant, but holding that this tension could have been resolved simply by Kant's taking a more staunch materialist line is hardly adequate to Kant's thought, for this obviously is to take up the mechanical materialism which has been rejected. There can be no doubt about the strength of the materialist impulse of the critical philosophy, and the ambivalent way in which this is ultimately maintained in that philosophy arises from Kant's being sensitive, in a way in which Lenin clearly was not, to the obstacles to a workable materialism.

Lenin's own materialism is founded upon a criticism of the possibility of granting the thing-in-itself even a wholly negative place in epistemology and then running this denial of its noumenal status into a declaration of its being phenomenally available. But though this is the correct way in which to move, of itself it can amount to only a covering up of the fundamental problems of the distance between the to-be-known and creative cognition which led to Kant's positing of the thing-in-itself in the first place. Lenin's basic idea that Kant is a materialist when he assumes that the thing-in-itself corresponds to our ideas is vague enough to lend itself even to a broadly pragmatist epistemology quite different from the position he wants to take up. Lenin gives no indication of what it is, if anything, that distinguishes his disposal of the thing-in-itself from the similar efforts made by either the idealist or (especially) the mechanical materialist oppositional currents of the interpretation of Kant which he identifies. Furthermore, his later acquaintance with the sources of Hegel's contributions to this issue seem to occasion no valuable change in this respect.[76]

All this, then, leaves a great void just at the point where a new development is needed, and into this void almost anything can be put. If these remarks seem harsh, it is because Lenin's simplistic confusion of an interesting preliminary comment with a fully worked out position must be opened up if the strength of Hegel's position is to be appreciated and thus new developments in this area of the study of Hegel and Marx are to be made.

It was quite open for Della Volpe to deepen Lenin's examinations of Kant[77] and insist that there is a strong materialist reference present in the critical epistemology which in the history of the development of empirical (social) science suffered profound suppression in Hegel[78] and was revived only in Marx.[79] However, when Colletti rather insensitively took over the same broad thesis with reference to Lenin,[80] but without Della Volpe's awareness of Kant's limitations in making materialism workable,[81] the result of the ensuing attempt to directly link Marx to the materialist intent in Kant is, as we saw in chapter one, a Kantianism. Though derived from Della Volpe to a pronounced degree, Colletti's intellectual history of Marx's epistemology is a regression and not a development from Della Volpe. What for Della Volpe are positions requiring improvement are taken by Colletti to be statements of a practicable materialism.

For Della Volpe, the "materialism" of Hume is as important as that of Kant, and this speaks volumes for the acute historical sense informing his account of Marx's epistemology. Della Volpe's discussion of Kant rather unusually - at least to British readers - attempts to outline the fundamentals of the critical philosophy by focusing upon Kant's attitude to Leibnizian rationalism, which in contemporaneous German philosophy was known through Wolff. Della Volpe stresses that the vigorous empirical impulse in Kant which inspired his attack upon Wolff is derived from Hume.[82] The materialist intent of the thought of *both* Hume and Kant is made clear, but coupled with an acknowledgement that a material reference in epistemology is very substantially vitiated as a resource for empirical science without a clear understanding of how that reference is available for and determines knowledge.

Bearing this in mind, I should now like to mention the antipathy to Bhaskar's attempt to give a transcendental realist basis to science displayed in Ruben's *Marxism and Materialism*. I am concerned here with only the first of a number of arguments which Ruben marshals against Bhaskar's transcendental mode of argument.[83] I have implied above that I think Bhaskar's efforts are an example of just the sort of ontological inquiry that might be made on the basis for realism which Hegel provides and that I regard it as important that such efforts be recognised as developments from a position fundamentally far more sound than that taken by Ruben. This latter is a position we will recognise.

Ruben believes, with Lenin,[84] that the possibility of materialist epistemology turns on the strength of a necessary presumption of an objectivity distinct from the subject.[85] Given what is common-sensically known about human beings, Ruben says, sceptical empiricist epistemology is literally incredible. In order to forestall the sceptical retort that such common-sense belief is open to doubt, Ruben argues that though this point can certainly be successfully made, this means that the whole project of foundationalism must not be answered but rejected. He is quite blunt; objectivity cannot have a philosophical justification.[86] But it is, I submit, quite unacceptable that an argument should be rejected because it is successful, and actually this is not what Ruben does. Beneath his blank statement of presumption he is in fact offering a challenge to empiricism based on common-sense experience's philosophical significance and empiricism's characteristic inability to come to terms with this. His argument as such is stunted - and Ruben offers no criticism of scepticism which can even be compared to that of Hegel[87] - because it is couched in what he takes to be self-sufficiently blunt terms. For Ruben, philosophy is reasoned thought, but reasoned thought can be dismissed as merely academic when it conflicts with being-in-the-world. The better way of putting this is, of course, to argue for the reason of being-in-the-world.

That Ruben's case takes this form at first glance appears to be because he identifies a possible philosophical defence of objectivity with an argument which is non-circular in the sense of in no way having its conclusions bound up in its premises.[88] As Bhaskar himself retorts,[89] this stipulation is rather unclear in that it would seem to rule out not only what are generally taken to be illegitimately circular arguments but also, certainly distinguishable from these, a great range of broadly deductive arguments, exemplified by aspects of mathematics and logic. Ruben's criticism as it stands is too vague to undercut the value of transcendental deductive arguments which may be made part of the philosophical task of revealing and clarifying the bases of given positions.[90] But within this broad claim lies the real problem for Ruben. Since he accepts the possibility of scepticism, in that he allows that as knowledge of objectivity must be founded in knowing and cannot have a ground elsewhere it is open to unrelievable doubt, Ruben's tack was to be to found objectivity upon a blunt presupposition. I think we can see that he is forced to do this by his paradoxical acceptance of the unassailability of the argument he wishes to dispute.

Though couched in marxist terms and taking its inspiration for a strong presumption of materialism from Lenin, Ruben's argument is in fact none other than a repetition of Moore's attempt to common-sensically ground our belief in the external world.[91] We should be familiar with the weakness of this position because Moore's defence itself is, I would say, in substance[92] no improvement at all on Hume's doctrine of natural belief. This would certainly explain Ruben's readiness to give up the idea of a philosophical defence of materialism, preferring to argue his case non-philosophically, a contradiction in terms which can be understood only within a Humean context. However, in the light of Hegel's discussion of these matters, I believe that we are able on the one hand to pay empiricism more respect than does Ruben, in that we can discuss its positions, and on the other hand have less respect for its conclusions. For we can say that it is going too far to allow that there is an irremediable element of indefensible presumption in materialism when the point makes sense only in the discredited terms of the criterion of truth demand by empiricism. Thus we are no longer hindered by the sort of scepticism which Ruben, in his own defence, has in the end to insist *can* be levelled at materialism.

The course of the full development of Ruben's position from his initial failure properly to confront scepticism is, I hope, now easily recognisable. As he allows scepticism he cannot defend any particular understanding of the ontology of knowing. Hence his rejection of the very idea of work such as Bhaskar's and his believing it necessary flatly to assert common-sense as an accurate intuitive understanding. If, however, we follow Hegel to the establishment of the transcendental unity of subject and object we find opening up a whole area of debate which Bhaskar enters, and which Ruben tries to close. It is not that the existence of objectivity is mediated by consciousness, but our knowledge of even its independent existence obviously is. Ruben is in error if he supposes that the acceptance of materialism will be guaranteed by surrendering philosophic explication of consciousness, the only ground upon which this acceptance may be won.

I feel sure that Ruben would agree that it is at best an unavoidable shortcoming of *Marxism and Materialism* that its statement of materialist presumptions tends to have a dogmatic form which is not entirely sanctioned by the literal incredibleness of the scepticism they are intend to displace. The whole tradition which I have called the classical epistemological project, and the thought of Hegel as well, is ultimately dismissed by Ruben on the grounds that it articulates a bourgeois understanding.[93]

Whilst this may be so, such a point is hardly directly pertinent to the truth of the beliefs thus criticised. In the face of accepting the strength of empiricist scepticism, to reflect the consequences of this because they stem from a bourgeois understanding in opposition to the presumptions needed to underpin marxist materialism is, to put the point strongly, a rather poor recourse to name-calling in the absence of a workable criticism. If, as I argue, Hegel makes possible rational debates in this area, then I feel that this should be welcomed. But perhaps more than this, the possibility of Ruben's materialism being at all convincing (outside of the Humean miasma which still clings to British studies in epistemology) turns on this. If it is the characteristic of modern epistemology that we must begin with subjectivity, then Hegel has shown that this must and can be the ground of philosophically defensible realism of united subject and object.

Notes

1   *Vide* Campbell, 'Rationality, Democracy and Freedom in Marxist in Critiques of Hegel's philosophy of Right', pp 2-4; Lubasz, 'Marx's Initial Problematic: The Problem of Poverty' and Perez-Diaz, *State, Bureaucracy and Civil Society*, pp 25-8. Since writing my own contribution to the detailed examination of the impact of the 1842 debates of the Rhenish Parliament on Marx, I have come across further evidence in support of the interpretation put forward by the above in certain of Engels' letters on this point. Nb Engels, 'To Fischer, 15 April 1895'.

2   EPM, pp 232, 332, 329.

3   Labriola's remarkable comments in *Essays on the Materialist Conception of History* are limited in the extent to which they can stand as interpretations as such

because many of the vital texts of the 1840's were not available. Nevertheless, indeed to some extent particularly because of this, Labriola shows how problematic is formalised marxism of the dialectical materialist sort in the light of any sort of sympathetic understanding of Hegel.

4   I have come across a number of references to a substantial course of study of the *Phenomenology* in the USSR in the twenties. For example, in *Let History Judge*, p 438, Roy Medvedev quotes Yevgeny Frelov, a friend of the leading Bolshevik philosopher Jan Sten, to the effect that around 1925 "dialectics was studied by a system that Pokrovsky had worked out at the Institute of Red Professors, a parallel study of Marx's *Capital* and Hegel's *Phenomenology of [Spirit]*". This must have been a significant course, for Medvedev quotes the episode in the context of describing Sten's personal tuition of Stalin. Within those materials accessible to me, I have been unable to find details of this course. One is obliged to fear the worst. Not only do orthodox Russian philosophical writings of the thirties show no qualities which could be derived from such a course, but the personal histories of many of the figures involved were tragic. Sten himself was not rewarded by success with his pupil, whom he regarded as most unpromising. He was rewarded by expulsion from the Party, exile, the publication of his works under author's name and execution on 19 June 1937.

5   This is of course, available to the reader of the *Science of Logic*, and Lenin was to some extent aware of it. Eg Lenin, 'Philosophical Notebooks', pp 230-1. But it is the *Phenomenology* which makes the absence of formalism a principle. For an outstanding statement of the results that can be gained for the interpretation Marx by, following Lenin, a concentration on Hegel's later works *vide* MacGregor, *The Communist Ideal in Hegel and Marx*, nb ch 8.

6   *Vide* Piccone, 'Lukács' *History and Class Consciousness* Half a Century Later'.

7   Popper, 'What is Dialectic?', pts 2-3.

8   DN.

9   Stalin, 'Dialectical and Historical Materialism'.

10   Eg Cornforth, *Dialectical Materialism*, vol 1, pt 2.

11   Eg note the effect of EPM, pp 330-46 on Kojève, *Introduction to the Reading of Hegel*, ch 1; Hyppolite, *Genesis and Structure of Hegel's 'Phenomenology of Spirit'*, pp 156-77 and Sartre, *Being and Nothingness*, pp 233-44.

12   To take but two examples selected because they were published recently, the first pointlessly paraphrasing the *Science of Logic*, Appelbaum, *Karl Marx*, pp 58-61, and the second similarly dealing with the lectures, Carter, *Marx: A Radical Critique*, pp 8-11.

13   *Vide* Hyppolite, *Studies on Marx and Hegel*, p viii.

14   The first part of this chapter will be a discussion of PS, secs 73-5.

15   Hegel's original manuscript did not contain a specific introduction. *Vide* Mueller, 'The Interdependence of the *Phenomenology*, the *Logic* and the *Encyclopaedia*', p 23.

16   LHP3, pt3.

17   Descartes, 'Discourse on the Method', pt 2. I am about to stress certain rather negative consequences of Descartes' positing of the classical epistemological project. Positive themes, to my mind rather anticipating some of Hegel's contributions, are emphasised in Cottingham, *Descartes*, chs 2-4.

18   This discussion of Hegel's views on scepticism locates them within a partial rational reconstruction of the development of modern epistemology. On the place of Hegel's views on ancient scepticism *vide* Forster, *Hegel and Scepticism*. Forster places a proper emphasis on Hegel's 1802 essay, 'The Relation of Scepticism to Philosophy'.

19   LHP3, pp 428-9 and L, p 14. On Hegel's relationship, especially as expressed in the *Science of Logic*, to the fundamentalist themes in Kant's epistemology *vide* Stern, *Hegel, Kant and the Structure of the Object*, chs 3-5.

20   This is the subject of the discussion of sense certainty in PS, ch 1. Some of Hegel's arguments in this chapter are extremely powerful. There is, for example, a refutation of the possibility of descriptions of singular sensations that, in my opinion quite adequately, more than one hundred years before this episode took place, covered the important issues in the collapse of logical atomism or logical positivism under the acknowledgement of the public interpretative framework upon which even natural scientific discourse is built. *Vide* Taylor, 'The Opening Arguments of the Phenomenology' and Westphal, *Hegel's Epistemological Realism*, ch 4.

21   Kant, *Critique of Pure Reason*, pp B131-6.

22   *Ibid*, pp B1-3.

23   *Ibid*, pp B10-4.

24   *Ibid*, pp B166-9.

25   Jacobi, 'David Hume über den Glauben'.

26   LHP3, pp 476-7, 505; L, pp 15-6 and PR, pp 2, 4-5.

27   FK, sec B; Hegel, *Lectures on the History of Philosophy*, vol 2, pt 3 sec 3, sub-sec A and L, ch 5.

28   DBFS, pp 174-95; LHP3, p 479 and L, pp 14-5.

29   Reinhold, *Beytrage Zur Leichtern Uebersicht des Zustandes der Philosophie*, vol 1.

30   Locke, *An Essay Concerning Human Understanding*, bk 4, ch 4, secs 3-4.

31   *Ibid*, bk 2, ch 21, sec 73.

32   *Ibid*, bk 2, ch 1, sec 24.

33   LHP3, pp 304-8.

34   The distinction, made in Locke, *An Essay Concerning Human Understanding*, bk 2, ch 8, is, of course, to be untenable in Berkeley, 'A Treatise Concerning the Principles of Human Knowledge', pt 1, secs 9-15 and, following this, in Hume, *A Treatise of Human Nature*, pp 192-3.

35 *Ibid*, bk 1, pt 4, sec 1, Of course, this conclusion is not nihilistic if one's goal is the thoroughgoing reduction of sense certainty to ideas or spirit. *Vide* Winkler, *Berkeley*. As I set out in chapter 4, however, a present rational reconstruction of modern epistemology must regard this development as unproductive.

36 LHP3, pp 428-9 and L, pp 14-5. Hegel's treatment of the metaphor of the instrument is derived from Spinoza, 'On the Improvement of the Understanding', pp 11-2. His parable of the man who would not enter the water before he could swim is taken from the *Philogelos*, a classical collection of jokes formerly attributed to Hierocles (as Wallace did in his notes to the *Encyclopaedia Logic*), but now regarded as of unclear origin. Anon, *Philogelos, or the Laughter-lover*, no 2.

37 Though the 'Introduction' does not do so until a later passage and in a somewhat different connection, at PS, sec 93.

38 Hume, *A Treatise of Human Nature*, pp 206-7.

39 Kant, *Critique of Pure Reason*, pp B19-24.

40 FK, pp 68-9; LHP3, pp 428-9 and L, sec 40.

41 Kant, *Critique of Pure Reason*, pp B294-315.

42 SL, pp 46-7.

43 FK, pp 76-7; SL pp 120-2 and L, sec 44. Hegel's criticisms here have been convincingly pursued even beyond the point to which he takes them in Hartnack, 'Categories and Things-in-themselves', pp 80-6.

44 Kant's pre-critical maintenance of metaphysical positions he eventually could not sustain is well enough known. What seems to be the case, and what surely calls for much greater investigation, is that Kant was not able to give these positions up entirely even after 1781. I will mention only one example. Kant's first, unsuccessful, application for a chair at Könisberg was supported by a dissertation on 'The Use in Natural Philosophy of Metaphysics Combined with Geometry', of which the published first part was a clearly Liebnizian 'Physical Monadology' derived through Wolff. Kant was, of course, obliged to relinquish monadology as relevant to the explanation of natural appearances as it is a form of dogmatic metaphysics. Interestingly enough, however, he seems never to have rejected its adequacy to the thing-in-itself as "a Platonic concept of the world carried out by Leibniz". Kant, 'Metaphysical Foundations of Natural Science', p 55. One is at least inclined to believe that Kant had more than a little regulatory idea of some details of the unknowable. The point becomes rather amusing in less sophisticated hands than Kant's as when, for example, one finds, Spencer spending almost 100 pages discussing "the unknowable" in his *First Principles*, pt 1.

45 *Vide* Mure, 'Hegel: How and How Far is Philosophy Possible?', sec 2.

46 This chapter now moves to consideration of PS, secs 78-9.

47 LHP3, p 223 and L, sec 64.

48   LHP1, p 14.

49   Descartes, 'Discourse on the Method', pp 117.

50   Eg LHP3, pp 233-40 criticises the purported establishment of the existence of God in eg Descartes, 'Discourse on the Method', pt 4 as resting upon a presumption of the idea of God's complete perfection and the inability of this idea to involve deception which simply should not survive Cartesian doubt. An ingenious - and it needs to be - defence of Descartes in the light of this is provided by Beyssde, 'The Idea of God and the Proofs of His Existence.' More sophisticated defences of Descartes do now, I think generally, concede that the Cartesian commitment to clear ideas is based on psychological assumptions. Eg Loeb, 'The Cartesian Circle'. Whilst this may well leave us with a Descartes of considerable interest to the analysis of thinking being-in-the -world, it does, of course, effect a surrender of Descartes' own epistemological aims.

51   *Vide* Weiss, 'Cartesian Doubt and Hegelian Negation', pp 83-94.

52   L, sec 40.

53   Hume, *A Treatise of Human Nature*, p 272.

54   LHP3, pp 370-4. This, of course, was the substance of Reid's criticism of Hume, Reid, *An Inquiry into the Human Mind*, ch 1 and *idem, Essays on the Intellectual Powers of Man*, essay 2, ch 12. On Hume and Reid *vide* Ferreira, *Scepticism and Reasonable Doubt*, chs 4-6.

55   *Vide* Smith, 'Hegel's Critique of Kant', pp 114-5.

56   For a detailed account of the substantial positions which can be based on the 'Introduction' *vide* Heidegger, *Hegel's Concept of Experience*; Lamb, *Hegel: From Foundation to System*, pt 1; Westphal, *Hegel's Epistemological Realism* and Westphal, *History and Truth in Hegel's 'Phenomenology'*, ch 1.

57   Cf Heidegger, *Being and Time*, sec 13. For an outstanding example of how far Heidegger can be taken in this respect *vide* Richardson, *Existential Epistemology*, pt 2.

58   *Vide* Cowley, *A Critique of British Empiricism*.

59   PS, p 79.

60   *Ibid*, p 49.

61   In the remainder of this chapter, *ibid*, secs 82-4 will be discussed.

62   Eg Ruben, *Marxism and Materialism*, pp 38-56

63   Bhaskar, *A Realist Theory of Science* and *idem*, The *Possibility of Naturalism*.

64   *Vide* Norman, Hegel's *Phenomenology*, ch 6, sec 3. Norman's argument here draws on the distinction between transcendental and empirical idealism in Kant, *Critique of Pure Reason*, pp A368-72. Transcendental idealism is an epistemological argument about the knowability of objects in consciousness, the latter an ontological claim about the ideal foundation of objects. Norman defends Hegel as holding to the former and attempts to separate this from the latter (to which Hegel also holds). This is a fruitful tack which I am trying to develop here.

But, although the terminology of transcendental idealism does serve to show how congenial Hegel's position is to modern transcendental realism, this way of putting the point is, I think, misleading. Hegel's criticism of classical epistemology is an immanent critique leading to the determinate negation of that philosophy. The convincing power of the argument depends on this form and failure to stress this leads to both ignoring Hegel's strength in one respect and weakness in another. First, one can find transcendental deductions of positions supposed to solve the problems left by Kant in Fichte and Schelling. As we shall see in the next chapter, it is the way these fail to relate to classical epistemology but merely stand as new solutions that is their weakness. Second, we might go on after accepting Hegel's argument so far, to examine knowing and transcendentally establish being-in-the-world committed to the reality of objects. But when Hegel puts forward such an examination, in the discussion of sense certainty in *Phenomenology*, ch 1 it is, as Norman points out in ch 2 of his commentary, precisely here that his conclusion is the ideal constitution of objects.

65   Kant, *Critique of Pure Reason*, pp B129-69.
66   *Ibid*, pp B10-4.
67   Fichte, *Science of Knowledge*, pt 1.
68   *Ibid*, pp 188-9.
69   *Ibid*, p 246.
70   *Ibid*, p 11-5.
71   *Vide* Collingwood, *The Idea of Nature*, p 120.
72   Fichte, *Science of Knowledge*, p 203-17.
73   As it enters into the ideas of concept formation that were developed in classical German historiography, Fichte's vitalist way of evaluating theories is the proximate source of the irrationality of value-relevance in Rickert and Weber. It is particularly interesting to note that Rickert supervised Lask's thesis which influentially drew from Fichte the conclusion that concepts and reality are separated by an *hiatus irrationalis*. Lask, 'Fichte's Idealismus und die Geschichte', pp 144-5.
74   Lenin 'Materialism and Empirio-criticism', p 198:
   When Kant assumes that something outside us, a thing-in-itself, corresponds to our ideas, he is a materialist. When he declares this thing-in-itself to be unknowable, transcendental, other-sided, he is an idealist.
75   *Ibid*, p 223.
76. Cf *ibid*, p 141 and *idem*, 'Philosophical Notebooks', p 173.
77   Della Volpe, *Logic as a Positive Science*, p 25 n 33.
78   *Ibid*, pp 53-4.
79   *Ibid*, ch 4 and *idem*, 'For a Materialist Methodology of Economics and of the Moral Disciplines in General.'

80   Colletti, *Marxism and Hegel*, p 84.

81   Della Volpe, *Logic as a Positive Science*, pp 93-4.

82   *Ibid,* pp 35-7.

83   Ruben, *Marxism and Materialism*, p 101:

> I dispute that legitimacy of producing any arguments of any kind which purport to justify philosophically (ie non-circularly) our belief in the essential independence of the world from mind, we do not argue to the extra-mental existence of tables and chairs, as does Bhaskar. On a naturalist perspective we begin with them. It concedes far too much to those who wish to impeach the mind-independence of the external world, or material reality, to think that we could take as premiss that science exists and argue from that to the conclusion that its objects are real. If we begin with science, then we begin with a particular human institution, and human beings are a special sort of physical object. To use hegelian jargon, Bhaskar takes it as immediate that science exists and as mediated by it that objects exists. In fact, to take science as immediate is to take real objects as immediate as well. No argument is necessary.

84   *Ibid,* pp 35, 168.

85   It would appear that the way that Lenin and Ruben identify basic realist claims with materialism is itself merely founded on an assumption. *Vide* Trigg, *Reality at Risk*, pp 27-37. However, I will allow this without comment here.

86   *Ibid,* pp 96-100.

87   Cf the scorn poured on the vulgarity of purported refutations of scepticism by reference to what are presented as the date of sensuous consciousness left entirely to itself in SL, p 832.

88   Ruben, *Marxism and Materialism*, pp 102-2.

89   Bhaskar, *A Realist Theory of Science*, p 257.

90   Ruben's own later work on *Explaining Explanation* contains many excellent examples of this sort of argument, which he himself calls "metapysical".

91   Moore, 'A Defence of Common Sense'.

92   In fact the power of trick is not really philosophical at all, it resides in style. And thus the best example of its modern employment is reported in Boswell's *Life of Johnson*, p 333:

> After we came out of the church, we stood talking for some time together of Bishop Berkeley's ingenious sophistry to prove the non-existence of matter and that everything in the universe is merely ideal. I observed that though we are satisfied that his doctrine is not true, it is impossible to refute it. I shall never forget the alacrity with which Johnson answered, striking his foot with mighty force against a large stone till he rebounded from it, "I refute it *thus*".

93   *Idem, Marxism and Materialism*, pp 99-100.

3 Hegel on the Structure of Learning

After having exposed those characteristics of the classical epistemological project which necessarily render any cognition flawed, Hegel goes on[1] to consider the possibility of dispensing with the inevitably bleak positions of that project and independently developing knowledge of the object to-be-known. This developed knowledge is, once established, to sustain its claim to truth through the then possible comparison of itself with classical epistemology or any other inadequate belief.

Hegel is referring here to Schelling's contraposition of objective idealism to subjective idealism as developed from Kant by Fichte.[2] We have seen in the previous chapter that Fichte's epistemology is entirely sceptical about any real ontological substance connoted by the sense of "objectivity" in truth. In Schelling this sense is to be restored by a statement of the identity of the subject and object in which the ontological import of an epistemology not in fact very different from that of Fichte is to be reversed by explaining subjectivity as a moment in the development of the objective world. Schelling holds that this truth, which he insists is quite different from ordinary beliefs and from classical epistemology,[3] is reached through an intuition of the identity of subject and object. He explains the ordinary empirical consciousness of a distance between subject and object[4] by a transcendental deduction from that intuition.[5] The intuition itself he eventually locates in an almost unconscious moment of aesthetic production.[6] This moment, it seems, represents an acquaintance with the truth specifically because it is mysterious and not able to be understood fully.

Hegel questions whether, whatever may be the rights of the matter, an inadequate belief might just come to accept true knowledge, even when directly confronted with such knowledge as Schelling's procedure envisages. The very problem is of course that such a belief is not able to recognise the truth. Were a true knowledge merely to insist upon its own truth and urge that it should be believed because of its insistence, then it could equally be met by a similar insistence made by the inadequate belief and any one such bare insistence as good as any other. The upshot could be only an unseemly haggling over rival "truths",[7] for why should any belief obey a demand that it stand on its head and accept its opposite?[8]

Whilst he had the greatest regard for the intent of Schelling's earlier philosophy, in the formulation of which indeed he collaborated,[9] Hegel's raising of these themes marks the extent of his departures from Schelling[10] at the time of the writing of the *Phenomenology*. Schelling's transcendental account of the empirical consciousness sophisticatedly develops ostensible forms from the principle of objective idealism. In this respect, Schelling's intellectual intuition is hardly comparable to intuitionism of Jacobi's type, which contents itself with the all encompassing, and therefore completely featureless, truth of God's infinite being.[11] However, with respect to the basic intuition, there seems to be little more to secure Schelling's philosophy than Jacobi's anti-philosophy. Hegel insists that Schelling's method of grasping true knowledge avoids the difficult but indispensable work of the reasoned establishment of itself as true.[12] The effect of this is that Schelling's position seems to be based on an assumption as it eschews coming to terms with the philosophic milieu which is its audience. Hegel accepts neither a simple intuitionist grasp of truth nor a statement of assumed truth accompanied by sophisticated philosophical development, because when it comes to establishing their vital basic truth, both are indifferent to reasoned criteria of proof.

Truth, Hegel says, actively must turn against inadequate beliefs and destroy their conviction in their own truth so that those beliefs might come to recognise the genuine truth as such. The full sense of such destruction, rather than the sense conveyed by suppression or its synonyms, can be accomplished only if it is effective within the inadequate beliefs themselves.[13] Unless it initially is secured within inadequate beliefs and organically develops from them, any change in the acknowledged truth will not, properly speaking, be an acceptance[14] of truth but a failure to win such acceptance. In so failing, though it might force an acknowledgement of its dominance, the truth will not gain recognition of its truth.[15]

There is a sense in which any important intellectual effort must be able to relate itself to its past, because in the past lies its own origins. Schelling's objective idealism must, unless it actually is arbitrary and unfounded in the most random way, potentially be communicable through dialogue with the classical epistemological project since, though Schelling effectively denies this, the significance of his work lies in the way it stands in relationship to that project. Not only will Schelling's work have roots in preceding philosophy, because this is necessarily the soil in which his thoughts will have grown, but the philosophic importance of that thought necessarily lies in its relationship to its own past. It would be to deepen Schelling's self-consciousness and consequently the foundations of his philosophy were he to be dissatisfied with intuition and attempt to ground that philosophy in the reasoned fashion of public dialogue. One cannot conclude these observations without mentioning that the early Schelling's continuous efforts to relate his thought to that of Fichte seems internally to contradict his reliance upon intuition.[16] His very addressing of this antithetical philosophy seems unnecessary were one able to be convinced by intellectual intuition.

Hegel expands this contradiction by arguing that the works of Fichte and Schelling represent the opposition of equally necessary aspects of truth. In an early work, Hegel addressed himself to *The Difference Between Fichte's and Schelling's System of Philosophy*, the use of "System" in the singular here turning on his conviction that these two writers represent moments in the overall development of an adequate philosophy.[17] Recalling his initial polemic against classical epistemology, Hegel will not allow Fichte's acknowledgement of subjectivity, with its concomitant erosion of the sense of objectivity in truth, and indeed he makes a rare direct statement to this effect in the 'Introduction'.[18] But equally he will not allow Schelling's simple establishment of an objective truth through an intuition which will, because it is an intuition, be powerless to win conviction. Rather he takes both of these positions as being constitutive of the point where objective truth is basically known, but awaits its full and clear demonstration as true, which can come only through the deliberately explicit awareness provided by philosophically reasoned cognition. He aims to enrich not only Fichte's empty subject but also Schelling's paradoxically equally empty object.

Hegel's critique of classical epistemology works by identifying it as an alienated belief. Whilst one cannot rest content with the inadequacy of such a belief, further criticisms, he is arguing against Schelling, cannot afford to simply pretend to take an entirely new position and claim that it is adequate. The price to be paid for so doing is to be dogmatic and, in so being, to lose all possibility of properly supplanting the inadequate belief. In any case, the claim of radical novelty is itself mistaken, for the origins of an adequate belief must lie in the belief's past. *The establishment of a non-alienated belief cannot proceed independently of the earlier alienated belief but must, and necessarily can, if the non-alienated belief is correct, relate the two.*

It is on this basis that Hegel goes on to set out explicitly his own proposal for carrying on the criticism of inadequate beliefs. He concludes his consideration of confronting inadequate beliefs with the truth by arguing that it is not open to the latter to demonstrate its truth by means of claiming that the former contains intimations of the truth as the beginnings of movement towards its, the latter's, own self. Fichte repeatedly claimed that Kant's work contained statements which were the precursors of the correct positions properly established in his own system.[19] Though this way of arguing seems to take up Hegel's point about the necessary connection of a true belief with its past and to develop this connection, it does so in a way which is subject to the criticism of dogmatism. Such a procedure turns on true knowledge being recognised as such in order that presentiments of it may be seen as leading to the truth. This procedure must be unconvincing because the truth will merely statically and dogmatically appeal to an untruth which precisely cannot express or recognise truth.

Though critical of the simple assertion implicit in this approach it is along these lines that Hegel thinks that a demonstration of truth can be achieved. For he closes his discussion of the procedure of bluntly opposing inadequate conceptions and the truth by declaring that it is because the static appealing to earlier intimation of truth will not win recognition that the *Phenomenology* is to undertake the exposition of the process by which truth came to appear. This exposition actually will illustrate the dynamic movement from inadequate belief to truth, not just claim this relation to be the case.[20] It will thus show how justified was an appeal to intimations of truth in earlier inadequate beliefs. The difference will be that Hegel is not to start from what asserts itself to be an adequate position and claim to see presentiments of that position in the past, but is to start from inadequate positions and be led by them to the truth.

That this procedure should be successful would appear not only not to be guaranteed, but the absence of any guarantee is its strength. It is open for any belief to try to show that it is the productive outcome of earlier beliefs, and to the extent that this is so the latter belief will win recognition of its truth. It will stand as true in that it constitutes what is valuable about earlier thought. But there is a hazard. If going through this procedure is necessary for a belief to establish its truth, it is by no means certain that at the end the effort will have been met with success. The belief claiming to be true may fail, for it may not have that significance. It is having run this risk that gives the successful belief its true quality.

Hegel holds, then, that it is the test of the true belief that it demonstrates its own truth. It can do so by giving an account of how truth came to appear, not by starting from the truth and comparing it to inadequate beliefs, but by starting from inadequate beliefs and, through analysis of them, moving to the truth. At the end of the 'Introduction' Hegel affirms what was to be the original title of the *Phenomenology*.[21] The book was to be the "Science of the Experience of Consciousness" in that it would develop a proof of truth from discussion of earlier experience. The truth will appear for inadequate beliefs, and inadequacy come to be realised for what it is, by developing truth from such belief.

That the *Phenomenology* will establish truth in this way potentially could satisfy Hegel's conditions for winning conviction. Not only does starting with inadequate beliefs secure the *Phenomenology* in those beliefs in the way Hegel feels is essential, but two further valuable qualities characterise the development which will lead to the recognition of the truth.

First, this development is to furnish a proof which is essentially empirical as opposed to merely speculative in the bad sense.[22] It is to win conviction by taking an inadequate belief and, by analysis of it, revealing that it is a moment of the development of truth. The understanding of such a belief will, on an in principle corrigible empirical truth claim, be shown to require the location of the belief within this development. The test of the true belief is that it is positively immanent in the beliefs it regards as inadequate.

It is this theme which allows us to identify what Hegel meant by "phenomenology". The term actually was not Hegel's own[23] and he included it in the title of the book only mid-way through writing it,[24] replacing what I have just mentioned was the original title: "Science of the Experience of Consciousness". "Phenomenology" was in fact coined in 1764 by JH Lambert, a distinguished predecessor of Kant at Königsberg, to describe, through an obvious Greek derivation, his doctrine of mere appearance as opposed to true essence.[25] Kant himself is known to have envisaged, in correspondence with Lambert and others, a similar project, a purely negative[26] exposure of the errors caused by exceeding in speculation the limits of empirical knowledge[27] as a propaedeutic to the examination of the pure reason.[28] He did not carry out this project as such, but of course it has its echo in the dialectic of the *Critique of Pure Reason*. The main difference between Kant's envisaged phenomenology and the dialectic of the *Critique* would seem to be that the former would have amounted to no more than the professed clearing away of mistaken ideas whereas in the latter certain inadequate beliefs are explained as the mistaken but nevertheless inevitable functions of human reason.[29]

Linked to his wider criticisms of the place of "phenomena" in Kant's philosophy, Hegel greatly extends this reincorporation of inadequate beliefs into philosophy by his phenomenology. Though retaining the sense of the examination of inadequate beliefs, phenomenology turns on the conviction that it is profoundly mistaken to treat of such beliefs as just obstructive of truth. Classical epistemology decays into unrelieved scepticism because its demonstration that our beliefs are all necessarily phenomenal is taken to mean that those beliefs are thereby separated from the truth. For Hegel it is precisely through inadequate beliefs that we can be lead to the truth, because the development of the truth must lie in such beliefs.

Typically, attempts to demarcate a boundary of truth/falsehood (or science/ideology, etc.) after the pattern set by Bacon's use of "idols"[30] consign the latter to a category whose very purpose is to contrast with the former. Such rigid demarcation of claims to truth from their past, ignoring the circumstances of their production, marks their own lack of self-comprehension, not an absolute break with the past. Having stressed this point against Schelling, Hegel presents phenomenology as an open commitment to an empirical encounter with a history of inadequate beliefs which will lead to a recognition of the truth. Through phenomenology, Hegel hopes to find a proof of truth by genuinely casting himself into inadequate beliefs.

Hegel is driving at a sort of benign circularity in his argument which later is stated explicitly in the *Science of Logic*[31] and the *Encyclopaedia Logic*.[32] A position such as Schelling's, posited just as an hypothesis rather than as a self-justifying intuition, *could* be regarded as true after phenomenological evaluation showed its claims about its own importance were true. For the empirical outcome of the evaluation would be to arrive at that position. The logical criticism of a circular argument vests on the demonstration of an unjustified foreclosure of alternative possibilities by the effective presumption of a conclusion and Schelling's intuitive stance, with its closed features, is susceptible to this. But if the free determinate negation of earlier beliefs immanently did produce the substance of what Schelling previously had only intuitively asserted, then the intuitive position retrospectively would be justified, though not as an intuition. The intuitive position would dissolve into the phenomenological movement described.[33]

This leads to the second important characteristic of the *Phenomenology* as a type of proof. This is the reflexive quality of the recognition of truth it is to furnish. Hegel's complete oeuvre does not lack a statement of true philosophy put forward quite internally, relying only on its own terms, "the true in its true shape" as he put it.[34] This is provided in the published system set out in the *Encyclopaedia of Philosophical Sciences in Outline*. But this is not the form of the *Phenomenology*. This latter work is to describe how the truth was developed as a way of leading up to the recognition of that truth, which can then be set out in the system. The *Phenomenology* is, then, to be a persuasive introduction to the system.

Though this is to allow the *Phenomenology* to avoid the strictures Hegel levelled at Schelling's contraposition of a system of truth to inadequate beliefs as a form of proof, it arguably brings the work under some of the criticism Hegel levelled at classical epistemology.[35] For, bearing in mind what was said of practically working with "truths" which are ultimately not thought to be true, what can we think of the *Phenomenology* working with this subject matter? Hegel initially regarded the *Phenomenology* as "the first part of the system", but in the second edition of the book, on which he had just commenced work when he died, he omitted this description.[36] This later placing of the *Phenomenology* outside of the system, in so far as it registers the important difference between the two, seems to be the more correct position.[37] But, as Hegel himself acknowledges,[38] this location itself places a question mark against the truth produced by phenomenology.

The *Phenomenology* does not, however, fall under Hegel's own earlier criticism of working outside of the truth, because its thrust is to show that the movement of inadequate beliefs is of the truth. Hegel's final thought on the role of the *Phenomenology* as an introduction would seem to have been that both articulate truth, but in two different ways which reflect two different standpoints. The former pursues the movement of inadequate beliefs from their own standpoints through to eventual truth. The latter reorders the product of this pursuit from the standpoint of having attained the later knowledge of truth previously missing from inadequate beliefs.

The possibility of setting out a system of truth which has a form differing from the phenomenological following of inadequate beliefs is predicated upon those who held those beliefs, in the act of recognising the truth, thereby reflexively being enabled to recognise the development of their own recognition as such. The winning of the recognition of truth involves those who now are enlightened looking back on their own earlier beliefs and seeing them in their true light, that is as overall inadequate. This they previously could not do, since they first experienced the development of which they were part as not as such a development but as "truth" itself. Hegel will convince those who held inadequate beliefs by showing that those beliefs both lead to truth and, from this, that those earlier beliefs were incorrect. Hegel does not shrink from emphasising that to follow the progression of the *Phenomenology* will entail continuously recognising that what formerly were held to be truths were not so. The *Phenomenology* follows, he says, the way of despair, the despair of rejecting earlier beliefs.

The whole impulse behind the *Phenomenology* is to carry out a necessary critique of earlier experience,[39] a critique which is to provide the double sense of enlightenment we have seen.[40] There is the initial recognition of the truth, and also a further securing of conviction by the implication of a reflexive critique of earlier experience by the very locating of that experience in the development of truth. In the

Phenomenology nothing can be presupposed, we merely go forward as we are led. Having reached the truth, in the *Encyclopaedia* Hegel reorders his material according to the acquired knowledge of the truth. This provides a new basis for deeper comprehension of the nature of earlier beliefs, once believed to be true and now known to be inadequate.

Hegel's proposal for the replacement of an inadequate belief with a true one turns not on the dogmatic contraposition of the beliefs but on the necessity of winning conviction. The inadequate belief is to be criticised, but the criticism, if it is to be successful, must work as a development from that belief. This is possible because if the true belief was conscious of its own production, it would recognise that it is the product of earlier beliefs, though those beliefs are now regarded as inadequate. Truth, then, though it has the external referent of objectivity, is located in the nature of earlier discourse and the procedure of establishing that truth is the clarification of that location. *This makes the criticism of inadequate beliefs a process of reflexive clarification, not one of dogmatic assertion.*

I present the foregoing as a carefully faithful account of Hegel's intentions in the *Phenomenology* and indeed of what he meant by phenomenology. I have tried to show - not to emphasise, for the emphasis is Hegel's own - that phenomenology is an empirically guided process of reflexive clarification through determinate negation of inadequate beliefs. It is metaphysical only in the sense that it is a successful rejection of the alienation which placed our power to know outwith this world.

Grasping this is essential to a proper understanding of what Hegel means when, later in the 'Introduction',[41] he describes this process as a dialectic. At this point of the 'Introduction' Hegel declares that he intends to add to the foregoing remarks about the necessity of undertaking the phenomenological inquiry something further on the method of carrying out this undertaking. Quite typically, his account of this method starts with an idea of what, in the end, we will find out it is not, the idea that criticism requires a fixed criterion of truth. If Hegel's project is to identify inadequate conceptions, and by so doing move closer to truth, then, he argues, the project would seem to require a criterion by which specific conceptions can be evaluated. But to say this immediately runs us into difficulties we have already encountered, particularly in respect of Schelling. For on what grounds could such a criterion by justified? Obviously such a criterion requires an agreement on truth but this is what is sought by the employment of the criterion. If we say that such agreement is unavailable, it becomes difficult to see how the examination of particular beliefs can take place.

If we take the problem of the complete dissociation of subject and object in consciousness to be solved, we now seem to be left with the problem of their relative dissociation. This is to say, Hegel is faced with the problem of learning. For though subject and object may be united on an ontological ground, they are not entirely one. Bringing them together is a perennial task. Dialectic is Hegel's method of bringing this relative dissociation within the unity of subject and object.

Hegel's solution of the problem of supplying a criterion to test knowledge claims is brief. We should not supply any such criterion. Indeed we need not even stage a testing of specific claims to truth. For since both claims and objects are, as we now know, for-consciousness, it is this very consciousness that stages their comparison. Consciousness itself *is* the awareness of any discrepancy between claim and object or, to put it this way, is the assessment of the adequacy of the former by use of the criterion of the latter. Hegel is continuing to press home his criticism of epistemological alienation by showing how the basic epistemological impulse distorted in the classical epistemological project actually *is* grounded. Determinate negation is explained as a process of the progressive evaluation of cognitions by the only criteria that are available for this, but which always *are* available, the objects cognition knows in consciousness. Learning is a process not of supplying outside criteria or objects but of developing awareness of the inadequacies of claims to knowledge to the objects known in consciousness.[42]

Hegel previously had argued, as we have seen, that to regard the thing-in-itself as the object of knowledge, and therefore as the criterion by which cognition should be judged, is an absurd epistemological position. The objects that can be of pertinence to knowing must be for-consciousness. He is now trying to set out the way in which these objects may serve as criteria for the testing of cognitions in the development of knowledge. Knowing consciousness is composed of cognitions and the objects they postulate. We now are discussing consciousness, and this identification of two elements in knowing, which amounts to the distinction of subject and object, must be justified without reference to an object-in-itself. This can, I think, readily be done, though I must point out that here I am reading what I think is implied in Hegel's position rather than directly interpreting it, for he is very brief indeed on this point.

Knowing consciousness "layers" its constituent beliefs, distinguishing by degrees of relative certitude attached to these beliefs between the relatively new and the more settled beliefs. These latter take on more the status of objectivity as they have gained a relatively large degree of corroboration in earlier investigations. New cognitions address issues which arise within the broad framework of these objects for-consciousness. These objects are, then, the criteria by which cognitions are assessed. As opposed to the objective inner core of knowing consciousness' set of beliefs, there are graduated belts of relatively fragile contributions to knowing which are, therefore precisely, subjective.

Though Hegel's argument depends on some such layering of subject and object in consciousness as I have set out, he devotes virtually all of his attention to a subsidiary position. This is the shift in the nature of the *object* which follows from the evaluation of any subjective cognition. Should a belief fail the test of comparison and be rejected, it must of course be regarded as inadequate. But, Hegel says, so too must the criterion be rejected. For that criterion is the framework in which the belief arose and when that belief is shown to be inadequate, this must call into question the criterion. This seems sophistic but, hardly unusually, it is the extreme economy of Hegel's manner of expression which more or less conceals an extremely valuable point. When a belief's being revealed as inadequate has led to the rejection of the belief and perhaps also to the rendering suspect to some degree of its object, then, Hegel says, this is not only a testing of what we know but of what knowing is.

Hegel rather overemphasises the degree to which patterns of objectivity can be called into question, as it is very doubtful whether the rejection of any one particular belief can of itself ever be crucial for the general framework in which that belief arose. Hegel himself is concerned with very major shifts in beliefs and in the organisation of ethical life and his studies in the body of the *Phenomenology* tend to have this acutely epochal form. However, the underlying commitment to openness in all our beliefs is a valuable one, as is the indication of how relatively settled structures of objectivity can be called into question. When these structures lead to the framing of new subjective conjectures that are found to do little or nothing to improve our knowledge in the areas they cover, then the possibility of a major shift in our understanding as a precondition of such improvement has to be countenanced. In this sense, earlier objects may become changed, for radical alterations in our understanding through reflexive reassessment of hitherto developed knowledge refashion even relatively stable sets of beliefs. They call, as we have just seen Hegel say, our very ideas of what knowing is into question.

It is the characteristic motif of dogmatism that such a call goes unheeded. Inadequacies are treated not so much as requiring explanation as requiring to be explained away in terms which preserve the original core ideas of the character of objectivity in the area of inquiry. Hegel's own criticisms of the classical epistemological project exemplifies authentic determinate negation which refuses to leave even the most apparently ineluctable beliefs inviolable. Hegel's particular contribution is to insist on the complete unacceptability of denying philosophic adequacy to cognition and to go on to have the faith to call into question the fundamental standard of knowledge that can yield only inadequate cognitions. As I will make explicit at the end of this chapter but as the reader aware particularly of Lakatos' work may well have realised, much of this idea of the treatment of subject and object in Hegel is revived in the treatment of degenerate research programmes in the modern philosophy of science. Now, there is a wealth of innovation in especially Lakatos that can in no way be traced back to Hegel, but there is a sense in which Hegel's treatment of subject and object is far more sound than avowedly post-empiricist philosophy's explanations. Hegel's treatment follows from a sound location of subjectivity and objectivity in the nature of knowing consciousness whereas, as we will see, post-empiricist philosophy of science is characterised by a fundamental acceptance of foundationalism which makes the name of post-empiricism an irony at its own expense.

With these comments Hegel details, as he now says, the dialectical movement which is the form of learning through experience. What characteristics of experience as Hegel depicts it are brought out by this discussion of the form of movement by which experience develops? One is emphasised above all others. Consciousness is the ground of its own development. Consciousness embraces both claim to knowledge and object and is their comparison. Attempts to close the distance between subject and object are the essence of dialectical development. Subjective beliefs are tested against the present object and, if they contribute to the object, they change it by expanding it. If they fail to contribute to the object, they eventually call for a shift in the very nature of the object, indicated by the nature of the determinate negation of these failures, as the condition of further progress in experience.

Of course, the dialectic does not have to be progressive, but there is a strong tendency for it to be so in that, as it is possible to draw upon the determinate negations of the past, it is possible to learn. Knowing then can be teleological in that it can be consciously guided according to an accumulation of determinate negations. It is in pursuit of the improvement of knowledge that consciousness must spoil the limited satisfaction which attends acceptance of any belief. In search of development, consciousness suffers the violence of the exposure of inadequate beliefs at its own hands.

Interpretations[43] and purported developments[44] of Hegel's dialectic subsequent to his death have repeatedly claimed that this dialectic has a triadic form. Of what hermeneutic value is this claim? It was Kant whom Hegel correctly identified as having initiated the modern revival of triadic dialectic, an infinite merit of the Kantian philosophy, Hegel believed.[45] Kant's transcendental dialectic is, as I have mentioned, an attempt to account for those illusions which arise when the understanding, driven by those perennially seductive speculative conundra which we can all readily call to mind, undertakes purely conceptual ratiocination beyond the empirical bounds of sense. Though in the dialectic Kant may revive an ancient form of argument, he does so in order to contribute to the polemic against speculation by which modern empirical thought explicitly distanced itself from its past. However, again as has been mentioned, unlike Bacon's use of "idols", Kant does not aim at the complete removal of speculative questions. Rather, their persistent presence is to be explained transcendentally, for they are given a fixed place in reason as a type of unrealisable longing.[46]

The presence of the speculative questions dealt with in Kant's dialectic is rendered harmless for the understanding, rather than perniciously misleading, because these questions are able to be rationally explained, if not answered as such. Kant's transcendental analysis cannot, by its very nature, seek to dispel what it reveals, but nevertheless Kant can claim that purely speculative questions are false questions in the sense that the understanding cannot make a coherent response to them in their own terms. Kant tries to show this by showing that attempted answers must fall into one of three types of inextricable confusion.[47] The second of these as he sets them out, the antinomies, is the most interesting for us here. An antinomy is a set of two propositions, each of which is required for speculation and indeed have, in one way or another, continually been put forward. However, these propositions are mutually antithetical, which of course precludes any consistent satisfaction of the need to hold them both.[48]

Kant was unable to restrict his attribution of an antinomical form to archaic cosmologies and the like, but carried this over to what still remain the fundamental problems of epistemology, knowledge of objects coupled with consciousness of subjectivity. In so far as he did so, then the essentially derogatory nature of the antinomical description cannot be maintained for pressing problems seem to have antinomical form. In the antinomies, Kant more or less gives the form not only of problems he would regard as fruitless, but also of ones he would regard as crucial. The feature of the antinomies which Kant takes to be the mark of incomprehensibility is the mutual antithesis of the propositions involved. It is very difficult indeed to base a sound rejection of the speculative issues involved here on this ground, for the overall impression which Kant gives is that he has just not made a sufficient attempt to resolve or synthesise the antitheses. Now, as we have seen, his own epistemology is based on a notion of synthesis and when he goes on to describe the categories of defensible reason, they themselves have a form very like that set out in the antinomical dialectic, only expanded to the third term missing in the antinomies. His presentation of the categories is of triplicities in which there is a mediate term formed by the combination of the other two[49] and there is no reason of form why this syllogism could not be expanded to the antinomies and their speculative problems. It is, Hegel believed[50] and he surely was right, more a matter of the way in which Kant sets out the account and proofs of the antinomies that blocks off their mediation, rather than any profound dislocation between their form and that of the categories. This is a point which Hegel settles by resolving the antinomies in arguments which are as sound as Kant's description of the categories (which sometimes is not very sound of course).[51]

Having looked at the fundamental substance of this explication earlier, we are now concerned with the form. Fichte claimed to overcome the flat opposition of antinomical thesis and antithesis in the *Critique of Pure Reason* by expanding these to a mediated third term of the synthesis of the two. The form of the self-positing of ego is conceived in a triadic fashion as a mediation of ego and posited non-ego. This basic form of Fichte's explanation of knowing[52] incidentally - for I do not intend further to discuss this point as the treatment is derived directly from Fichte though, of course, subjected to a change of object - is also found throughout Schelling's early philosophy.[53] Now, as we have seen Hegel to be in broad sympathy with the aims of Fichte and Schelling, we can expect him to more or less endorse their responses to the Kantian dialectic. Though this is so,[54] we equally can expect that the formalism of this application - and this is the right word - of thesis-antithesis-synthesis would be anathema to him.[55] Hegel indeed is withering in his criticism of the use of this scheme by Fichte and Schelling as a "monotonous formalism".[56] This criticism must, I think, be accepted without reservation, for in its formalistic use this scheme repeats a dry reduction of all moments of determinateness to moments of synthetic mediation which is entirely abstract and barren.

It must categorically be stated that one cannot even begin successfully to interpret Hegel's own writings through the employment of the heuristic of a stiff thesis-antithesis-synthesis template.[57] For one thing, these terms are but very rarely to be found in Hegel's writings,[58] other than where he takes them over in commentary, and never, subject to this proviso, to my knowledge together.[59] More importantly, if one forces the text into the mould of this syllogistic scheme, then the very vivacity, in the fullest sense, that distinguishes the Hegelian phenomenology from the philosophies of Fichte and Schelling[60] thereby is lost to view. Hegel's dialectic of determinate negations is to proceed, as we have seen, by following the self-movement of consciousness. It is in no way to impose a pattern upon this development. Its of consciousness. It is in no way to impose a pattern upon this development. Its mechanism of movement, immanent critique structured by the moments of subjectivity and objectivity, in no sense was to follow a fixed pattern of theses and antitheses, much to the embarrassment of attempts to criticise Hegel for not providing a clear enough triadic pattern to his dialectic such as the critic's formalistic understanding requires[61] or for carrying out formalistic deductions of specific phenomena.

In respect of the latter criticism, we are fortunate in being able to draw upon a polemical clarification of his views which Hegel provided in 1802[62] and repeated in 1827.[63] In response to the claim that a completely adequate philosophical system would be able deductively to derive all existent phenomena, one WT Krug, a distinguished contemporary of Hegel's (he was to succeed Kant at Königsberg), challenged such a system to deduce the pen with which he wrote his criticisms of it.[64] Krug may have some licence to direct this barb at Schelling,[65] but Hegel's response has great power. Hegel turns the attempted sarcasm back against itself. The task which Krug would wish to see performed is indeed, Hegel agrees, a trivial one. Krug therefore must wait until far more pressing matters have been dealt with before he can hope to see his pen being glorified within a system of true philosophy. Now, it seems clear that Hegel allowed that, in principle, Krug's pen could be found such a place[66] and there is no point in trying to defend Hegel by withdrawing from the strength of this claim.[67] We would hardly have such confidence as Hegel today, for reasons I will discuss in the next chapter, but this is not because we would deny what Hegel is fundamentally trying to say, that an explanation of the pen can be put forward. Hegel is not saying that the existence of the pen can formally be deduced but that, in principle, the pen can be accounted for, its use explained, according to whatever are the requisite explanatory materials. The issue is one of adequate *comprehension*, in the form required by the subject, rather than a presumption of formal deduction.[68] In this sense, to hold out the hope of Krug's pen being brought under a true philosophy is hardly fancifiul, it is merely a way of saying that its existence is in principle explicable and to say this seems to be as valid holding out any other possibility of explanation.[69] It must also be said, of course, that this explanandum seems as little worthy of the effort as Hegel himself thinks.

We are not, however, entitled to conclude from all this that Hegel's dialectic displays no intimate connection with a triadic form.[70] The essentially approving character of Hegel's comments on Kant's revival of this form should alert us to this, as should the marked literary predilection for overall triadic arrangements which he displays throughout his work - as a brief perusal of any table of contents which he provided would reveal. The fundamental point which Hegel is trying to capture in dialectic - that it describes the progressive subject-object structure of learning - is well set out in the *Encyclopaedia Logic*:

> by dialectic is meant the indwelling tendency outwards by which the one-sidedness and limitation of the predicates of understanding is seen in its

true light and shown to be the negation of them...Thus understood, the dialectical principle constitutes the life and soul of scientific progress.[71]

This is to say that, as with Fichte or Schelling, Hegel sets his overall solution to epistemological problems within a broad triad. But Hegel's triad is to be immanently developed from the given forms of consciousness and is to stand or fall by the plausibility of its immanent development, quite in opposition to the abstract formality of Fichte and Schelling. The dialectic is the broad description of the general subject-object form of learning understood as a process of determinate negations. Far from being objectionable, it is, as we have seen it so far, a rather substantial contribution to the philosophy of scientific development.[72]

This attitude to the interpretation of Hegel can, I think, be brought out by some comments on the discussion of Hegel in Popper's 'What is Dialectic?' In the famous criticism of Hegel's broadly social philosophy which he wrote at about the same time, Popper, in virtually his first words about Hegel in *The Open Society and Its Enemies*, gives his opinion that Hegel would have been a fit subject for psychoanalysis.[73] (This seems particularly cruel as Popper seems to have substantially reached his unfavourable conclusions about that discipline at that time). In 'What is Dialectic?' we are presented with what is presumably an aspect of Hegel' pathology - his notion of truth is utterly absurd.[74] Now, although Popper's paper is as shot through with coarse misrepresentation of Hegel as is his book,[75] there is doubtless and inevitably some important ways in which Hegel's work is unsatisfactory. But I will try to show that this sense is hardly akin to flat incomprehensibility but is rather that of the unsatisfactory resolution of some very real issues. To ignore these means that one falls beneath the level of Hegel's thought.[76]

Popper's own work provides, I think, a case in point. It was Popper's claim to have solved the problem of induction in the philosophy of science, that is to say understanding the movement from particular statements (of events) to general ones (of a law-like form)[77] by adopting what he called a deductive system.[78] In this system the issues are the criteria of the falsification or refutation of theories in science understood as the continuous replacement of theories. Typically Humean scepticism based on objections to the possibility of induction are thereby rendered immaterial as science is to proceed without recourse to that operation.[79] Now, as Popper himself says,[80] his basic shift in the focus of the philosophy of science did not really involve nor require a notion of truth. We can agree with him that the displacement of scientific theories by others does not of itself necessarily imply a movement, intended or actual, towards truth. However, when we invoke a general philosophy of science based on agnosticism on this point, then "science" can retain few of its nobler connotations of the valuable provision of knowledge and becomes merely an academic, in the bad sense, enterprise. Popper gives an analogy between his envisaged process of continuous criticism and a game[81] and I would say that this is uncomfortably true. For all its overt polemic against inductivism, indeed probably because of this, Popper's philosophy of science is readily assimilable to the basic programme of the Humean philosophy of science. As such it stands, despite Popper's quibbles, as *the* twentieth

rationalisation of technical rational science's eschewing of all social goods but its own[82] practical[83] ones.

Popper frequently has characterised science as a process of progressive discovery[84] and the inconsistency of such a characterisation, involving as it does some idea of truth, speaks of his reluctance to grasp the rigorous conclusion of his own philosophy.[85] Relatively recently he has openly admitted both his earlier inconsistencies and the absence of a motivational rationale for a science without truth, and has tried to set both right by bringing into his work some idea of truth having a necessary regulatory function in scientific development.[86] His aim is to be able to describe his philosophy as setting out the process by which we may actually *learn* from our mistakes.[87] Though in my opinion this is a valuable direction for Popper to take, it is instructive to see why he is unable to establish any real regulation of criticism of truth.

There is obviously going to be a forcedness about such a saving development in Popper's representation of science, for if this representation could be formulated without use of a notion of truth, then the later inclusion of some such notion to save the representation from certain criticisms is not the actual involvement of truth in the core formulation. This is a crucial point. Popper's tack when faced with scepticism about induction was not to refute that scepticism[88] but rather to accept it, give up the aim of verification and set criteria for falsifying theories.[89] On this basis, to recognise that truth is needed even as a motive for falsification and therefore to include it in such a role does not allow Popper to claim, as he does,[90] that his description of science is now of an approach to truth. Having failed to reject an inductivist understanding of truth, truth, for Popper's philosophy, remains above human authority.[91] Despite Popper's use of some picturesque metaphors which conceal this,[92] he cannot come to terms with Hegel's criticisms of the idea of being in possession of approximations of truth when what is properly true is unreachable. Perhaps the clearest indication of this is that Popper's idea of the way in which we might speak about truth, which he purports to derive from Tarski, is an attempt to make this possible through discussion about the form of linguistic statements and their implication of correspondence to facts.[93] This is to say that, as with all of this sort of underhand ontology in analytic philosophy, it is hopelessly trivial in respect of, indeed eschews consideration of, understanding how we may claim to know real states of affairs.[94]

Now, I think Popper falls beneath Hegel's demonstration of the possibility of knowing through critique of those epistemological positions which terminate in unbelievable scepticism. Indeed, there arises a rather peculiar situation in Popper's understanding of Hegel. I would say that the closest Popper comes in all of his writings on the topic to a representation of Hegel's views that is not wildly inaccurate is in the *first* section of 'What is Dialectic?' - section *two* is at the same level as Popper's claim that the dialectic of lordship and bondage is a defence of slavery. This happy coincidence with respect of the critical features of the dialectic is not, unfortunately for Popper, repeated in its positive aspects. Obviously leaving aside the hugely authoritative technical detail, what is best about Popper's own work in respect of establishing a philosophy of science against scepticist philosophy is presaged, indeed rather better done, in Hegel. One - surely - can hardly postulate a relationship of conscious intellectual indebtedness here, though Popper has acknowledged, with rather better done, in Hegel. One - surely - can hardly postulate a relationship of conscious intellectual indebtedness here, though Popper has acknowledged, with respect to the Peirce, that though many of his ideas have been presaged, he has been put to the labour of developing them independently.[95] However, there is an attempt to deal with this ticklish problem in Lakatos. Lakatos thanks Popper for help in breaking from Hegel,[96] and yet Lakatos' extensions of Popper are, I would say, basically correct in so far as they repeat Hegel's directions of thought. I do not mean by this to refer to the strong Hegelian cast of some of Lakatos' ideas, of which the rational reconstruction of intellectual disciplines, so reminiscent of Hegel's own histories of thought, is the outstanding example.[97] I mean that when, having pushed Popper's work to its sceptical conclusion, Lakatos makes a plea or a whiff of inductivism,[98] the way he does this directly recalls the positive side of determinate negation. Having immersed ourselves in science and presumed science's ability to know, Popper's philosophy, Lakatos argues, gives us many valuable reflections on how to judge the value of now criticised theories. Of course, it is quite unprincipled to ask for a whiff of inductivism within Popper's philosophy, which is founded in the rejection of just such a possibility. In fact, Lakatos does not really want the return of inductivism but of the sort of confidence in truth to which it aspired. To achieve this he puts forward a truly lame attempt to close the distance between wishing for something and achieving it.[99] The weakness of this in an oeuvre as brilliant as Lakatos' makes one despair of the power of philosophic knowledge of faults ever to eradicate them from one's own practice.

Overall, and ironically enough, it would seem that there is a great deal in Hegel which would give a more sound footing for the achievements of twentieth century philosophy of science by eradicating, in the way Hegel does for classical epistemology, the bad consciousness of doing something one denies one can be done.[100]

For the interpretation of Marx's relationship to Hegel, I hope that the preceding two chapters have shown a Hegel more or less entirely lost in interpretations of his work outside of pure Hegel scholarship. Hegel's dialectic, viewed in this way, is manifestly not just "a simple internal principle"[101] and, crucially more than this, should it become so, then it would do so in complete contradiction of its own methodological canons. I do not mean only that its results would be arrived at in defiance of these canons, but that the method by which Hegel could arrive at such results also would be corrupt.

Now, to anticipate the next chapter, it is undeniable that Marx found it essential to reject the "one-sidedness and limitations"[102] bound up in "Hegel's familiar trick of the self-distinction of man in thought".[103] But if we allow that "Hegel is indeed an idealist and a monist", we should go on to recognise that "what deserves admiration...is his unfaithfulness to this monism"[104] which follows from "the astonishing self-subversive movement of Hegel's dialectical thought".[105] I will argue that Marx understood this in a way that the interpretations of his work have not been able to reproduce. The key to this understanding lies in the use of the notion of inversion as a metaphor for the critique of alienated beliefs by Hegel and Marx.

Notes

1   PS, secs 76-7, 88-9 will be discussed here.

2   *Vide* Caird, *Hegel*, ch 3 and Pippin, *Hegel's Idealism*, pt 1.

3   Schelling, *System of Transcendental Idealism*, p 1.

4   *Ibid*, pt 1.

5   *Ibid*, pt 3.

6   *Ibid*, pt 6, sec 3.

7   PR, pp 2-3.

8   PS. p 15.

9   DBFS and LHP3, pt 3, sec 3, sub-sec D.

10   Hegel's correspondence with Schelling is somewhat equivocatory on this point. *Idem*, 'To Schelling, 1 May 1807' and Schelling, 'To Hegel, 2 November 1807.'

11   LHP3, pp 519-20.

12   *Ibid*, pp 522-5, 550; PS, pp 489-90 and L, sec 229 addn.

13   *Vide* Norman, Hegel's *Phenomenology*, p 14.

14   Hegel's thought on the pedagogical relationship involved here is based on Rousseau *Emile*, nb p 19.

15   *Vide* Lukács, *The Young Hegel*, pp 428-32.

16   Schelling, *System of Transcendental Idealism*, pt 3.

17   *Vide* Kaufmann, *Hegel*, pp 72-3.

18   PS, p 52. Cf DBFS, pp 119-54; FK, sec C; LHP3, pt 3 sec 3, sub-sec C1 and L, sec 194 addn.

19   Fichte, *Science of Knowledge*, pp 1-2. That this method of proceeding is arrogant and ungrateful is clear. The unseemly character of the philosophic milieu at the end of Kant's life and in the period immediately after his death is amply demonstrated in Kaufmann, *Hegel*, sec 26. The paradox of the episode is that by stating his positions in this way, regardless of decorum, Fichte was unable to show why those positions were so important.

20   That the theme of movement as opposed to stasis characterises Hegel's differences with Schelling is emphasised in Kierkegaard, *Journals and Papers*, vol 2, p 223.

21   *Vide* Mueller, 'The Interdependence of the *Phenomenology*, *Logic* and *Encyclopaedia*, p 23.

22   *Vide* Kojève, *An Introduction to the Reading of Hegel*, ch 7.

23   *Vide* Kaufmann, *Hegel*, p 148.

24   *Ibid*, p 413.

25   Lambert, *Neues Organon*, vol 2 pt 4.

26   Kant, 'To Lambert, 2 September 1770', p 59.

27   *Ibid* and *idem*, 'To Herz, 21 February 1772', p 71.

28   *Idem*, 'To Lambert, 2 September 1770', pp 59-60.

29   *Idem, Critique of Pure Reason*, pp B354-5. As I have mentioned in the previous chapter, examination of Kant's pre-critical writings shows clearly enough that he himself once held to some of these positions, including an extended rationalist metaphysics and even, one should add, an empirical proof of God's existence. *Idem*, 'A New Exposition of the First Principles of Metaphysical Knowledge' and *idem, The One Possible Basis for a Demonstration of the Existence of God.*

30   Bacon, 'The New Organon', aphs 41-68.

31   SL, pp 67-78. *Vide* Findlay, 'Reflexive Asymmetry: Hegel's Most Fundamental Methodological Ruse', pp 154-73.

32   L, sec 17. The name "*Encyclopaedia*" can be seen as a play on this theme. *Vide* Mueller, 'The Interdependence of the *Phenomenology, Logic* and *Encyclopaedia*' pp 30-3.

33   *Vide* Heidegger, *Hegel's Concept of Experience*, p 44 and Kojève, *An Introduction to the Reading of Hegel*, pp 93-9.

34   PS, pp 3, 22.

35   *Vide* Hyppolite, *Genesis and Structure of Hegel's 'Phenomenology of Spirit'*, pp 5-7, 53-5.

36   PS, pp 13-7 Cf BP, p 88; SL, pp 27-9 and L, sec 25.

37   *Vide* Rosen, GWF *Hegel*, pp 123-30.

38   PS, p 22.

39   *Vide* Heidegger, *Hegel's Concept of Experience*, pp 59-64.

40   *Vide* Hyppolite, *Genesis and Structure of Hegel's 'Phenomenology of Spirit'*, pp 24-5.

41   We will now consider PS, secs 80, 81, 85-6.

42   *Vide* Collins, 'Hegel's Redefinition of the Critical Project', sec 2.

43   Eg McTaggart, *A Commentary on Hegel's Logic*, sec 4 and *idem, Studies in Hegelian Dialectic*, sec 80.

44   Eg LF, p 589.

45   LHP3, pp 439, 477-8; PS, p 29; SL, p 837 and L, p 117.

46   Kant, *Critique of Pure Reason*, pp A297-8, 462-76; B354-5, 490-504. I repeat that Kant himself succumbed to this longing.

47   *Ibid*, pp A339-40; B397-8.

48   *Ibid*, pp A405-567; B432-595.

49   *Ibid*, pp A76-83, B102-13.

50   L, sec 48.

51   SL, pp 190-9, 234-8.

52   Fichte, *Science of Knowledge*, pp 105-19.

53   Schelling, *System of Transcendental Idealism*, pp 34-41.

54   DBFS, pp 119-73.

55   *Ibid*, pp 155-60.

56   PS, pp 29-31.

57   *Vide* Kaufmann, *Hegel*, sec 37.

58   *Vide* Findlay, *Hegel: A Re-examination*, pp 69-70.

59   *Vide* Mueller, 'The Hegel Legend of Thesis-Antithesis-Synthesis', p 412.

60   *Vide* Royce, *Lectures on Modern Idealism*, pp 95-114, 187-212.

61   Pace McTaggart, *Studies in Hegelian Dialectic*, sec 213.

62   Hegel, 'Wie der Gemeine Menschenverstand die Philosophie Nehme', pp 178-9.

63   PN, sec 250 remark n. This remark was added to the second edition of the *Encyclopaedia*.

64   Krug, *Briefe über den Neusten Idealism*, pp 72-3.

65   Eg Schelling, *System of Transcendental Idealism*, p 74.

66   *Vide* Plant, *Hegel*, pp 129-30.

67   *Pace* Stace, *The Philosophy of Hegel*, secs 425-8.

68   PS, pp 24-7 and SL, pp 27-8, 43-59.

69   *Vide* Kaufmann, *Hegel*, sec 17.

70   *Vide* Norman, *Hegel's Phenomenology*, pp 25-6.

71   L, p 116.

72   *Vide* Williams, *Hegel, Heraclitus and Marx's Dialectic*, chs 3-4.

73   Popper, *The Open Society and Its Enemies*, vol 2, p 8, n 25.

74   Idem, 'What is Dialectic?' pp 325, 329.

75   *Vide*, Kaufmann, 'The Hegel Myth and Its Method'.

76   Indeed, this element of Popper's work is reactionary in a strict sense, for it intends to lead a return to a classic liberalism by attacking the economic and political tendencies critical of it. The trick, which Popper, Hayek, *et al* have been performing for fifty years, is to ignore the fact it is classic liberalism and *laissez faire* capitalism that have themselves generated these tendencies and that returning to them (were it possible) would merely commit us to the cycle again. *Vide* Marcuse, 'Karl Popper and the Problem of Historical Laws'. That this remarkably weak idea has such currency at the moment is a graphic illustration of a corresponding weakness in the progressive tendencies being attacked.

77   Popper, *Objective Knowledge*, p 1.

78   *Idem*, The Logic of Scientific Discovery, sec 1.

79   *Idem* 'On the Status of Science and Metaphysics', p 200.

80   *Idem*, The Logic of Scientific Discovery, sec 85.

81   *Ibid*, sec 11.

82   *Ibid*, sec 10.

83   *Ibid*, sec 85.

84   *Ibid*, p 278.

85   *Ibid* p 281.

86   *Idem*, 'Truth, Rationality and the Growth of Scientific Knowledge', p 229.

87   *Idem, Conjectures and Refutations*, p vii.

88   *Idem*, 'Back to the Pre-socratics', p 157.

89   *Idem*, 'On the Status of Science and Metaphysics', p 192.

90   *Idem*, 'Truth, Rationality and the Growth of Scientific Knowledge' p 1.

91   *Idem*, 'On the Sources of Knowledge and Ignorance', p 30.

92   *Idem* 'Truth, Rationality and the Growth of Scientific Knowledge', p 226.

93   *Ibid*, pp 223-4 and *idem, Unended Quest*, ch 32.

94   In this connection it is instructive to note that Popper's argument decays into merely reformulating the problem, which he himself insists is a real one, contained in the question 'Why are the Calculi of Logic and Arithmetic Applicable to Reality?', nb pp 204-6. Incidentally, for an authoritative modern answer to this question which, by the commitment to explanatorily necessary metaphysics wittily expressed in its title, would rather discomfit Popper *vide* Barrow, *Theories of Everything*.

95   *Vide* Bird, 'A Giant's Voice from the Past'. A further joke likes here in Peirce's own acknowledged indebtedness to Hegel.

96   Lakatos, 'Popper on Demarcation and Induction', p 139 n 1.

97   *Idem*, 'History of Science and Its Rational Reconstructions'.

98   *Idem*, 'Popper on Demarcation and Induction', pp 159-67.

99   *Ibid*, p 165.

100 Which Popper is entirely ready to criticise when he identifies it in Hume. Popper, 'On the Status of Science and Metaphysics', p 200.

101 Althusser, 'Contradiction and Overdetermination', p 103.

102 EPM, p 333.

103 HF, p 100.

104 Hyppolite, *Studies on Marx* and Hegel, p viii.

105 Findlay, 'The Contemporary Relevance of Hegel', p 2.

4 Inversion and the Critique of Alienation

What, I have no doubt, will be troubling many readers of the previous two chapters is the absence of reference to "spirit", the predominant translation of Hegel's use of *Geist* to refer to his conception of God. Previous discussion of Marx's relationship to Hegel has been dominated by a stress on the theological elements in the latter's thought represented by his use of this concept of "spirit". Given the overall tenor of these discussions, my failure to refer to spirit so far will no doubt be regarded as provocative but I do feel I have taken this line for what is really a quite unproblematic reason. I do not find Hegel's concept of spirit useful and I think that what *is* most useful in his work can best be stated without reference to it. In this position, it is, of course, necessary to unpack Hegel's own statement of his epistemological positions by reference to spirit, and I will now do so.

In the briefest outline: Hegel holds that spirit posits the appearance of its own finite limitation in the initial estranged form of nature, and that human history is the progressive recognition, or realisation, of spirit's own absolute self. Spirit's real struggles travelling this route are the necessary means by which it comes to be aware of its own infinitude. Let me try to make this more clear, in part at least, by showing how it is to constitute a source of productive development over Schelling's positions.

Hegel believes that his conception of spirit allows an answer to his own criticisms that Schelling fails to pay attention to the winning of conviction in the truth because it has, at its heart, a crucial role for just such an effort. It is Hegel's basic contention that it is radically insufficient for God to be understood merely as objective, even were He all infinite objectivity, for even such all embracing omnipresence, though it is certainly a characteristic of God, is meaningless unless God knows Himself to be omnipresent. In part, this is an argument of logical entailment. On occasion Hegel seems to be saying that, for example, infinitude can have no meaning unless it is contrasted to finitude. For God to be the infinite unity, He must have overcome the limitations of finite individuality, otherwise His infinity cannot have any sense.[1] However, such logical arguments obviously turn upon adopting an epistemologically subjective standpoint in the assessment of the requirements of certain types of knowledge, and it is Hegel's point more generally that God must see his own constitution of all objectivity if He is to know it in a full sense.[2] That is, God must come to know this from the position of subjectivity. He must be not only object but also subject.[3] It is only by becoming aware of His own presence in objectivity and thus, in an important sense which follows from the conterminity of what God may know and what He Himself is, overcoming the distinction of subject and object,[4] that God may recognise His own omnipresence. God thus *has to* posit finite subjectivities[5] within an initially independently objective realm[6] as the vehicles through which He may come to know His own infinitude. Human history as the overcoming of the alienation of lack of self-knowledge is central to Hegel's spirit. Hegel does not shirk from accepting the positions to which this account of God's reliance on the world must lead. The core of the argument is that God may recognise His character only by striving after the realisation of it. That is, the very comprehension of the existence of both human beings and God turns on recognising in God some of the characteristics - particularly characteristic needs - of personality.[7] This, then, is the crucial feature of Hegel's understanding of God as spirit,[8] a conception of God needing to posit human history as the fulfilment of the requirement of subjectively coming to know Himself. History is, in essence, God's autobiography.[9] In sum, Hegel argues that God must be conceived not only as objective substance but as the subjective realisation of His own constitution of objectivity.[10]

The obvious - but nevertheless very forceful - critical response to all this is to insist that there is absolutely no reason to accept it in its own terms. Let us allow that there is great interest in Hegel's conception of spirit. This idea indeed is surely one of the most striking and fruitful allegories of human existence in modern thought. Let us even further allow (though I think this is to go too far) that this conception of alienated spirit may serve as a coherent understanding of God and His creation of humanity which overcomes the traditional theological conundra associated with these matters. Even so, this formulation remains purely speculative, a mere spinning of ideas. As it stands, it is merely an ingenious construction of God's image.

Now, attempts to entail God's existence in the very possibility of conceiving of Him have of course played a major part in the history of theology. Such attempts are particularly strong forms of a more general argument which in one form or another is more or less coeval with western philosophy but which has as its modern statement the idea that existence is a predicate whose denial is absurd. After Kant's insistence upon the synthetic character of knowledge of existents, his argument that existence cannot be regarded as a predicate amply provided a convincing refutation of the ontological argument,[11] including the version to which he himself previously was committed. I do not think it is now for us or was then for Hegel an issue that such attempts could be regarded as in themselves successful. Hegel, as is well known, did defend the ontological proof against Kant, but, as we shall see, this defence comes, so to speak, at the end of his own proof of absolute spirit rather than at the beginning; for Hegel certainly did not think that the ontological argument could be just re-asserted in even its best pre-Kantian forms.[12] To see how Hegel did restate the proof, we must conclude the discussion of his critique of classical epistemology.

For, as should be made perfectly clear, Hegel's critique of classical epistemology by defence of the power to know is carried through to a claim, of which this particular argument is part, that spirit should be recognised as absolute truth.[13] Hegel's fundamental intent is to bridge the gap between knowledge and faith[14] and to establish a belief in God which is subject to and confirmed in reason. Hegel regards philosophy as the highest form of belief in God, higher than that which he thinks he shows in art and religion,[15] because of the manifest clarity of, precisely, philosophy.[16]

If my interpretation of Hegel's argument in the previous two chapters be accepted, it remains of course the case that his negative achievement of a convincing criticism of the barriers to a workable realism in classical epistemology requires much development before it can itself claim to be such a realism. Amongst the number of ways in which this is so I would like to mention one in particular. If, as I suggest, we accept a restricted sense of "consciousness" as corresponding to Hegel's usage of this term so far, as a reference to only epistemology, then further development must surely raise questions about the ontological sources of the character of this consciousness. Indeed, the full understanding of the alienated positions which have been criticised must involve some reference to this, in the form of a grasp of the non-alienated conditions which give counter-factual sense to the explanation of the classical epistemological project as alienated. Now some such developments are put forward by Hegel, but in a fashion the peculiarity of which it is vital to grasp.

Hegel does not broaden out epistemology into an empirical investigation of the acquisition of knowledge, neither in the sense of the general transcendental ontology which I have argued he makes possible, nor even in the more restricted sense of an examination of the subjective psychological processes involved in coming to know. In failing to take up even the latter, Hegel does represent a regressive step from the psychological efforts of empiricism and Kant. He does not proceed in these ways because he is attempting to develop a most radical idealism in which the objects of knowing can be directly predicated of consciousness. Hegel does not even seek to pursue a line such as that of Descartes when the latter attempted to divorce subjectivity from the materiality of the body.[17] The idealism which Hegel envisages is one in which epistemological statements about consciousness can also *immediately* stand as ontological statements about the objects of consciousness. Obviously a consciousness in which not merely all knowing but also all being is grounded is a rather different consciousness to the one we have so far discussed, and we must look into the difference between these more deeply.

After having located within consciousness the criterion by which specific cognitions may be judged, Hegel sums up his argument in the following way.[18] If knowledge is designated as the notion, he says, and the true as the object in-itself, then examination of the truth of a cognition does indeed turn on whether notion corresponds to that object. We have seen that such a procedure yields nothing. However, Hegel now proposes, in opposition to this fruitless project, that we should call the object in-itself the notion, and with this call the object for-consciousness as established in any particular cognition the object. Now examination of the adequacy of cognition consists in seeing whether object corresponds to notion. It is evident, Hegel claims, that the two are the same.

Hegel's way of putting his point is extraordinarily difficult, and I have thought it best, as far as I can, to initially simply put forward his own statement and then try to explain it. For the first thing we must note is that he does not even convey what he wants his readers to believe. If the two ways of setting up the examination of the adequacy of a cognition were the same, having argued that the first one is fruitless, there would seem to be little point in Hegel's turning to the second. What he is, in fact, claiming is that the two procedures describe the same state of affairs, only the second, unlike the first, allows us to see what that state of affairs is.

Hegel is suggesting that as an object for-consciousness is the only criterion that can possibly be relevant to the assessment of a particular cognition, this amounts to saying that objectivity is constituted by consciousness. His use of the term "notion" or "concept" (*"begriff"*) here arises from his thinking of this issue within the framework of his idea of spirit. Here the place of the object in-itself is taken by absolute truth, or the adequate notion of spirit's self-consciousness. In calling beliefs objects, Hegel is immediately representing these beliefs as concrete externalisations of spirit, particular forms of objectivity being given by particular stages in the development of absolute spirit. Understood in this way, object eventually must have to correspond to notion because the truth of all objectivity is spirit's self-consciousness. This is the basis of Hegel's solution to the problem of dissociation. Subject may know object because both are of spirit.[19] In Hegel's vocabulary, the object in-itself is absolute spirit. We can, however proceed to knowledge of the absolute through objects for-consciousness because these are also of spirit. The consideration of a succession of objects for-consciousness will lead to absolute truth because, far from such truth being unreachable for the subject, it will be found to be only the notion, the subject's own presence.[20] The dissociation of subject and object is to be shown to be spirit's self-alienation, and this will be overcome as spirit is progressively revealed to be the foundation of objectivity.

We can, at this point, return briefly to an earlier passage in the 'Introduction'[21] where Hegel, having preliminarily outlined the development of the *Phenomenology*, says that the goal of this development is as necessarily fixed as the development itself. This goal is the point where knowledge no longer needs to go beyond itself, where notion corresponds to object and object to notion. The sense to be made of such a goal is, I hope, now apparent. It is Hegel's explicit statement of the situation in which he envisages the solution to the problem of dissociation in the complete identification of what were earlier thought to be separate.[22]

The force of Hegel's solution of the problem of dissociation, if I may stress the point, is to lie in the way that the stressing of the grasp of an object for-consciousness can, within the framework of spirit, amount to the same thing as grasping the object in-itself. That is to say that, to all intents and purposes, the object in-itself in the Kantian sense must lose all relevance because the brute objectivity which it registers is made a product of the subject. To be sure, a certain difference between object for-consciousness and object in-itself remains in the 'Introduction' in that Hegel notes their difference at this early stage of the phenomenological investigation. But the recognition of their difference is now split from the initial understanding of them in consciousness as separate categories, the former denoting being and the latter being that is known.[23] Hence the possibility of their reconciliation through complete mutual identification is opened.

The key to understanding Hegel's own solution the problem of the dissociation lies, I would say, in recognising that this solution contains a great deal more that requires detailed scrutiny than the brevity with which it is expressed would lead us to believe. I note this further instance of this stylistic feature of Hegel's writing in full awareness that the first three chapters of the *Phenomenology* purport to argue the movement from perception of objectivity to self-consciousness. Let us consider the relevant aspects of these three chapters.

The notion of spirit positing objectivity and eventually realising in this the subject obviously owes a great deal to Fichte. What can be identified as characteristically Hegelian about the discussion of this in the *Phenomenology* is the manner of the development of self-consciousness. For when, by the end of the chapter on 'Force and the Understanding', Hegel declares the truth of consciousness of objectivity to be self-consciousness, this position has been argued in the most intimate, if allusive, relation to Kant as the first stage of the phenomenological movement.[24] Hegel's argument in the section on 'Consciousness' has a form very substantially set by an attempt to immanently develop, to use the Kantian terminology, intuition into understanding and then on into the unity of apperception. That is to say, Hegel tries to move from perception of objectivity (intuition in Kant) to conceptual comprehension (understanding in Kant) to the fact that all knowing is predicated of a subject (the transcendental unity of apperception in Kant),[25] these three being related by the last being the immanent truth of the first.

The difference of the form of Hegel's response to Kant from that of Fichte's similar response is enormous. I have mentioned in the previous chapter that it was a principal, and eventually somewhat notorious, claim of Fichte's that the content of his philosophy was but the Kantian categories set out in a coherent deductive relationship to the basic principle of human knowledge - the absoluteness of the ego.[26] Of course Kant encouraged this, one of the first post-Kantian "completions" of the critical philosophy, by setting out the categories in seemingly arbitrary manner,[27] and Hegel certainly agreed with Fichte upon the necessity of some proper linking of (again to use the Kantian terms) the unity of apperception to the specific categories of experience, such as Fichte had provided.[28] However, Hegel found the deduction by which Fichte claimed to have accomplished this[29] to be wanting.[30] It is in the very movement of spirit itself - in this case in Kant's and his successors' thought as the philosophic expression of consciousness - that Hegel sought to locate self-consciousness as the truth of objectivity. One need only read these brilliant first three chapters to see the power this phenomenological method grants to Hegel's arguments - though of course this is not to say that one must agree with them, merely that one must register their marked superiority to presentations such as Fichte's.

The progress of the first part of the *Phenomenology* is recapitulated in the *Encylopaedia*,[31] in line, of course, with the wider character of Hegel's relation of phenomenology and system proper. This particular moment of absolute truth has its place in the system because Hegel is trying to argue that there is a necessity in encountering the problem of dissociation, in that it is in the very overcoming of this that the self-awareness of spirit begins to emerge. In sum, in all these passages we have discussed Hegel is locating the form of consciousness as a moment of spirit, with a profound change in the meaning of "consciousness" being effected. As opposed to facing a distinct objectivity, consciousness as a moment of spirit has to face, essentially, only its own self.

It would seem, then, that what is required in order to evaluate Hegel's full solution to the problem of dissociation is to turn to the first section of the *Phenomenology*.[32] However, I do not propose to do so, for I believe that for the purposes of a deeper understanding Hegel's own thinking on this point, it is crucial to realise that the basis of this solution is to be found in the passages of the 'Introduction' which we have preliminarily discussed.[33] I have claimed that Hegel's criticisms of classical epistemology lead towards an examination of the character of subjectivity given in relation to distinct realm of objectivity; and yet he himself has summed up his argument in a fashion which undoubtedly expressed one of the most thoroughgoing idealisms in modern philosophy. If my understanding is correct, Hegel has run his polemic against the classical epistemological project immediately into the broader setting out of his own conception of the gaining of truth without acknowledging that he has done so. What is vital here, both for assessing the strength of Hegel's eventual position and for gauging the felicity of my interpretation of this position, is that, as I will now argue, what Hegel accomplishes in this surreptitious way is not defensible under open scrutiny under the protocols of his own dialectic of immanent critique.

In the shift in the meaning of "consciousness" on which Hegel's conclusion of his argument rests, an essential characteristic of consciousness is, without any warrant, simply eliminated by not being carried on into consciousness as a moment of spirit. It will be recalled that from the very outset Hegel's discussion of classical epistemology has turned on showing how it is unable to ground truth once it has recognised the creative contribution of cognition to knowledge. Hegel's solution to the problem of dissociation turns on making this essentially synthetic understanding of cognition redundant by identifying subject and object. Hegel claims not only to have shown that any potential criterion of truth must be found in consciousness, but also thereby to have shown that there is no distance between what is found in consciousness and objectivity. Or rather, there is the illusory show of distance created by the alienated form of spirit's externalisation which must be overcome. In Kantian terms, what Hegel is doing is reducing the effect of the categories on judgments to the unity of apperception, reducing the cognitive contributions of the subject to the mere fact of subjectivity.

Hegel makes this quite clear when he says that the point arising from these observations which we must grasp in understanding the method of phenomenological proof is the following. As particular cognitions (being-for-another) and the object as criterion (being-in-itself as it is for-consciousness) fall within knowledge, it is just when we abandon all our presuppositions and simply follow the developments of successive cognitions we will eventually reach an exhaustive, an absolute, knowledge of being.

This idea of knowing exhausting being makes sense given the way in which, on Hegel's understanding of consciousness as a moment of spirit, objectivity itself drops out of consideration. As there is no object, there can hardly be the category of subjective *contributions* to synthetic judgments. The subject constitutes all there is to "judgments", and to have truth we must immerse ourselves in the subject. Hegel is here advocating a kind of optimistic direct perception (I hope this vocabulary is not misleading) in which the source of epistemological problems is nullified at the point of the object rather than the subject.

Taking up the problem of knowing in the light of subjective contributions to cognition has, however, another side to it than the one which in the classical epistemological project leads to the positing of the thing-in itself. This is the registering of, again of using Kant's terms, an intuition of materiality as the recognition of objectivity distinct from the subject. Whatever difficulties there may be in understanding knowing after registering this intuition, there is no sense in which the original setting up of the problem ever conceives of knowing actually breaking down the distinctness of object from subject. Knowing *in the light of* this distinctness is the epistemological problem. Hegel's solution to this problem is to dissolve the very distinctness, as we have seen. However, there is no warrant for this outside of immediately understanding consciousness to be a moment of spirit.

Hegel substantially does this. In the course of setting out the above argument, Hegel wavers between two meanings of "consciousness". One meaning, with which we are familiar, is that which we have seen Hegel sometimes call "natural consciousness", which is the consciousness described by the classical epistemological project. Now, as a *beginning*, this characterisation of the dominant epistemologies of natural consciousness is acceptable, indeed it shows something of a remarkable aptitude for synopsis. We have seen how productive the discussion of this consciousness can be. However, by referring to this as "natural consciousness", Hegel is also trying to identify it as *the* consciousness of all ontologically distinct objects, which it is not.[34] Far more defensible accounts of knowing ontologically distinct objects can, as I have argued, be constructed than are available in classical epistemology and certainly they have enough plausibility to make this simple elision untenable. If this is untenable, then so is the way Hegel goes to talk about consciousness throughout the rest of the 'Introduction' and the first part of the *Phenomenology*, for he treats the necessary critique of classical epistemology as amounting to the rejection of material sensation when he sets out the entire movement of the dialectic of consciousness.

There is a radical difference between the meanings of consciousness Hegel runs together and, in quietly shifting between them, he fails to translate the ineradicable sensation of materiality which, certainly for Kant, identifies knowing consciousness.[35] His argument that in Kant this sensation becomes posited as an absurd thing-in-itself is, though correct, not nearly sufficient to dispose of the underlying sensation, even when absurdly conceptualised.[36] Of course, were Hegel's argument in the first three chapters successful, then he could claim his epistemological argument to be the solution of a fundamental ontolological problem. But I think that we can see that it is here, in the 'Introduction', that he effects a shift in the meaning of "consciousness" that makes the nullification of objectivity possible. Instead of thought and being standing as ontologically distinct, a characteristic feature of consciousness, Hegel now construes the latter as predicated by the former. In his discussion in the course of the first three chapters, forms of objectivity are always considered to be exhausted through treatments of ways of knowing them.[37] Hence, by merely following successive cognitions without making any contributions of our own to the process, Hegel is able to claim to be able to reach the absolute truth of being.

I have already mentioned that Hegel is sure that previous forms of the ontological proof cannot hold against Kant's post-critical attack upon them. His acceptance of this is always coupled with the reservation that there is a fundamental truth indicated by the proof which can and should be recovered in a more adequate formulation. In this light, Hegel holds that Kant's thoroughly critical dismissal of the proof constitutes a mistaken rejection of a most valuable philosophical resource.[38] Not only did Hegel famously try explicitly to revive this truth after Kant,[39] but, as I think we can now see, his attempt was based upon the principal thrust of the whole of his fully developed response to Kant.[40]

For natural consciousness, Hegel concurs, the concept of God and His existence are radically different. However, he manages to turn even this to his own ends. He argues that Kant's refutation of the proof acquired a rather flawed brilliance by being given in a polemic against the weakest possible rendering of the proof, that given to it most famously by Mendelssohn,[41] in which existence certainly is thought of as a formal logical predicate and in which, therefore, "the identity of idea and reality was made to look like the adding of one concept to another".[42] Hegel's revival of the proof seeks, as we might expect, to break with the natural consciousness' way of treating knowledge itself, this being a way of securely defending the proof against attacks such as Kant's which are based on natural consciousness' categories. Hegel's reply to Kant takes the tack of stressing that the proof is not referring to natural consciousness' concepts but to the notion of God; and, he says, there is a greater difference between these two types of "concepts" than between thought and being.[43] Taking consciousness to be a moment of spirit, it becomes quite open for Hegel to claim the fundamental truth of the ontological proof, because the essence of consciousness understood in this way is that it is part of a movement in which is to be shown to be itself the ground of existence. What remains ineluctably formal in the proof, and therefore seemingly sophistic, is its logical predication of existence. However, for Hegel this can be recovered and entirely vindicated in its essentials by being made part of a full argument which sets out the role of consciousness in the development of the adequate notion of absolute spirit.[44] If this overall argument is successful, then the empirical sensitivity to materiality which stands behind Kant's rejection of the proof can be of no consequence, for it is this materiality itself that is to disappear.

My own understanding of the rights of the matter has lead me to argue that Hegel's conception of the unity of subject and object contains a central and yet indefensible elision of two senses of "consciousness" which makes crucial epistemological problems dissolve by being artificially integrated into a theocratic scheme. However, we must remember that this elision comes at the end of a determined polemic made not expressly against objectivity but against the thing-in-itself. Here we must draw on Hegel's valuable arguments, and not attempt to return to the genuine, but nevertheless inadequate, materialist aspirations in Kant for the advance of realist, empirical epistemology. There is no productive fashion in which we can simply return to Kant as a response to Hegel's arguments.[45]

Hegel leaves us with very serious problems arising from his coupling of a successful description of aspects of what epistemology can and must do to an unacceptable depiction of the character of the operations which he tends to think are thereby also established. Not least in its contribution to the unacceptable character of Hegel's depictions is the way he entails their specific forms in the earlier, quite open and general, often merely negative (albeit in a positive way) arguments.[46] In this instance, criticism of the demand that the thing-in-itself be the criterion by which particular cognitions be judged, which grounds a compelling realist commitment to the knowability of objects in consciousness, is summed up in such a way that it seems to entail the disappearance of objectivity distinct from the subject. By this elision, Hegel has contributed to the subsequent marginalisation of his own work, for the issues of lasting epistemological interest left by Kant, those of coming to terms with the distance between subject and object known to be mutually constitutive moments of knowing, are, in the end, of no concern to him.[47]

Hegel's argument for shunning all preconceptions in order to follow the course of given beliefs ends with epistemology being denied any distance from the essence of objectivity. In the way in which cognition's contributions to knowing are rendered meaningless as they are now all of knowing, Hegel is putting forward a construction of the unity of subject and object which is a simple break with the basis of classical epistemology and his criticisms of that project. There is no immanent development here, merely the erasure of what had earlier been the starting point of productive development. What is more, the identity thinking at which Hegel thereby arrives can have only pernicious epistemological consequences. There can be no corrigible check upon Hegel's conduct of the phenomenological progression, because when treating cognitions as objects he is now claiming to directly represent them. Absolute presuppositionlessness is the methodological injunction arising from his doing away with an effective moment in knowing of objectivity. When we reject this injunction, indeed reject its very possibility and restore the essential sense of the subject making contributions to knowing, then Hegel's construction of phenomenology must be seen as giving far too much licence to his own representations of those cognitions. The check on speculation provided by respect for the object is removed, and the overall implausibility of the *Phenomenology* as a history to which disregard of this check leads finally refutes Hegel's phenomenological method.

For we are now hard up against the vital question: is it possible for Hegel to sustain his essentially empirical treatment of forms of consciousness - including consciousness itself - and yet bring them within his overall theological scheme? There is really only one way in which one can judge the veracity of this opinion in a way sufficiently sympathetic to Hegel's profoundly important way of setting out his argument and to the extraordinary interest of the substance of that argument. This is to read his works; but most especially, for reasons with which we are familiar, to read the *Phenomenology of Spirit*. However, I do not feel that anything is to be gained for the appreciation of Hegel's achievement by failing to state my opinion that it is absurd to regard the dialectic of the *Phenomenology* as successfully bearing the enormous weight placed upon it,[48] or, indeed, more generally that Hegel's attempt to establish his core theological beliefs is an unarguable failure.[49] It is enough to say, from the epistemological point of view taken in this commentary, that it is trivially easy, and in itself unrewarding, to insist upon the many discontinuities, and unfounded elisions that paper over these, in the book's movements through and transitions between forms of consciousness and ethical life. (Such elisions are equally present in Hegel's other writings). This response to Hegel must be made if one is to assess his work in the light of his own evaluations of and professions about his philosophy, which are a failure and have diminished the relevance of his work to the formulation of an adequate historiographical method.[50] But this response had largely served its purpose as soon as Trendlenburg first made it in 1840,[51] and a positive way to approach these continual break-downs in Hegel's argument is to recover from them the resources they obscure.[52]

On one point we must be particularly careful. The arguments of the *Phenomenology* may follow in a literary sense as internal to the book. I personally do not find this to be so, but distinguished opinion to the contrary is readily available.[53] This is, however, an issue quite distinct from taking those arguments to be empirically and necessarily secured in the way that Hegel requires for the public winning of conviction. Though the studies are without doubt of the utmost interest as allegories on more or less all characteristic features of modern society and on certain basic issues of human existence,[54] it is simply unwarranted to regard them as succeeding precisely at the point where Hegel needs them to stand not as allegories but as explicit truth.[55] Those qualities of rational, empirical openness which Hegel identifies as the essence of what is valuable in philosophy must, in the end, be seen to be lacking in the *Phenomenology*, and certainly so in respect of the terms of necessarily compelling circularity which he seeks for proof of the absolute.

What in fact goes on throughout the book's remarkable combination of forms of argument is a most massive effort to continually force his basically empirical materials into the presumptive speculative mould in which they then play their part. Much more than forms of consciousness showing themselves to need to be understood within the framework of Hegelian spirit, the reading of Hegel's work, at least after his death, has continually testified to the need to draw out what is valuable in his treatment of these forms from the encumbrance of that framework. We must note the indefensible elisions which this forcing introduces into the book, not because they could be removed, but because they could not. Hegel's dissatisfaction with the 1807 edition of the *Phenomenology* led him to commence revisions shortly before his death and presumably these would have involved significant changes.[56] However, such an effort of revision is irrelevant to the point I am trying to make.

The *Phenomenology* combines erudition, philosophic ability and substantive philosophic and social theoretical illumination, all of the highest degree, in a way that make it, in my opinion, the greatest work of modern human studies. Nevertheless, as an attempt to dominate its enormous material in a way that satisfies Hegel's theological claims, it is naive, breaking down at just about every point. This contradiction, which might be expanded to that between the speculative-objective demands of Hegel's theology and the empirical-subjective demands of his philosophic proof, the latter continually ridiculing the former, is stopped from splitting the work apart by a continuous forcing that is an astonishing effort of dogmatic conviction and style.

An important consequence of this contradiction in the *Phenomenology* is that the motive power of the movement described becomes impossible to understand coherently. I have mentioned that it is essential to the concept of spirit that its externalisation be a commitment to open self-discovery. Equally the open character of the progression of forms of consciousness is of the essence of phenomenological proof. Despite the depth of Hegel's setting out of the ways in which forms of consciousness can be seen to be their own ground of development, it proves impossible for him ultimately to ward off the impression that the phenomenological progression is teleologically directed. I do not mean this in the acceptable, indeed important, sense that new forms of consciousness may direct themselves by learning from the past. I mean that Hegel's representation of forms consciousness gives a direction to the movement which stands as an outer teleology, a direction outside of the movement itself. One should not make too much of this.

In his later writings, Hegel attempts, from the point of view of the system, to extol as a virtue just that ambiguity which we have seen in the *Phenomenology*. The empirical following of history's own movement is to reveal the process of the externalisation of spirit,[57] and spirit's method of realising itself through the alienated conduct of human beings is shown to be a work of absolute cunning - the ruse of reason.[58] The essential truth of the system is that in striving for their own goals, human beings actually act out the purposes of spirit. It is not, of course, by any means impossible that (in alienated societies) the behaviour of men and women is influenced by social forces they do not comprehend. Adequate explanation of that behaviour reveals those influences and hence those forces. The full recognition of this possibility of unacknowledged social determination is indeed, in my opinion, Hegel's most important achievement. This is not to say that we must accept his specific understanding of the issues involved, which explains them through the scheme of the externalisation of spirit. This is surely a separable matter.[59] What is more, if we do not so separate the general possibility of the penetration of alienated consciousness from Hegel's specific construction of it, then when, as we must eventually do, we come to regard that construction as an ultimate failure, we stand threatened with losing the entire possibility of the critique of alienation.[60] We must allow ourselves the hope of rebuilding the ground on which we can claim the epistemological privilege of penetrating alienated consciousness after seeing in Hegel why this task is indispensable and why it cannot be performed in the way he imagines.

In sum, Hegel leaves us in this position: we are shown by him to be committed to the knowability of objects in consciousness. His own argument that this knowability rests on the grounds of an assumed identity of subject and object is a failure in terms of his own protocols of critique. The task that remains, then, is one of comprehending knowability, which posits the unity of subject and object, in the knowledge of the perpetual non-identity of these two moments of knowing, that is to say in the knowledge of the "untruth of identity, the fact that the concept does not exhaust the thing conceived".[61] All this amounts to a radical failure in Hegel's work, but one that, because I trust that it is pointed out on the basis of some real knowledge of Hegel's work rather than crude misrepresentations or blunt ignorance of it, offers the possibility of some positive immanent critique and this possibility is realised in what we can gain from reworking the notion of inversion. For, having set out the aims and method of phenomenology, Hegel makes certain observations at the end of the 'Introduction' which directly raise the idea of inversion, and it is to these that we must now turn. If we are to understand Marx's purported "inversion" of Hegel, the first task, one we can now straightforwardly address, is to see the way "inversion" figures in Hegel's own thought.

After setting out his instructions on how to follow the course of experience, Hegel allows that they contain a moment which does not seem to follow him what is ordinarily understood as experience,[62] and thus, I should like to add, can only with difficulty be said to be directly derived from the study of experience. This moment is the transition from immediately undergoing experience to the comprehension of what experience actually is. Let us take the course of any episode described as a determinate negation as it is actually experienced. It is understood as a change of some sort no doubt, and perhaps elements of comprehension of the immanent criticism of existing positions are available to the participants. But it certainly is not understood as a point in the progressive realisation of the absolute. This can come only afterwards, when we may look back upon and reflexively re-comprehend experience with the privileged hindsight of knowledge of the realised absolute. What we are dealing with, says Hegel, is an inversion of consciousness' normal perspective.[63]

We can recall Hegel's rejection of what he described as Schelling's asking of inadequate belief to stand upon its head, to invert itself when faced with its opposite in the truth and thereby to rise to the truth by assuming what that belief must regard as a quite unwarranted posture. Obviously, we must ask in what crucial way Hegel's phenomenology is different to this. Hegel says that this inversion of consciousness' perspective on experience is something contributed by "us", by Hegel himself and his readers. He explains "our" ability to contribute this inversion in the following way. He claims that the entire progression of spirit does not amount to nothing, it amounts, as the summation of determinate negations in a final negation of the negation,[64] to our knowledge of what experience actually is. The awareness of this reveals patterns of consciousness as moments of spirit, and in this awareness we have a deeper knowledge of experience than those who initially made that experience. We can, of course, agree with this, which is but a resume of Hegel's conception of phenomenological proof, and allow that it can explain how an inversion in consciousness' perspective on experience may come about. However, it is also necessary to say that it cannot explain this in the way Hegel requires, for the chronology of the contribution to phenomenology that is made when "we", as Hegel says, adopt this inverted perspective, is all wrong. It is clear that a great deal turns on the position of the "we" who are able to make this contribution.[65]

Let me dispose of an ancillary point first, Hegel imposes exacting requirements upon those who would follow his argument, requirements of, as has been seen, being prepared to follow a way of despair as the cost of adopting an open-minded stance. It is necessary to be dissatisfied, or at least not content, with one's present positions, and being ready to undergo the arduous task of reaching the absolute through intellectual effort.[66] (The extreme labour of reading the *Phenomenology* manages to even exaggerate this latter condition). In an interesting convergence with later phenomenology's fundamental requirement for breaking through the natural attitude,[67] what Hegel firstly needs his readers to be is engaged in intellectual criticism of existing reality; that is to say, to be engaged in philosophy.[68]

If this condition is both recognised and allowed, it is still clearly an insufficient qualification for reaching the position of Hegel's "we". There remains an irremediable difficulty in ascertaining who it is that will be able to contribute to and who will receive phenomenological enlightenment. If, as it has centrally been argued, the *Phenomenology* is written for those whose beliefs constituted the earlier, inadequate conceptions, then there are surely major confusions involved. For the *Phenomenology* is written to demonstrate that the truth is on the scene, and could be written only after this was so. Ordering the material in the light of knowledge of the absolute is, precisely, "our" contribution. But to say this is to say that the progression outlined in the *Phenomenology* has been completed. The reflexive commentary and the enlightenment it is to bring becomes rather pointless if the possibility of making this commentary turns upon the truth it is to reveal having already been realised. In so far as Hegel located the possibility of this enlightenment in the complete identification of the absolute and the form of its progressive realisation, then I contend that he makes the function of the *Phenomenology* either redundant or indefensible in the terms of the sought after phenomenological proof.

There really does seem, in the end, to be no ground of the conception of absolute spirit from which Hegel could deflect even manifestly hostile and relatively uncomprehending criticisms of that conception.[69] The radical shift in the most basic of the aims of the project of "phenomenology" in and after Husserl, although by no means always providing a contrast unfavourable to Hegel, does speak of the way this project has proceeded in contradiction of Hegel's theocratic aims,[70] even when other Hegelian themes have proved to be of the greatest interest. From the opposite point of view, as it were,[71] Kierkegaard's so completely negative later evaluation of Hegel[72] has turned on an explicit relocation of Christian religious belief in a specifically incomprehensible leap of faith which it was Hegel's central concern to make redundant.[73] In the 'Preface', Hegel tells us that the *Phenomenology* is written in order to provide the ladder which it might reasonably be requested be made available in order to climb to the absolute.[74] Whatever one makes of this, indeed whatever one makes of religious belief, Hegel has left unanswered the obvious question about his own ladder.[75]

Now it might be thought that this question is unacceptably rude. The ready availability of a common-sense construction of Hegel's position would seem to make the contradiction in the *Phenomenology* at which I am aiming hard to identify. It could be said that Hegel is putting forward his account of the realisation of spirit as an explanation of world history, and he is seeking to win acceptance of the truth by gaining acceptance of his explanation. Though I have rendered it in what to Hegel would be an extremely banal fashion, I think this is what he thought he was doing. However, this cannot be what he actually does. The strength of the phenomenological proof is to lay in the complete identification of the phenomenological account and the course of the development of spirit. Philosophy may paint its "grey in grey" only when "a shape of life has grown old",[76] and the shape of absolute spirit is, amongst other things, consciousness in the shape of realised absolute knowledge, the shape which Hegel would have "us" both contribute to and find in the *Phenomenology*. There is difficulty in understanding exactly in what sense the truth can, in Hegel's terms, be both on the scene and yet require actualisation.

Hegel's philosophy has its most important shortcoming at just this point. Hegel's statements of actualised rationality have to have an ambiguous form. For the reason I have just mentioned, one finds that they contain statements which both affirm the rational character of the world and also set out changes necessary for the actualisation of that rationality. As Hegel bases his arguments on the ultimate dogmatism of cognisance of the absolute he must find realised rationality in the world, and yet the fact that realisation is incomplete is the rationale of the phenomenological effort. I do not mean to argue that there is no, as it were, middle ground possible here, of identifying the potential of rationalisation in the existent. My point is that for Hegel to put things this way is impossible because he continually draws upon achieved rationality as the absolute justification of his philosophy. The consequence is of course that identifying rational potentials and ways of actualising them is, remarkable enough to have to say, the greatest lacuna in Hegel's thought.[77] It seems as if Hegel thought that as he set out the rational in thought this served to make the rational truly actual[78] and this serious weakness emerges from the absolute justification which he seeks for an attempt to move to the absolute. Hegel's inversion of consciousness is an unacceptably abbreviated statement of what is in fact a task, both for him and for us. This task is the actualisation of the rational, a task we must approach, though he did not, in the knowledge that there is no available absolute to justify our conduct.

Hegel does not in the end wish to remove alienation in order to leave us free of past inadequate beliefs. He rather wants to turn them on their head to to show their truth. On this basis, he is not really seeking to put us in a position to find out new things. He wants us to find the truth of old things through their inversion. Against this it must be insisted that the uncovering of alienation does not produce absolute knowledge, it produces the freedom to know.

Many of the, on a first look, outright silly features of Hegel's thought which have been fastened on by subsequent criticism arise here, around his idea of "the end of history".[79] Let us first dispose of a distracting vulgarisation of this idea. Hegel is by no means denying that new events can or will take place. He makes it plain even in so famous a text as the introduction to the lectures on the philosophy of history, in which he refers to North America as the land of the future,[80] that this is not what he means. What he does mean is that at the point of absolute knowledge, the basic principles of knowing have been developed and no *fundamental* improvement on these principles will ever be possible.[81]

As we now have ample historical testimony to show, this conviction is not so much ridiculous as terrible in the power of the dogmatism it can generate.[82] Awareness of historical relativism lapses when the historical location one grants oneself transcends history, and this, incredible enough to say after what we have seen of determinate negation,[83] is just what Hegel does.[84] Hegel holds that, as he writes, "truth is on the scene" and he writes to flesh that truth out.[85] The task of philosophy, then, is integrate all phenomena into a totality of understanding based on the now available principles, a sort of (perhaps infinitely extended) filling in: "The truth", Hegel famously declares, "is the whole".[86]

This idea, and the way it runs against determinate negation, becomes clearer if we return to Hegel's polemical exchange of views with WT Krug. At the most fundamental level, of insisting on the in principle possibility of basically explaining Krug's pen, I have argued that Hegel was right. But there undoubtedly is an uncomfortable tone to all this, and I think we can now see what causes it. When Hegel says that the task Krug wants performed will have to wait, he *is saying* that it is just a matter of time (if anyone could ever be bothered) before the pen would adequately be explained. This attitude is possible only if one thinks that the fundamentals of explanantion are now so absolutely settled that eventually even phenomena as insignificant as this could be brought into the settled system. This attitude is very seriously mistaken.

With respect to Krug's pen, the adequate form is that of the philosophy of nature. Now, as Hegel says, no philosopher can be bothered to carry out the comprehension of Krug's pen. Whilst the solar system itself remains to be comprehended - and this therefore faces philosophy as its most sublime and supreme task - Hegel says that Krug's pen will have to wait. Hegel used a very similar locution when describing his own earlier attempt to perform this "supreme task".[87] His dissertation on the orbits of the planets is most often remembered for Hegel's explanation of the relatively (by comparison to the distance between the orbits of the inner planets) vast emptiness between Mars and Jupiter, which was put forward just at the time when the discovery of asteroids in this space was being made. But the last thing that can be said is that Hegel was speculatively deducing a necessary emptiness which outlawed, and thus was ridiculed by, the discovery of these asteroids. Rather, using the extant empirical evidence (the discovery of the asteroids was not available to him), Hegel tried to furnish an explanation of the relatively vast distance. His explanantion not only strenuously tried to fit the facts but actually did so in express polemic against the idea of there being a strict mathematical relationship in the distances between the planets.[88] This is but one example of the way in which the philosophy of nature, which is a system of flat exteriority which exhibits no dynamic in a dialectical or any other sense,[89] is an attempt to comprehend a system in nature[90] and not impose a deductive or any other system on it.[91]

But the real shortcoming of Hegel's idea of the absolute emerges here perfectly clearly. It is as little scientific to accept given data, such as that about the planets' orbits, as ineluctable and then set about comprehending them in some final way[92] as it would be to impose a deductive scheme on nature. This data, and the fundamental ways in which it is understood, will shift the more we know. But this is just what the end of history denies. All that is required is the further extension of what is now known and, given this purely qualitative attitude to the growth of knowledge, even Krug's pen would eventually be found a place. Hegel turns what he allows us to recognise as true, that epistemology must pursue ever more adequate accounts, and turns it into a closed totality which, in many forms, has proved to be wholly repugnant[93]: "the whole is the true, and the whole is false".[94]

With this conclusion we would seem to have come right round to the very beginning of Hegel's mature project. However, in doing so we have not arrived at the promised conviction in the absolute but at a rejection of the essential aims of that project. Hegel's phenomenology is ridden with a contradiction between its theological ends and its philosophic means, and this contradiction is summed up in the very way Hegel himself adopts the perspective of an inverted consciousness which in the end he can only hortatively say he would have us also take up. The flat undercutting of all his remarkable gains compels the refusal of his request. Let us recap on why this is so.

Hegel's epistemology is dominated, as of course was that of all his contemporaries, by an awareness of the shortcomings of the first *Critique*, shortcomings which most obviously disrupt Kant's thought at the point of the concept of the thing-in-itself. Though Hegel was by no means unique in disposing of this concept, he did so in a uniquely productive fashion. In criticism of what he goes on to show to be an unsupportable presupposition of the radical dissociation of subject and object, Hegel unites these sundered moments of knowing by giving them a common ground in consciousness, by which he initially conveys a sense of the domain of cognition, that is, of all possible experience. By doing this, he takes a distance from Kant's aims as they exemplify the classical epistemological project, and is able to show those aims to be self-defeating ones which themselves alienate our power to know. The identification of the basic problems of philosophy with foundationalism which has proven so absurdly destructive of the whole philosophical enterprise is thereby broken, and epistemology freed for more valuable work.

The essential work Hegel sets is the construction of a rational awareness of the inadequacies of present beliefs by a scheme of progressive critique. This scheme is the dialectic of determinate negations, about which three characteristics are particularly important. The first is its sensitivity to any given belief. Hegel insists upon immersing critique in the phenomenological character of such belief, and thereby gaining access to one's audience by the empirically adequate fashion in which one addresses it. The second is the way movement from any such belief takes the form of developing the belief's productive potentials to the point where they exhaust the core of that belief and call for a radical change of viewpoint. Hegel, in effect, "layers" determinate critique. A new, relatively subjective, line of development is contrasted to the wider, more entrenched, relatively objective framework of belief which generated that line. The exhaustion of the ability of that framework to generate new and valuable subjective conjectures calls for a shift in even our most settled beliefs. This is a negation of given belief, but it is a determinate negation for it issues from the empirical character of that belief. Phenomenology is the pursuit of that character through to its eventual self-criticism. The third point I should like to mention follows from this determinateness. The dialectic of determinate negations is potentially progressive because it may incorporate awareness of earlier errors.

It is out of an awareness of the futility of foundationalism that the idea of determinate negation itself arises. Thus this very idea is itself an example of the application of the principle involved. This method is, then, given in a critique of a specific alienation, the alienation of our power to know by the classical epistemological project. However, this method also addresses alienation as such more widely. Hegel treats all of history as the movement of self-estranged spirit, and attempts to cast a reflexive illumination on that history from the position when, as he has it, the truth of spirit is on the scene and alienation is essentially overcome. The dialectic of determinate negations is to culminate in the negation of the overall negation of the self-awareness of spirit that characterises all previous history. This is obviously a different idea of negation, but it is to be generated as a determinate negation. Rigorous phenomenological pursuit of present beliefs is to lead to an appreciation of the possibility and necessity of the totality of comprehension which emerges from seeing history as spirit.

Hegel's project is, in his own terms, the "inversion" of contemporary consciousness, for understandings which are marked by the alienation of spirit present the opposite of correct comprehension of the character of history. However, this inversion is not successfully accomplished in the *Phenomenology*, in fact Hegel ends up asking his readers to effect an inversion in their perspectives themselves, as a requisite of then grasping the dialectical progression. The break in what should be the continuous flow of determinate negation is marked by a number of unfounded elisions in the way Hegel sets out the truth, perhaps the most important of which is that between two distinct notions of consciousness. Having secured knowability in consciousness, Hegel goes on to speak of this consciousness as mere natural consciousness, and the phenomenology is carried on through a consciousness in which knowledge exhausts all being. His explanation of history as the externalisation of spirit involves a conterminity of knowing and being which follows from the way spirit's self-knowledge constitutes all phenomena. But the ideality which allows this explanation is not secured from within the phenomenological position constituted by the classical epistemological project. Though Hegel shows the idea of exteriority in that project to be an absurd one, he does not, as he seems to think, thereby immanently negate exteriority as such. At this point, the point where Hegel's own theocratic aims are to be realised, the *Phenomenology* breaks down, and the complex of positions that is to demonstrate the absolute truth - such as the end of history and the necessity this can give to Hegel's explanations - collapses.

Though coming to an essentially unfavourable conclusion about Hegel's project's ability to satisfy its own aims, I have meant to do so in a radically different way than has characterised recent marxist criticisms of Hegel. The interpretative paths through Hegel taken by Althusser and Colletti (and, more or less by default, Cohen and Elster) which lead them to try to separate Marx from him completely show a most interesting similarity. Though dealing with different aspects of Hegel's thought - Althusser with the teleological structure of the dialectic, Colletti with its idealist formulation - they both insist on an extremely strong coherence in Hegel's work. They do this in order to successfully criticise what they characterise as the naive extant attempts to borrow from the dialectic and develop it in a non-teleological, non-idealist fashion. We cannot dispute their conclusions about such naivete. However, beneath this ostensible criticism, they both introduce a far stronger claim, and it is this claim that makes their positions ultimately unacceptable. This is the claim that any attempt to link Marx and Hegel must be naive. What they at first seem to be arguing, for example against Engels, is that his attempt to make this link is weak. But rather they are claiming that this is so as a result of another argument, that any such an attempt *must* be weak. They give to Hegel's arguments such a degree of internal coherence that any such link becomes impossible. His thought is so monolithically consistent that one must take all or nothing from him.[95]

Now this is very dubious in a number of ways. Firstly, their choice of the alternatives they establish - to take nothing from Hegel - is hardly rationally defensible in their own terms. The internal consistency they find in Hegel is surely a strong ground for belief in any opinion. This would be so particularly for Althusser, who adheres to a pure coherence criterion of truth. We know why they turn away from Hegel, but their own interpretations tend to remove the rational ground from what is thereby exposed as a political decision in the bad sense. Secondly, on general hermeneutic grounds into which I will not go here, the attribution of such a degree of consistency is quite simply illusory and off the point of any interpretation. Thirdly, we must see that in this specific case there is indeed a profound fissure running through Hegel's thought which not only allows but demands a creative utilisation of elements of that thought if the enormous significance of Hegel for social theory and its development is to be recovered. As justification for saying this I can only refer the reader to what has gone before, and in summary of this say that recognising the strengths and weaknesses of Hegel's thought is necessary both for understanding Hegel's work and, because that work is of the first philosophical importance, for the setting out of a principal resource for contemporary philosophy in full knowledge of the difficulty of utilising it. In his critique of classical epistemology, Hegel outlines both the necessity of criticising alienated beliefs and a method - immanent critique - which in principle can allow us to set about satisfying that necessity.

It is in this context that I would like now to turn to the work of Marx, and particularly to *Capital*. I make no secret of my belief that rather than having to distance himself from Hegel's thought in order to make his own work valuable, such is Hegel's stature that it is in the ways in which he might make Hegel's insights philosophically and scientifically corrigible that Marx's importance will lay. I shall now, therefore, turn to the major instance of the use of these insights in social theory, *Capital*.

Notes

1   LHP1, pp 90-100.
2   L, sec 237 remark.
3   PS, p 10.
4   *Ibid*, p 103.
5   PM, sec 381.
6   PN, sec 247.
7   SL, p 824.
8   LHP3, pp 280, 281.
9   *Vide* Hook, *From Hegel to Marx*, pt 1, ch 5.
10 *Vide* Findlay, *Hegel: A Re-examination*, ch 2.
11 Kant, *Critique of Pure Reason*, pp A592-602, B620-30.
12 FK, p 85; LHP3, pp 63-4; L, pp 258-8 and LPEG, pp 353, 363-4.
13 *Vide* Copleston, 'Hegel and the Rationalisation of Mysticism'; Fackenheim, *The Religious Dimension of Hegel's Thought* and Westphal, 'Hegel's Theory of Religious Knowledge'.
14 FK, pp 53-191; PS, pp 1-45 and *idem*, 'Hegel's Foreword to H Fr W Hinrich's *Die Religion in inneren Verhaltnisse Zur Wissenschaft*', pp 227-44.
15 PS, chs 7-8 and PM, secs 553-77.
16 *Vide* Taylor, *Hegel*, pt 5.
17 Descartes, 'Meditations', no 6. Cf the critique of "rational psychology" in Kant, *Critique of Pure Reason*, pp A341-405, B 399-432.
18 PS, paras, 84-6.
19 *Vide* Maier, *On Hegel's Critique of Kant*.

20   SL, p 827.

21   PS, p 51.

22   *Vide* Norman, *Hegel's Phenomenology*, pp 16-8.

23   Cf the first movement of the logic, the running together of pure being and determinate being. SL, pp 82-108 and L, secs 86-8.

24   *Vide* Gadamer, 'Hegel's Inverted World', p 36.

25   Cf PS, pp 58-103 and Kant, *Critique of Pure Reason*, pp A95-130, B 129-69.

26   Fichte, *Science of Knowledge*, p 100.

27   Kant, *Critique of Pure Reason*, p 113.

28   L, sec 42.

29   Fichte, *Science of Knowledge*, pp 93-102.

30   DBFS, pp 79-82.

31   L, chs 3-5.

32   Furthermore, this would seem particularly to be the case with regard to our concerns, for the conclusion of 'Force and Understanding' itself utilises an idea of inversion. However, discussion of this use of "inversion" is, I believe, obviated by the argument I am about to make. For such a discussion *vide* Bossart, 'Hegel on the Inverted World'; Flay, 'Hegel's Inverted World'; Solomon, *In the Spirit of Hegel*, pp 376-85; Verene, *Hegel's Recollection*, ch 4 and Zimmerman, 'Hegel's "Inverted World" Revisited'.

33   It goes without saying that I do not by this mean to imply that there is nothing of interest or lasting value in that first section which, as I have said, works very well against many twentieth century empiricist philosophies.

34   *Vide* Marx, *Hegel's 'Phenomenology of Spirit'*, pp 2-3.

35   *Vide* Bird 'Hegel's Account of Kant's Epistemology', pp 69-70.

36   *Vide* Ruben, *Marxism and Materialism*, pp 38-49.

37   *Vide* Della Volpe, *Logic as a Positive Science*, pp 41-9.

38   FK, p 67; LHP3, p 66 and LPEG, p 353.

39   SL, p 70.

40   *Vide* Lauer, 'Hegel on Proofs for God's Existence', p 455.

41   Mendelssohn, 'Morgenstunden' lecture 17.

42   FK, p 85.

43   SL, pp 86-90; L, sec 51 and LPEG, pp 354-9.

44   L p 259 and LPEG, pp 363-4.

45   *Vide* Solomon, 'Hegel's Concept of Geist', p 149.

46   On this weakness in relation to Hegel's critique of Kant *vide* Guyer, 'Thought and Being', p 204.

47   *Vide* Adorno, *Negative Dialectics*, p 8.

48   *Vide* Plamenatz, *Man and Society*, vol 2, p 147.

49   *Vide* Tayor, *Hegel*, p 538.

50   *Vide* Dilthey, 'The Construction of the Historical World in Human Studies', p 194.

51   Trendlenburg, *Logische Untersuchungen.*

52   *Vide* Pippin, 'You Can't Get There from Here.'

53   Eg Gadamer, 'Hegel's Inverted World', p 36 and Verene, *Hegel's Recollection.* Verene tries to give metaphor the status of explicit argument, but whilst the light cast on Hegel is often very valuable indeed, the effort really runs counter to Hegel's own views of philosophy.

54   *Vide* EPM, pp 332-46.

55   The rigidity of the rod Hegel fashions for his own back emerges in a contrast with a book of similar scope to the *Phenomenology*, Vico's *New Science*. Vico's account of the common history of (gentile) nations matches its own stress on unifying poetical themes in that history with a form and style more (sometimes wildly) lyrical than "scientific" - the whole is hung from the interpretation of a picture (Vico, *The New Science*, pp 2-26). Vico cannot avoid rational criticism in this way (though his strengths have often escaped formulaic analytical criticisms), but nor can he be said to *demand* it in the way Hegel did.

56   Though, interestingly enough, in that part of the 'Preface' which he did revise he did not make other than trivial alterations. *Vide* Kaufamnn, *Hegel*, pp 368-405. This was, on the other hand, the part of the book written with most knowledge of where the argument was going.

57   LPH, p 10.

58   L, sec 209 remark and LPH, p 33.

59   *Vide* O'Brien, *Hegel on Reason and History*, pp 104-16.

60   Pace Kaufmann, *Hegel*, pp 262-3. When faced with objections to the ruse of reason, Kaufmann's tack is to reduce it to a very general idea of "unintended consequences" which would cover almost all of the uses of this idea in social theory of which I am aware. This removes what is objectionable about the ruse of reason, but only by removing much of what is characteristically Hegelian about it. One might as well defend a natural scientific account of the trajectory of a moving object by saying that the account involves no more than a reference to "motion".

61   *Vide* Adorno, *Negative Dialectics*, p 5.

62   PS, secs 87-9.

63   *Idem*, 'Phänomenologie des Geistes', p 61. Of course, I by no means insist upon "inversion" as the translation of "Umkehrung", though, in truth, it seems to be the best of the synonyms available. In using "inversion" I follow Dove (Heidegger, *Hegel's Concept of Experience*, p 122), Miller and Findlay (PS, p 15) and Kaufmann (*Hegel*, pp 398, 400).

64   Cf eg SL, pp 114-6.

65   *Vide* Dove, 'Hegel's Phenomenological Method', pp 44-56.

66   PS, pp 3, 43 and L, pp 7-8.

67   Eg Husserl, *Ideas*, pt 2.

68   *Vide* Marcuse, *Reason and Revolution*, p 94.

69   Eg Russell, *History of Western Philosophy*, pp 701-2.

70   Husserl, 'Philosophy as a Rigorous Science'; Heidegger, *Being and Time*, sec 82 and Sartre, *Being and Nothingness*, pt 3, ch 1, sec 3.

71   *Vide* Löwith, *From Hegel to Nietzsche*, p 137.

72   Kierkegaard, *Concluding Unscientific Postscript*.

73   *Vide* Thulstrup, *Kierkegaard's Relation to Hegel*, pp 380-1.

74   PS, p 14.

75   *Vide* Rosen, *GWF Hegel*, pp 129, 272-3.

76   PR, p 15. Cf Goethe, *Faust*, pt 1, p 98.

77   *Vide* CHPL.

78   *Vide* Habermas, 'Hegel's Critique of the French Revolution'.

79   PS, p 426.

80   LPH, pp 86-7.

81   *Vide* Kojève, *Introduciton to the Reading of Hegel*, p 168.

82   *Vide* Kolakowski, *Main Currents of Marxism*, vol 1, ch 1, sec 14.

83   *Vide* Lukács, *History and Class Consciousness*, p 147.

84   *Vide* Mure, 'Hegel: How and How Far, is Philosophy Possible?', p 22.

85   PS, pp 6-7. Cf LHP3, pp 551-2, PR, pp 13-4 and LPH, p 442.

86   PS, p 11. Cf SL, p 840 and LPH, p 78.

87   Hegel, 'Dissertatio Philosophica de Orbitis Planetarium', p 92.

88   *Ibid*, p 117.

89   PN, secs 247-50.

90   *Ibid*, sec 246.

91   Pace eg Rosen, 'Hegel', p 283.

92   It would hardly be fair to identify Hegel as the sole perpetrator of this idea in respect to natural science, in fact, when practising natural scientists hazard epistemological speculation, it is not uncommon to find a similar view expressed. So, in what is probably the most widely read recent popular cosmology by a highly distinguished natural scientist, we find Stephen Hawking postulating the discovery of "a complete theory" which would be "the ultimate triumph of human reason" as it would allow us to "know the mind of God". Hawking, *A Brief History of Time*, p 175. This passage undoubtedly does strikingly echo similar ones in Hegel, eg L, p 70.

93   *Vide* Jay, *Marxism and Totality*.

94   Marcuse, 'A Note on Dialectic', p 451.

95   Althusser, 'Contradiction and Overdetermination', pp 101-2 and Colletti, *Marxism and Hegel*, pp 46, 51.

5 Use-value and Exchange-v?
in the Analysis of the
Commodity

In Marx's presentation of his political economy of capitalism, the first dichotomy into which the commodity is shown to resolve itself is that of use-value and exchange-value.[1] What is at issue in this dichotomy is the analytic separation of the material content of a good, which is its use-value, from the social form of the production of that good, which is as a commodity with exchange-value. In order to explain exchange-value, it is necessary to make reference not only to the natural properties of commodities but to those properties as grasped through a historically specific mode of production, capitalism, which has its own form of social organisation of production, value. This involves a criticism of bourgeois political economy as a form of alienated consciousness in which social relations are obscured by being conflated with naturally given qualities, an alienated belief which Marx calls commodity fetishism.

Let me briefly illustrate this theme by turning to that place in *On Protection to Agriculture* in which Ricardo contrasts the economics which will hold "as long as society is constituted as it now is" to that which might apply to "Mr. Owen's parallelograms", by which he meant, of course, Robert Owen's "new towns".[2] Marx regarded this passage as testimony to the poverty of Ricardo's ability to conceive of society in any way other than as presently constituted. Indeed, when Ricardo elaborates on Smith's description of the economics of the "early and rude state of society" in order to illustrate his analysis of the magnitude of value by descriptions of the economic conduct of primitive hunters and fishermen,[3] one finds, as Marx says, that these primitives calculate the value of their tools and labours as if " in accordance with the annuity tables in use on the London Stock Exchange in 1817".[4] Other than Owen's parallelograms, Marx concludes, bourgeois society is the only society Ricardo seems to have been able to countenance. That Ricardo could not even conceive of non-capitalist forms of economic calculation and organisation has the direct consequence that in his political economy the form of value is nowhere examined. Value is regarded as *the* principle of economic life and, therefore, neither requires nor indeed permits social investigation.[5] This is an explanatory limit which must be broken. It is a limit which is set by regarding capitalist production not as historically specific but as a general, natural form. Accordingly, the price of a good which enters economic life as a commodity is believed to be a given quality of the same sort as its physical properties and is not recognised to be the result of the social fact that the good has the form of a commodity. This belief, which amounts to thinking that the commodity is the only form of a good, is commodity fetishism. Even Ricardo, Marx concludes, has his Robinson Crusoe stories.[6]

I wish to stress that this view of capitalism and of the mistaken beliefs to which it gives rise sets up a most difficult test of Marx's own positions and the understanding to which they give rise. Marx is attempting a critique of alienated beliefs and must face the epistemological problems of such critique. The issue which is raised is whether *Capital's* description of modern society can carry social scientifically informed conviction beyond the point where the *Phenomenology of Spirit* cannot do so. To put this another way, can Marx push the criticism of alienation beyond Hegelian limits?

Marx's argument for the separation of the material content and the social form of a good is given in his analysis of the commodity as the statement of the first positions of the labour theory of value. Let us begin, then, with Marx's beginning, the commodity. Adapting, as he so often does, one of Hegel's famous locutions, Marx allows that selecting a point at which to begin any science is difficult[7] and tells us that in his science the commodity is chosen as the economic cell form of bourgeois society.[8] Leaving aside the rather sweeping analogy with the entire history of western science by which Marx arrives at this metaphor, we are led quite directly to the reasons for his choice of beginning by this hint. We now can see from the *Economic and Philosophical Manuscripts* and the *Grundrisse* that Marx did not begin his own investigations in this way but, of course, had to begin his studies with ostensible (and, it turns out, very complex) facts - let us say poverty in the former and the use of money in the latter.[9] Nevertheless, he surely was justified in believing that his presentation of his economic investigations has as its beginning the simplest element of contemporary economic life as it appears to the common consciousness.[10]

Two senses of "simple" are played upon here. The commodity does, at every moment in the vast majority of transactions, present itself as the unit of economic life and, therefore, is a simple, easily recognisable beginning. But, as it is to be argued throughout *Capital*, it possesses this character only because it is simple in that it is the unit (the cell, we might agree, bearing the biology of Marx's time in mind) of bourgeois wealth.[11] To look at everyday economic transactions would reveal a great number of possible common determinations: the use of money, the motivation of utility, etc. Furthermore, the commodity can itself be analytically broken down - Marx himself proceeds to do this. However, it is the commodity that is the end point of any heuristic abstraction or simplification which preserves in their unity the specific characteristics which identify the capitalist mode of production.[12] The commodity is, in a phrase, the fundamental element of generalised commodity production and, by virtue of this, is the proper place to begin an explanation of capitalism.[13] Marx's choice of beginning is intended to direct our attention to the fundamental unit of capitalism as a *specific* mode of production.[14]

This is a beginning which can be justified only by the explanatory power of what follows from it, for the identification of capitalism as a particular mode of production obviously must underpin, after being shown to be demonstrable from, the singling out of the commodity as the fundamental element of a specific form of production. It is our grasp of this specific form that will enable us to understand the peculiar characteristics of a historical type of production. This would not be possible if we took an element to be found in all economic transactions, say the element of utility, as our starting point in explaining specific transactions. Indeed, a counterpoint between the two senses of simplicity we have discussed here, between the simple because commonplace character of the commodity as it appears and the simple because analytically irreducable element of specifically bourgeois wealth, is a persistent ordering theme of the three volumes of *Capital*, as Marx sets about explaining the former simplicity by means of the latter. What is more, as the explanation proceeds, marked peculiarities are uncovered in the commodity which rather alter our perception of its commonplace character.[15]

Marx is trying to establish a real social structure, of specifically capitalist social relations of production, as necessary for the explanation of the features of a specific set of economic transactions. The structure is posited through explanatory requirements which subsequently it is to satisfy.[16] Marx undoubtedly has a certain realist confidence in the presence of this structure as an actually existing determining influence on empirical human conduct which he will pit against alternative understandings of that conduct which tend to deny the influence, or indeed existence, of that structure. These understandings are alienated beliefs in the inevitable givenness of bourgeois society.

The use-value and exchange-value of a commodity are distinguished by Marx under the dualisms of quality and quantity and substance and magnitude. The particular use-value of a commodity rests in the peculiar qualities which it possesses by virtue of its intrinsic natural properties. Though Marx was well enough aware that such properties may constitute a use-value only though being recognised as useful,[17] he emphasises the intrinsic character of the use-value[18] by, in line with classic philosophic usage, denoting this quality as the commodity's "substance". Equally in line with this usage is the problem which arises immediately upon turning to the exchange of these substances. It is precisely the qualitative differences between use-values that is the reason for the exchange of commodities, but how might the exchange of different qualities be proportionally regulated when those qualities constitute different, incommensurable substances? How can one table equal two chairs?

Certainly when first taken up in this way, any exchange would seem to be purely arbitrary. Quite accidental exchanges of various proportions of commodities turning on any number of easily imagined reasons, such as a parent giving a valuable gift in return for a less valuable one from a child, arguably generate ratios of exchange specific to each instance and do not involve any proportional regulation at all.[19] Indeed, as the purposefully comic examples of exchange given in the *Critique of Political Economy*[20] indicate, and as Marx observes in so many words in *Capital*,[21] the idea that such regular exchange could take place, according the commodity an inseparable exchange-value, seems absurd. Nevertheless, Marx proceeds to investigate how it is that such regulation can take place, taking it from the outset of both this section of *Capital* and the latter, more detailed discussion of the elementary or accidental form of value, that exchange-value expresses some regulated commensurability.[22] On what grounds did he do this?

These grounds are not readily apparent. Marx's overt argument for taking this course is, following an insistence that exchange requires equalisation of the goods to be exchanged which is to be found in the *Nicomachean Ethics*,[23] that two different qualities can be exchanged only after they have been reduced to quantitative differences of the same unit, that is to say, after they have been rendered commensurable. He drew support for this logical case from analogies to geometry,[24] physics[25] and chemistry.[26] But we can see that the whole argument which Marx formulates itself presumes the proportional regulation of exchange and, being an inquiry into how it takes place, hardly can prove that it does.

It is not correct, however, to say that Marx provides no argument which supports his making this presumption.[27] There are brief comments on Samuel Bailey at points throughout the section on the elementary form to the effect that he paid insufficient attention to the very form of value because he focused exclusively on its quantitative aspects. These seem promising, but were only very brief summations of a longer discussion of Bailey in *Theories of Surplus Value* and therefore pursuing these points was not possible before Kautsky. We now can, of course, turn to the unfinished script and to the quite long section in which Bailey's contribution to the disintegration of the Ricardian school is considered.[28] From this, together with the discussion of the anonymous *Observations on Certain Verbal Disputes in Political Economy*[29] which Marx thought Bailey closely followed on these points,[30] we can glean support for Marx's stance on proportional exchange by following the thinking by which he arrived at this stance.

Bailey's polemic against the entire Ricardian attempt to determine a measure of value took the form of an accusation that there were really only an infinite number of accidental equations of the relative values of various commodities and that therefore a theory of value such as that sought by Ricardo illegitimately attempted to render absolute that which was purely relative.[31] The cause of this scholastic illusion on the part of Ricardo was a misunderstanding of money's role as a universal mediator of exchange. That money could play this part did not mean, as Bailey alleged Ricardo took it to mean, that it was an absolute, invariant measure of value, for it could and did vary infinitely in value. It could nevertheless be a universal mediator, as its variations did not of course affect the relative magnitudes of commodity values expressed in it as these would vary uniformly. Money thus, in fact, expressed the essential relativity of value.[32]

Marx recognised that Bailey had in this way cast a valuable light on the manner in which money could function as a measure of value and he evidently drew to some degree upon this[33] when reaching his own conclusion that money must have a variable value.[34] But as Marx's own going on to incorporate this within the labour theory of value testifies, Bailey's disposal of the idea of an invariant measure hardly secures the position that value was thereby only relative. Drop the requirement that value be invariant, and Ricardo's commitment to this is by no means as clear cut as Bailey assumes,[35] and the argument against an "absolute" value formally falls. This cannot, I think, be shown more clearly than it was by Marx himself in criticism of the use of such an argument by Broadhurst. Broadhurst's argument would seem to have been used in *Capital* to exemplify the critique of "absolute" value only because of the economy of his formulations, as he is not discussed elsewhere in Marx's published economic writings and as he obviously was not the first to state the case. I therefore quote; first, the relevant passage from Broadhurst:

> Once admit that A falls, because B, with which it is exchanged, rises, while no less labour is bestowed in the meantime on A, and your general principle of value falls to the ground...If [Ricardo] allowed that when A rises in value relative to B, B falls in value relatively to A, he cut away the ground on which he rested his grand proposition, that the value of a commodity is ever determined by the labour embodied in it; for if a change in the cost of A alters not only its own relation to B, for which it is exchanged, but also the value of B relatively to that of A, though no change has taken place in the quantity of labour needed to produce B, then not only the doctrine falls to the ground which asserts that the quantity of labour bestowed on an article regulates its value, but also that which affirms that the cost of an article regulates its value;[36]

and, second, Marx's comment on this:

> Mr. Broadhurst might just as well say: consider the fractions 10/20, 10/50, 10/100, etc. The number 10 remains unchanged, and yet its proportional magnitude, its magnitude in relation to the numbers 20, 50, 10 continually diminishes. Therefore, the great principle that the magnitude of a whole number, such as 10, is "regulated" by the number of times the number 1 is contained in it falls to the ground.[37]

The exposure of such an error in itself if of much less significance than noting the step in the direction of vulgar economics which allows it. Bailey's writings of the 1820s were part of a polemical attack against the Ricardian theory of value's inability to square with certain immediately available characteristics of the capitalist economy such as the equalisation of the rate of profit and it was spurred on by Ricardo's frank but nonetheless increasingly disingenuous admission of exceptions to his theory.[38]

Clearly Bailey's efforts, and those of others at the time, were aimed not at developing Ricardo but at doing away with the core of his work, dismissing as a scholastic invention the very basis of any investigation of regular exchange. Bailey's political economy was to *end* with relative exchanges of commodities, the values entering those relative exchanges accordingly being regarded as naturally given properties.[39] This result was used by Marx in *Capital* to illustrate the nadir of the fetishistic confusion of the natural and social.[40]

Obviously an explanation of exchange-value, given Marx's establishment of the necessity of social explanation, must go further at precisely the point where Bailey breaks off and would have Ricardo break off.[41] Time and again Marx insists that the point is to examine how regular proportional exchange can take place and that there must be a qualitative equalisation of different use-values into commensurable quantities for it to do so. The argument worked up in *Capital*, even down to a version of the analogies with geometry and physics,[42] is given many times in this section of the *Theories*, and Marx had little difficulty in formally refuting the logic of Bailey's attempt to treat value as purely relative. But the acceptance of the plausibility of Marx's particular explanatory tack and the formal arguments for this cannot be secured without explication of why that tack is necessary and why it allows convincing formal arguments to be marshalled to its aid. However, the display of the conviction that Bailey is fundamentally diminishing political economy's explanatory power, which emerges far more clearly from the *Theories* than from *Capital*, gives us all the lead we need in this respect.

In arguing about what is necessary for exchange to take place, Marx is not giving a second-order rationalisation of exchange, but an, as it were, first person account of what goes on in the capitalist mode of production. I have mentioned that we can conceive of many rationales of certain acts of exchange which certainly are specific to only those acts and recognising this would seem to undercut Marx's ground for the necessity of undertaking his projected explanation of regular exchange. But he is directly drawing our attention to an actual process of reduction to qualitatively equalised units and quantitative commensuration of the magnitudes of these units that *does*, as a matter of fact, take place, allowing the generalised exchange of innumerable goods in regular, definite proportions that is the principal characteristic of bourgeois economic life.[43] He is, in a phrase, trying to describe the real social structure of capitalist exchange.[44]

This becomes rather more clear in later passages of *Capital*,[45] where Marx describes the actual historical development of the specific form of proportionally regular exchange which he wants to investigate.[46] This interpretation of Marx's taking regular exchange as given is directly confirmed by certain passages of the *Grundrisse* and the *Theories*[47] and it is also supported by following up the textual links between such passages and Marx's writings of the early 1840s. This reveals that Marx initially took up these themes in an ethical evaluation of capitalist universal exchange as constituting the universal venality of bourgeois society.[48] It is a requirement of the explanation of capitalist production that justifies Marx's criticism of Bailey for neglecting the qualitative aspects of exchange.

As we have seen, Marx gives a number of logical arguments and natural scientific analogies in order to demonstrate that for proportionally regulated exchange to take place there must be a reduction of the qualitatively different objects to be exchanged to commensurable quantities of the same unit. Though I have said that these devices cannot, as Marx seems to think they can, establish proportional regulation as essential for exchange, once we accept exchange in this sense as taking place they do show, and Marx wants them to do this as well, that some quantitatively commensurable common denominator is necessary.[49] Such a conclusion can claim realist support as it is arrived at by the use of formalised argument to deepen given experience, in this case of capitalist exchange. Everyone knows, as Marx later says, that distinct from their various shapes as use-values, commodities have such a quantitatively mensurable denominator - money.[50] Let us note here only the force of the observation of the denominator; to consider money itself at this point is to run rather ahead in the argument.

In turning to the examination of this denominator, Marx's first conclusion is that it cannot inhere in commodities' use-values. Two related arguments to this effect may be found in *Capital*. First, as it is the qualitative differences between use-values that motivate their exchange, this aspect of the commodity does not have the essential uniformity which allows of quantitative comparison - one bed is equal to two chairs is an absurd statement.[51] This again is a formal explication of the experience of capitalist commodity exchange, making clear what goes on in the typical obliteration of the qualitative differences of use-values when commodities are assessed in respect of exchange-value; when £100 worth of anything is equivalent to £100 worth of anything else.[52]

From this argument we reach a second. If we bring two different use-values together, though we may well express their worth in relative amounts of each other, this cannot be done by actually equating them themselves, but only through the mediation of a third quality, one which is common to, but distinguishable from, both. Thus one bed can equal two chairs because both constitute the same amount of their denominator. The thing to note in this context is that the denominator cannot be the actual object of the exchange but must be a third quality.[53] Now, for some purposes this denominator can, as Marx's analogies infer, refer to the natural characteristics of the commodity which go to make up its use-value. A bed and a chair can be equated in terms of mass, volume, analysis of composite materials, etc. But it is the *unique* configuration of an object's properties that makes it desirable as a specific use-value and, therefore, resolution into these properties, though perfectly possible, cannot lead to the *common* denominator we are seeking for as a regulator of exchange.

The aim of this argument is to criticise the direct attribution of exchange-value to the intrinsic qualities of natural objects, so that a commodity seems naturally endowed with a certain worth. It is the making of such an attribution in the earliest formulations of marginalism (apart from Gossen of course, of whom it would seem that Marx, hardly uniquely, was unaware), that draws Marx's only comments on this then nascent current of economic thought. In the first volume of *Capital* he briefly observes that the sorts of information that are gathered in attempts to relate worth directly to natural properties belongs only in commercial catalogues[54] and not, by implication, in political economy. Against such blunt attempts to derive value from inner worth, Marx's arguments show that what attempts to explain exchange-value as a natural property rest upon is not acceptable as such a residuum. Explanation of exchange-value calls for some further account of how the purported equation of different qualities can take place. To put this another way; it is no explanation of exchange-value tautologically to ascribe it to an intrinsic worth of the commodity when not only has natural science never revealed exchange-value in a natural object[55] but when, even if it did so, it would remain to be understood how judgments of worth based upon it can be made in a proportionally regular fashion.[56] It is even less of an explanation when in fact such judgments seem quite impossible on the basis claimed. How *can* one bed equal two chairs?

Marx so far concludes that such an equality cannot inhere in the natural properties of commodities as it is impossible to see how a proportionally regular equation of them is to be constructed out of these properties. The thrust of such direct attributions of worth to natural properties is to remove the distinction between use-value and exchange-value, but I believe that Marx has successfully demonstrated that explanation of the latter calls, at least at an initial stage, for their analytic separation.[57]

If then, continues Marx, we disregard use-values, only one property is left common to all commodities - that of being the products of labour. Once we have abstracted from use-value, all commodities tell us is that they are congealed quantities of human labour. It is as units of this social substance that they have value, the common denominator of their exchange.[58] We have reached the first expressions of the labour theory of value. I should like to leave aside for the moment the description of "human labour" by which Marx tries to show how this is to play the part of the quantitative denominator which we are seeking and consider the very plausibility of the basic idea of the labour theory of value as so far expressed.

Before proceeding, it is necessary to note a shift in the subject of our discussion. Labour is put forward as the constituent of value and value as the basis of proportionally regulated exchange. Though the entire argument so far would lead one to expect that value is directly related to price, Marx, although not sufficiently clearly, leaves the character of this relationship quite open and in fact he will argue that it cannot be one of direct proportion. Recalling the earlier argument that the common denominator cannot be either of the objects to be exchanged but must be a third quality, we can see how Marx leaves a space for his later distinction. An exchange-value, strictly speaking, is a relational term expressing the proportional exchange of two or more objects. One bed is equal to two chairs is an exchange-value. But this is only the form of the expression of the denominator which sets the proportionality and mediates the exchange. What is actually going on in the equation of the bed and the chairs is the recognition that these things may be mediated by a common denominator - value. This is all one can say so far. It would be wrong to move immediately on to saying that a bed has twice as much value as a chair because this would presume that exchange-value is a direct expression of value and we do not yet know whether or not this is so. Exchange-value is then, to be quite precise, the form of expression of value,[59] which form will be subjected to detailed investigation later in *Capital*.

The commodity is now shown to be analytically resolvable into a dichotomy of use-value and value, not use-value and exchange-value, and in the development of this third term of "value" Marx gives a name to the real social structure at which he is driving in his comments on Bailey. As Marx says, initially treating exchange-value and value as equivalent could do no harm so long as we are aware of the problem of the value-form. This tack did give us a certain purchase on the immediately accessible characteristics of the commodity from which we could begin.[60] But now we must be sure in our grasp of value as that component of the commodity other than its use-value, as that component which is the ground of exchange and as that component which represents the labour expended in realising the use-value of the commodity.

What we have, of course, immediately to ask is whether this presentation, stated generally in order that we might avoid qualifications which could as yet only obscure the main point, is correct? There are at first glance some anomalous cases which run counter to the constellation of the concepts of commodity, use-value, exchange-value, value and labour which Marx has now presented[61] and in explanation of those concepts he takes up such cases.[62]

A thing can be a use-value and be a product of labour without being a commodity. We have, I trust, already dealt sufficiently with the identification of capitalism as generalised commodity production to see that this case is not really an anomaly but directly follows from and strongly supports the depiction of capitalism as a specific mode of the general production of use-values. However, a number of further points of importance follow from this case and these will be discussed in a moment. Rather of the same theoretical consequence as this first case is a second, which arises when a commodity is a product of labour but has no value as the commodity produced has no use-value and thus cannot be exchanged. Again this case can be easily seen to fit in with what Marx has said of the dichotomy of use-value and value rather than to pose a problem for that dichotomy, though again some interesting corollaries remain to be discussed.

Amongst the anomalous cases which Marx sets out, the one we are about to discuss is distinguished from the other two in that it by no means easily falls into place in Marx's analysis of the commodity.[63] A thing, Marx observes, can be a use-value without being a value. This is a rather imprecise way of putting the case, for if we quite properly regard value as the representation of labour in commodity production, then this anomaly merely restates the first which we have discussed, where labour is present in a form other than value in a different mode of production. But, as is made quite clear by a brief look at the list of things Marx gives, including air and natural meadows, this case actually is the one of the possession of value by objects which are not the products of labour.

Even with this made clear, there are still difficulties in seeing what Marx means. Considering the two examples of air and natural meadows which have been mentioned, it would seem that including both in the same list is to ignore important distinctions. Air, let us allow (subject to certain modern day exceptions I will consider below), has never appeared as a commodity and thus regarding it as a use-value presents no difficulty for the labour theory of value. Indeed we might say that air is a use-value but not a commodity because it has no value. This would however be very rash, because natural meadows, which may also have a use-value not produced by labour, do of course appear as commodities. Marx noted this problem in the *Critique of Political Economy* of 1859 and, in fact, had set out the essentials of its solution before this[64] and this solution is given repeatedly in the script for volume three he had drafted before the list in volume one went to press.[65] We can be sure, then, that we are not dealing with some terrible slip[66] and, bearing in mind the earlier distinction between value and exchange-value, it is possible to look forward to Marx's thoughts on rent and such matters without being convinced beforehand that they are casuistic.

It transpires that Marx has, in fact, chosen his words rather carefully in this particular respect. He does not deny that natural meadows may have an exchange-value, rather he denies that they have a value, though he claims that rent is based upon and determined by the basic structure of value, though the meadows themselves have no value. We must then suspend our judgment until we have considered his account of the distance between value and its expression in exchange-value, of which the theory of rent is an important part. However, some general comments on the character of this distance are in order at this point, for we are not pursuing the knowledge, uninteresting in itself, that exchange of use-values unmediated by labour is reconcilable with the labour theory of value, but rather Marx's claim that we need this theory in order to explain even these exchanges. Natural meadows have use-value; they also can be commodities. Now, there can be nothing in their use-value that makes the meadows necessarily commodities, for that use-value can be realised without the meadow entering economic life as a commodity at all. We need a further account of why the potential to be commodities which the meadows' use-value affords them is realised. This way of putting the issue here sets out one explanatory aim of the labour theory of value,[67] the aim which concerns us here.

Let us take a rather simple model of commodity production.[68] Goods are produced and are to be exchanged. They have no use-value for their producers, who wish to realise their exchange-value in order to purchase other goods which do have a use-value for themselves. Such producers produce independently, or rather individually, for they require each other for the full satisfaction of their needs. In the production of commodities for exchange, deliberate regulation of this social interchange typically is absent. Individual decisions about what to produce and what to exchange in what proportion for what other goods can only be arrived at in the market place. That is to say, after the act of individual production. Such decisions obviously are made with reference to the use-values of the commodities, but we must note that investigation of this reference is theoretically subsequent to recognising that these decisions are situated at a distinct ontological level of the social relations of the division of labour.[69]

We can recall Marx introducing the labour theory of value by saying that if we abstract from their use-values, commodities are congealed labour and that it is as units of this social substance that they have value. This formulation immediately runs together private labour and social exchange in a way which in retrospect reveals that we are dealing with the set of social relations which govern even the individually undertaken labours of commodity production. That is to say, we are dealing with the social relations which form the division of labour in commodity production, social relations which posit seemingly independent individual producers. In so far as these relations are mediated through the value which appears intrinsic to the commodity when the commodity is brought to the market place and the exchange of commodities takes place, then value is the social component of the commodity.

I have mentioned that it is rather stretching a point to say that a commodity's use-value is inherent in it. However, so long as we remain aware that the specific relationship between a commodity's natural properties and its use-value is a product of use, this way of speaking provides a useful contrast with which to address value. For looked at in this way, use-value is distinguished from value in that it has ontological foundations directly in the natural properties of the commodity which are quite absent from the social relations of production which make that use-value present itself as a commodity. The difference is not so much that labour is present in value. This is a misleading way of putting the point, as we can see from noting that labour usually is present in use-values as well. It is that the command of labour is the object of the social relation of value, whereas utility is the object of use-value. If it is human relations with nature that are described by use-value, it is the social relations of production which governs those relations with nature that are described by value. The distances between natural properties, use-value and the social relation of value are opened up by the separation of use-value and value.

Examination of these distances can, as they must, now follow. But any such examination will necessarily be inadequate if it does not start from the knowledge that what are at issue are the social relations of the direction of labour. Moving from positions where we (necessarily of course) begin with the phenomenal appearance that exchange-value is a natural property of commodities, we must first show that labour is the principle of the social direction of labour in capitalism. When accomplished, this task becomes the preliminary to the explanation of why labour is socially directed through the mystified form of value, which is the real crux of the identification of capitalism as a generalised commodity production.

Value emerges as a mystified principle of the social direction of labour, which principle remains to be investigated. It is basically only a presumption, then, to imagine that value is the directly proportional measure of labour. Such a presumption has no relationship to actually understanding what value is as a given social structure. Marx continually urged this point against the utopian socialism of especially Proudhon,[70] which sets its desired measure of labour against what, because they do not conform to this ideal standard, are the defective measures of capitalistic value.[71] Marx continually stresses that what he is dealing with is value as it is actually present for empirical investigation, dealing with understandings and assessments of value as they have become, as a matter of fact, cemented by custom.[72] Value might be a perfectly irrational measure of labour, or it might measure it with complete precision. We do not yet know. Though we have to come to some opinion about the validity of value's representation of labour in order to understand that representation, what we must not thereby do is simply give a moralistic pronouncement based on that opinion without understanding why that representation has become socially dominant.

However, I must say that Marx continually allows some determinations of the relationship of value and labour which belong to this latter part of the investigation to enter into his presentation at far too early a stage, giving the erroneous impression that he himself conceived of value as some precise measure of labour by the use of which he will recalculate capitalistic assessments of labour's just economic desserts[73] in precisely the way he regarded as utopian. This has proven to be a shortcoming of very considerable consequence and I will have to return to it at various points below.

Bearing the substance of Marx's idea of value in mind, we can now see our anomalous cases in another light. Marx can, we recall, allow that something may be a product of labour but not have a value because it cannot be exchanged. This obviously could not be so if he regarded value as his own measure of labour, for then an input of labour would constitute value irrespective of other conditions. But equally obviously Marx can allow this denial of value to some labour if we take value as the given principle of the social direction of labour under generalised commodity production, a principle which is quite prepared to negate any amount of labour if that labour's product has no use-value which will lead to its exchange. This is to say, in fact, that the labour's product has no socially endorsed use-value. It is the production of goods not merely for the use of someone other than the producer but for exchange understood as this oblique general social direction of individual producers that distinguishes commodity production.

Natural meadows can, of course, be said to have a use-value which is in no way the product of labour. But if we regard value as the principle of the social direction of labour under commodity production and not as a substance composed of labour, then the possibility that the utilisation of the use-value of the meadows should come under that principle, irrespective of that use-value's not initially being a product of labour, clearly emerges as one it is important to pursue. For we see that this case certainly falls under what we are trying to understand; the direction of labour. Natural meadows may have an exchange-value because their, as it were, original use-value can be ultimately utilised only through labour, and that labour is organised through the structure of value. Air, by contrast, has not been regulated by value or any other form of economic organisation because its utilisation in breathing defies the mediation of labour.[74] Or, more specifically with regard to capitalism, air defies subordination to the position where it is utilisable only through such mediation, that is to say, being rendered private property.

Air is a gift of nature as much as natural meadows, and yet its economic position is significantly quite different. If it should be quibbled that in some special modern day cases - aqualungs, compressed air, respirators, etc - air is rendered subject to commodity production, then this quibble, which certainly turns on the provision of air through the mediation of labour, surely reinforces the belief we have reached that with value we are dealing with a social ontological structure which must be distinguished from the given natural and which we must allow an effective place in the determination of specific form of human relations with nature.

In claiming that when we disregard the use-values of commodities only the common property of being the products of social labour remains, Marx observes that our view of the commodity has radically altered. Its sensuous characteristics and the use-value which is based upon these are removed; it remains only as a product of labour. Having grasped this dual character of the commodity itself, we are able to recognise that the labour involved in its production must also have a dual character, a new side to which character now also has emerged. For labour is no longer to us a specific act or type of work. If the sensuous characters of commodities no longer interest us, then neither do the particular types of work - tailoring, spinning, metalwork, etc - which realise those characters as use-values. As opposed to these, as it were, concrete labours, what Marx is now trying to drive at is the idea of abstract labour.[75]

If we abstract from the characters of concrete labours, we are left with just the simple fact of the expenditure of human effort. Marx's argument certainly makes it seem that he conceives of arriving at abstract labour through some reduction of different labours to a common index of biological energy expended or some such physiological quanta. Now, such a reduction from tailoring to amounts of energy is impossible, as has often enough been pointed out in criticism of the idea of abstract labour.[76] However, not only does such a reduction speak of a kind of materialism which Marx himself thought mechanical, thereby contradicting the way Marx posits conscious intention as integral to the labour process,[77] but Marx himself is in fact here affirming this impossibility. As there can be no reduction of qualitatively different use-values to a common denominator, there cannot be such a reduction of the labour which produced those use-values. And even were such a reduction possible, the resulting physiological quanta would remain in the realm of the natural and we know that the common quality of the commodity which we seek is social.

Indeed, the peculiarity of the dual character of labour lies in the necessity of concrete labours being different, for their products must have different use-values in order to exchange[78] whilst abstract labour must reduce to units of a single commensurable quanta. The abstract side of labour's dual character is the mechanism of social or mutual command of labours in commodity production; the analogue in wage-labour of value in the commodity. Abstract labour is the aspect of wage-labour which allows the social interdependence of specialised individual labours that is of the essence of the division of labour (which is, of course, a condition of generalised commodity production although, as Marx tells us,[79] the converse does not thereby follow).

If commodity exchange is in essence proportionally regular, as value is determined by the amount of capitalism's resources of productive labour needed to realise the use-values of particular commodities, it follows that the social side of the dual character of labour must equally render labour quantitatively calculable. This is the specific quality of abstract labour. In it, all types of labour and all degrees of skill displayed in labour are reduced to the exercise of a general labour capacity or labour-power, whose measure is duration in time.

Marx immediately tries to leave no doubt as to what he means by abstract labour by saying that if the value of the commodity is determined by the quantity of labour needed for its production, then it would seem that the less able the worker who produced it the more valuable would be the commodity, as that commodity would then take a longer time to make. This is not so, however, because we are dealing with socially necessary labour-time, that is, "the labour-time required to produce any use-value under the conditions of production normal for a given society and with the average degree of skill and intensity of labour prevalent in that society".[80] In a competitive market, this average is rigorously enforced. The law of commodity production is that anybody whose productive activity chronically falls beneath the average may not be able, due to competition, to valorise her or his product as a value proportionate to the time he or she spent on it. The producer will be left with unsaleable goods. And under established capitalist production, this market necessity is transmitted to wage-labourers through factory discipline[81] in what Marx called the real subsumption of labour to capitalist production.[82] By the same social token, the degree of productivity in use-value terms of this average or simple labour will vary with changes in productive resources. Or, put another way, what counts as simple labour at one point may well be below average after a rise in the general level of productivity.

The dichotomy of concrete and abstract labours is by no means an ideal way of describing the social direction of labour at which Marx is trying to drive. In this respect a better, and seemingly more natural, dualism might well be that of individual and social labours.[83] But we must be careful not to extinguish an important shade of meaning in abstract labour, for by this term Marx means not only social labour, common to all modes of production, but the *specifically capitalist* form of social labour. This specific form is abstract in the sense of being based on a quantitative abstraction from qualitative forms of labour and the absurd confusions this no doubt puts in the way of grasping the sociality of labour follows from the capitalist form of social labour. If, as I would say is the case, the social character of abstract labour emerges more clearly in the *Grundrisse, Critique of Political Economy* and *Wages, Price and Profit* because of the direct social locutions Marx uses there, this is because in *Capital*'s various editions the presentation becomes increasingly intimately bound up with the statement of specifically capitalist conditions. Undoubtedly this was a serious shortcoming in presentation, leading to the appearance that Marx was himself committed to the capitalist operations he was criticising.

Though we have arrived at abstract labour as the social denominator of individual productive effort which allows of their mutual command through exchange, this is not to say that we have discovered some easily realisable socialist truth of capitalism. Capitalism certainly does rest on an essential sociality which it denies and it is impossible to exaggerate the significance of knowing this. But it does this by resting on a sociality which denies itself. Formulating the labour theory does not socialise capitalism, because ultimately the sociality it reveals is one which obstructs the conscious grasp of its own existence.[84] In abstract labour, what is missing is precisely the recognition of the fundamental equality of all labours, as exercises of human power, which would stress their mutually interdependent, social character and would allow of their common, conscious, planned direction. Such conscious regulation recognises all labours as instances of an essential human activity, conterminous with human life, mediating human existence in nature.

The development of conscious economic planning requires a recognition of human equality as a minimum condition. If it takes one day to build a wall and two days to make a coat, then planning must take note of this, of course, and such recognition involves some commitment to being able to place both labours under the plan. But in abstract labour we have the quantitative equalisation or equation of labours, which is something quite different, a perverted form of equality. We say that a coat is worth twice as much as a wall. But this is absurd. It is in itself meaningless and really comprehensible only through a distanced commentary. Such expressions are, however, the only bourgeois way of grasping the social equality of labours.

This may seem a nice point but rather it is of the very greatest importance. The difference of worth and planned allocation of labour emerges most clearly when we consider that plans could embrace criteria of production - say organisation of labour to maximise enjoyment of that labour or to minimise environmental damage - which are externalities when judged by their worth. And here we come to what is peculiarly capitalist about abstract labour as a specific form of social labour. Abstract labour is the abstraction of concrete labours down to a unit expenditure of effort. It may be retorted that there is no way of doing this and indeed there is no defensible way. But it is, as Marx says, an abstraction that is performed every day in capitalist society.[85] It is a suppression of the concrete individualities of labours and skills in performing labours[86] in order to make them available to a production that is interested in their contributions to quantitative value only,[87] the measure of that quantity being time.[88]

With the commodity being assessed in this way, so is the labour which makes it up. Abstract labour is not labour shown to be mutually social, but rather labour reduced to quantitative units. Value is the necessary quantitative measure of the proportional exchange that is the social bond of bourgeois society. Labour which constitutes value can be socially relevant for production only in so far as it can be reduced to quantitative value components. This reduction is a real process conterminous with capitalist production, though of differing significance at different periods of capitalism's development. It is a process often called de-skilling, a name which captures the abstraction in abstract labour most neatly.[89] This abstraction is an important source of the instrumentality of working class attitudes to labour.[90] As such, abstract labour is a very substantial political economic fleshing out of Marx's early characterisation of capitalist wage-labour as an alienation of the quintessential human activity of conscious, productive work.[91]

If we have found labour to be the content of value, we must be clear that it is not the labour of citizens who overtly unite their efforts but abstract labour that leads to value; the labour which is given as wage-labour. In uncovering abstract labour, we uncover the ground of value. It is not a form of labour which makes clear the social ground of the individual giving of labour, but rather socially unites individual labours in an absurd and mystified way by reducing them, as Marx puts it, one-sidedly to their duration in time. This reduction is to the quantitative, mechanical side of labour, and this militates against the development of other sides. Paradoxically, then, abstract labour's suppression of its social dimension has the direct result of extinguishing individual satisfaction in the giving of labour.

So far my account of the first chapter of *Capital* basically has moved from the immediately available characteristics of the commodity to the labour theory of value, following the development of Marx's own argument in the first two sections of the chapter. A quite crucial element of this argument is that Marx intends it to refute what he identifies as the fetishistic ideology through which the commodity's characteristics are normally understood. Let us now turn to this part of his case.

Marx sets out from the simple, isolated or accidental form of value,[92] in which the single statement x commodity A is worth y commodity B describes the principle of the exchange of two goods. What we have here, in a sort of rationally reconstructed history,[93] is a description of the historically earliest and thereby equally the most intrinsically simple form of exchange, in which isolated acts of exchange take place in a context of basically non-exchange (though with various sizes of subsistence unit) economies. These exchanges will be almost accidental initially, but with increasing volume of exchange, a proportional regulation develops in custom which cuts against this accidental quality and begins to develop all the essential characteristics of value. For the proportions are, with development of the volume of exchange and of competition, fixed not by traditional assessments of merit in the work or its just price but by evaluations of necessary labour-time established through what, in increasingly a context of competitive selling, the commodity will realise in exchange.

The simple form automatically passes into a distinct form with expansion of the volume of exchange. This is the total or expanded form,[94] in which a whole series of goods find commodity expression in equivalents of each other. Thus x commodity A is worth y commodity B, z commodity C, etc. Instead of being brought into relationship with one commodity in an isolated act of exchange, each commodity is known to be in proportional relationship to a large number of others, these relative valuations being established through a large volume of exchange. The possibility of this attests, as we have seen, to the real existence of some denominator of the social exchange of these naturally distinct goods and here, in the existence of the expanded form of value, we have reached the position where value is the medium of a large amount of economic activity. The bringing of commodities to market in enough volume to form this expanded idea of a good's worth testifies to value's supplanting traditional organisations of labour.

This expanded form clearly does not meet the requirements of generalised exchange and it has itself passed into a further form with the development of this level of exchange, the general form.[95] In the expanded form, no commodity can really be said to have a clear, definite exchange-value, for that value is given in a virtually infinite and ever-changing set of relative expressions. General exchange on this basis is impossible, for the form speaks of production that is still linked to specific acts of barter, though increasingly barter conducted according to calculations of value, and not to the mere possibility of exchange as such, to exchange with anything. In the general form, one commodity is singled out as the general equivalent and all other commodities have a quantitative value relative to the general equivalent.

From the point of view of social relations of production, any commodity could of course stand as this general equivalent. In pre-capitalist modes of production, the development of a large volume of exchange may lead to the singling out of the commodity in most general demand as the general equivalent - the cow, grain, the goat, etc. Here again we see that it is basically the resolution of the demands of barter with a developing volume of exchange that orders the development. Another form of development from the general form is possible, however, the money-form[96] and this form is essential for (though not of course unique to) capitalism.[97] For in the money form, it is not the common utility of the general equivalent commodity that is its most important property. It is rather, we might say, its lack of direct utility. For the money commodity functions as the repository of exchangeability as such. It is set apart from all other commodities by virtue of being the general equivalent. It is the mark of the well developed possibility of exchange, for possession of money does not itself afford any utility (or very little) to the owner. Rather, through possession of money, the owner has a special command on all other commodities. The money form can be distinguished from the general form as such because of the clear representation in the former of exchangeability as such in a well developed commodity economy. The precious metals have conquered the position of money in bourgeois societies and, amongst the reasons why this is so, are their ability, because they are so difficult to come by, to encompass a great social value in relatively little bulk; their ability as metals to be divided into precise quantitative units by weight and their ability to be made into a form which will facilitate circulation.[98] The progressive replacement of precious metals by paper and, since Marx's time, by direct electronic transfer merely emphasises Marx's point that the function of precious metals as money cannot be a direct natural product.

The most important thing to understand about Marx's discussion of the money-form and the value-form generally is the great distance he means to travel in moving from value to exchange-value or price. We can see from the *Grundrisse* that he arrived at his most sophisticated views on the fetishistic character of money in a critical dialogue with what he thought were utopian attempts to make money directly represent labour-time,[99] as part of what we have already discussed as his general attitude to Proudhonism. The large time spent on this in the *Grundrisse* is written up only briefly in the *Critique of Political Economy*[100] and appears merely as footnotes in *Capital*.[101] The positive side of this contraction is that the heart of the issue of the difference between price and value is available in very brief form in *Capital*.

Why money does not directly represent labour-time, Marx says in the last of his footnotes on the point, "comes down simply to the question why, on the basis of commodity production, the products of labour must take the form of commodities". For any medium of circulation directly to represent labour-time, labour itself must be undertaken through a general social plan. In such a plan, a certain amount of labour-time might well be directly credited to whoever performed it by its meriting a certain amount of medium of circulation. For the labour is socially credited as deserving the reward of that amount of the medium before the labour is carried out. Such social recognition is precisely what is absent from commodity production and *money* is a development of commodity production. As we have seen, labour in commodity production is invested in a commodity for sale, and that labour is socially credited only through the sale of the commodity. It is not the labour which is the subject of sale, it is the commodity. We know that the very possibility of proportional exchange involves recognition of labour-time and that it is the social bringing together of individual labours invested in commodities that is the real issue in the general division of labour under commodity production. Nevertheless, these social relations are established only through the exchange of commodities. It is commodity exchange that is the object of this exercise, not the direct representation of labour-time.

It follows from this that there is the possibility of quantitative divergence between value and price bound up in the very existence of a developed money-form.[102] Of course, a commodity may not be bought because it has no use-value, and therefore the labour in it is not socially rewarded at all, but let us leave this aside and consider the following. Two people produce the same desired use-value. It may take the first one day and the second two. If price directly measured exchange-value, the latter product would exchange for twice the former product. But, of course, such an exchange is not what would take place. The former person would be able to sell his or her product and expand his or her production if he or she so wished, whilst the latter typically would be unable to sell his or her product at all. It may be thought that price is therefore an imperfect measuring device. But rather we should not regard the direct measure of labour as leading to the development of money price, but rather see the exchange of commodities as the peculiar basis of general money. When the issue is the buying and selling of commodities, and when the production of commodities will be open to continuous competition in methods, money's diversions from value are an absolute necessity. Under *laissez faire* capitalism, competition will constantly alter the rewards for different labours according to the changing of the socially necessary conditions of production that is endemic to the search for surplus value. Indeed, Marx thought that competition between capitals for commodity sales realising the highest possible profit would always, as it were, redistribute surplus value. Because greater amounts of capital would be attracted to areas of higher surplus value, commodities would more or less never sell at their value under capitalism but at a production price set by the effect of supply and demand on the profit of different branches of production.[103]

To regard Marx's labour theory of value as a direct quantitative account of price is, then, a mistake.[104] Not only is money fetishistic in that it allows of the understanding of social relations only through a mystifying material form, making all commodities and especially money itself seem to have an intrinsic natural value, but also money is necessarily not a direct quantitative measure of labour-time. This produces a real distance between price and value. The result of this foremost social scientific analysis of the *laissez faire* stage of the capitalist mode of production reveals the recognition of value, however, both qualitatively to describe the real social structure of that production and then quantitatively to orient the account of price to an influential starting point which we can consider supply and demand as modifying.[105]

Of course, the political economy of capitalism must be able to explain price as such and, given enough boundary data,[106] specific prices.[107] That Marx's own attempt[108] to transform values into prices carries a vitiating error would seem to be clear,[109] but this is not to say that, as a technical matter, a generally acceptable redrafting of the econometrics of this attempt might not be made[110] (or indeed have not been made).[111] The present problems with achieving this general acceptance repeat past experience[112] in that the technical solutions really are rather hindered because of a lack of clarity about what the explanation of prices really is meant to do. The ability to calculate price in itself, without extension backwards into the understanding of the specific relations of production,[113] can make no verifiable contribution to political economy[114] because there is no clear idea of what the calculations show. This surely is a clear limit to the value of the explanations of allocations offered by neo-classicism, and by neo-Ricardianism to the extent that it tends to relinquish interesting sociological content, for the assumptions on which the explanations are based are never examined but contain all the real interest. I must make it clear that I regard the sociological content of value theory the most important issue and, to the extent that value theory remains the economics which seems best to be able to explain fetishism, regard the present issue as being one of the quantitative development of value theory.[115] However, there is no doubt that an acceptable quantitative method for the calculation of price is required to give a complete account of the capitalist mode of production.[116] Were alternative quantitative explanations of price able to include the sociological insight of value theory, there would, of course, be no good reason to remain wedded to value theory.[117]

We can mention one further point at which a distance between value and price can be seen. Money is a command of social labour through its ability to be exchanged for all other commodities. It takes this position through a process which is predicated upon value. Once having gained the social pre-eminence of being the general equivalent,[118] however, money can of course be used to buy things which do not have a value, and, to put this the other way around, things which do not have a value can have a price. For those who sell the thing without a value will thereby gain a command over almost all other products through possession of money. What is involved here is merely the impinging on other social relations of the economic relationship at the heart of the capitalist production.

The rent or purchase of land from land owners whose private property in that land is of pre-capitalist origin is the most economically important such case. The very structure of Marx's explanation of rent shows his overall conception of value most clearly. He makes it explicit that he is investigating the particular capitalist influences upon the rent paid to non-capitalists and not any other form of land charges (though some extension into other forms are, and could further, I think, be made).[119] Marx certainly believed that the explanation of this rent required the labour theory of value. He accounted for it as being paid out of the super profits available to investment in agriculture due to the typically relatively low organic composition of agricultural capital. The volume of rent is clearly delimited by the size of the deduction from super profits which is possible before agricultural profit to the capitalist declines below that which would be available from industrial investment.[120] Such an account of the source of rent obviously does require the labour theory and, as such, is to describe the incorporation of pre-capitalist land-holding into the developing value economy.

Perhaps a more generally significant social consequence of the dominance of money over other than value relations is the possibility of purchasing human qualities, such as conscience, honour, etc. These might even come to have a fixed price through custom. With this observation, we have returned to a central theme of Marx's early works - the universal venality of money.[121] This is now an ethical condemnation backed by an unparalleled understanding of the capitalist economy that makes this venality not only possible but, as the spirit of the age, to be expected.[122] This is not a matter of a rather distasteful materialist tone to cultural life - though there is this. It is a question of an absurd misdirection of human effort. An outline of Marx's basic tools for the analysis of capitalist production shows that he saw economic life under capital as a fundamentally alienated set of practices.

In any specific mode, production will require the application of labour via tools to raw materials and any growth will require the production of a surplus. But under capital, this becomes an awful self-enforcing, ineluctable necessity. An individual capital, C, is composed of constant capital (raw materials and tools), c, and variable capital (labour power), v.[123] The goal of the capitalist is the growth of C, accumulation.[124] There simply is no limit to the pursuit of the growth of C, for, as an exchange-value, C has nothing but quantity as its measure. An infinite, purely quantitative growth is the capitalist's aim and no more absurd purpose surely can be imagined.

The fund for accumulation is surplus value, s, given by C - (c + v) *after* a productive cycle.[125] As the values of c, v and s also are all perceived in terms of exchange-values, the use of c and v must be directed by the pursuit of the quantitative growth of s.[126] There is no necessity at all for the capitalist directly to pursue use-values in determining the composition of C's output.[127] Nor, as c and v are perceived only as costs,[128] is there scope to decide that certain uses of v should be eschewed because of their effects on the workers[129] or certain uses of c be eschewed because of their effects on the natural environment.[130] Most importantly, the reduction of labour time cannot feature as a goal because it would counter the potential growth of s and of C.[131] In sum, the whole direction of the system falls under the absurdity of the reduction to quantity that is of the essence of money and this *is* a fetish. As such, of course, it demands its sacrifices. These are described well enough in volume one of *Capital*.

If, under planning, some unit of circulation was provided which was directly representative of judgments of labour-time, it would not lead to these consequences of money and capital except under circumstances which would lead to condemnation of the planning authority. This unit could be called money but would *be* money only by the most forced stretching of the term.[132]

Much criticism of Marx's political economy has simply read those economics as a piece with the aims of neo-classical economics when really the two pursue such different aims that their mutual dialogue, though essential as I will argue in the next chapter, requires a careful preliminary elaboration of the terms in which it will be conducted. If Marx is taken to be claiming that he can explain prices as the rational outcomes of the labour theory in the sense that prices are the "correct" expressions of labour inputs, then what he says is absurd. But it is just this line that was taken in the first serious criticisms of *Capital* and has continued to be taken in neo-classical economics. Böhm-Bawerk argues that the passages of *Capital* we have just discussed contain more or less as many errors or even falsifications as words.[133] He allows that the basis of exchange cannot be directly derived from the natural properties of goods. His own rather more sophisticated marginalism turns on relating prices to scarcity, scarcity being determined both by natural supply of and individual demand for a good.[134] Searching for the error in Marx's political economy from which the shortcomings in price calculation which he believes he has revealed in *Capital* stem, Böhm-Bawerk attempts to lodge it here, in the adoption of value based on labour as the denominator of exchange rather than allowing scarcity this role, a move which he claims pushed volume three into all sorts of difficulty in order to reconcile volume one with reality.[135]

Böhm-Bawerk's objections are given in two stages. First, he notes that Marx presents his case as an argument by elimination, elimination of other claimants for the position of denominator leaving value. Böhm-Bawerk quite rightly observes that this type of argument must satisfy a rather difficult boundary condition if it is to be valid, the condition of considering each and every possibility. This condition, it is claimed, Marx entirely fails to observe. When examining commodities, Marx surreptitiously includes only the direct products of labour in the set of relevant objects, which set is not, as Marx would have us think, the same as the set of all commodities. Examination of the former set may allow value to emerge as the common denominator, but examination of the latter, which includes gifts of nature, certainly would not.[136] We have dealt with this point as one of the seeming anomalies for the labour theory of value and I will not repeat myself. However, I would like to say that as Böhm-Bawerk is approaching these passages of volume one of *Capital* from volume three, it is a failing that he provides no discussion of Marx's account of the value determination of the commodity exchange of gifts of nature. Though the point is surely not made very clear in the first chapter of *Capital*, it would be a better reading to relate the many pages of volume three on rent to this first chapter than to imply that they do not exist, their theoretical space being filled in by a piece of dialectical sleight of hand. At the bottom of this failing there is the fact that Böhm-Bawerk does not seem to be able to countenance value as other than a flat measure of exchange-value in terms of a substance composed of amounts of labour. If we were to allow that value is such a measure, then Böhm-Bawerk would be right and Marx would look so foolish in holding to such an obviously absurd position that it would seem that he could reach his conclusions only through self-delusion at best.[137]

It is on this understanding of value that Böhm-Bawerk repeats these mistakes in respect of another of Marx's anomalous cases, arguing that value cannot be composed of labour because in some cases labour creates no value as its product cannot be exchanged and concluding that this profoundly embarrasses the labour theory of value.[138] Knowing that Marx himself was aware of this case does not alter Böhm-Bawerk's opinion.[139] Such a reading is fashioned by Böhm-Bawerk's not stepping away from the neo-classical economics concern to rationalise capitalistic assessments of value when turning to a theory which centrally tries to distance itself from and therefore to explain the very idea and the form of such assessments. If neo-classical economics can construct some measure of value which is able to arrive at decisions rather like exchange valuations, it considers itself to have explained the latter. Thus, for Böhm-Bawerk, Marx's theory cannot be empirically justified because it is impossible to construct with impeccable mathematics a scale of value of units of labour which can plausibly recreate exchange valuations. Marx's actual aim in the labour theory of value, to try to understand why economic organisation takes the form of value and what value assessments are, is completely lost. As we will see in the next chapter, Marx accords to value a great advance in economic organisation, but this is a vast scientific distance away from the presumption that value is (the only form of) rational economic judgment. Indeed, it is the inability to imagine economic judgment in any other form than value that underpins Böhm-Bawerk's economics and his submersion of Marx's attempt to open up value for investigation.

At this stage of the argument Marx has, says Böhm-Bawerk, managed to include labour amongst the list of candidates for the position of denominator of commodity exchange, a candidacy which it does not actually deserve. Let us now follow Böhm-Bawerk's exposition of how Marx makes labour the successful candidate, the second stage of his objections to the labour theory of value.

Böhm-Bawerk sets out the abstraction from use-values and the conclusion that after this abstraction all commodities have to tell us is that they are congealed labour. The error by which this conclusion is reached, is, according to Böhm-Bawerk, a confusion of abstraction from the genus and abstraction from the specific forms in which the genus manifests itself. Thus when we abstract from the use-value of commodity, this is not to say that we abstract from the category of use-value itself, which can remain common to all commodities and mediate their exchange, though in this mediation we no longer consider use-values' particular forms. The conclusion that labour is the only common denominator of commodities is therefore wrong.[140] However, again Böhm-Bawerk does not grasp what is actually going on in the passages which he criticises. On his own understanding, labour must be the only common denominator of commodities if it is to serve the function of calculating their exchange-values. If we are attempting to construct some such means of calculation, then Böhm-Bawerk's objections again are sound. But Marx is not. Thus, instead of taking it, as Böhm-Bawerk does,[141] as evidence of a gross inconsistency that Marx in fact allows use-value in general to be common to all commodities, we can see that Marx can do this and still abstract from use-value as such. The great deal of time which Böhm-Bawerk spends in trying to prove a common quality of use-value in commodities against Marx, though realising that Marx allows this, can count for little, for Marx is able nevertheless to abstract from this quality on ontological grounds for the purposes of explanation. The validity of the abstraction can indeed be proven only by its explanatory power, but such an abstraction cannot be closed off or even really adjudicated by the formal disquisitions on the logic of common properties which Böhm-Bawerk provides. The possibility that value is to be investigated in its form and not just used in its given form in order to recalculate prices is simply beyond Böhm-Bawerk's attempt to read the labour theory of value, testimony enough to the complete obliteration of these concerns in neo-classical economic thought.

The *Theories of Surplus Value*, and hence Marx's comments on Bailey, were not, of course, available to Böhm-Bawerk as he wrote *On the Conclusion of the Marxist System*. Perhaps because of the lack of the materials necessary to have knowledge of what has gone before, a remarkable irony of historical repetition surely occurs, linking Böhm-Bawerk to Bailey, when the former criticises Marx's attraction to an equivalence theory of exchange as "scholastico-theological", after the fashion in which the latter criticised Ricardo. Böhm-Bawerk, accurately enough, detects an Aristotelian influence here, but he obviously means Aristotelian in the bad sense.[142] Böhm-Bawerk leaves no doubt that he thinks the equivalence theory is flatly wrong. Why, he asks, when there is equivalence between goods, should there be exchange? This argument seems to be deceitful, as Böhm-Bawerk appears to be completely overriding the qualitative difference between use-values which Marx gives as the motive for the exchange of equivalent quantities. But it is, or course, precisely this radical separation of use-value and exchange-value which Böhm-Bawerk simply cannot see as an issue.

Wicksteed's criticism of the labour theory of value antedates Böhm-Bawerk's essay by some twelve years and, of course, therefore was made on the basis of knowledge of only volume one of *Capital*. That Wicksteed looks forward to the resolutions to be offered in the later volumes to the contradictions between obvious economic phenomena and the theses of volume one, and that Böhm-Bawerk considers these resolutions casuistic, obviously makes the latter's criticism the more complete. It is perhaps more fair, then, to compare Wicksteed's paper with the chapter of *Capital and Interest* on Marx which appeared almost simultaneously.[143] However, I want to draw attention to the overall similarity of Wicksteed's arguments of 1884 and those of Böhm-Bawerk of 1896, for this comparison does not embarrass Wicksteed. For, after setting out the argument by which Marx reaches the labour theory of value, Wicksteed identifies the central mistake of that argument as that which we have seen Böhm-Bawerk call confusing abstraction from the genus with abstracting from instances in which the genus is manifested. In short, Wicksteed says that though Marx is right to abstract from individual use-values, he is wrong to think that this means abstracting from the category of utility, which category must in fact be used in explanations of exchange-value.[144]

Wicksteed's application of this to abstract labour goes as follows. Having taken Marx's argument up to abstract labour, he says that he awaits the later volumes of *Capital* in order to set the surprising conclusion that labour is the sole constituent element of value in illuminating context. However, displaying the tolerance characteristic of his article and of his political and academic attitudes more generally, he proceeds to go on to find in Marx a less surprising conclusion on the content of value. This is provided when Marx says that labour which actualises no use-value cannot have a value, into which Wicksteed proceeds to read the whole apparatus of accounts of exchange-value in terms of utility. Not surprisingly, he concludes that this other line which he finds in Marx surrenders the previous analysis. Abstract labour, on Wicksteed's new understanding is "abstractly useful work", conferring "abstract utility" on wares. Despite Wicksteed's constructive tone, there is no doubt that criticism such as this represents a serious failure of interpretation.[145] Obviously Wicksteed's paper collapses into the complete reading of his own positions into Marx's text. My point is that even Wicksteed's constructive attitude to Marx ends up in the same position as Böhm-Bawerk's destructive one, for both are given by a complete inability to hold value up as an investigable form and consequently to grasp that Marx may not wish to give immediate accounts of exchange-value but to inquire into what exchange-value can mean.

The fundamental conclusion of Marx's analysis of the commodity is that capitalist production engenders a pervasive social alienation represented in the direction of economic life by capital and in the ideology of fetishism. When economic life is dominated by capital, a serious distortion of the human comprehension and control of that life necessarily follows. The centrality of Hegelian themes of the critique of alienation in Marx's very concept of capital is quite clear.[146] But, of course, when judged by the standards of political efficacy which Marx set himself, this critique obviously has not been a success and commodity fetishism still characterises the common consciousness. There are hugely important reasons for this which I will try to set out in the remainder of this work, but for now I will merely comment on the positive features of the critique of commodity fetishism as developed so far.

The essential positive feature is that it seems to be fundamentally correct. When properly understood, as it was in numerous works of what I have called the initial interpretation of *Capital* and in untold numbers of subsequent works, chapter one of volume one has, of course, proved enormously productive. It seems soundly to base its critique of commodity fetishism on showing that moving beyond that alienated belief is necessary for an expansion of the understanding of basic features of modern life. Not all of what is said is acceptable, but it is only the ridiculous hagiographical tone in which both defence *and* criticism of Marx often have been conducted that makes necessary this disclaimer of the idea that all that is said could be expected to be acceptable. What is said is at least as interesting as, and in my opinion is more defensible and thus of more importance than, any other argument establishing the existence of the social ontology which calls forth social science.[147] It does seem to bring Hegel's project into the realm of scientifically corrigible discourse. And when we turn, as we now will, to consider how Marx set about explaining and defending his own penetration of the contemporaneous alienated belief of commodity fetishism, we will find that it was through a dialogue with capitalist theoretical political economy that gains its power largely because it satisfies the requirements of the dialectic of immanent critique.

Notes

1   C1, pp 125-8. Cf EM, vol 29, pp 252-3; CPE, pp 269-70; C, pp 7-8 and VF, p 134.

2   Ricardo, 'On Protection to Agriculture', p 141. Cf Owen, 'Report to the Country of Lanark'.

3   PPE, ch 1, sec 3. Df WN, p 65.

4   CPE, p 300 and TSV3, p 55.

5   PP, p 162 and C1, pp 173-5.

6   *Ibid*, p 169 n 31.

7   *Ibid*, p 89. Cf SL, p 67.

8   C1, p 90.

9   *Vide* Sayer, *Marx's Method*, pt 2.

10   NW, pp 198-9.

11   *Ibid*, p 112 and RIPP, pp 494-51.

12   TSV3, p 112 and RIPP, pp 949-51.

13   *Vide* Banaji, 'From the Commodity to *Capital*' and Wilson, *Marx's Critical/Dialectical Procedure,* pp 113-9.

14   The procedure of beginning with the commodity in order to identify a specific capitalist mode of production was grasped perfectly clearly in what I will call the initial interpretations of Marx's economics. Engels' comments on *Capital* were, strictly speaking, the first commentary on the book. However, these can hardly be said to amount to a full interpretation of the economic content of the work. The third part of his review of volume one, the part actually dealing with the economics, never appeared. By the "initial interpretation" I mean that body of economic explication and extension of *Capital* produced around the time of the publication of volume three and the life of the Second International, up to and including the first products of Soviet scholarship in the twenties. Rubin's *Essays on Marx's Theory of Value* is perhaps the most accomplished of these works but undoubtedly Kautsky's own gloss on *Capital, The Economic Doctrines of Karl Marx*, was the most important general formulation of this initial interpretation. The very start, *ibid*, pp 2-3, of Kautsky's textbook sets out the historically specific qualities of the commodity. Kautsky then develops, *ibid*, pp 3-11, a line of inquiry which was of interest to Marx and particularly Engels themselves. He draws on comparative ethnographic materials to support the specific identification of the commodity. The most substantial development at this time of this ethnographic line, a description of earlier property forms which provides

a context for bourgeois property, was that of Marx's son-in-law, Lafague, in his 'The Evolution of Property'.

15   C1, p 163.

16   Vide Sayer, 'Science as Critique: Marx Versus Althusser', sec 5.

17   CPE, p 269.

18   TSV3, p 129.

19   *Vide* Cutler *et al, Marx's 'Capital' and Capitalism Today*, vol 1, pp 12-9.

20   CPE, p 270.

21   C1, p 126, Cf C, p 8.

22   C1, pp 127, 140-1. Cf CPE; p 270, WPP, pp 200-1; C, pp 8-9 and VF, p 136.

23   Aristotle, *Ethics*, pp 185-6.

24   C1, p 127. Cf WPP, p 201 and C, p 8.

25   C1, pp 148-9. Cf VF p 139.

26   C1, p 141.

27   Pace eg Arnold, *Marx's Radical Critique of Capitalist Society*, p 80.

28   C1, pp 133-47.

29   *Ibid*, pp 110-7, 125-33.

30   *Ibid*, pp 111, 125, 144, 128.

31   Bailey, A *Critical Dissertation on the Nature, Measure and Causes of Value*, pp 1-36 and *idem, A Letter to a Political Economist*.

32   *Idem, Money and Its Vicissitudes in Value*, pp 9-11.

33   EM, vol 28, pp 168-9, 189.

34   C1, pp 192-3. Cf CPE, pp 308-10 and TSV3, p 133.

35   PPE, pp 43-4.

36   Broadhurst, *Political Economy*, pp 11, 14.

37   C1, p 146 n 21.

38   Eg the addition of "almost exclusively" in the third edition of PPE, p 20.

39   Bailey, *Money and its Vicissitudes in Value*, p 165.

40   C1, p 177.

41   *Vide* Dobb, *Political Economy and Capitalism*, pp 9-10.

42   TSV3, p 143 and n.

43   C1, pp 155-6. Cf TSV2, p 495 and VF, pp 145-6.

44   *Vide* Sayer, *Marx's Method*, pp 37-42.

45   *Vide* Meek, *Studies in the Labour Theory of Value*, pp 162-4.

46   C1, ch2

47   Eg EM, vol 28, pp 127-8 and TSV3, p 129.

48   Eg cf EM, vol 28, pp 99-100 and EPM, pp 323-4.

49   C1, p 127. Cf CPE, p 271: WPP, p 201 and C, pp 8-9.

50 C1, p 139. Cf EM, vol 28, pp 78-9.

51 *Ibid,* vol 28, pp 78-9.

52 C1, pp 127-8. Cf C, pp 8-9.

53 C1, pp 127, 139-41. Cf EM, vol 28, pp 80-2; TSV3, pp 128-9; WPP, p 201; C, p 8 and VF, 134-6.

54 C, p 9. Cf CPE, p 270 n and NW, p 198.

55 C1, p 177.

56 Marx, 'To Engels, 25 July 1877'.

57 NW, pp 196-9.

58 C1, p 128. Cf C, p 9 and CPE, pp 270-1.

59 C1, p 128. Cf WPP, p 205 and C, p 11.

60 C1, p 152.

61 CPE, pp 301-2.

62 C1, p 131. Cf C, p 11.

63 CPE, p 302.

64 Eg EM, vol 28, p 511.

65 Eg C3, p 760. Cf *idem,* 'To Schott, 3 November 1877.'

66 *Pace* eg Parkes, *Marxism: An Autopsy,* p 62.

67 *Vide* Kay, 'Why Labour is the Starting Point of *Capital',* pp 49-50.

68 C1, pp 178-83. Cf EM, vol, pp 93-7, 172-7 and WPP, pp 201-2.

69 C1, ch 2. Cf GI, pp 32-3, 44-8, 59-60, 62-8; Vol 28, pp 93-8, 172-7 and TSV3, pp 268-9.

70 Proudhon, *What is Property?,* ch 3 and *idem, The Philosophy of Poverty,* ch 2.

71 C1, p 178 n 2. Cf HF, pp 31-4; PP, pp 120-44; EM, vol 28, pp 180-2; CPE, p 301 n; TSV3, pp 523-7 and RIPP, pp 971-4. I have tried to apply a similar criticism to one of the most substantial present analyses of the law of contract as a system of exchange in 'The Social Theory of Relational Contract: Macneil as the Modern Proudhon'.

72 C1, pp, 166, 168-9, 182. Cf EM, vol 28, p 139-40 and CPE, pp 299-300.

73 *Vide* eg Acton, *The Illusion of the Epoch,* p 26.

74 EM, vol 28, p 174.

75 C1, pp 129-37. Cf CPE, pp 272-8; WPP, pp 203-4 and C, pp 13-6.

76 *Vide* eg Acton, *The Illusion of the Epoch,* p 30. To the extent that Marx's purported defenders *have* attempted to purse the "labour reduction problem" as if it were rationally soluble, they have been misled by Marx's exposition of the idea of abstract labour and have wasted rather a lot of effort. *Vide* Blaug, 'Another Look at the Labour Reduction Problem in Marx'.

77 EPM, pp 275-7; G1, p 31 and C1, pp 283-4.

78 C1, p 132. Cf C, p 12 and *idem,* 'On the Division of Labour', p 617.

79   C1, p 132. Cf EM, vol 28, pp 39-40; CPE, pp 299-300 and C, p 12.

80   C1, p 204, ch 4.

81   *Ibid*, ch 14, sec 5.

82   *Ibid*, pp 645-6 and RIPP, pp 1019-38.

83   *Vide* Kay, *The Economic Theory of the Working class*, pp 23-4.

84   C1, pp 166-7.

85   CPE, p 272.

86   *Vide* Rowthorn, 'Skilled Labour in the Marxist System'.

87   *Vide* Kay, 'A Note on Abstract Labour'.

88   *Vide* Thompson, 'Time, Work, Discipline and Industrial Capitalism'.

89   *Vide* Braverman, *Labour and Monopoly Capital*, nb pp 181-2.

90   *Vide* Willis, *Learning to Labour*, pp 133-7.

91   C1, pts 3-4. Cf EPM, pp 270-82.

92   C1, pp 139-54. Cf, pp 21-5 and VF, pp 134-45.

93   Marx and particularly Engels made rather heavy weather of this method of historical and theoretical presentation. Eg Engels, 'Review of Karl Marx, *Critique of Political Economy*', sec 2. An in the end impenetrable miasma continues to distort even otherwise valuable modern discussions of this "method", eg Uchida, *Marx's 'Grudrisse' and Hegel's 'Logic'*, which undoubtedly follows from an attachment to hegelianism in the bad sense. A simple dose of Lakatos is the cure. Eg Lakatos, 'History of Science and its Rational Reconstructions.'

94   C1, pp 154-7. Cf C, pp 25-6 and VF, pp 145-6.

95   C1, pp 157-61. Cf C, pp 26-33 and VF, pp 146-8.

96   C1, pp 162-3. Cf VF, pp 149-50.

97   EM, vol 28, pp 102-3.

98   C1, pp 183-4. Cf EM, vol 28, pp 103, 110-21 and CPE, pp 385-8.

99   EM, vol 28, pp 51-110.

100 CPE, pp 322-3.

101 C1, p 161 n 26, 181 n 4 and 188 n 1.

102 *Ibid*, pp 195-6.

103 C3, pt 2.

104 *Vide* Arthur, 'Dialectic of the Value-form.'

105 *Vide* Dobb, *Political Economy and Capitalism*, ch 1.

106 There sure must be a major issue whether, after the fetishisations involved in capitalist calculation are taken into account in the way which I will do in chapter 8 below, this data can ever become corrigibly available. The seeming necessity the authors feel to turn every statement into a *reductio ad absurdum* should not undercut the power of the recognition of this point in Cutler *et al, Marx's*

'*Capital*' *and Capitalism Today*, vol 2, pt 2. In this sense, the problem with measuring dated labour inputs indicated by Sraffa, *Production of Commodities by Means of Commodities*, secs 68, 79, may cut too far for the comfort of those who attempt to remodel the explanation of prices on Saffian lines as the commodity production data may not be available. (Of course, it is similarly unavailable for value theory).

107 *Vide* Steedman, *Marx After Sraffa*, p 14.

108 C3 pt 2.

109 *Vide* Von Bortkiewicz, 'On the Correction of Marx's Fundamental Construction in the Third Volume of Capital'.

110 *Vide* Desai, 'Methodological Problems in Quantitative Marxism'.

111 *Idem,* 'The Transformation Problem', p 40.

112 The transformation problem as such was really of minor interest in Böhm-Bawerk's 'Criticism of Marx'. The issue was the taking of labour and utility accounts of value to be flatly contradictory.

113 *Vide* Meek, 'From Values to Prices: Was Marx's Journey Really Necessary?' and Sweezy, 'Marxian Value Theory and Crises', sec 1.

114 *Vide* Shaikh, 'The Poverty of Algebra'.

115 *Vide* Desai 'The Transformation Problem', p 40 and Mohun, 'Value Theory', p 48.

116 *Vide* Gerstein, 'Production, Circulation and Value', pp 55-7 and Itoh, *The Basic Theory of Capitalism*, ch 6.

117 In his essay on 'Marx on Ricardo', however, Steedman actually emphasises the degree to which neo-Richardianism contains a strain which simply denies any value, or even sense, to the sociological question. It is one thing, for example, to say that Marx's analysis of labour-power as a "peculiar commodity" is uncomfortable, and I will take this up at length in chapter 9. But is quite another thing to say, as Steedman does, that analysis sets up a "non-issue", for labour-power is not a commodity at all! (pp 149-50). If only this were so, but of course it is not. The whole historical sense of what it means to treat human effort as a commodity, and the point of the struggle against this, is just extinguished. It is instances, like this, of valuable social issues simply dropping out of Steedman's own work that one finds most undercut his strong statements that value is irrelevant (*idem*, 'The Irrelevance of marxian Values') or, indeed, that progress can be made only by eschewing its consideration (*idem, Marx After Sraffa*, p 207).

118 C1, p 162.

119 C3, ch 37.

120 *Ibid*, pt 6.

121 EPM, pp 322-6.

122 This theme has recently been interestingly discussed - though in a way in which the ethical critique is rather unclear and is certainly more muted than Marx's - as market colonisation of other areas of life in Walzer, *Spheres of Justice.*

123 C1, ch9.

124 Surplus is understood by the capitalist in the form of profit. C3, ch2.

125 *Ibid,* ch 4.

126 C3, ch 2.

127 C1, ch 7, sec 2.

128 C3, ch 1.

129 C1, ch 15.

130 C3, ch 5.

131 C1, ch 10.

132 *Pace* Nozick, *Anarchy, State and Utopia,* p 18. This argument for the necessity of money, taken from von Mises, *The Theory of Money and Credit,* pp 30-4, is but a tedious repetition of some of the commonplaces of classical political economy, albeit an unknowing repetition which is ignorant of those developments which were more than commonplace. Nozick's work's remarkable vogue simply shows that there now exists such a high degree of ignorance of the classicals that foolish defences of capitalism as if it was a system of simple commodity production are thought to have a plausibility.

133 Böhm-Bawerk, 'Karl Marx and the Close of His System', p 69.

134 *Ibid,* p 74-5.

135 *Ibid,* pp 64-8.

136 *Ibid,* pp 70-3.

137 *Ibid,* pp 77-80.

138 *Ibid,* p 65.

139 *Ibid,* p 75 n 1.

140 *Ibid,* pp 73-6.

141 *Ibid* p 75.

142 *Ibid,* pp 68-9.

143 *Idem, Capital and Interest,* bk 6, ch 3.

144 Wicksteed, '*Das Kapital:* A Criticism', p 712

145 *Pace* Steedman, 'PH Wicksteed's Jevonian Criticism of Marx', pp 138-40, which flatly repeats the failure.

146 Additionally, there are profound similarities of substance between Hegel's and Marx's views of political economy. *Vide* Lukács, *The Young Hegel,* pp 168-78, 319-97.

147 *Vide* Benton, *Philosophical Foundations of the Three Sociologies*, ch 8; Bhaskar, *Scientific Realism and Human Emancipation*, ch 2 and Keat and Urry, *Social Theory as Science*, ch 5.

6 Marx and Marginalism as the Successors of Classical Political Economy

We have seen that an Hegelian project of the critique of an alienated belief - commodity fetishism - is at the heart of Marx's political economy of capitalism. I want in this chapter to ask upon what basis he claimed to penetrate this necessary concomitant of capitalist production. I have argued, and Marx certainly believed, that there are definite limits to the dialectic in Hegel. I now want to consider how far Marx can be regarded as having gone beyond these limits and succeeded in placing his critique of an alienated belief on a firmer ground than Hegel's. The most obvious, but nevertheless the best, way to do this is to explore the ways in which *Capital's* arguments for the labour theory actually work as a critique of classical political economy. This critique is Marx's dialogue with the body of bourgeois thought through which he developed - having to start with this thought but hoping to change it - his socialist account of the capitalist mode of production. I will examine the strength of this critique. I also shall examine, in what I hope will be an illuminating contrast, the ways in which the classicals have been represented in the subsequent rejection of the labour theory in neo-classical economics.

There is a difficult manoeuvre at the heart of Marx's critique of classical political economy which I want carefully to describe. This manoeuvre involves, first, separating out the historically specific elements from the general elements of capitalist production and showing how bourgeois political economy commits serious mistakes in failing to do this. Second, just as importantly but far less widely recognised, Marx *has* to show how the scientific resources for his critique of political economy are *generated* by capitalist conditions. For scientific illumination as well as ideological fetishism can *both* only spring from the given social life. The first part of this manoeuvre emerges clearly enough when we recall Marx's observation that even Ricardo has his Robinson Crusoe stories. That Marx's aim is to expose the explanatory limits of Ricardo's ahistorical view of value is, of course, very familiar. However, Marx's opinion of Ricardo's idea of value contains, I submit, a second, positive, element to which we should be alerted by the way in which Marx insists on the quantitative power of Ricardo's analysis.

Marx says "even Ricardo" because it was, of course, his opinion that though the explanatory power of Ricardo's writings is bounded by the limitations of historical imagination that identify bourgeois political economy, those writings were the highest achievement of that body of thought. Ricardo's work was the culmination of the productive lines of classical political economy because of both - related points - its firm commitment to labour as the content of value and the quality of its analysis of the magnitude of value.[1] Of course, Marx had to recognise the inadequacies of Ricardo's analysis. In the period between Ricardo's death and the writing of the *Economic and Philosophical Manuscripts*, exposure of these inadequacies had, as I have mentioned, almost buried the basic labour theory. That Marx himself moved from an initial rejection of the labour theory[2] to his eventual characterisation of the disintegration of the Ricardian school as a large regressive step into vulgar economics[3] was possible only because[4] he spent an enormous effort on completing Ricardo's reconciliation of the influence on price of differing organic compositions of capital and of competition with the labour theory.[5] Now, we can hardly say that these considerations on price are external to the labour theory as they are crucial to the determination of cost price[6] and, therefore, to the adequacy to the theory as such. However, I would say that Marx added *nothing* to Ricardo's determination of the magnitude of value itself, value rather than price.[7] Let me briefly defend this claim.

Marx mentions Ricardo's Robinsonade because, as political economists are so fond of these fables, he wants to give one of them himself.[8] We are shown Marx's Robinson organising his economic life in a way which is intended to make clear the basic labour theory of value, even to the least penetrating economist. As anyone who compares the relevant pages of *Capital* and *On The Principles of Political Economy and Taxation* will see, there is no difference in method between the calculations of Ricardo's primitives and Marx's Robinson. The basic assessments of value according to, in a phrase, the rarity of the use-value and therefore the amount of labour needed to actualise it in so far as possible the desired quantities, or in a word, scarcity, remain the same. What I believe Marx thought he was doing here was simply taking over the evaluations of the expenditure of labour, the various forms reduced to a common denominator, which he found in the tradition which he identified as classical political economy, certainly as he considered it to culminate in Ricardo.[9] At least with respect to Ricardo, we can understand this taking over quite literally. Marx merely on occasion repeats some of the basic evaluations for his own purposes.[10] One should stress the obvious, direct intellectual debt here. Marx thought that in classical political economy, in its examination of the determination of the values of different durations and intensities of labour for example,[11] there were the most refined reflective contributions to the fixing of values through competitive commodity production that was of the essence of the development of capitalist relations of production. All the principal works of at least English classical political economy display something of the essentially pragmatic tone which emerges so clearly from *The Wealth of Nations*. Ricardo's *Principles* was, of course, written up from a polemic against the corn laws and this shows throughout the book. In the directness of his borrowings in respect of the labour theory of value from, as he knew well enough,[12] epitomically bourgeois works, we can see that Marx learned the principles of his political economy in a most important sense from capitalism.

We have seen that Marx's formal case for the necessity of reduction to equivalents draws upon the insistence that exchange requires equalisation of the goods to be exchanged which is to be found in the *Nicomachean Ethics*. Aristotle himself, however, was driven to relinquish a strong argument for equalisation, and to regard money as merely a makeshift estimate of value fixed on by (in itself arbitrary) custom, when faced with the qualitative differences between the articles exchanged. In *Capital*, Marx gives the following explanation of why Aristotle was unable to explain equalisation.[13] The key to the solution of the commensurability of different use-values lies in their being common expenditures of human labour and therefore subject to social equalisation (whether in value or in other ways). However, the slave labour of ancient society involved an ideology of the essential inequality of people and their labours which prevented such a theoretical insight. It is only, Marx says, after the event of the social equalisation of labour powers that the theoretical comprehension of the content of value is possible, a resource obviously denied to Aristotle. Aristotle's own deliberations on value lapse more into philology than social analysis when faced with some puzzling equivalences,[14] but, of course, he could hardly explain value as an overarching social structure when it did not exist. Marx, by contrast, is trying to refer to a facility for the understanding of general production provided by value, or more precisely for our concerns at present, by abstract labour.

If abstract labour is the basis of the comprehension of the social reality of labour, then it must be said that capitalism provides this basis. Production for exchange-value accumulation is fetishistic, but in subjecting nature and all traditional practices to the demands of even a fetishised expansion of productive powers, capitalism makes essential human material intercourse its object.[15] By disruption of all traditional impediments to the most technical-rational disposition of productive forces,[16] that is to say, human labour-power, capitalism constructs for the first time the potential for social self-consciousness of the organisation of that intercourse. Co-operation, albeit under the limited form of the division of labour in the production of commodities, is itself made the fundamental productive resource.[17] It is a mode of production whose historically unprecedented social spirit is the judgment of all human effort in terms of its production of value, which is prepared to direct and redirect that effort according to those terms and subordinate all other values to that redirection, that has laid the foundation of the comprehension that not only is labour the substance of value, but that the fundamental issue of economic life is the social organisation of labour.

In recognising this potential for understanding, we must immediately add, as is immediately added by capitalism itself, the limitations on this potential. It remains a long way from seeing labour as the content of value to actually grasping what value is in its historical specifics. It makes all the difference in the world that Marx's Robinson, who is unique amongst the pantheon of heroes of such economic fables in that he emphasises rather than extinguishes the period features of Defoe's character,[18] could at least plausibly and without anachronism conceive of calculating according to annuity tables. Classical political economy expresses the quantitative elements of value quite clearly in its labour theory. On this basis, because it *is* possible clearly to set out the quantitative side, it must also be possible to develop the qualitative side of value. The former may be accomplished only when the latter is possible, for the carrying out of the latter - even without full consciousness of what one is doing[19] - is a condition of the former. It must be possible to equalise labours in order quantitatively to assess them. The assessment can, then, be pushed on to explication of the equalisation if we are to become fully conscious of what we are doing.

Marx argues that capitalism provides an historically unique, invaluable resource for understanding. But adequately grasping the value of that resource depends on grasping it as, precisely, historically unique. In doing this one must move from using the resource only quantitatively to using it qualitatively. The concepts of classical political economy are invaluable and Marx makes full use of them, but those very concepts are changed even in the course of being used by being used self-consciously.[20] What is at issue here is Marx's insistence on clearly situating bourgeois knowledge with reference to its past, present and future. We have seen how describing value in terms of the bourgeois present, which is its ground, is central to Marx's criticism of fetishism and, from this position, we can set about relating value to the past and the future without committing anachronistic category mistakes.

With respect to the future, there are of course fetishistic influences just as intrinsic to capitalism as are enlightening ones and a crucial strand of Marx's conception of socialism is altering the balance between these. That the possibility of enlightenment be bound up in capitalism is essential to Marx for two reasons. One, obviously, is that without this possibility socialist aspirations would be utopian,[21] for those aspirations would have no ground in the present, which is the only possible resource for their development. The very possibility of conceiving of socialism - as opposed to utopia - can arise only when the conditions for that effort of imagination are present. Socialism, in other words, must be a task mankind can solve from the position of the bourgeois world as a condition of the formulation of the project of socialism. This is to put the point rather too dogmatically. Marx must continually *show* by the adequacy of his socialist account of capitalism that socialism is on mankind's agenda, or his notion of socialism falls into utopianism. On the other hand, however, the adequacy of that account will tend to justify the socialist goal. Socialism is depicted as the realisation of capitalism's potential for social self-consciousness against the restrictions on this realisation equally bound up in this mode of production, a depiction made perhaps most clear in Marx's insistence upon realising the liberatory potentials of large-scale industry against its appalling capitalist consequences which he did so much to document.[22]

All epochs are distinguished by their historical features, features irreducible beyond a social to a directly natural ontology. What has been absolutely unique about capitalism is that it created the potentials for the socially self-conscious recognition of this, the promise bound up in its being the end of mankind's pre-history. The unique feature of socialism is to be its actualisation of capitalism's promise of general self-consciousness of social self-determination. This future potential can also be used to illuminate the past. Once we have grasped the limits of bourgeois knowledge and have thereby broken its typically ahistorical perspective, that knowledge can be applied to earlier societies.

For clearly the uncovering of the social organisation of labour is, if it is truly the key to understanding economic life, going to prove most informative about earlier epochs. Marx's opinion, it is quite clear, was that a reflexive application of bourgeois knowledge to earlier societies allows us a clearer comprehension than was available to those who lived in them.[23] With the advantage of hindsight and a distance from the prevalent ideologies of modes of production alienated from consciousness of social organisation, Marx envisages a privileged dialogue with the past. Of course, crucial problems of understanding remain, but I think we can allow this and yet still recognise the privilege of reflexive re-comprehension at which Marx is trying to drive.

Marx's main concern in setting out this re-comprehension is to distance it from the platitudes which result unless the historical character of bourgeois knowledge is kept in view; even when, and this is the vital point, that knowledge is of general elements of production. If the understanding of value leads to the recognition of the social organisation of production that is a general element of production, this is not to say that in all epochs this organisation takes the form of value.[24] Value is a unique form of the social organisation of labour, one that marks the end of the pre-history of mankind, in that it offers the possibility of social self-consciousness of that organisation. The question might well then be to investigate that organisation in earlier epochs. It is, however, at best pointless to attempt to work out value calculations for the economic conduct of those epochs. This is not because value is itself still a mystificatory form of economic organisation. Even planning cannot be retrospectively applied. These forms of economic principle simply cannot be applied directly to those pre-capitalist epochs, though they indicate the existence of some economic principle in them. Attempts to impose value on those epochs because value is thought the only comprehensible principle of economic organisation has the immediate effect of making the economies of those epochs incomprehensible because the first thing that emerges about them is that they were irrational. It is this issue in historical understanding that informs Marx's insistence upon the inner rationality of mercantilism (at a time of burgeoning trade and merchant capital but of limited, pre-industrial production of wealth) against the scornful dismissals of it in bourgeois political economy ultimately pointing to free trade.[25] We might add that the regarding of pre-capitalist economics as irrational is a necessary consequence of the application of more or less value criteria to them in the foremost sociological underpinning of neo-classical economics - the later writings of Max Weber.[26] The very universality claimed for the categories of neo-classical understanding implies, as I will later argue at length, a certain explanatory sterility.

In all, then, in moving from the grasp of labour as the quantitative content of value, which I would say he thought he inherited in its fundamentals in a more or less adequate form, to regarding value as the capitalistic form of the social organisation of labour, Marx makes an enormous step. This step involves important enough refinements of the qualitative connotations of even the key concepts of classical political economy. The making clear of the two-fold character of wage-labour was, for example, a development of an idea traceable to at least Steuart.[27] But Marx is able to insist upon a substantial originality in his own relatively clear formulations of this two-fold character,[28] which are based on a comprehension of the distinction of general use-value and specific exchange-value productions denied to classical political economy.[29] This originality improves the clarity of the application of bourgeois knowledge, of which let me take as an example Marx's use of the distinction between productive and unproductive labour in Smith.[30]

There is no doubt that Marx drew on this distinction in reaching his conclusion about the general requirement of a degree (itself historically variable) of necessary labour in all modes of production, above which surplus labour time might be available for various purposes.[31] But he equally recognised that the narrow idea of productive as opposed to unproductive labour has an intrinsically and ineradicably bourgeois meaning. What was in question in this dichotomy was not the production of use-values but the production of surplus value.[32] Now, productive and unproductive labour is that form of the distinction of necessary and surplus labour time which Marx is able to use to gain knowledge of the general distinction, but it is not the general distinction itself. It has specific characteristics and Marx, indeed, argues that it is a contradictory expression of the general distinction. Accordingly, Marx heaps scorn upon the bourgeois conceit of the likes of Senior who took exception to the distasteful consequences of Smith's admittedly cynical evaluations of productive and unproductive labour. Against the cynicism of judging everything from the bourgeois standpoint of the production of surplus value, it is spurious of Senior to argue that even the lawgiver of the Hebrews would be an unproductive labourer according to Smith.[33] Senior is certainly more arrogantly bourgeois than Smith, for he wishes to hold on to bourgeois judgments and to extinguish the bourgeois limits of their applicability which permeate almost every word of Smith's economic and social studies. As Marx observes, Senior would hardly get the grateful response he expects were he able to acquaint Moses with the honour of being a labourer, even a productive one.[34]

Equally, if we look to the future, the idea that under socialism productive labour should receive its product in full makes, for example, the provision of social services in that society impossible[35] or makes it very difficult to see how socialist equality can be extended to women, given the typical gender roles in the nuclear family and that housework is not productive labour in this sense.[36] This idea is a socialist conclusion which, as with the comparable bourgeois ones,[37] follows from the plethora of category mistakes in the use of historically specific terms. That labour is productive of surplus value is by no means directly connected to the ethical character of the labour and judging the latter by the former is unacceptable[38] - the two very well might be contradictory. A great deal of rather worthless casuistry intended to make plausible Marx's seemingly arbitrary distinction between the moral worth of various employments could have been saved if this arbitrariness had been recognised not as his but as capitalism's.[39]

What Marx fundamentally draws from value is, I would say, this. Basic calculations of utility, scarcity, demand, supply, etc - however one wants to put it - are made in any mode of production and have been developed to an unprecedentedly high level of sophistication in capitalism. They will continue to be made under socialism.[40] Marx describes this as general use-value production, metabolism with nature, etc., and I would say his terms are less likely to carry unwanted historically specific connotations. *But the point remains that the same marginalist technique is to be found in Marx as neo-classical thought now makes the whole business of economics.* This technique is the general examination of the production of use-values in those material relations with nature that are conterminous with human existence.[41] But what is valuable to say about those relations for historical purposes is, in the first instance, very limited *and cannot stand on their own without historical mediation.*[42] For people enter into those relations only, Marx argues, within a further set of *social* relations and this further set of relations exercises a determination on the form of production which is irreducible to any initial set of basically naturally given conditions of human life. Hence there is no point in directly applying one specific form of calculation to all epochs. The distance between even utility in a mode of production which subjugates all of nature to the fetishised pursuit of the seeming intrinsic profitability of things and the analogical considerations of utility in all modes of production is vast - for one thing it is the proper subject of the whole of political economy. The first task preparatory to studying these relations with nature as socially modified is to distinguish general and specific elements of production. The labour theory of value is not so much a quantification of value in amounts of labour as recognition of the social ontology of a mode of production in which such quantification is made the essence of the age.

Confusion arises because we have to understand a general characteristic of human life through the particular specific form in which the general is made a subject open to clear understanding. Marx tries to both make clear the specific location of value, in the capitalist mode of production, and also, as part of identifying what is historically unique about value, show that value has furnished the opportunity of self-consciously understanding the social organisation that is a general element of production. Given all of this one can begin to understand the difficult, oblique fashion in which Marx goes about identifying value as a mode of the organisation of labour. The crux of this understanding turns on relating his seeming concern with quantitative reduction to its intellectual background in the bourgeois computation of the magnitude of value. Marx himself was very dissatisfied with what we now have as chapter one[43] and continually reworked it.[44] It would appear that despite these efforts, he never succeeded in properly distancing his own social analysis from the historically naive magnitude of value analyses from which it was developed. And I repeat that it has proven most significant that the most directly clear statements of Marx's own positions are to be found at points in the *Grundrisse*, *Critique of Political Economy* and *Wages, Price and Profit* and not in the versions of volume one of *Capital* on which he laboured so extensively. Indeed, one could claim that a very sad irony arises in that the real social content of chapter one actually became more difficult to grasp in the course of these revisions and this content is far more clear in the other places I have mentioned.

In fully working through his position, to some degree in the *Critique* but especially in the second edition of *Capital*, Marx was unable to secure a proper position in which his, as it were, first person statements of what goes on in the capitalist mode of production would be understood as historically specific. When Ricardo writes: "If a commodity were in no way useful...it would be destitute of exchange-value..." and Marx puts: "If the thing is useless, so is the labour contained in it",[45] the historical contextualisation through which Marx intends to give full sense to Ricardo's descriptions obviously does not emerge and Marx slips into locutions derived from what he himself insists was only magnitude analysis. In this circumstance, the very radicalness of Marx's critique of the value-form is all that is needed to push the first part of *Capital* into an incomprehensibility that yields only to a most determined interpretive effort.

Let us focus on abstract labour. What Marx means to say is that the general equalisation of all labour-powers allows penetration of the mutual sociality of the organisation of labour that is general economic life. This insight into the fundamental equality of all human effort is gained from a mode of production in which all labours are quantitatively equated. But in the form of quantitative equation, the penetrative resources are limited. This is so because, amongst other reasons, this form of equalisation is itself absurd. To repeat a point already made, from the perspective of conceivable economic planning it is one thing to say that a particular use-value takes so long to produce and that the act of production requires a certain prior investment of effort in order to secure the requisite materials, tools and productive skills. It is quite another to say, at the further limits of bourgeois comprehension, that a commodity has a price related to so much labour expended in its production. If the first is the rational comprehension of economic activity manifest in its consciously planned organisation, the latter is a mystification so absurd as to be literally meaningless. It takes a distanced commentary to understand the in itself senseless equation of labour with quantities of money. The way in which Marx's own presentation is dominated by forms of thought which affect the very transformation of quality into quantity which he wants to criticise is one of the elements that has quite blunted the general comprehension of his work.

The point I wish to make is not that *Capital* has not had a mass readership - this could hardly be expected. It is that chapter one of volume one has proved very resistant to correct interpretation when read. Althusser's injunction to omit this chapter when reading *Capital*[46] is ridiculous but must unfortunately be taken to be an attempt to turn into principle what, one confidently suspects, is general practice.[47] By using, if I might put it this way again, first person capitalist locutions to set out the labour theory, Marx seemed to be making acceptance of that theory turn on the very capitalist processes he was in fact claiming were absurd. It cannot be doubted that this misled even the most sympathetic readers. To take but one example of the interpretation of abstract labour, when in 1957 the gifted, indeed in my opinion the best, Fabian theorist, GDH Cole, wrote an introduction to the Everyman edition of volume one, he said:

> All actual labour, it is argued, can be resolved into so much...abstract labour, skilled labour counting as a multiple of it [and] the "amount of labour" that enters into the "value" of commodities is not the actual amount expended on the production of each commodity but the amount that is "socially necessary"...The socially necessary amount of this abstract labour is the sole factor that can influence the value of any commodity. All this Marx says.[48]

Now, if Marx says all this and means it,[49] then what he is saying is absurd and Cole, politely saying that the labour theory is evidence of the "mystical view of reality" Marx derived from Hegel, is driven to try to argue that "It is...fully possible to hold to the theory of Surplus Value without holding the Labour Theory of Value [!]".[50] Cole's views are wrong, but were one to look at the passage he is attempting to gloss, the first section of the first chapter of volume one, then the least that can fairly be said is that Marx invited Cole's - very common - reading.

We must, then, register some serious shortcomings when evaluating Marx's immanent critique of classical political economy.[51] From a dialogue with this body of thought Marx hopes to generate a socialist account of the character of capitalism. The possibility of doing so is in a very important sense the crucial test of his socialist understanding. Without having yet turned to the way in which Marx conceived of the mechanisms of socialism's determinate negation of capitalism, we can see that there are weaknesses in his attempt to generate socialism as the truth of capitalism. Nevertheless, these weaknesses are not, in my opinion, fatal to the critique of commodity fetishism - indeed I would say they are of a character which speaks of a sort of strength. There are too many instances of claimed "strengths" in Marx's apparent weaknesses for one to feel really comfortable in putting the point this way, but nevertheless I do. If my remarks on Marx's critique of classical political economy are allowed, it emerges that this critique's shortcomings are bound up in the way it fails to gain sufficient distance from the forms of expression of bourgeois thought. However, this does mean that it has a ground in that thought and is not a speculative construction divorced from its objects of critique, based on an unjustified, and therefore from an epistemological point of view presumptive, position. Marx's stylistic revisions of chapter one, volume one are obviously a failure. Nevertheless, this effort of revision was, I think, properly directed. It shows Marx's concern to immerse his critique in the alienated belief he was criticising and this is extremely important.

We must hold it open, of course, whether Marx's specific claims are sound. Applying Hegel's idea of reflexive proof, only the adequacy of Marx's account of capitalism and of bourgeois economic thought can justify his socialist understanding. I do not think that ultimately it does. But, preparatory to turning to this question, I want to argue in the rest of this chapter that Marx's critique can gain strength from its ability to inform us of the character of bourgeois economic thought. I will say something more about Smith and Ricardo, but I also want anachronistically to show how Marx's thought is the indispensable framework within which to embrace even marginalist developments in economics.

If my account of Marx's relationship to classical political economy's fundamental treatments of value is correct, then this only underlines the most obvious lesson of the history of economic thought after the publication of volume one of *Capital*: that Marx relies far too heavily on his opinion that Ricardo especially had essentially won the basic positions of the labour theory of value. We have, as I have mentioned, only sketchy comments - all more or less contemptuous - by Marx on the origins of neo-classical economics in German national economy (apart from Gossen). But when the initial dissemination of *Capital*'s arguments had to battle against an increasingly intellectually dominant neo-classicism, a crucial point of the interpretation of the history of political economy up to Ricardo was at issue. As Jevons put it in 1879: "When at length a true system of economics comes to be established, it will be seen that that able but wrong-headed man, David Ricardo, shunted the car of economic science on to a wrong line".[52] The intellectual history in which this was definitively argued was provided by Schumpeter.[53] The picture of lines of intellectual development here is, as always, somewhat confused by the way that some contributions are claimed by both of the alternative interpretations. Ricardo's analysis of differential rent is, for instance, a veritable blue-print for the very notion of marginal returns and, when coupled with an appreciation of the intensive as well as the extensive margin, has entered very directly into accounts of diminishing returns on investment in land.[54] Leaving such cases aside, I would like to look in detail at the issue of social scientific substance bound up in the neo-classical interpretation of classical political economy, or at least of Smith and Ricardo, as a counterpoint to what I have said about Marx's efforts at such an interpretation.

Though for neo-classicism the shunting of economic science on to a wrong line was the work of Ricardo, the points at which this was done were located in Smith, and it is with Smith that we must start. The vital question for the neo-classical reading of Smith is, I believe, the possibility of describing the theory of value in *The Wealth of Nations* as a circular movement, from an initial rejection of the consideration of utility to an eventual framing of the central parts of that theory through just such a consideration. This work is necessary because, before turning to prices, Smith takes up a common theme in contemporaneous political economy by noting the distinction of use- and exchange-values. He contrasts the high amount of the former and the low amount of the latter in the case of water and the reverse situation in the case of diamonds.[55] But if this is a paradox, Smith shows no interest in resolving it; he invokes it to make clear that he is interested in *The Wealth of Nations* with exchange-value or price alone.

There are, however, two senses of price for Smith. Price as a measure of labour inputs into the production of a commodity he calls real price. Price as a measure of the labour, not the fruits of labour it must be stressed, that may be commanded by the exchange of a commodity he calls nominal price.[56] In early societies, what labour was expended in the production of a commodity will be matched by the amount of labour able to be commanded by the commodity's exchange. For at the more or less uniform level of productivity which is implied by general subsistence production, there can be no grounds on which a certain labour input could expect to command more than an equivalent amount of (similarly productive) labour.[57] In improved, commercial societies, real price typically is lower than nominal price. This is because, consequent upon the vast increase of specialised productive powers by means of the division of labour,[58] the cost of production of a commodity is far less to those engaged in that production than is its worth to those who are not so engaged and who would therefore find that particular commodity so much harder to make.[59] Smith is perfectly well aware that the accumulation of stock necessary for the generalisation of the division of labour had been a matter of private property charging a revenue.[60] Nominal price is therefore composed of the revenues of labour (wages), stock (profit) and land (rent), the latter two being paid from the excess of nominal over real price.[61] It is this excess that is the fund for accumulation and expanded production.[62]

Smith's distinction between early and commercial societies clearly involves the impossibility of value in the latter being determined by labour inputs. This is warrant enough for broadly neo-classical developments from Smith, which have taken two lines. First, having found nominal price to consist of wages, profit and rent, Smith proceeds to reverse this and to construct nominal price as the sum of the natural prices of each of these three when independently determined.[63] This cumulative mutual determination may be seen as a rudimentary equilibrium theory foreshadowing Walras.[64] Second, a general utility theory analogy to regarding nominal price as what a commodity is worth established by what will be given for it in exchange presents itself.[65] Taking up this latter tack, it becomes natural to suggest that if Smith had been acquainted with a workable marginalist apparatus, he would have been able to recognise the way his ideas of value in commercial societies had worked around to a position where it was important to resolve utility/value paradoxes such as the water/diamond one he mentions, not the attempt to exclude value in use from political economy that he actually did pursue.[66]

Though these ways of taking up Smith have a ground, and to that extent represent valid applied readings of his work, they are hermeneutically weak. The interpretation they put forward involves emphasising part of Smith's work which is thought valuable and imputing a rejection of the rest which is regretted. The rejection is clearly that of the interpreters - eager to quash the labour theory at its main source in favour of a militant neo-classicism - rather than that of the interpreted. As I say, this sort of eclectic borrowing has its place, but in this case the sacrificing of fidelity to Smith in order to justify later positions means that one falls beneath some very valuable ideas which would emerge if we try to understand his work as a whole, rather than as anachronistically fractured by subsequent divisions in the history of economic thought.

How in detail does Smith himself account for the difference between real and nominal price? If we take his solution to be that the former is composed only of labour inputs and the latter of the sum of wages, profit and rent, then this is certainly very weak as an explanation of the difference. The natural prices of labour and means of production by which Smith assesses wages, profit and rent is arrived at merely as their average price as opposed to their market prices, which vary according to competition.[67] Natural price is thereby no explanation of *why* these three revenues should enter into nominal price. In respect of wages, Smith of course has such an explanation in the basic labour input theory of value. His explanation of why profit and rent enter into nominal price is very different, not turning on production but upon the exacting of those revenues by those who want to reap where they have not sown and are able to do so. Profit and rent are merely the monopolistic charges able to be imposed after the appropriation of stock and land into the hands of private property owners.[68] Those who have private property in stock or land must be paid something for their use or they would not allow them to enter into production. This payment must be in proportion to the amount of their possessions allowed to be utilised in production as otherwise there would be no incentive to put larger resources into productive employment.[69]

Smith's account of why the three revenues enter into nominal price embraces two types of explanation which are by no means compatible. His comments on profit and rent involve rather too radical an idea of exploitation for them to be accepted, for its reliance on flat parasitism cannot explain how the excess of nominal over real price is *produced* in line with the way the labour input theory explains the production of real price. Smith is in fact rather badly confusing production and exploitation in the most vulgar sense. When Smith's own Robinsonade on early and rude societies gives an account of the economics of hunting, this account does not refer only to direct labour inputs into real price, despite Smith's own opinion to the contrary. No doubt even his hunters had to reckon the value of their kill not only by the time spent in the chase but also by the time spent in the making of their weapons, though Smith's picture of them glosses over this. What actually emerges from Smith's contrast of early and commercial societies is not that in the former value was determined purely by direct labour, but rather that in these societies the means of production were certainly individually but also generally owned. Smith shows production taking place using materials available to everyone, not concentrated in the hands of private property owners.[70]

The difference between real and nominal price is not one of the *factors* entering into the production of a commodity which it seems at first, because in early societies Smith is including means of production as a labour input. Making this inclusion so quickly as not to see what he is doing, Smith draws the wrong conclusion from his historical contrast. It is the alienation of labour from the means of production as the latter are appropriated as private property which is really illuminated by Smith's contrast. But the economic consistency of Smith's thought is disturbed by the way in which Smith himself understands this illumination. It is not, as Smith thinks, that the labour theory of value must be thought to have ceased to operate in commercial societies, but rather that we must recognise its operation in the provision of labour-dated means of production in early societies and we must apply this to the privately owned labour-dated means of production of commercial societies. But Smith carries his immersion of means of production into immediate labour right throughout his work. In his path-breaking analysis of capital reproduction, to take the main example, Smith always resolves price into merely the forms of revenue. That is to say, he always fails to consider the reproduction of constant capital.[71] This is, as we will see below, a paradigmatic instance of where the improvement of the labour theory turns on showing the productive place of (constant) capital, and not on the mere condemnation of private ownership of the means of production as a parasitic form of exploitation.

However confused, there is the strongest theoretical interest in Smith's concept of nominal price, a theoretical interest which amply displays the strength of the social philosophical milieu in which that concept was formulated. Let us ask what is left of Smith's idea of the fund for accumulation in commercial societies, which we have seen him locate in profit and rent, after the above critique of his confusion of ownership and role in production? The excess of nominal over real price would seem to be the very work of exchange, as we have to account for the production of the excess of labour commanded in exchange over labour input when the two components which take up the excess of nominal over real price are presented by Smith not as themselves productive but as only revenue charges. This is in a strong sense what Smith believed. Not that he conceived of surplus as a product of exchange itself. Smith is rather beyond mercantilism in what are thereby the most interesting parts of his work. Surplus is certainly something added in production: "the value which the workmen add to the materials", as he puts it.[72] However, his whole account of commercial societies, aptly named by him, turns on making exchange the paramount productive force. Given the division of labour, a great deal more wealth of use-values is of course produced. The division of labour implies the renunciation by more or less everyone of the possibility of subsistence production. Irrespective of the appropriation into private property of stock and rent, specialisation destroys this possibility. The absolute pre-condition for the division of labour is, for Smith, the exchange economy.[73] In this sense, exchange is itself the productive power of commercial society, which is a most interesting position to take up.

Smith puts the essence of this position in a way which is not immediately clear when he says that labour is the real measure of exchangeable value.[74] Now, on the basis of what we have seen of the way labour and profit and rent enter into the account of production, Smith cannot mean what one would might naturally expect, that the exchangeable value of a commodity is measured by labour inputs into it. Rather, when Smith describes nominal price, he says that it is measured by commandable labour; that is, the amount of labour which the exchange of the commodity *can command in return*, not labour inputs into the commodity. Of course, these two senses of "labour" are radically different for Smith. Though generating profound confusions as we shortly shall see, there is a most valuable explanatory benefit in the way Smith speaks. For Smith is able to focus in his account of accumulation in commercial societies on the relations of commandable labours rather than on relations between people and goods. Not only is the organisation of labour through general exchange made the key to understanding commercial societies, but furthermore accumulation is shown to be an issue of the command of new labour by those who gain the revenues of profit and rent. The, as it were, qualitative sociological thrust of Smith's notion of commandable labour is towards making clear the specific social relations of production in commercial societies and how these ground an historically unprecedented level of productivity. The issue is the new social structure. We should remember that in Smith's pin factory no new technology but merely the division of labour is the cause of the vast increase in pin production.[75] And we can add that it was factory organisation that called for the employment of increasingly large-scale machinery and not the other way round.[76]

Much of the sociological content of *The Wealth of Nations* - based on the four stages theory - is common to other outstanding Scottish Enlightenment accounts of civil society.[77] No doubt the peculiar elevation granted to Smith's book in large part follows from the way in which it captured the spirit of, and therefore had much of direct practical interest to say to, the rising industrial bourgeoisie. The obvious example is the staunch criticism of luxury consumption, more as policy recommendation than as a theoretical choice, on the ground that this is hardly the best way to make use of the possible fund for accumulation.[78] Smith's book is unique within this extremely productive tradition in social thought in the way it unreservedly falls into political economy, though he was, in fact, following particularly Hutcheson's example[79] in focusing upon economic questions. We must say, then, that the exchange relationship between the various types of specialised labours in the division of labour and their command for the purposes of capital accumulation is put forward in *The Wealth of Nations* together with the first reasonably clear grasp of the capitalist social equalisation of labour at the heart of political economy. However, this unity of social philosophy and economics is very precarious in Smith and in fact his qualitative account of capitalist social relations of production is put forward in a way which militates against the development of such an account into compatible quantitative accounts of value through the labour theory. Smith's confusion over the factors entering into production and the economic significance of their private ownership ensure this. Let us try, then, to give an overall evaluation of Smith's description of commercial society.

It is clear that Smith is unable to give any account of the production of the excess of nominal over real price in terms of exchangeable value. What he seems to do is take the undoubted increase in wealth, in amount of commodities for use, in commercial societies as immediately an exchange-value category. Smith's essential problem is to come to terms with the historically unique expansion of the production of use-values in the historically unique social relations of commercial society which, as he clearly saw, operate through exchange-value. What is absolutely necessary here is a proper ordering of the relationship of historically specific exchange-value production, general use-value production and their relationship in a specific form of use-value production organised through exchange-value. But of course this is precisely what we may expect to be absent from the ahistorical perspectives of what remains in the end a bourgeois vision and Smith's attempt to contextualise capitalist economic forms is in the end a failure. One example, on a fundamental point, will suffice. The reason given for the development of the social form of commercial society is a purported natural instinct of exchange,[80] a pitifully weak fetishisation by comparison to the social theoretical importance of Smith himself and his intellectual background in the Scottish Enlightenment.[81] Smith's errors in comparative value calculations for early and commercial societies are, then, of the greatest importance, for they are the nexus of the shortcomings of his attempt to describe the social relations of developing capitalist production and their historic significance.

Smith is fundamentally concerned to describe the new criteria of economic life which inform capitalism and these criteria essentially are those of the allocation of labour according to scarcity and demand under competitive pressures which are now central to marginalist technique. However, for Smith, this is an important point, but one which can be dealt with briefly, for what he saw as the real task, running together the practical need to criticise pre-capitalist relations and the theoretical task to grasp the character of capitalist ones, is to come to terms with the new social form which has brought about these novel types of technical-rational economic conduct. This is the significance of the labour theory of value. The theory does not dispute the new criteria but provides the context of those criteria as a new form of the economic organisation of labour. The point remains, however, that Smith develops the fundamental social theoretical content of the labour theory in a way which obstructs its adequate narrowly economic, quantitative development. Let us now turn to the way Ricardo sought to remedy this.

Ricardo's *Principles* were, of course, written in the closest relationship to Smith's thought in *The Wealth of Nations*. He draws upon the labour theory of value in *The Wealth of Nations* in the very first section of his book and we can see that this is no mechanical borrowing but that Ricardo deserves to be regarded as the principal carrier of Smith's description of specifically capitalist economics. Ricardo's very first words invoke Smith's distinction between use- and exchange-values and he adds a most interesting qualification. Ricardo goes on to say that, given that they have a use-value, commodities derive exchange-value from one of two sources; either from scarcity or from the amount of labour required to obtain them. This seems like two ways of saying the same thing, but in fact by "scarcity" Ricardo means something more like "uniqueness", referring to such goods as oil paintings by Rembrandt, the value of which is economically quite arbitrary. As these goods are not reproducible and are therefore not open to determination of value through competitive production, their value boils down to what it is possible to get for them (though given enough potential customers, a competition of merely buyers may make their price subject to convention). Without forcing Ricardo's meaning, I think we can say that he is here detailing an instance of the impinging of money on the sale of other than "true" commodities. For in making this quibble, Ricardo is displaying a keen grasp of the economic conditions which do enforce value. Leaving aside more or less unique goods, Ricardo means by commodities only those which "can be increased in quantity by human industry, and on the production of which competition operates without restraint".[82] He has in mind, of course, commodities produced in a developed capitalist economy of generalised exchange and competition. From the outset, then,

Ricardo has his eye fixed firmly on production in bourgeois society and properly identifies exchange-value as value fixed by production within these conditions.

It is the genuine taking up of Smith's standpoint of social observation coupled with a concern to remedy his errors in delimiting the applicability of the labour theory of value to capitalist institutions that give the essential shape to Ricardo's book. (Or rather, gives the shape to the first six chapters in which he puts forward this theory of value, the theory merely being amplified or applied in the later chapters). Ricardo takes the labour theory straight from Smith[83] and exposes, amongst other shortcomings,[84] the errors in Smith's restriction of its applicability to early societies.[85] He then takes the main economic institutions of the developed capitalist economy one by one and tries to show that they do not contradict but are subject to the labour theory of value.[86] Ricardo essentially argues the mistake in Smith's inclusion of means of production in direct labour in early societies which I have - following Ricardo - described. He then shows that though capitalist institutions based on private property may charge revenues other than, or indeed antagonistic to, wages, their ability to do so is based on their entrance into the production process as labour-dated means of production. Whatever weaknesses are left in Ricardo's quantitative determination of price, it is clear that he here provides the coherent foundation of bringing bourgeois economic life within a unified reference to capitalist social relations of production.

Why Ricardo should set out the *Principles* as a contribution to a political economic science dominated by Smith is obvious and the approach does, as I say, serve to extend Smith's legacy of the labour theory most clearly. However, that Ricardo felt able to present his work in this way, in which capitalist institutions are taken as given and then reconciled with the labour theory, shows the historical explanatory limitations of his whole concept of political economy. One need not agree with Marx that one should begin with the commodity in order to fully explain value in order to see that Ricardo begins very substantially with what he should end. In Ricardo, then, we have the paradox of the possibility of bringing bourgeois institutions into a single set of relations of production expressed through a complete lack of penetration of the historicality of these relations. Let us look at this paradox more closely.

Ricardo attempts to improve the coherence of political economy's handling of the distinction of use- and exchange-values. Ricardo understands perfectly well that improvements in setting the forces of nature at work can wonderfully increase riches, but not only does nature create no use-value but also improved use-value production will typically lower exchangeable value per good.[87] Ricardo makes this point against Say,[88] defending the importance of Smith's distinction of value in use and exchangeable value. But, as his having to add these passages in order to address himself to Say here makes us aware, Ricardo could hardly be thought to be holding to a clear line from Smith. Rather Ricardo is trying to clear up the confusions of Smith's running together of the use- and exchange-value components in his characterisation of commercial society and he does this by expunging use-value considerations completely. Ricardo included chapter twenty in the third edition as an expansion and defence of the essential position taken up in the first paragraphs of the book. Its purpose is to make it quite clear that the best way to move on from Smith is to restrict oneself to exchange-value. In claiming this, he advances the arguments later used by Marx to show the necessity of a common denominator of exchange in order for exchange to take place, making labour that denominator. This is a rather pure form of the labour theory, for it is achieved by expunging the use-value observations on capitalism to be found in Smith in order to leave (on, in the end, inconclusive quantitative grounds it must be said) labour organised through exchange-value as the sole determinant of value.

Of course, in Ricardo these social phenomena they become so extended beyond their proper historical context that they become almost natural in their generality. What I want to point out is that this extinguishing of historical location is linked to the loss of consideration, however confused, of use-value. For use-value production is the context of all social relations of production. What is at issue here is the clear understanding of the general production of use-values and, undoubtedly, some of Ricardo's fetishisations of capitalist forms could not have taken place with a more clear grasp of this. But the fundamental issue is that capitalism is not just a specific mode of production, production just as a noun or as a disposition of pure labour, but a mode of the production of use-values as the general process of human metabolism with nature. Comparative studies of forms of production may be rather simple catalogues of differing forms set out in relativistic juxtaposition. This is all that comparative study can amount to without some common thread by which the mutual evaluation that is the essence of real comparison can take place. By employing, as Smith does, use-value production as this criterion, the contrast of early and commercial societies is brought out in an historically significant fashion. Abstraction from use-value to the point where the naturalistic context of all social forms is lost destroys the context in which those forms take their shape. There is an interpenetration of the natural and the social in the very identification of the latter, as looking at any attempt to come to terms with the specific characteristics of capitalism, which must involve reference to its historically unique capacity to dominate nature, would show.

In Smith and Ricardo there is a substantially correct description of the specifically capitalist relations of production, though a grasp paradoxically characterised by an inadequate appreciation of the historical bounds of those relations. What is more, the extension of the unified description by Ricardo is accompanied by a loss of Smith's greatest contribution to the recognition of those bounds, his attempt to come to terms with the specific use-value consequences of capitalist production. In Ricardo, only the social relations of production are examined, in the terms of the labour theory of value describing exchange-value. The labour involved here is a mysteriously spiritual labour, divorced from its material location and considered only for its disposition. By contrast, labour in its relationship to nature and the natural disposition of materials is the very object of marginalist technique. To some extent as a result of this, the neo-classical articulation of marginalism loses any grasp on what is specifically capitalist, for in it, let me repeat, the specific social relations that have made human relations with nature the dominant object are lost to view.

What Marx attempted to do in *Capital* was to draw upon the social *and natural* elements in the identification of capitalism by Smith, re-uniting them in a way which overcomes Smith's shortcomings. If he celebrates Ricardo's refinement of the description of specifically capitalist relations, we must also recognise the positive advances on the development of the other side of Smith's thought in marginalism. Saying this obliges me to take up two positions: a first on the attitude one should take towards utility theory on the basis of a fundamental acceptance of Marx's critique of bourgeois economics and a second on the character of Marx's own political economy.

An antagonistic attitude to neo-classical uses of marginalism on the part of those who wish to defend Marx tends in fact to undermine an important prop of Marx's position. For Marx is ultimately trying to say that in value capitalism begins, in however difficult and convoluted a way, to make the key to rational, social self-consciousness of economic organisation available. What we must add is that marginalist technique is the leading bourgeois statement of these rational potentials, as technically developed both in econometrics and in the various applied analyses of the organisation of labour. That technique draws on just those observations about value being determined in relationship to scarcity, that is to say, to the amount of labour required to actualise a use-value in as far as possible the required amounts, that Marx finds in Smith and Ricardo.[89] To make this clear, some errors often displayed in Marxist attitudes to marginalism must be cleared up. For one thing, marginalism can by no means be considered to directly fall under Marx's criticisms of fetishism. Marginalist technique is neither content with surface appearances, for it always wants to operate an explanatory regress to utility, nor does it consider utility to be an intrinsic property of a good, for it always emphasises that utility emerges in human relations to nature.[90] Some confusion arises here because Marx is, I think, far more directly critical of the commodity fetishist depiction of relations between people and things than he would have been of a marginalism in which the refinements involved in the concepts of utility and scarcity as opposed to the concept of inherent value were made clear. For I think that, in fact, the reference to utility takes over substantially the grasp of the principles of rational organisation of labour which Marx considers capitalism to have made available.[91] Of course, the tendency of neo-classical thought is precisely to forget the specific social relations which have made this rational comprehension available. This both makes the neo-classical reading of the classicals on even these points seem very forced,[92] but more than this it makes neo-classical economics collapse into a vacuously general psychology of rational economic behaviour.[93] Although it is essential that we acknowledge that a vital insight into technical-rational use-value calculation is given, this is in terms which allow little or no purchase on specific economic conditions. In particular, this knowledge quite subdues the power of marginalism to give an account of present day forms of the contradiction of rational use-value production by exchange-value.

The ugly continuing coexistence of starving needy and rotting food "surpluses", to take but one glaring example, makes one a little impatient of the modern neo-liberal economics which fail even to register the serious problem here. But we must not be too hasty even over this. In especially welfare economics, marginalist technique pushes rational use-value economics through to what is in fact a criticism of capitalist production - albeit a criticism which emerges only after one looks at the distance between the prescriptions for rational utility and employment and the actual capitalist economy.[94] In Keynes this distance is, of course, made the object of study, and there seems to have been no real limit to the social reorganisation in order to reduce this distance that Keynes could at least contemplate.[95] If, as seems clear,[96] Keynes' radical ideas of economic reform are bounded by an insufficient appreciation of the capitalist restrictions on the pursuit of the extension of social justice he envisaged,[97] nevertheless these ideas have led to a profound socialisation of the capitalist economy, adjusting exchange-value's departures from optimum use-value production (though this fundamentally is conceived only in terms of the extent of the employment of economic resources rather than the directions of that employment).[98] What, I am sure, is basically operating here is the use-value criticism of exchange-value, albeit in a muted form.[99]

What I have called the initial interpretation of *Capital* was substantially formed in more or less total opposition to the attitude I am trying to advocate, for the polemical separation of use- and exchange-values was its paramount concern. Though Gossen published his book in 1854, it was of course only after Jevons, Menger and Walras published in the early 1870s that neo-classical economics became such an important force. Against a militant neo-classicism, overt polemic against a focus on general use-values which suppressed conscious consideration of historically specific social relations of production, especially the contradiction of optimal use-value production by capitalist exchange-values, became an even more pressing concern than it had been for Marx. Böhm-Bawerk put forward his famous criticisms within two years of Engels' making available the third volume of *Capital* and it is important to note that, as I have mentioned, in those criticisms the discussion of price calculation principally serves as the occasion for an argument that utility is a far more defensible central concept of economic analysis than is value.

The polemical character of the initial interpretation's response to neo-classicism does make a reference to an important element of Marx's criticism of fetishism and the separation of use- and exchange-values was essential to make the case that capitalistic economic conduct typically makes no direct reference to utility at all, being conducted in terms of the accumulation of exchange-values   The separation of use-value and exchange-value and the establishment of the pressing reality of the latter, not least when it obviously contradicts the former, are vital for the appreciation of the principal determinants of bourgeois economic life. The initial interpretation involves a stress, then, on a specifically capitalist construction of exchange-value, distinct from and often in opposition to use-value, as governing bourgeois economic activity. Though heavy-handed, the ridicule[100] to which works of the initial interpretation are able to subject attempts to give purportedly marginalist explanations of the conduct of major companies in terms of concern for use-value provision (attempts now largely given up and replaced by the flat tautology of regarding market outcomes as analytically the expression of consumer preferences), is considerable evidence of the superior productivity of these marxist social explanations.

More generally, in terms of setting up economic explanations, Böhm-Bawerk centrally argues that Marx did not take up the possibility of giving psychological explanations of the worth placed upon commodities which would explain their exchange-value.[101] In Sombart, the marxist response to such a claim was to contrast Marx's "objective" treatment of value to this "subjective" one, arguing that the former and not the latter was the proper one for political economy. Subjective valuations of commodities, even supposing that such data were scientifically corrigible, were still uninteresting unless set in the context of the objective, in the sense of socially rather than individually based, determinants upon those valuations. The very principles by which subjective valuations were reached remain to be explained without the objective investigation.[102] Much of the especially epistemological apparatus of this contrast of social and individual has proven not only inadequate, as is the fate of all ideas, but very dangerously mistaken, reflecting a principal shortcoming in the philosophical explication of marxism after Marx's death, and would not repay discussion. However, I would say that it is an achievement to have even posed this contrast. I will not say it was posed as a problem, for taking what were only the beginnings of analysis as something solidly cemented was a principal reason for the unsatisfactory state of the treatment of the social and the individual by these marxist writers. Nevertheless, they show, correctly I think, that in the psychologistic reconstruction of economic valuation, the boundaries within which the psychology may correctly apply are left quite unexamined, for they are, in fact, the ultimate basis of the explanation of the valuations put forward.[103] That these boundaries themselves call for an explanation which it would seem has to be social rather than psychological is the principal thrust of these marxist criticisms of marginalism.[104]

I would add that if these criticisms are good ones, then remedying the shortcomings of neo-classical accounts of exchange-value cannot be a question of adding a social component to a given psychology. For that psychology is arrived by a negation of social determinants and thus misunderstands its own data. What are social influences on the psychology of the bourgeois individual in his or her economic life are taken to be directly psychological phenomena; that is, as structures of consciousness, structures of nature. Recognition of social determinations on psychological phenomena would have to intrinsically alter our understandings of those very phenomena. The obvious facts of economic life of which Böhm-Bawerk makes so much crumble away from his purportedly commonsensical refutations of Marx's analysis when we see that those facts claim to be "facts" in this absolute sense only because they embody conceptions of their own character which, far from being the arbiters of science, are inevitably condemned as bad consciousness by radical scientific efforts to understand.

Despite these important virtues in the initial interpretation, I believe that it adopts an overly polemical attitude to marginalist technique which leads to a limiting tendentiousness in its interpretation of the separation of use-value and exchange-value. This interpretation essentially claims that Marx registers the use-value of a commodity in order to relegate this element to a background of the general, ahistorical production of goods conterminous with human life. Against this background, the exchange-value which arises when goods generally are produced as commodities is shown to be the specific element indicating the individual capitalist mode of production. The focus of political economy is upon the latter. Against the characteristic tendency of bourgeois political economy to conflate use-value and exchange-value, the initial interpretation focuses more or less exclusively on the specific social relations of production. Whilst, let me repeat, there is much in this that has made the sense of Marx's concept of fetishism available to us, I think it fails to grasp the way in which Marx tries to explain social relations as definitely linked to a particular level of human knowledge of, and ability to work within, nature.

This polemicism has contributed not only to a severing of relations with neo-classicism but also to a fracture which has been perhaps the principal feature of socialist political economy in this century. For since the demise of the Second International, social democratic parties have not followed the intial interpretation's line but have been overwhelmingly influenced by welfare economics and by Keynesianism. It just is not good enough to say that those economics have thus been weakened by being at a distance from Marx, for, of course, they have, but the aim of closing the distance has hardly been strenuously pursued by avowed marxists whose tone towards the social democratic parties has been condescending in the extreme.[105]

A great deal of the marginalist determination of the magnitude of price is to be found in Fabianism, the earliest socialist development of welfare economics. A particularly clear case is the collapse of Shaw's almost light-hearted scorn for the principle of utility[106] into more or less total acceptance of this principle upon appreciating the place of competition in marginalist theory.[107] Perhaps for us now the most important task set by this fact is the assessment of the productive resources of welfare economics as a response to the socialisation of capitalist production. However, a description of the theoretical positions actually adopted at the time would have to conclude that Fabianism fell very far indeed beneath the social understanding being generated in the initial interpretation and that the valuably organic conceptions of socialist development which Fabianism maintained remained poorly articulated. One has only to recall the unconvincing optimism by which mysteriously democratised state action is so often invoked to fill in the gaps left by these conceptions.[108] Perhaps the most important characteristic of the Fabian attitude to Marx was, amidst all the admiration, an almost total failure to understand the first part of *Capital*. The consequences of this for the popular comprehension of Marx in Britain are perhaps best displayed in the ludicrous inadequacies of Russell's account of the labour theory of value.[109] But we have seen that even Cole gave an introduction to *Capital* which contains a total failure to understand all those issues of social analysis illuminated by the initial interpretation.

The complete scorn for marginalism in the initial interpretation had then its socialist opposite in a Fabian distaste for those parts of *Capital* beyond its marginalist comprehension, which Fabianism came to regard as metaphysical or some such positivist synonym for nonsense. Represented here is the fracture in socialist political economy at which I am trying to drive. If Fabianism had access to relatively popular understanding, it did so by falling far beneath Marx and standing on day to day opinions about price which it turned to socialist purposes as far as it could. The initial interpretation accompanied its depth of knowledge by refusing to allow everyday conceptions of value any other place than that of ideology in the most derogatory sense. Standing thereby in opposition to, rather than a development of popular consciousness, this most vital area of marxist theory militated against its own popular understanding, even in the in other respects most favourable political situation in which initial interpretation addressed its audience.

Still the outstanding (and here Marx's comments on JS Mill must apply) attempt to forge any links between these two stances on common understandings of price and their explanation by the labour theory is Bernstein's *Presuppositions of Socialism*. Bernstein's biography tells of a surely unequalled opportunity to both recognise the necessity of better marxist response to marginalist economics and to provide such a response. When at one point Bernstein quotes a sentence from volume three of *Capital* in which Marx makes consideration of use-values intrinsic to important political economic issues and adds the comment: "This sentence alone makes it impossible to make light of the Gossen-Böhm theory with a few superior phrases", we are given a, to my knowledge unique, western attempt of the period to reach some cross-fertilisation.[110] Bernstein was in an excellent position to draw on the milieu of the initial interpretation as well as of Fabianism, and the historical failure of his attempt to make any real progress in economic, if not in political, theory must be regarded as being in some part due to his own shortcomings. For Bernstein himself continually falls beneath the social understandings available in German theoretical marxism into a philosophically naive defence of the given empirical so little theoretically re-worked as to be more or less ideologically reproduced. Given Bernstein's advantages, the character of his articles and book go a little way to warranting the contumely with which they came to be held.[111] Unfortunately, this was almost the direct opposite of the reaction which would have been most fruitful.

Rather similar positions, indeed including some directly influenced by Fabianism and by Bernstein, were taken up in "legal marxism". Certainly the political economy of the likes of Tugan-Baranowsky[112] bears little comparison with the flat inadequacies found in Bernstein. But equally certainly legal marxim's economic and political theories have been as much the object of polemical attack by marxist orthodoxy as Bernstein himself. Attempts to utilise marginalist insights were rejected as the watering down of marxism.[113] As one might suspect, there are far more than merely theoretical questions involved here; but nevertheless legal marxism has been substantially lost to present assessments of marxism's historically developed theoretical resources. As the waning of Stalin's baneful influence has lead to the excellent works of such as Rubin, Pashukanis and Vološinov being made available in the west, perhaps a waning of those influences of Lenin of similar character will allow of a reconsideration of Struve and others.

Unfortunately, marxist examinations of the development of neo-classical economics predominantly continue to take a militant and polemical interpretative tack. Writing against an intellectual background, in economics at least, in which Marx's work continues to be dismissed as ideological, as opposed to the science put forward in neo-classicism and its underpinnings in sociology, marxist writers have have tried to reverse the labelling. Now, one may sympathise with the motive behind this attempted reversal, but this does not relieve one from an overwhelming impatience in reading works of this type. Though concerned to be historical, they are sadly lacking in knowledge of their own history - of the evaluations of economic theory to be found in the initial interpretation of *Capital* which they more or less repeat. This would not matter so much were it not that this lack of self-awareness reflects the fact that all the potentially productive issues of critique in this area are more or less lost in the repetition of a wholly unsympathetic line, and that the possible dialogue - however limited - between two bodies of thought which seem typically only to swap derogatory epithets is frustrated. I will focus, unfairly enough, upon Clarke's *Marx, Marginalism and Modern Sociology* as an example, for its particular stress on sociology brings out the essential social issues most clearly.

The characteristic themes of the critical - in the derogatory sense - marxist interpretation of the history of late-nineteenth and early twentieth century social thought are virtually all displayed in Clarke's work. His book is set out as something of a purported reply to *The Structure of Social Action* as a history of ideas,[114] and its central thesis is that Parsons, though certainly correct in identifying the emergence of a voluntaristic theory of action, is wrong to identify this as a scientific development.[115] Parsons in fact missed the real scientific development in nineteenth century social thought - by Marx.[116] I am sure that there is a great deal that is defensible in this. Indeed, as it is developed into an exposure of the essentially abstract character of the voluntaristic theory,[117] it is novel and illuminating. But this valuable defensible element is not made the basis of a generous attitude towards the criticised thought, but is rather only the springboard for intentionally hostile, destructive criticism.

The essential issue is Clarke's attitude towards reform informed by marginalism. This attitude is deprecatory, focusing upon the undoubted limits which such reform accepts and works within.[118] But if it is not difficult to see how this criticism is intended to work as criticism, it is difficult to see what purpose such criticism is meant to serve. If it is meant to argue for the superiority of Marx's science, it adopts the unfortunate form of preaching to the converted and reviling the unconverted for their sins. No real effort is made to speak to marginalists on any other basis that they initially reject their own beliefs, so the potential for winning conviction in the superiority of Marx's thought is lost. When Clarke writes that he believes that it was "important to take liberal social theory more seriously than did the 'radical' social thought of the 1970s",[119] what he means is that we should take greater pains to show how very wrong it is. This hardly suits a book originally written for a series which proclaims that it "aims to create a forum for debate between different theoretical and philosophical traditions in the social sciences".[120] Of course, the celebration of Marx's correctness may have a ritual function.

If, on the other hand, Clarke's book is meant to help the development of marxist theory, then its form is equally unsuited to its task. An essential correctness of the positing of revolution, from which all reform can be condemned for being such, is the starting point of Clarke's main thesis. Even if one accepted the fundamental correctness of this evaluation on the most general terms, this does not carry Clarke's point. It is surely impossible to argue that twentieth century marxism has had any real success is specifying the precise mechanisms of revolution in the western (or for that matter, the eastern) world. When assessing real social improvements, the type of revolutionary marxism Clarke seems to have in mind does not have a list of achievements which even begins to compare with the reformism he deprecates, even when assessed by those also critical of that reformism.[121] Clarke obviously then has to couple his attack on marginalism with an assault on "orthodox marxism" for having "neutralised" the power of Marx's work,[122] for surely something has to be responsible for the failure of marxism to oust so weak an opponent as Clarke argues marginalism to be. The essential theme remains, however, one of lack of fidelity to Marx, which is as "orthodox" a criticism as one could imagine.

All this is not to celebrate the limits of reformism but to draw what I cannot but feel is the obvious lesson here: that the task facing us is to deepen both revolution and social reform. If the limited ambitions of the latter can be expanded through dialogue with the former, the former, probably to a greater degree, requires some teaching on how to immerse itself, or rather to find itself, in the given social world. A dogmatic stress on their own correctness by proponents of either one or the other prevents this.

Works like Clarke's - first published in 1982 - seemed unhelpful when written. They seem downright wrongheaded now, after the hypocritical confidence in the socialisation of the advanced capitalist economies which obviously underlied this type of criticism has been shown to be misplaced by more than a decade of outright reaction. As one might have expected, the overall socialist response to the rejection of welfare economics[123] and broadly Keynesian economic planning[124] by a literally reactionary neo-liberalism has been utterly disingenuous, now regretting the disappearance of a system which has more or less suffered nothing other than calumny at socialist hands until regression from it cut back the socialisation of the economy.

Of course, broadly marxist political economy can show how limited Keynesianism is and how nevertheless it is insupportable for the capitalist organisation of production.[125] But this did not have to be a destructive statement of the bourgeois limitations of Keynes, but could have been one of the socialist directions which must be taken even to secure his limited gains and not lose them.[126] This is more a question of the generosity with which one examines social theories than any fundamental change in the evaluation of those theories.[127] However, the consequences which could flow from the dialogue which can follow only after the adoption of such a generous attitude still are invaluable.[128] If my argument is accepted, it is clear that a broadly Marxist intellectual history of marginalism needs to be re-written. It is encouraging that the second edition of Clarke's book, written in the light of changes in "the intellectual landscape"[129] since 1982, expands the criticism of marxism which were vestigial in the first edition[130] and, were Clarke able to recognise that this is a criticism of what certainly were once his own beliefs, this should allow of the re-evaluation of others' positions.

However, as I have said above, there is a second task which a reorientation towards marginalism puts on the agenda and it is this which I will take up. For if use-value consideration in marginalism at least presents a muted form of the criticism of exchange-value, I now want to argue that Marx himself criticised capitalism in essentially this way, contrasting the use-value potentialities of capitalist production with exchange-value restrictions on that potentiality. The crucial point is that whereas the play of use- and exchange-value components of the description of capitalism in Smith is confused, Marx is, with his much firmer grip of the general and specific elements of production, able to make this play coherent. In Marx, after the distinction between general use-value production and historically specific exchange-value production is made, there is a consideration of the form of use-value production undertaken in those particular relations of production. In the next two chapters, I will carry this discussion of Marx's utilisation of the resources of classical political economy further by examining the play of use- and exchange-values in Smith and Ricardo's explanations of the tendency of the rate of profit to fall and in Marx's own account of capitalist development.

Much of what I am ultimately going to say about Marx's account of capitalist development will be critical and I must preface it with some remarks about the status of his critique of classical political economy which will serve as a conclusion to the previous two chapters. It should go without saying that this critique is a marvellous achievement of scholarship. It represented a huge personal investment by Marx and the returns are huge - at least as great as any other work of social science. I think that, if we set it the test of the dialectic, it stands as an outstandingly brilliant, if flawed, instance of immanent critique. It exposes an alienated belief, but does so only through proper immersion in and development of that belief. I regard the critique of commodity fetishism as we have seen it so far a major success. However, it has not, of course, proved to be a success, as watching the grotesque spectacle of any current financial news bulletin confirms. It is the principal task of social theory to determine why - beyond the stylistic shortcomings of the presentation - this is so. Let us, accordingly, now turn to how Marx set out his account of the developments in capitalism which would provide the basis for overcoming capitalist alienation. And because this is such a soundly based critique, we are obliged to start not in Marx but in classical political economy - in Smith and Ricardo.

Notes

1   PP, pp 120-5; CPE, p 300 and C1, p 173 n 33.

2   Eg *idem*, 'Comments on James Mill', pp 211-28.

3   TSV3, ch 20.

4   *Vide* Mandel, *The Formation of the Economic Thought of Karl Marx*, ch 3.

5 WLC, pp 222-5 and C3, pt 2. Cf PPE, chs 4, 30.

6 TSV2, ch 10 and C3, p 305 n.

7 For intimations of a similar interpretative stance, though taken towards the theory of surplus value generally, *vide* Wilson, *Marx's Critical/Dialectical Procedure*, p 13.

8 C1, pp 169-70.

9 CPE, p 310 and C1, p 174 n 34.

10 CPE, pp 269-72; C, pp 10-1 and C1, pp 130-1. Cf WN, pp 47-8 and PPE, ch 1, sec 1.

11 WN, pp 27, 176-221 and PPE, ch 1, sec 2.

12 EPM, pp 284, 291, 310-1 and PP, p 125.

13 CPE, p 306 n; VF, pp 141-2 and C1, pp 151-2.

14 CPE, p 306 n.

15 EM, vol 38, p 336-7.

16 MCP, pp 486-9.

17 C1, ch 13.

18 *Ibid*, pp 169-70. Cf Defoe, *Robinson Crusoe*, pp 87-117. The editor of this edition of *Robinson Crusoe*, Ross, makes a common mistake at pp 16-7 when he mistakes Marx's passing of bourgeois value judgements for the judgements Marx himself would make. That Marx would, one imagines, always mean more or less the opposite of what he is taken to mean in these instances does, of course, raise serious questions about the way he conducts his critique of political economy which I will address at more length in this chapter.

19 C1, pp 166-7, 168-9.

20 *Vide* Foucault, *The Order of Things*, p 176.

21 EM, vol 28, p 97.

22 *Idem*, 'On Friedrich List's Book', p 281 and C1, ch 15.

23 EM, vol 28, p 42.

24 *Ibid*, vol 28, pp 43-4.

25 *Ibid*, vol 28, pp 157-8; CPE, pp 389-90 and C3, pp 440-55, 920-1.

26 Weber, *Economy and Society*, pt 1, chs 1-2. Cohen, *Karl Marx's Theory of History*, pp 320-1 draws attention to an acute example of the superiority of Marx's historical understanding here which emerges in a comparison of Weber, *General Economic History*, pp 260-1 and EM, vol 28, p 251. I have discussed this example in analysis of the interpretative shortcomings of Weber's reproduction of bourgeois value judgements in 'Truth Claims and Value-freedom in the Treatment of Legitimacy: The Case of Weber', pp 217-22.

27 EM, vol 29, pp 162-4 and CPE, pp 297-8. Cf Steuart, *An Inquiry into the Principles of Political Economy, etc*, pp 361-2.

28 C, p 11; 'Marx to Engels, 24 August 1867' and C1, pp 132, 173 n 33.

29   CPE, pp 271-6; C, pp 11-3 and C1, pp 131-8.

30   WN, bk 2, sec 3.

31   C3, pp 957-9.

32   TSV1, pp 152-3 and RIPP, pp 1038-49.

33   Senior, *Principes fondamentaux de l'économie politique*, p 198. I am unable to trace this passage in the English *Outline* or in any of Senior's published lectures. It would appear that it was one of the extracts from the manuscripts of Senior's lectures which his French translator, Arrivabene, added to the English text of the *Outline* for the French *Principes fondamentaux*.

34   TSV1, p 287.

35   COGP, p 318.

36   *Pace* eg Della Costa, 'Women and the Subversion of the Community', p 52.

37   Describing this type of mistake is one of the ways in which Marx used the term "petty bourgeois" Eg PP, p 178. However, if it ever had any productive use in this way, which I doubt, that use has surely been lost in the course of subsequent employments.

38   RIPP, p 1044.

39   EM, vol 28, p 231.

40   *Vide* Lange, *Political Economy*, ch 5. In an exemplary fashion, Lange distinguishes the science of the application of rational economic technique, which he calls "praxiology", from political economy. The technical insights of the outstanding planners of the communist economies are being positively drawn into western socialist economics after the collapse of those economies. *Vide* Brus and Laksi, *From Marx to the Market*, pp 11; Estrin and Winter, 'Planning in a Market Socialist Economy' and Winter, 'Market Socialism and the Reform of the Capitalist Economy'.

I leave aside as too large a subject, certainly in proportion to the value of discussing it, the conundra in which communist economists placed themselves over the application of "the law of value" to their economies, which seems to represent a more or less continuous decline from the early high point of Bukharin, *The Politics and Economics of the Transition Period*, ch 9 to the low manifested in Stalin, 'Economic Problems of Socialism in the USSR', sec 3. Unfortunately, even after the collapse of Soviet communism, it is not a purely historical matter. Whilst it is of great importance that the degree of sophistication of some of the technically competent planners (eg Li Fuchun, 'For the Sake of Socialist Construction Strengthen Planning Work Throughout the Country') who were simply overridden by Mao be not overlooked, it would appear that, so far as a commentator without Chinese can say, China has yet to produce a Brus, Lange, Kalecki, Kornai, Pybyla, Sik, etc, and even the best of the contemporary Chinese economists (eg Xue Muqiao, *China's Socialist Economy*) struggle with pointless issues. Hsu, *Economic, Theories in China* 1979-88 thoroughly examines the baneful effects of communist jargon.

41   Eg Robbins, *The Nature and Significance of Economic Science*, pp 4, 15.

42   *Pace* Roemer, *Analytical Foundations of Marxist Economic Theory*, pp 1-10.

43   The remarkably diffident tone of Marx's letter to Kugelmann of 11 October 1867, that is to say, within weeks of volume one's appearance, is striking evidence of this. A diffident tone is not a common characteristic of Marx's correspondence.

44   Most notably by dropping VF, an appendix to the first German edition, from all subsequent editions.

45   PPE, p 11 and C1, p 131.

46   Althusser, 'Preface to *Capital* Volume One', p 80. It can hardly be denied that understanding the material set out at the beginning of volume one is hard to read - I am arguing that this is so here. But the problem is not that Althusser recognises this, it is that he does not *want* this material to be understood. *Ibid*, p 91.

47   Not least because Engels and Marx themselves would seem to have advocated it on occasion. Eg Marx, 'To Kugelmann, 30 November 1867' and *idem*, 'To Engels, 23 May 1868'.

48   Cole, 'Introduction', p xviii.

49   The obvious line to take, then, is to doubt he said what he meant, so we find Cole giving two chapters (7-8) of his tellingly titled *What Marx Really Meant* to the refashioning of the theory of value.

50   Cole 'Introduction', pp xxiv, xx.

51   On the basis of similar evidence, Boss, *Theories of Surplus and Transfer*, ch 5 goes rather further than I do in criticism of Marx in her very interesting discussion of "the factory paradigm" in his thought.

52   Jevons, *The Theory of Political Economy*, p 72.

53   Schumpeter, *History of Economic Analysis*, pp 590-8.

54   Eg Marshall, *Principles of Economics*, bk 4, ch 3 and Appendix L.

55   WN, pp 44-5.

56   *Ibid*, pp 47-51.

57   *Ibid*, p 65.

58   *Ibid*, bk 1, ch 1.

59   *Ibid*, p 47.

60   *Ibid*, pp 65-7.

61   *Ibid*, bk 1, ch 6.

62   *Ibid*, P 71.

63   *Ibid*, bk 1, chs 6-11.

64   Walras, *Elements of Pure Economics*, lesson 12.

65   Eg Marshall, *Principles of Economics*, pp 627-8.

66   Eg Jevons, *The Theory of Political Economy*, pp 128-31.

67   WN, bk 1, ch 6.

68 *Ibid*, p 67.
69 *Ibid*, p 66.
70 *Ibid*, p 276.
71 Eg *ibid*, pp 68-9.
72 *Ibid*, p 66.
73 *Ibid*, bk 1, ch 2.
74 *Ibid*, p 47.
75 *Ibid*, bk 1, ch 1.
76 *Vide* Landes, *The Unbound Prometheus*, pp 55-63.
77 Eg Ferguson, *An Essay on the History of Civil Society*, pt 2, sec 3 and Millar, *The Origin and Distinction of Ranks*. The ultimate sources of the four stages theory would seem to be in the social thought of the French Enlightenment. Turgot, 'On Universal History'.
78 WN, p 47.
79 Hutcheson, *A Short Introduction to Moral Philosophy*, bk 2, chs 12-3 and *idem, A System of Moral Philosophy*, bk 2 chs 12-3
80 WN, bk 1, ch 1.
81 Cf eg Ferguson, *An Essay on the History of Civil Society*, pt 4 sec 3.
82 PPE, pp 11-2.
83 *Ibid*, pp 12-3.
84 *Ibid*, ch 1, sec 1.
85 *Ibid*, ch 1, sec 3.
86 *Ibid*, chs 1-6.
87 *Ibid*, ch 20.
88 *Ibid*, pp 279-81. Cf Say, *Treatise on Political Economy*, bk 1 ch 4.
89 Eg Marshall, *Principles of Econmics*, Appendix B.
90 Eg Jevons, *The Theory of Political Economy*, p 59.
91 *Vide* Meek, 'Marginalism and Marxism'.
92 *Vide* Myrdal, *The Political Element in the Development of Economic Theory*, pp 77-8.
93 *Vide* Bukharin, *The Economic Theory of the Leisure Class*, ch 1.
94 Eg Pigou, *The Economics of Welfare* pt 2,
95 Keynes not only welcomed the eventual "euthanasia of the rentier" ('The General Theory of Employment, Interest and Money,' p 376) as a consequence of abundant investment funds but also saw an end to human beings' domination by the impulse to accumulate as a consequence of the achievement of abundance. *Idem*, 'Essays in Persuasion', pp 326-32. Keynes' broad opinion that the eventual possibility of the achievement of abundance meant "the economic problem is not...the permanent problem of the human race" (*ibid*, p 326) is an idea wholly

compatible with the strains of Marx's thought that I am trying to emphasise in this work.

96   As early as 1939, Ward had made it perfectly clear that, behind their substantial degree of overlap "the final rift between Marx and Keynes...is on the sociological point of...whether capitalism is *based* on exploitation" ('Marx and Keynes' *General Theory*', p 165, my emphasis).

97   Eg the wholly implausible political quietism which he displays when discussing the euthanasia of the rentier. The tone of the keynesain attitude to politics, in its positive and negative sides, was perhaps most clearly expressed by Meade in *The Intelligent Radical's Guide to Economic Policy*, ch 1. Meade's own keynesian achievements are, of course, very considerable indeed, perhaps the most important being his major influence on the Beveridge Report on *Full Employment in a Free Society*, which still stands as the most nearly successful attempt to turn high human aspiration into policy under advanced capitalism.

98   Keynes, 'General Theory of Employment, Interest and Money', p 379.

99   *Vide* Magdoff and Sweezy, 'Listen Keynesians', pp 48-9.

100   Hilferding, 'Böhm-Bawerk's Criticism of Marx', pp 125-6.

101   Böhm-Bawerk, 'Karl Marx and the Close of His System', pp 66-7.

102   Which Sombart, in particular, exhaustively supplied from the marxist perspective in *The Quintessence of Capitalism*.

103   Eg Robbins, *The Nature and Significance of Economic Science*, p 19. Even explicit attempts to make this type of understanding realistic must founder on the basic lack of historical appreciation. Coase's brief remarks by way of economic philosophy in 'The Firm, the Market and the Law' are a perfect example. Donald Harris and I have tried to make clear the bizarre nature of Coase's "realism" in Campbell and Harris , 'Flexibility in Long-term Contractual Relationships: The Role of Co-operation', pp 177-80.

104   Bukharin, *The Economic Theory of the Leisure Class*, pp 36-46, 62-4 and Hilferding, 'Böhm-Bawerk's Criticism of Marx', pp 131-3.

105   The tone was set by Lenin, 'Two Tactics of Social Democracy in the Democratic Revolution'.

106   Shaw, 'The Jevonian Criticism of Marx', pp 726-8.

107   Idem, 'The Economics of Socialism', pp 12-8.

108   Eg Webb, *Socialism in England*, ch 8. The best defence of this optimism is provided by Laski, *A Grammar of Politics*, ch 1.

109   Russell, *History of Western Philosophy*, p 612.

110   Bernstein, *Evolutionary Socialism*, p 36 n.

111   Eg Plekhanov, '"What Should We Thank Him For?" An Open Letter to Karl Kautsky'. This is a criticism of Kautsky's own attitude to Bernstein. Kautsky was editor of *Die Neue Zeit* when it published Bernstein's articles and his own spoken and written responses to them were of a polite tone.

112 Tugan-Baranowsky, *Grundlagen des Marxismus.*

113 Bukharin, 'The Policy of Theoretical Conciliation'.

114 Clarke, *Marx, Marginalism and Modern Sociology*, pp 1-3.

115 Ibid, p 290-8.

116 Ibid, p 4. This line is developed at even greater length in Therborn, *Science, Class and Society.*

117 Clarke, *Marx, Marginalism and Modern Sociology*, chs 5-8.

118 Ibid, ch 7.

119 Ibid, p viii.

120 Publisher's note inside the front cover of the first (1982) edition of *ibid.*

121 *Vide* Hamilton, *Democratic Socialism in Britain and Sweden.*

122 Clarke, *Marx, Marginalism and Modern Sociology*, p 306.

123 Eg Coase, *'The Lighthouse in Economics'.*

124 Eg Friedman, *The Counter-revolution in Monetary Theory.*

125 Eg Pilling, *The Crisis of Keynesian Economics.*

126 Eg Cutler *et al*, *Keynes, Beveridge and Beyond*, ch 4.

127 Of course, the lack of generosity creates serious weaknesses in the interpretation of Keynes himself. *Vide* Vicarelli, *Keynes: The Instability of Capitalism*, ch 11.

128 *Vide* Hansen, *The Breakdown of Capitalism*, p 143.

129 Ibid, p viii.

130 Clarke, *Marx, Marginalism and Modern Sociology*, ch 9. It undoubtedly is the case that the second edition of the book is far better than the first, for, although it is an incidental side-effect of the way he approaches the subject, Clarke's attack on orthodox marxism, provoked by the collapse of communism, necessarily tends to balance his attack on marginalism.

7 Smith and Ricardo on the Falling Rate of Profit

I want now to set out the main lines of Marx's account of the development of the capitalist mode of production, intending to deepen our understanding of that account by showing how it articulates the immanent positing of a higher social form in existing society. I will specifically argue that socialism is posited within capitalism as a set of potentialities created by, and also necessary measures in order to deal with, the burgeoning forces of use-value production when these, inevitably, push beyond the social relations of production of exchange-value and capital. Marx claims that a chronic tendency towards over-production, which becomes acutely manifest in increasingly profound crises, is the signal to the capitalist mode of production that it both contains potentialities which it cannot realise and that the pressures of this containment are bound to accumulate.

I hope, of course, to show how my interpretation of Marx's attitude of Hegel can help us to understand Marx's substantive work. More than this, however, I want to continue to ask how far that work manages successfully to carry on Hegel's legacy and allows Marx to give an account of socialism that properly sets out their, as it were, joint proposals of the overcoming of alienation in modern society. The strength of Marx's account of the development of capitalism substantially rests on the closeness of the relationship of his thought to classical political economy, specifically in that his views on the limits to capital accumulation rest on the basis of similar ideas in, particularly, Smith and Ricardo centring on the idea that the rate of profit will fall with the progress of accumulation. We must first, then, examine this idea in Smith and Ricardo.

Smith quite forthrightly declared that there is a tendency of the rate of profit to fall proportionate to the degree of improvement of commercial society,[1] his grounds being the following. Accumulation means a growing stock[2] and the expanding market that characterises a society undergoing improvement provides greater possibilities for the productive utilisation of that stock, thus allowing an increasing proportion of profit and rent revenues to be productively rather than unproductively consumed.[3] However, there is a point, Smith says it in so many words, when it becomes increasingly difficult to convert this growing proportion seeking productive employment of an in any case increasing stock into new productive stock.[4] Being able to export a surplus produced when the home market for a product is satiated is given by Smith as an important function of foreign trade - "Without such exportation a part of the productive labour of the country must cease, and the value of its annual product diminish".[5] The volume of the carrying trade is hence a reliable indicator of the wealth of improved societies.[6] Beyond this point, however, Smith seems to envisage a general difficulty in finding new outlets for the productive investment of revenue. In this situation, competition between revenues to secure their own productive investment must force down the rate of profit. Each revenue is forced by competition to pay more for its inputs and charge less for its outputs when productively utilised in order to be so utilised. In particular, continuously expanding demand for productive labour must push up wages at the expense of profits.[7]

Smith does not clearly identify the cause of either the partial or the general over-production to which he refers. At first glance, Smith seems to regard the possibility that consumption requirements of use-values in specific and general markets may be satiated as the basic reason for the rate of profit falling. Smith's foretelling of England's future in Holland's present lends direct textual support for this interpretation. In Holland, approaching near to the state of "a country which had acquired its full complement of riches, where in every particular branch of business there was the greatest quantity of stock that could be employed in it", the rate of profit was so small that only those who owned a great volume of stock could live on profit and interest and more and more owners were being reduced to superintendence of their own productive workers.[8] The unprecedented ability of improved commercial societies to furnish riches is to run into contradiction with the satiation of use-value consumption, the development of which contradiction is manifested in a declining rate of profit returned upon productively invested stock.

Ricardo would, I think, have regarded this last sentence as a fair summary of Smith's ideas on the fall of the rate of profit, but he treats it as an indefensible slip rather than as a line of thought which has a ground in Smith's basic theory. Ricardo makes short work of the slip and, because of the shortcomings of Smith's treatment of use-value, of Smith's whole idea of satiation as well in *The Wealth of Nations*. If the problem is of over-production of specific goods, then, Ricardo says, nobody has shown better than Smith that capital will flow from a sated branch of production where the rate of profit will be declining into a branch where profits are higher. Smith's specific examples were of Britain's production of more corn, woollen goods and hardware than the home market could absorb and the consequent need to export these products. One would think, Ricardo observes, that Britain was under some compulsion to produce those particular goods. Even if export outlets dried up, the capital could be shifted to other branches of production.[9]

When turning to general over-production and decline in the general rate of profit, Ricardo's opinion of Smith's conclusions is no less critical, but the issue is a little clouded. For Ricardo himself held that there was a tendency for the general rate of profit to fall with progressive accumulation, but he attributed this to the restraint of non-capitalist factors on accumulation, not to a development intrinsic to capitalist accumulation itself. A few words first, then, on why Ricardo himself thought that the rate of profit would decline.

Though Ricardo was well aware of increases in profits deriving from the development of labour productivity with the improvement of society,[10] he identified an increased demand for labour with such improvement, as he was historically warranted to do in the midst of primitive accumulation. This demand for labour translates into demand for the necessaries which wages purchase,[11] most importantly for foodstuffs. Ricardo focuses upon corn.[12] Ricardo knew, of course, of historical improvements in agricultural productivity,[13] but he regarded these as being exceptional occurrences with little prospect for continuous future development.[14] There is a historical warrant for this too in the great discrepancy between the relatively low degree of real subsumption to capital of agricultural as opposed to industrial production in Ricardo's time, a discrepancy which has been only reduced and by no means removed at present and which arguably never will be totally removed. For Ricardo, this intensive margin of increases in agricultural productivity was of little significance beside the extensive margin of bringing more land into production.[15] In what he felt was an acute contrast to the virtually limitless capitalist expansion of the production of industrial goods,[16] Ricardo saw corn production being pushed onto decreasingly fertile land and thus corn rising in value because more labour would be required to produce a given amount. The consequence of this is that differential rent must rise with increased agricultural production.

Ricardo accounted for all rent as a charge on the super profits accruing to agricultural production on relatively fertile land as total demand for corn pushes agriculture onto less fertile land. Prices must allow profitable production on this poorer land, but such a level of prices provides great profits for production on the better land, which land can thus charge differential rent.[17] In the condition of rising demand for corn, to maintain even a minimum standard of living,[18] labourers would have to be paid an increasingly large money wage, even if the corn wage which represented the real wage[19] remained stationary or even declined.[20] As Ricardo treated wages and profits as directly competitive shares of revenue,[21] then this would imply a tendency for profit to decline, or, more precisely, for rent to absorb profit.[22] If initially the expansion of capital's revenue would exceed the rate of increase of the money wage because of the relative under-utilisation of the better land,[23] this could be so only for a limited period which the pressure of accumulation must eventually end. Ultimately, corn production would be pushed on to such poor land that the tendency of profits to decline would predominate as the rate of growth in money wages overcame the rate of growth of capital's revenues.[24] Then return to capital investment would be so low that no such investment would take place and obviously growth would stop.[25] This would be a position in which - Ricardo's armageddon - the country's whole produce would, after paying wages, be in the hands of the land-owners.

This argument clearly contains a number of errors which basically turn on Ricardo's underestimation of capitalism's ability to increase agricultural productivity, but it is not really to these that I should like to turn but rather to the overall direction of Ricardo's argument. At one point Ricardo seems to be saying that in a situation when all the world's possible land was brought under corn production, then progress would be halted by a law of nature.[26] This is nonsense which exposes the limits of Ricardo's historical imagination rather starkly, for that land can charge a rent to capitalist production has everything to do with forms of land ownership and nothing to do with the volume of agricultural land. Ricardo's vision is much more acute in the short term, as opposed to this fanciful speculation at the limits of bourgeois thought. The whole thrust of Ricardo's argument up to the end of chapter six is against the corn laws in particular and the landed interest in general - showing the *Principles'* origin in his earlier polemic against those laws. A small but fertile country, Ricardo tells us, "particularly if it freely permits the importation of food, may accumulate a large stock of capital without any great diminution in the rate of profits, or any great increase in the rent of land".[27] Ricardo's overall position is confused by a typical fetishisation of private property, even of agricultural land, which it seems he could not abandon even when it would serve him to do so, but its thrust is clear. Ricardo can see no internal bounds to capital accumulation, but rather accounts for any such bounds in the survival of pre-capitalist fetters on capitalist production, which he understands as natural limits. Ricardo explicitly argues against there being any such *internal* limits,[28] and does so against Smith.

The attempt to bestow on the claim that general over-production in a capitalist economy is impossible the title of a law is identified with the name of Say. However, Say's law of markets is characteristically Ricardian, and is so not merely because the formulation of the law owes at least as much to the elder Mill as to Say himself.[29] For this law sets out what is quite characteristically Ricardo's fundamentally optimistic attitude to capital accumulation. It is true that as it is given by Say and Mill themselves the law is either a flat tautology, cancelling out the distance between production and valorisation by means of an unhelpful definition of sale and purchase, or a failure to distinguish between simple commodity production with use-value production almost immediately in mind and developed capitalist production for exchange-value accumulation. We should not expect to find this sort of thing in Ricardo. When Ricardo approvingly refers to Say, he does so in a fashion which brings out the point of substance in the law. As Ricardo renders it, Say's law has the form of a proposition that any amount of capital may be productively employed in an economy, because the only limit to demand is production.[30] There is no limit to what might be demanded should it be produced, for having sated oneself of a certain product there is always something else which one may wish to have.[31] If nature has limited the possible amount of food one may consume, there remains an infinite amount of the conveniences and ornaments of life which would be in demand once productive resources had been turned to furnishing these.[32]

Ricardo takes this distinction of food and the conveniences and ornaments of life from a passage in which Smith argued there were natural limits to the former but not the latter.[33] As with over-production of particular goods, Ricardo's tack in dealing with general over-production is to turn Smith's own arguments against themselves. This polemic seems spectacularly successful, but it seems so only by virtue of being hermeneutically tendentious. Ricardo seeks consistency by pushing the consideration of the ultimate consumption of use-values right out of the analysis of the capitalist economy and claims that his warrant for this is that Smith was inconsistent in undertaking any such consideration. "It follows", says Ricardo, "from these admissions" by Smith against his own position, "that there is no limit to demand".[34] That we can conceive of infinite demand for luxuries, Ricardo is arguing, means that there is no reason for Smith to think capital can ever satiate its markets and thus ultimate use-value consumption is irrelevant in determining the course of capitalist production.

As Smith's consideration of use-value consumption in commercial societies gives only a most confused account of the specific influences of exchange-value production on use-value production, Ricardo is of course right to claim that it is inconsistent. As Ricardo himself attributes an exemplary degree of rigour to Smith's distinction of value in use and in exchange,[35] Smith's departures from this seem to be just lapses. But Ricardo's general elimination of consideration of use-value here in fact rules out a substantial point in the very understanding of the social form of capitalism. I think that a dialogue aimed at expanding our knowledge of Smith's thought (beyond his self-comprehension) rather than outlawing part of that thought, just the opposite to that part outlawed by neo-classical economics, will raise points of great substance.

These points are, I believe, raised by Marx in the discussion of these parts of Smith and Ricardo through which he arrived at much of the economic detailing of his broad conception of the limitations of capitalism as a historical mode of production. Let us turn to the passage in the *Grundrisse* in which Marx notes that Smith's conception of the falling rate of profit is characterised by the excessive amount of theoretical work which is to be carried out by competition.[36] Smith evidently meant competition to be the mechanism not only of the levelling of the rates of profit accruing to different sectors of production but also of the lowering of the general rate of profit. The actual competitive mechanism is the same in both cases, but acceptance of the former, with its background substantiation in Smith's account of transfers of capital to their most profitable employment, does not imply acceptance of the latter, as Smith seems to think.[37] Without some auxiliary theoretical statements about the finitude of potential accumulation, the latter case cannot be regarded as substantiated, and we have seen Ricardo demonstrate that Smith does not provide this. Ricardo, of course, uses competition to achieve a general rate of profit,[38] but insists, against Smith, that competition cannot lower the general rate of profit.[39] Marx, who, of course, also equalises profit rates through competition,[40] as always recognises Ricardo's superior consistency.[41] However, what for Ricardo are merely slips by Smith are taken rather more seriously by Marx, who claims that at issue in the competitive lowering of the general rate of profit, and in the development of external trade to overcome satiation of the internal market,[42] is some comprehension of over-production as a limit to capitalist accumulation. For it is Marx's opinion that in the very consistency of Ricardo's corrections of Smith, in the very purity of the labour theory in Ricardo, something - a productive theoretical resource - is lost.

When Ricardo pushes consideration of the consumption of use-values out of the formulation of the tendency of the rate of profit to fall and depicts a completely production led demand which poses no internal limit to capital accumulation, we can hardly say, in initial response, that by such consistency in the distinction of use- and exchange-values we have come any closer to crucial features of the capitalist economy. Against the requirement of explaining what at least provisionally had to be regarded as crises grounded in over-production (or its broad synonyms), Ricardo's attitude, perhaps with a degree of hindsight available to Marx,[43] appears as a restriction on understanding. Maintaining such an attitude would appear to owe much to a pious wish that there were no such crises and to a consequent effort not to explain these episodes but rather to explain them away.[44]

Marx recognises that by comparison to the obfuscatory character of Say's law in Mill and in Say himself,[45] Ricardo's formulation of the idea does at least make the point at issue relatively clear. The question of the unlimited potential for capital accumulation is brought into focus rather than being completely conjured away. It is true to say, however, that though Marx spent some time on learning from Ricardo's formulation, his opinion of Ricardo's attitude towards questioning the potential for capital accumulation was that it was very weak - "Could there be" Marx asks, "a more childish argument?"[46]

There is, of course, something to be said for Ricardo's taking ultimate consumption to be infinite (that is to say, limited only by the volume of production) and therefore irrelevant to economics. It has proven possible in bourgeois society to identify virtually all human values with consumption as an end in itself, and if this identification is accepted, as it was by Ricardo and has been by more or less all bourgeois economics, then consumption can have no limit placed upon it even in the imagination. Marx violently disagreed with this taking of all human goals to be consumption needs, the diminution of necessary labour time being a far more important goal for him than unlimited increases in consumption. But even so he accepts that there has never been and nor could there be (in other, perhaps, than the very long term future) over-production in terms of what Marx himself calls "absolute needs".[47] Even in those periods which he regarded as being ones of over-production, Marx did not for a moment think that absolute needs had been even nearly satisfied, much less over-fulfilled. But what, Marx goes on to ask, has over-production to do with absolute needs?[48]

That Ricardo's position is impossible to maintain is easily seen. Judging by the criteria of absolute needs, even the relative over-production of *certain* goods, which is both an obvious phenomenal characteristic of capitalism and theoretically essential for Ricardo's account of profit,[49] could never have taken place. The competitive forcing down of profits in a particular branch of production could not be attributed to the absolute satiation of demand for that product, certainly not in the vast majority of cases.[50] Leaving this aside, and moving to the crucial point, in capitalism needs are effective, that is to say have a social command over production, only when backed by money. The creation of absolute needs might well be directly connected to bourgeois standards, but they remain outside of capitalism because needs not supported by money might as well not exist in so far as they are typically recognised by that mode of production.[51] Marx spent a great deal of the time in which he learned his political economy describing the capitalist historical form of the distinction of production and consumption[52] by way of a criticism of the attempt simply to elide the gap between production and the valorisation of surplus value connected with Say's law. If we recognise this gap, the question which Ricardo tries to answer definitely in the negative in his formulation of the idea behind Say's law, is whether consumption can, under capitalism, furnish adequate demand for continuously expanding production.[53] Marx's opinion is that this is not so, and further that this is intimately bound up with a tendency of the rate of profit to fall.

I intend to set out Marx's ground for this opinion at length in the next chapter as I believe it can easily be expanded to cover all of Marx's account of capitalism, but for the present I would like to sum up these remarks, as it were preliminary to my discussion of this account, by making explicit what is involved in Marx's being able to offer any opinion on this whatsoever.

I do not think that it is an adequate interpretation of the attitude Marx is taking towards Ricardo to say that Marx insists on the historically specific forms not only of production but of consumption, and that Smith is to be congratulated for having, however unclearly, anticipated such an insistence. For this is to dodge the real issue, of why consumption must be considered, and this pushes one into an artificial construction of Marx's relationship to Smith. Smith has tried to deal with a whole set of issues relating to the very identification of the character of modernity - the issues with which we can identify the very beginnings of social science - which are suppressed by the economist Ricardo as a consequence of the way he makes the labour theory a coherent measure of the magnitude of value. Marx tries to take over this coherence, drawing on Ricardo's relatively clear description of the specific structure of value, but then also to return with this to revive Smith's social issues in a more clear way.

For the crux of Marx's argument against Ricardo is not, in the first instance, a historical one.[54] Clearly, when consumption plays a determining role in a mode of production, it can do so only in a historically specific form. However, that consumption has such a role *is* a natural given, a necessity with which no conceivable historical mode of production can dispense. What is essentially the shortcoming of Ricardo's attitude to over-production is that it considers production in isolation from consumption.[55] It is true that Ricardo gives some account of the character of consumption, but the effect of his account is to make consumption irrelevant to his political economy. Production becomes, to all intents and purposes, an end in itself, for it is not understood as the furnishing of use-values to satisfy consumption demands but as merely production for exchange-value, that is to say, limitless production, production which an infinite desire for use-values will underwrite. It would seem that Ricardo is saying something like the infinite possibilities of demand are the, as it were, vacuum in which infinite capital accumulation could take place, other things being equal. He denies use-value consumption any theoretical space in the analysis of capitalism. Marx insists that this is unacceptable. Though production and consumption are subject to historical determination, the fact of their intimate relationship is not, and the study of historical forms of that relationship must begin by registering its ahistorical influence.

This is not a case where use-value components of explanation can be thought to have been added to exchange-value components, because here we have no ground for ever doing other than analytically separating those components. Though their analytical separation is vital, this must not disrupt, in fact it must deepen, our grasp of their real unity. We must grasp the implications of our dealing with a specific form of general material intercourse with nature, that is to say with properties that have a general basis but owe their specific character to their historical form. Nevertheless, the development of that historical form is in conjunction with nature; it is a product of a specific form of work on nature. We are dealing in fact, with an inter-penetration of the natural and social components of explanation, fusing them into one history,[56] because the very understanding of the particular consequences of the capitalist mode of production for the ahistorical production and consumption of use-values directly enters into the description of the social form itself.[57]

Marx begins *Capital* by reference to "The wealth of societies in which the capitalist mode of production prevails". Against the background of the use of "wealth", or sometimes "riches", as opposed to "value" in classical political economy, there can be no doubt that Marx is referring to the wealth of *use-values* in those societies, though he then goes on to say that that wealth " appears as an 'immense collection of commodities'".[58] The very description of capitalism involves historical locutions which can be made only through comparisons with other modes in respect of their wealth,[59] though the identifications of any specific modes of production at all obviously requires historical abstraction to the isolation of those modes in the first instance. Capitalism poses potentials of use-value production, in the organisation of labour through exchange-value, which are historically unprecedented. It also actualises these potentials to an unprecedented degree - in recognising this amongst the horror of primitive accumulation and the production of absolute surplus value Marx shows a remarkable depth of historical imagination. However, as I will go on to discuss in the next chapter, Marx also tries to argue that capitalism, through its positive features, posits socialism as the condition of further substantial development of the use-value productivity it has made possible.

Both Ricardo's response to Smith and the neo-classical interpretation of this are distinguished by tendentiousness. An interpretative deficiency is manifest from the very outset in the way they both celebrate Smith's inconsistency in order to discard parts of his work and emphasise others. However, the substantial point is that crucial issues are lost to both attitudes to Smith in the way they seek to be improvements upon him. Marx's position, I would say, would be that both of these responses to Smith are progressive developments, though I do not doubt that in terms of explaining capitalism he would maintain that Ricardo's is the far more valuable contribution. In Smith, a jumble of general and specific determinations flows from the inability to maintain his distinction of use-and exchange-values, but in this jumble issues which must involve the interpenetration of both of these distinguished values is present, and is lost when sorted out by, in their differing fashions, Ricardo and neo-classical economics.

Marx's attitude[60] is stronger in that it recognises in Ricardo the establishment of the specific historical structure of the capitalistic organisation of labour that is described - in an unrivalled fashion - by the labour theory of value. He goes on to insert this, in a rather more clear way than Ricardo himself (though hardly in a fashion beyond improvement), between the extant empirical world and what inevitably is given by nature in his account of capitalism, manifestly as a criticism of commodity fetishism. He does not thereby go so far as to deny a theoretical role in political economy to the relationship between people and nature that is the object of marginalist technique. Marx identifies the distance between the social relations of capitalism and the possible relations between people and nature fostered under those relations as the fundamental contradiction of that mode of production that posits socialism. This is the progressive element of marginalism set in an enlightening historical context which is more or less absent from neo-classical economics. When we now turn to Marx's own views on the limits to capital accumulation, we will see this strength, derived from immanent critique, quite clearly.

Notes

1   WN, p 266.
2   *Ibid*, p 71.
3   *Ibid*, bk 2, ch 3.
4   *Ibid*, p 352.
5   *Ibid*, p 372.
6   *Ibid*, p 373.
7   *Ibid*, p 353.
8   *Ibid*, p 113.
9   PPE, pp 290 n 291 n.
10   *Ibid*, ch 1, sec 4.
11   *Ibid*, ch 5.
12   *Ibid*, pp 121-5.
13   *Ibid*, p 80.
14   *Ibid*, pp 93, 120.
15   *Ibid*, pp 69-72.

16   *Ibid*, p 120.
17   *Ibid*, ch 2.
18   *Ibid*, p 118.
19   *Ibid*, p 93.
20   *Ibid*, pp 101-2.
21,   *Ibid*, ch 6.
22   *Ibid*, pp 125-7.
23   *Ibid*, p 71.
24   *Ibid*, pp 98-101.
25   *Ibid*, pp 120-1, 122.
26   *Ibid*, p 126.
27   *Ibid*.
28   *Ibid*, p 289.
29   Say, *Treatise on Political Economy*, vol 1, p 167. The first edition of this work contained at best only intimations of the law and before the second edition expanded these a detailed exposition of the idea had been given in Mill, *Commerce Defended*, pp 81, 83.
30   PPE, p 289.
31   *Ibid*, p 292.
32   *Ibid*, pp 293-4.
33   WN, pp 180-2.
34   PPE, p 296.
35   *Ibid*, ch 2.
36   EM, vol 29, pp 135-6.
37   WN, p 105.
38   PPE, ch 4.
39   *Ibid*, p 291 n.
40   C3, ch 10.
41   EM, vol 29, pp 136-8.
42   TSV2, p 525.
43   *Ibid*, pp 497-8.
44   *Ibid*, p 519.
45   EM, vol, pp 228, 351-2; CPE, pp 332-3; TSV2, pp 493, 502-4, TSV3, pp 100-4 and C1, p 210 n.
46   TSV2, p 506.
47   *Ibid*, p 527.
48   *Ibid*, p 506.
49   *Ibid*, p 529.

50   *Ibid*, p 507.

51   *Ibid*, p 506.

52   EM, vol 28, pp 85-7; 171-82; CPE, bk 1 pt 1, ch 2, sec 2; TSV2, pp 500-5 and C1, ch 3, sec 2 and ch 4.

53   TSV2, p 520.

54   *Vide* Groll, 'The Active Role of "Use-Value" in Marx's Economic Analysis'.

55   EPM, p 310.

56   *Ibid*, p 303.

57   Pace Mandel, 'Introduction to Volume One', pp 12-3. Mandel more or less realises that his attempt to treat general elements of production as economic trivialities is very suspect and he goes on to say that they may well figure not in "economics" but in "historical materialism, the science of modes of production". This would mean, if anything, that economics is concerned only with social statics and social dynamics are to be dealt with in historical materialism, a position the detail of Mandel's own work has always denied. Mandel is so concerned to oppose what he says to marginalism that he lapses into the dogmatic application of talismanic labels, a level of argument which, though common in his work, is far beneath what is best in it.

58   C1, p 125, quoting CPE, p 269. Cf WN, bk 1, ch 5 and PPE, ch 20.

59   GI, p 54.

60   TSV1, p 151.

8 Marx on the Limits to Capital Accumulation

Marx's own account of the limits to capital accumulation has a two-stage form, discussing the problems of simple and then of expanded reproduction, and we shall consider these in turn. In part three of volume two of *Capital*, Marx takes up again the concepts of total, C, constant, c, and variable, v, capitals and of surplus value, s, which he used to describe the structure of capitalist production in volume one, and employs them, in the context of volume two's examination of circulation, to ask two questions of the capitalist economy. First, what are the conditions of commodity exchange which would allow a given level of commodity reproduction to take place - simple reproduction? Second, what such conditions would be needed to allow this production to continue and to generate capital accumulation - expanded reproduction?

Marx approaches reproduction in this two stage fashion in order theoretically to isolate growth. Now, leaving aside accumulation is to leave aside the very goal of capitalist economic effort and involves supposing that the conditions of production remain constant when capitalism typically revolutionises them.[1] Marx insisted on these two characteristics of capitalism as much as anyone. However, it certainly is necessary to grasp the conditions of simple reproduction in order to assess potential for growth, because any level of expanded reproduction is a surplus over simple reproduction. What is more, analysis of the requisite of simple reproduction in capitalism can allow us to ask whether there is the possibility not only of stagnation in the capitalist economy but also defective simple reproduction?[2] That is to say, we can examine the strength of the capitalist process of reproduction as such.

Marx divides the capitalist economy into two departments, i producing means of production and ii producing means of consumption, giving the following model:[3]

$$\text{department i } c_i + v_i + s_i = C_i$$
$$\text{department ii } c_{ii} + v_{ii} + s_{ii} = C_{ii}$$

Of course almost any number of departments could be depicted. Marx had himself worked with a four department model in the *Grundrisse*[4] and, as he deepens his discussion of the two department model in volume two, we are given the materials, such as the distinction between necessary and luxury consumption, for a schema detailing many more departments.[5] A two department model, however, is all the apparatus needed to focus on the fundamental sociological problems of reproduction. A general element of all modes of production is that their production is directed at the satisfaction of the consumption needs of the people within them and is also directed at the provision of the means of production with which new production can take place. It is the ability of capitalism to satisfy this requisite that Marx's two department model of simple reproduction is able to put to the test.

The conditions for commodity exchange in and between departments for simple reproduction are:[6]

$$c_i + c_{ii} = C_i$$
$$v_i + s_i + v_{ii} + s_{ii} = C_{ii}$$

To reach these equilibrium conditions, constant capital reproduction charges must equal the product of department i and revenues to the labour force and capitalists (ignoring other claimants upon surplus value), that is wages and profit, must equal the product of department ii (all profits being unproductively consumed as there is no accumulation). These conditions can be determined by the most simple mathematics; mathematics that could get only increasingly complicated due to the multiplication of data and not really intrinsically more complex as one enlarged the number of departments in the reproduction model. A similarly complicated picture to the one presented by such value calculation would emerge were one to attempt, following particularly Leontiev, to chart the material inputs and outputs of decreasingly abstract departmental schemas. But when we turn to the investigation of the means by which equilibrium would actually have to be reached in the capitalist economy, the picture is not merely complicated, but is convolutedly complex as simple reproduction is shown to have to be realised through a number of economic mechanisms which are by no means in economic harmony.

As I am interested not so much in detailing these mechanisms themselves but in the overall character of the reproduction process they constitute, I will make only a few observations. Though conducted in terms of exchange-values in the capitalist economy, reproduction in that or any other economy is a question of the distribution of use-values. The difficulties inherent in this are not really adequately described by conceiving of the capitalist circulation process as a dual flow of exchange- and use-values.[7] There is only one flow, and in it the imperative distribution of use-values can be achieved only through the exchange of exchange-values.[8] We should note further that in circulation conducted in terms of exchange-values, even value equilibrium cannot be the object of bourgeois calculation.[9] It is in the spaces between values and exchange-values that the rushed destruction of capital that attends the pursuit of surplus profits by productive innovation takes place.[10] Much less than even this can the division of the production process into c, v and s as reproductive sectors be made a conscious object, for these sectors are perceived through forms of revenue - wages[11] and profit -[12] which obscure the sectors' real productive roles.[13]

One could go on, but I would like to merely add to these obstructions to simple reproduction which we must note when considering the nature of capital as a whole some mention of the obstructions which emerge when we consider that the whole capital is necessarily made up of individual capitals. These capitals typically not only lack an overall view of the economy, but conduct themselves in ways which, in their competition between each other, certainly need not even embrace their dim perception of the general economic interest and may well be antithetic to this.[14]

Even from this brief list of factors (which excludes the complications of arbitrage, interest and rent), the conclusion to which recognition of the separation of use- and exchange-values must lead, when that separation is understood not as a sundering but a mediation, is that the possibility of defective valorisation embodied in this real separation is not an isolable malfunction of the capitalist economy but a disproportionality endemic to it.[15] This disproportion can be the ground of crises through the multiplier effect of a sufficiently large initial dislocation in the allocation of resources.[16] In its characteristically unplanned outcomes,[17] *laissez faire* capitalist circulation, if not perhaps chaotic as there are certainly determinate influences at work in it,[18] has as its first and foremost law that it is conducted as if it were chaotic. That the law of the capitalist economy is chance[19] was one of the first conclusions Marx, following Engels, reached in his political economic studies,[20] and in volume two we have the full development of this central idea.

This link between Marx's earlier and later writings illustrates what I think is the main characteristic of Marx's account of the mechanisms of simple reproduction in capitalism, that these mechanisms engender a more or less complete lack of social self-consciousness of the conduct of economic life. At the end of the process of capitalist circulation, very little indeed can be seen of the social organisation of labour that is at the heart of the process. True enough, Marx believes that even the most disparate phenomena of capitalist reproduction are to be explained through the labour theory of value, but this is not to say that those phenomena easily or clearly represent the essential organisation of labour. In a sense, the science of political economy arises in order to penetrate exactly the alienation which capitalist economic mechanisms must create,[21] robbing the members of bourgeois society of social self-consciousness of their economic life. The economic phenomena of the capitalist mode of production are the material foundations of alienated social consciousness and when crises of disproportionality arise, they are grounded in this lack of social self-consciousness.

We have seen that the conditions of commodity exchange in and between the departments for simple reproduction are:

$$c_i + c_{ii} = C_i (c_i + v_i + s_i)$$
$$v_i + s_i + v_{ii} + s_{ii} = C_{ii} (c_{ii} + v_{ii} + s_{ii})$$

If we eliminate those commodity exchanges which are to take place within departments, that is, c_i will partially valorise C_i and $v_{ii} + s_{ii}$ will partially valorise C_{ii}, then we are left with the following condition of exchange between the departments for simple reproduction:[22]

$$v_i + s_i = c_{ii}$$

By reducing to this condition I do not of course mean to imply that the other exchanges will take place unproblematically. But this reduction facilitates a change of focus from problems of the very carrying out of reproduction at all in a capitalist economy to some structural contradictions which that economy presents to such a state.

In order to turn to this we must appreciate how expanded reproduction modifies this condition of exchange between departments and so must now consider accumulation. What distinguishes expanded from simple reproduction is that, in the former, part of s is reinvested in the next production cycle, augmenting the capital which enters that cycle with the aim of producing more s which can itself then be a fund for further expansion.[23] Of course, all investment for expanded reproduction in this model is, as it were, a saving by capitalists out of the possible fund for luxury consumption. The very expansion of the capital invested involved here means, however, that after a certain point both luxury consumption *and* investment can expand. Though I will discuss the relationship of luxury consumption and accumulation later, I will assume growth in both here. We must then divide up s for any capital according to where it will enter into the next cycle of production. If we let s1 be a sum which would maintain luxury consumption at its previous level, s2 be a sum which is used to increase that consumption, s3 be a sum used to increase c in the next production cycle, and s4 be a sum used to increase v in that coming cycle, then we can state the following conditions of exchange in and between departments for the, as it were, dynamic equilibrium of expanded reproduction:

$$c_i + s3_i + c_{ii} + s3_{ii} = C_i (c_i + v_i + s1_i + s2_i + s3_i + s4_i)$$
$$v_i + s4_i + s1_i + s2_i + v_{ii} + s4_{ii} + s1_{ii} + s2_{ii} = C_{ii} (c_{ii} + v_{ii} + s1_{ii} + s2_{ii} + s3_{ii} + s4_{ii})$$

Again we may reduce these conditions to the requirement of exchange between the departments:

$$v_i + s4_i + s1_i + s2_i = c_{ii} + s3_{ii}$$

This condition is obviously very similar to that for simple reproduction and indeed will simplify further when we remember that $v_i + s1_i = c_{ii}$, as this is the component of simple reproduction that must be accomplished even in expanded reproduction, and that therefore we are left with:

$$s4_i + s2_i = s3_{ii}$$

The multiple obstructions and detours through which expanded reproduction must be mediated can and do enter into contradiction with these exchange conditions, requiring us to regard instances of disproportionality here and in the consideration of simple reproduction as actualisations of chronic latent contradictions. However, a rather stronger notion of contradiction, of contradiction necessarily arising from the very working of the system, is also displayed by the capitalist economies as an obstruction to expanded reproduction. Consideration of the dynamic equilibrium conditions of exchange between the departments which we have just discussed is a good place to begin in the description of this contradiction. Marx argues overall in *Capital* that there is a chronic tendency for $c_{ii} + s3_{ii}$ to rise in value at a greater rate than $v_i + s4_i + s1_i + s2_i$. If this is so there will be a tendency for a specific disproportion in the economy, of failure to valorise $c_{ii} + s3_{ii}$, which for capitalist production will mean a breakdown in expanded reproduction.[24] This is of course an instance of disproportionality in a sense. However, as I have already intimated, we are not really dealing here with the shortcomings of the very matching of commodity flows in the capitalist economy, but with a specific structural tendency to obstruct expanded reproduction. We are dealing, in fact, with the particular disproportionality which I shall follow Marx's most common - though not completely consistent - usage in calling over-production.

From our earlier discussion of the way that capital posits an infinite urge to accumulate, we can go on to say that expanded reproduction is undertaken in order to furnish the greatest possible amount of s.[25] Two importantly distinct ways of doing this are open to the capitalist. One is to increase the mass of s by absolutely increasing v. This is the extraction of absolute surplus value that Marx describes as the formal subsumption of production to capital,[26] a process of the increase of the number of wage-labourers[27] and of the amount of time they each spend in wage-labour.[28] More important once production has been, as Marx puts it, really rather than only formally subsumed under the capitalist mode,[29] is the increase of s not through the mass of v but of the rate at which v produces s.[30] This is the production of relative surplus value.[31] If we assume that the number of wage-labourers and the length of the working day are fixed and the possibilities of increasing absolute surplus value are thus exhausted, it remains possible to increase s by increasing the part of the working day in which s is produced. s is not increased by increasing v but by increasing the rate at which v produces s, that is to say, the rate of surplus value,[32] s', which is given by $\frac{s}{v}$. Let us look at how relative surplus value may be produced and s' increased.

The increase in surplus labour-time involved in increasing s' means, of course, a decrease in necessary labour-time,[33] that is, a decline in the value of labour-power. The reduction in the value of labour-power is the mechanism of the production of relative surplus value. Now, no individual capitalist has this as a goal. It is the unplanned outcome of the invisible hand's aggregation of the drive to lower the costs of each competitive capitalist's product.[34] Furthermore, the lowering in each individual case is pursued in exchange value terms, the only terms of which the capitalist is cognisant. But the lowering must be pursued by increasing the ease of supply of the capital's product in order to lower its scarcity based value. The value of labour-power is governed by the value of the consumption goods necessary for the reproduction of the labour force.[35] Ultimately, therefore, relative surplus value is produced by increases in the use-value productivity of the labour-time spent on the commodities which go to necessary consumption. We have here Marx's formulation of Smith's insight into the unprecedented use-value productive capacity of capitalism. Marx does not place any reliance on Smith's unacceptable delimitation of the possible capacity of want, however. Marx does, it is true, see this unprecedented increase of use-value productivity as burdened by limits, but these are located in the value consequences of the technical changes required to furnish relative surplus value.

This massive impulse which capitalism gives to the improvement of the productivity of labour is obeyed basically by alterations in the composition of capital itself. The natural character of the labour process, in which use-values are produced by transforming raw material with the aid of tools,[36] means that increases in use-value productivity are gained by increases in the amount of raw material which a given amount of labour can transform, which implies an increase in the, as it were, mechanical assistance offered by the tool. This is a shift in the technical composition of the labour process; a relative increase in the means of production over living labour. All such natural considerations on the production of use-values are in themselves quite immaterial to the capitalist, except in so far as they are the technical requisite of reduction in the value of labour-power. But alterations in technical composition of course alter the value composition of capital, though of course the two are by no means the same thing.[37] There are a number of ways of assessing the value composition of capital, but the way which has proven most fruitful focuses on the amount of c in c + v, that is the organic composition of capital, given by $\frac{c}{c+v}$, which is usually designated by q.

On a cursory look at this issue, it would seem that the pursuit of relative surplus value must raise q, for the technical composition of capital is altered in favour of c by this pursuit. This conclusion directly follows, however, only given that the level of technique remains constant, so that the values of c and v per unit do not change, only their absolute amounts are increased by differing degrees in favour of c. But the very point of the effort is, we recall, precisely to increase the level of technique. Part and parcel of reduction in the value of labour-power will undoubtedly eventually be a reduction in the value of the means of production. The value of c could, then, fall as much if not more than v in the effort to produce relative surplus value, leaving net alterations in value composition quite indeterminate as to overall direction in changes in q even when we can say that the technical composition of the labour process will change in favour of the amount of means of production.[38]

Marx was of course quite well aware that reductions in the value of c per unit will follow from attempts to reduce the value of v,[39] but he did not seem to regard this as disturbing an unproblematic, virtually tautological, proportionality in the changes in q brought about by alterations in technical composition.[40] In volume three, as part of his formulation of the law of the tendency of the rate of profit to fall, he implies that there is a basic tendency for q to rise which is only, as it were antecedently, slowed by reduction in the value of c per unit.[41] I will discuss in general the presentation of "counteracting tendencies" to the falling rate of profit in volume three below. But for now we must deal with the specific point that if we are unable to really say anything about the directions of change of q, this listing of reduction in the value of c as a counteracting force to a basic tendency would be a wholly unwarranted way of speaking.[42]

Though I have followed Marx and labelled q "organic composition', I have so far spoken of the "value" and not the "organic" composition of capital as I think the essential requisite of understanding Marx's attitude to reductions in the value of c per unit as they affect q is to give organic composition a different meaning than the mere expression for value composition which it seems in much of volume three. There is some textual warrant for this. In his scripts of around 1863 Marx seems to identify organic composition with technical, not value, composition.[43] The passage in volume one where technical, value and organic compositions are defined shows that organic composition is value composition "as it is determined by and mirrors the changes in technical composition".[44] Of themselves such narrow philological issues are of little interest, but we are driven to them because there is a muddle in Marx here, but one which can relatively easily be straightened out. Establishing a distance between value and organic compositions along the lines which these passages indicate allows us ground Marx's way of presenting reductions in the value of c per unit as a counteracting force to overall increases in q in, it must be said, a clearer way than Marx himself, and this plays an important role in, to return to our starting point, the explanation of the pursuit of relative surplus value.

At time T^1, the pursuit by capital C of increased relative surplus value by increase of its technical composition will in fact take the form of a, to all intents and purposes, direct increase in its value composition. Though there may well have taken place a change in productivity that will eventually lower the value of c per unit, at time T^1 this change will not have taken place. Even if C produces a means of production only remotely related to the production of the objects of necessary consumption this will be so. For the value of c per unit is the social value and at time T^1 this remains as it was before the change in the technical composition of C. In the time lag before the recomposition of C works its way through the economy, C will, by its unequalled rate of relative surplus value, be able to win surplus profit over the general rate and may well be able to increase its market by cutting the price per unit of its product. The competitors of C will have to recompose their own capitals to compete with C and this will ultimately generally lower the value of c and v as the increase of productivity and therefore s′ become generalised. Marx uses this very explanation to account for the general rise in relative surplus value by the actions of individual capitals when those actions clearly are not in their long term interest.[45] Distinguishing organic composition from the direct value recomposition (that is, based on old values) of C due to its technical recomposition at T^1 allows us to assess both the short-term behaviour of C and its effect on the economy and the long-term changes in s′ due to the production of relative surplus value. Certainly, the effects on q of direct value recomposition and of q taken as the net value composition after reductions in c and v per unit consequent upon the multiplier effect of the technical recomposition of C would seem to be open to quantification.[46]

Let us turn to the long-term considerations which arise here. The value recomposition of a capital will, then, always represent a rise in q. However, this is not to say, to turn to this more important point, that organic composition will tend towards ever increasing values of q, for of course in assessing the overall change in value composition over successive episodes of value recomposition, we have to take into account the revaluing of c that will take place between those episodes. But with further consideration it does become necessary to say that successive value recompositions will increase the overall value of q.

At time T_1 the technical recomposition of capital C will give it a value composition in which value of q has increased, that is, in C, c will be larger and v relatively smaller than before the technical changes. Any multiplier effect of this alteration as it reflects on the new value composition of C at time T^2 can only be to lower the value of v even further. But what of the value of c? Eventually the value of c per unit certainly will be lowered, the speed of this consequence depending on the location in the economy of C's product. However, whatever this location, the reduction in the value of c per unit *ultimately* will be lower than the reduction in v. If we recall that the value of v is the value of the objects of necessary consumption, v (together with luxury consumption) represents, then, the end point, to put it this way, of the capitalist economy, consumption. Now, technical recomposition of even the most insular sphere of production of department i, producing means of production which make parts of parts of new means of production let us say, ultimately must depend on a reduction in the value of v, because the ultimate valorisation of the investment in even these recompositions remote from department ii must come from the sale of objects of ultimate consumption. New investment in any sphere of production in the *laissez faire* capitalist economy ultimately must be funded by gains in some capital's market for the production of objects of consumption. Lacking this ultimate valorisation, no investment made with the aim of producing valorisable surplus-value will take place. Obviously, for certain capitals, investment in c is so remote from the production of wage-goods that it seems as if there was no relation here, but this speaks of the limitations of an individual capital's grasp of the total economy more than of the true state of affairs.[47] The competitive accumulation impulse must eventually work towards reduction in v in order to fund any development in the productivity of c. (Though, of course, given other principles of economic organisation, increases in consumption need not be the pre-requisite of investment in the productivity of the furnishing of means of production. Investment in this area could be undertaken, let us say, simply to reduce, as an end in itself, necessary labour-time in these industries).[48] I would say, then, that c will be reduced in value per unit at a lower rate than v, because the former can typically be undertaken only in order to do the latter. Successive value recompositions will, therefore, take place on the basis of earlier value compositions which had had the overall effect of raising q.[49] In sum, organic composition, that is, to repeat, "value composition as it is determined by and mirrors the changes in technical composition", will rise cumulatively.

The tendency of q to rise with, but typically at a greater rate than,[50] capital accumulation was of the greatest interest to Marx, because he gave it a central role in his account of the law of the tendency of the rate of profit to fall,[51] a law, there can be no doubt, he thought, as much as Smith and Ricardo, of the utmost importance in the analysis of the historical location of capitalism.[52] I will for the moment exclude other variables and simply set out Marx's way of linking rising organic composition and falling profit rate, and then discuss the strength of this link in the light of the re-introduction of those variables. In this presentation I am following the way (to which I will return) in which "the law itself" is set out followed by "counteracting forces" in volume three. As the live issue is whether, in the light of the counteracting forces, the law itself can be said to describe a real tendency, this way of proceeding obviously has its shortcomings.[53] I am no doubt betraying my eventual conclusion in the very way I set about the task of examining this law. It is because I do feel the basic law to be valid for *laissez faire* capitalism and that grasping it is a pre-requisite to correctly understanding its counteracting forces *as such*, that I take over this two part way of formulating the law.

The basic point is simple enough - indeed a (mathematical) tautology.[54] Seeking relative surplus value is a contradictory goal, and therefore developed capital accumulation is a contradictory process, for the relative decline in v at which the capitalist aims must relatively reduce the source from which s is produced, for of course c does not produce s.[55] Let us calculate on the basis not of s', that is to say on $\frac{s}{v}$, but in the terms with which the capitalist is concerned (indeed even cognisant of) the rate of profit, p', that is, surplus over total capital advanced:[56] $p' = \frac{s}{c+v}$. It is evident that there is a fundamental proportionality between s' and p' determined by the amount of v in c + v such that (s' : p') : (v : c + v).[57] We can see therefore that the capitalist is faced with a relative reduction in that part of the total capital which can produce a surplus. Holding other influences constant, it is obvious that an increasing q must lower p', a tendency which will be more manifest with increasing accumulation.

One important difference, of which Marx himself made a great deal,[58] between his theory of the falling rate of profit and Ricardo's is that Marx is by no means committed to the direct opposition of profits and wages which forms the basis of Ricardo's thinking. In Marx's terms, Ricardo does not ever deal with profit. In calculating on the basis of only variable capital and surplus he deals only with surplus value, and not with surplus against total capital advanced, that is, with constant capital as well. Marx's introduction of c frees the theory of the falling rate of profit from having to rely on direct deductions from profit, the essential shortcoming of Ricardo's formulation.[59] This is of the greatest significance, for capital accumulation will involve pressures to increase c, v, s and C. Marx was able to set out the relationship of p' to s' in the light of changes in isolated aspects of production treated as variables.[60] Accumulation will give definite positive directions to the absolute growth of these variables, and by considering these we can assess the specific effect of the accumulation process on p'. I do not intend to deal with all the factors treated by Marx as countervailing forces, much less with all the other possible influences on the rate of profit of which one could conceive. Rather I mean to treat of only those which enter into the issue not because of some possible empirical conjuncture of factors, but because they are directly related to the basic structure and must therefore be part of any theoretical statement of the law of the tendency of the rate of profit to fall. Allowing what I have said about q, there remains the behaviour of s' and of the absolute growth of C.

On the first page of the chapter on 'The Law Itself', Marx illustrates the law of the tendency of p' to fall by a table in which v, s and hence s' are the same for five capitals but c is increasingly large, and shows that p thus decreases over the five capitals.[61] It has therefore seemed to some commentators that the law presupposes s' to be constant.[62] Presupposing this, the law would certainly be proven once one had established that q must rise, but of course to do this is wholly unwarranted as increases in q are the very means of increasing s'. Marx's subsequent listing of "the more intense exploitation of labour" as the first of his counteracting forces[63] would thus seem quite disingenuous. In the absence of further argument we have every right to think that counteracting force might quite annul or even reverse, indeed deny existence, to the law itself.

As a matter of fact, it is only this juxtaposition of the first page or so of chapter thirteen and the first few pages of chapter fourteen of volume three that provides textual evidence for this attribution to Marx of holding s' constant. Not only is it rather implausible to imagine that Marx forgot that he had laid the basis for part three of volume three in part four of volume one but it is made explicit enough in the rest of chapter thirteen and elsewhere[64] that Marx thought of the law as covering the rising values of s' which could be expected with accumulation. It obviously is possible to take the table in which Marx gives s' as a constant and substitute quite steeply rising values of s' and still show p falling.[65] Of course, these values are all quite arbitrary and were one to give even higher values of s', then p could be shown as stable or even rising. What we have to do in the absence of firm empirically derived figures,[66] is to try to assess theoretically the likely relation of q and s' with the progress of accumulation. Marx actually did consider this at some length in the *Grundrisse* and reading the relevant pages would seem to be - judging by the history of the understanding of Marx on this point - a pre-requisite of evaluating the statement of this argument in *Capital*.

The fundamental point is that, as Marx puts it when introducing the importance of s' in determining its absolute mass in volume one, "there are limits, which cannot be overcome", to the compensation for a relative decline in v by a rise in s'. As long as necessary labour has any positive value, the amount of surplus labour must be less than 24 hours in a day[67] and, of course, the working day is shortened by political action beneath this absolute maximum.[68] Marx seems in *Capital* to have thought this sufficient. In volume three, he briefly repeats that there are definite limits to the degree to which a rising s' can compensate for a relatively declining v and gives the illustration that "two workers working for twelve hours a day could not supply the same surplus-value as twenty four workers each working two hours", even if the former "were able to live on air and hence scarcely needed to work at all for themselves".[69] As I hope to make clear, I have little sympathy with the lament that all would have been well had Marx finished volumes two and three, but it is to be regretted that Marx did not make as clear in *Capital* the relation of these limits to the actual working of the law of the tendency of the rate of profit to fall as he did in the *Grundrisse*.

In the *Grundrisse*, Marx outlines, through some rather weakly worked out examples in fact, what must mathematically follow from the statement of the above limits, once one had secured, and this is all implied in allowing a rising value of q, the real significance of those limits. Although this is not necessary, let us follow Marx's numerical examples, though making necessary corrections. Let us take necessary labour time as ½ the working day. Let us further assume that labour productivity doubles. Necessary labour time is therefore now only ¼ of the working day. However, though the productive force has doubled, surplus labour time and surplus value have grown by only ¼. "If the productive force is quadrupled, then the original relation (between necessary and surplus labour) becomes ⅛ and the value grows by only ⅛". To go even further: "If necessary labour were only 1/1000 (of the working day) and the productive force tripled then it (necessary labour) would fall to only 1/3000, or surplus labour would have increased by only 2/3000".

What these examples illustrate is that the surplus value of capital cannot increase as does the multiplier of the productive force and that the disparity here will increase with every previous raising of the level of productivity. The pursuit of relative surplus value must involve diminishing returns in the terms of the improvement in s' gained by a raising of q and this pursuit must become increasingly difficult with every succeeding effort.[70] It is this development of the need to recompose ever-larger capitals, in which c must be growing far faster than v, in order to gain ever smaller improvements in s' as capital accumulation progresses that Marx begins to describe with the law of the tendency of the rate of profit to fall. There are two cumulative multipliers cutting away at the rate of profit. Doubling productivity requires c to double, and redouble, and so on. But doubling productivity can only halve v, and then cut that half by half, and so on. Given any more than an infinitesimal increase in q, and one intuitively allows vast increases, this relationship of s' to c must rapidly threaten p'.

It is important to bear in mind that these statements of a relation do not tell us anything about the absolute amounts of c, v and s involved in any C.[71] Marx is speaking of total capital, capital in general, and the outlook for individual capitals of varying absolute sizes can be very different within this overall picture. I will discuss the absolute dimensions of capital in a moment, but first, I would like to complete these remarks on the relation of s' to q by offering some explanation of how "more intense exploitation of labour" can sometimes feature entirely as a counteracting force to the tendency of the rate of profit to fall. What Marx seems to have in mind here - and his unfinished exposition is very confused at points - are exceptional (if common in many areas or even prevalent in some areas) ways of increasing p other than by raising s'. These can include sweating, an extraction of surplus value by consistently paying less than the market price of wages for all the hours spent in labour, which is in fact a sort of peculiar increase in absolute surplus value; or fixing wage levels per hour less than the value of labour power; or any of a number of other possibilities. Marx feels able to set out such methods as counteracting factors because the usual method of raising s' is, precisely, to raise q, and these other methods which do not raise q are exceptional. They certainly would counteract the basic tendency of p' to fall because they raise s' without the usual consequence of this, a further increase in q, following,[72] but their relatively exceptional character allows them to be treated as a secondary consideration.

I intend now to turn to a factor which in a sense does not have a place in a discussion of p' as it does not directly affect that rate. However, I consider this factor, the possibility of absolute growth in C, indispensable to setting out the context in which the tendency of p' to fall works. In other words, I would say that the consideration of this factor by "under-consumption theories"[73] which give alternative accounts of crisis to that of the law of the tendency of p' to fall is a mistake, for these two main lines of the explanation of capitalist crises are mutually complementary, indeed are mutually constitutive.[74]

A rise in q would have no detrimental effect on the absolute mass of profit, though the profit rate would fall, if the accumulation of C took place at such a pace that the absolute growth or restricted absolute decline of v produces, even at the increasing values of s', a mass of s that counterbalances the influence of the relative growth of c on the profit rate.[75] A capital will, of course, always seek to employ as much v (and c) as possible,[76] and in fact for larger capitals this mass of v has served very well as the base of continued accumulation,[77] giving these capitals a great advantage over small capitals.[78] Though in the absence of firm statistics about increases in q one can really only guess, we might straight away suspect that the rates of growth in C required for this compensatory effect are, after a certain point has been reached in concentration and centralisation, fanciful.[79] However, we can get rather closer to an examination of this possibility by focusing upon what must certainly be part of it, and which is something we might initially imagine to be part of accumulation as such, a tendency to full employment.[80]

An obvious consequence of increasing accumulation would be a growing demand for labour-power. For Ricardo, as we might expect from his conception of the relationship of wages to profits, this was a serious obstacle to capitalist progress. But if he saw nature eventually posing difficulties for such progress by the recalcitrance of agricultural production, nature fortunately came to the rescue in this instance. The doctrine of population identified with Malthus' name[81] has a central place in classical political economy largely through that body of thought's reliance upon the doctrine for the restriction of wages to a level commensurate with capital accumulation, a reliance from which Ricardo was not exempt. The argument runs basically thus: as accumulation progresses the demand for labour will rise and wages will increase. This will be an increase in real as well as money wages. In this position, the market price of labour being above its natural price will represent an improvement in the labourers' conditions. Profits will by this very token be restricted and an obstacle to further accumulation will have arisen. However, the rise in the labourers' conditions will eventually be reflected in an increased labouring population, due to this population's peculiar tendency to expand (geometrically) to the maximum possible given a certain level of provision, and this will redress the balance of supply and demand for labour even at the new level of accumulation. This reduces wages to their natural level or even, by a reaction, for some time below that level.[82]

Marx's analysis of capitalism clearly required some similar tailoring of the price of labour-power to the needs of accumulation, but this solution given by Ricardo was anathema to him and is undoubtedly that part of *The Principles* from which Marx gained the least. Looking at the tone of Marx's writings on this issue, it seems that Marx's ability to see the recurrent cynicism of Smith and Ricardo in a light which set it off to best effect quite left him in the case of Malthus' population theory.[83] However I would certainly place great weight on Marx's own account of why this was so.

Marx unambiguously placed Malthus' general political economy[84] in the category of a vulgar economic regression from Ricardo, and he saw the population theory not as wedded to the progressive capitalist interests of the time when the bourgeoisie played a historically revolutionary role, but as a reactionary response to capitalism's contradictions as it establishes its historical limits.[85] The spectacle of a cleric urging the rich to consume unproductively in order to maintain in the face of its contradictions an economic system whose imposition of narrow necessity on the labouring population was nonetheless to be brutally enforced was no doubt somewhat hard to bear to a humanitarian who saw in those contradictions the possibility of the end of all domination by necessity.[86] However, our judgment must, as Marx would surely have said, turn on our evaluation of the theory of population as a scientific theory. If we can say that Malthus had a brutal (by our standards) disposition and Marx an (overall) generous one, whether Malthus was a cynical reactionary or Marx a utopian idealist turn on whether the theory of population is true.

On this point, Marx's scholarly contempt was profound, exposing through his enormous acquaintance with the political economic and related literature such a degree of intellectual indebtedness on Malthus' part that Marx thought him a plagiarist.[87] The basic line of Marx's substantive criticism runs as follows. Malthus' geometrical reproduction law is, because it sets out to describe a natural difference between human and other animal reproduction, not a human law but a natural one. The theoretical formulation of this law is very shaky,[88] but this shakiness is a necessary result of what is an attempt to subordinate all the particular historical forms of the influences on human population which have obtained to one supra-historical formulation. There are no doubt real determinations on population growth in all historical epochs, but they are certainly set by modifications on the natural basis of population that must be historically, as they cannot be naturally, explained.[89] In the case of population under capitalism, Marx has no doubt that Malthus has seen a real phenomenon of this mode of production - surplus population.[90] In his theory of relative surplus population or the industrial reserve army, Marx gives an account of this phenomenon quite parallel to that of Malthus,[91] but an alternative historical account.

Let us consider again the impetus to wage rises given by capitalists' competition for labour-power during a period of expansion. Given the expanded scale of reproduction with accumulation, it would seem certain, Marx allows, that the demand for labour-power would eventually exceed customary supply and wages thus rise.[92] During the period of the formal subsumption of production to the capitalist mode, the basic solution to this was expansion of the number of wage-labourers. Though Marx mentions this in *Capital*,[93] it is *Wage-Labour and Capital* (to which Marx refers in the passage in *Capital*) that is the foremost explanation of this process which Marx gives. An assessment of this solution should bear strongly in mind that this published speech was given in 1847. In the developed capitalist production described in *Capital* we can disregard the possibility of recruiting wage-labour from non-capitalist sectors of the economy, but nevertheless Marx still thought wage rises would be restricted to a level compatible with accumulation.

The basic reason for this is that the purchase of labour-power is conditional upon the capitalist's being able to produce a valorisable surplus-value with that labour-power.[94] Assuming a rise in wages which makes v dearer for C, one of two cases might obtain. The price of v may continue to rise because this rise does not interfere with the progress of accumulation. Though the increasing cost of v may be a deduction from possible profits, the growing mass of profit that is the desired effect of accumulation might easily outweigh this unavoidable cost of such growth. What we are dealing with here is the mass of profit accruing to large capitals compensating them for declines in rates of profit, which essentially is Marx's explanation for the nineteenth century co-existence of the vast accumulation of British capital and the rise in the real wage of the British worker.[95] The second possible case is that the wage rise does interfere with accumulation. To the extent that it does so, the profit incentive for accumulation will be lessened and accumulation will slow down. But in slowing down, the cause of the wage rise, the disproportion between the demands of expanding capital and the labour force, will tend to disappear. The price of labour will again fall to a level corresponding to capital's requirements for self-valorisation, whether this level is the same as or lower or higher than before.

For Marx, it is this characteristic of the accumulation process to remove the very obstacles it temporarily creates that explains the cyclical character of *laissez faire* capitalist accumulation, or to put this the other way around, crises. It is not, as the population theory has it, fluctuations in population that affect accumulation, but rather the reverse which is the case.[96] Marx not only was quick enough to observe that the real crises he had seen were describing a cycle of far too short a period to be linked to generational population shifts, but also that the range of capitalist responses to these difficulties were by no means limited to passively waiting for population growth, but embraced actively changing the pattern of accumulation.[97] Fundamentally, however, what he stressed in his foundation for an explanation of the cyclical character of capitalist accumulation is that such a movement was historically impossible before the establishment of the developed capitalist economy. The possibility of bringing great productive resources to bear in a short time is the requisite of an equally rapid contraction. This is quite unimaginable without the development of the economic mobility that is the essence of ever-accumulating capital and ever fluid wage-labour.[98] The, as it were, reflected consequences of accumulation for the labour force cannot have a directly natural cause. They are inconceivable without a specific historical structure of production - capitalism.

The relinquishment of the population theory in later economic explanations of the industrial cycle has resulted (disregarding the biological criticisms) from the evidence of the persistence of that cycle in a capitalism socialised to the point where the clear correlation of labour force changes and economic growth can by no means be linked to the mortality rates of the entire working class. Marx grasped this point the other way around. Were capital to wait until, to speak bluntly, enough workers had starved to death to make accumulation profitable again, capital might find that its dominance of the production process had been wrested from it by those who wanted to work in order to live even when they could not work in order to make a profit.[99]

It might be thought that this foundation for a theory of crises can allow of only a very limited degree of accumulation before any further capital expansion would necessarily run into labour shortage. However, this is not to take into account those consequences of accumulation which free it from a direct tie to the labour force. Leaving aside the consequence of concentration and centralisation that they would allow expanding capitals to absorb the labour forces of now liquidated other capitals, what I am speaking about is of course the accumulative spur to productivity. Accepting a rising value of q and a rising s' as bound up in accumulation, there will be, Marx says, the tendency for relative surplus population, or an industrial reserve army, to be built up with capitalist progress.[100] Although aware that the English and Welsh birthrate was steadily falling[101] (a phenomenon we can now say is common to all the advanced bourgeois societies), Marx evidently thought that such was the rate of rise in organic composition and relative surplus value that the production of the industrial reserve army would continue. In this, Marx followed Ricardo's change of mind over the possibility of labourers who were "set free" from one branch of production always having an opportunity to be re-employed in another branch - the compensation theory as it was called.[102] Instead of this constant smooth redeployment, the aftermath of each capitalist boom and slump would be a recomposed capital in which q was higher and the relative surplus population greater. This population serves as an industrial reserve army, the especially fluid labour resources that are needed to undertake the great new venture of the boom and which by their expansion of the available labour force at these times lower the pressures for wage rises. Marx distinguishes three forms of existence of the relative surplus population - the floating, the latent and the stagnant - depending on their place in the industrial reserve army determined by their distance from taking up employment,[103] but this need not concern us here.

What is fundamentally different between Marx's idea of relative surplus production and Ricardo's eventual rejection of the compensation theory is that whereas the latter is, as it were, an adjunct to a doctrine of wages and relies on an avowedly biological theorem extrinsic to political economy, the former is an integrated whole. The ground of Marx's tying of wages to the requirements of accumulation and of the formation of relative surplus population to the progress of capital accumulation is his basic characterisation of the capitalist mode of production. We are dealing here with the relationship of paid to unpaid wage-labour as it develops in the mode of production predicated upon wage-labour.[104] When in a boom period the unpaid labour extracted from the labourers would require too much paid labour in order to be reconverted into capital, that paid labour will be curtailed to a degree which re-establishes the dominance of unpaid labour. Equally, when the reconversion of unpaid labour into capital with ever increasing amounts of c relative to v takes place, the consequence is that paid labour will again be curtailed to the best situation for the unpaid labour.[105]

In the industrial reserve army, Marx's critique of the alienation consequent upon capitalist production reaches its most developed point. When the products of labour have been given such a form that living labour is subordinated to them, and not the other way around,[106] then and only then is it possible that the development of productive power will be carried out in order to augment the size of the productive forces as an end in itself and not, for example, to diminish necessary labour. The ultimate result of the vast expansion of productivity through capital accumulation is not that necessary labour is reduced for all, but that some population becomes relatively surplus. Having described the massive powers of machine production, Marx goes on approvingly to quote JS Mill to the effect that "It is questionable if all the mechanical inventions yet made have lightened the day's toil of any humn being"[107] and, if this now somewhat exaggerated, the point still strongly obtains that gains in productivity are normally not channelled into reduction of necessary labour time.[108] Every working day, indeed, increases the domination of the fetishised products of men and women's work over their living labours.[109]

The competitive raising of wages is not the only, indeed it is not the most fundamental, obstacle to an absolute growth of production that would provide for large individual capitals a mass of s that can compensate for relatively low values of v and p. A truly basic difficulty in the way of this possibility arises with the establishment of the capitalist form of the relation of production and consumption itself.

Let us again consider the position of capital C as it seeks to accumulate. There can be no mistake about the strength of the intention here - the aim is an infinite, because purely quantitative, growth. Recognition of this consequence of the very nature of capital not only tells us a great deal about the absurd fetishism of capitalist production as such, it is also of the first importance in understanding specific acts of capitalist marketing strategy. When C expects to expand, it typically does so with unlimited ambition. C's aim is not to satisfy a certain need for a use-value to a required degree. It cannot with any reliability know of such needs, for we are specifically not dealing here with the pre-planned allocation of resources, and in any case such knowledge is not what is most important to it. If C can expand its market for a relatively frivolous use-value it will do so, even if this is at the expense of the existing volume of consumption of another capital's relatively essential use-value. C will attempt to expand its market as far as possible and, under the pressures of competition, so must C's rivals. The form of capitalist growth is, then, to seek the infinite expansion of each individual capital.

If it could, C would all at once produce an infinite surplus value.[110] But we are dealing here with a form of general productive intercourse with nature and though C's aims may be posited in the terms of only quantitative value, it may realise those aims only through the production of specific commodities with specific use-values. These commodities must be valorised if they are to serve the purposes of C's accumulation.[111] With the vast increase in productivity that characterises capitalism, very soon indeed in the history of that mode of production this means an expansion of consumption.[112] Extrinsically Marx thought the construction of a world market for goods as much part of the dynamic establishment of capital's domination as the creation of general wage-labour.[113] Intrinsically, Marx took the historical expansion of needs through the creation of the means by which those needs may be realistically conceived to be a most important part of capital's unprecedented civilising influence.[114] Such expansions of consumption ultimately must be of wage-goods or luxury goods, for as I have mentioned in another context, investment in, and we can now say consumption of, the means of production is limited in the *laissez faire* capitalist economy by the final sale of consumption goods.

There are definite limits, however, to consumption under *laissez faire*, limits which contrast rather starkly with the ideology of infinite want which accompanies the capitalist form of efforts to expand production. I will continue to assume that luxury consumption by capitalists and necessary consumption by wage-labourers are the only forms of consumption and that the fund for accumulation is a deduction from the possible fund for luxury consumption.

The in some respects characteristic capitalist attitude to luxury consumption has, as is well enough known, been an abstemious one,[115] an attitude representing a time when individual capital formation did, as a matter of fact, substantially depend on the personal savings of a capitalist. Of course, to treat this as an act of abstinence by the capitalist which is paid for by profits, the capitalist's wage for renunciation,[116] is apologetic nonsense. But if the source of profits in this idea is fictitious, the abstemiousness which the idea rationalises was not. The temptation to invoke such a useful defence of the very existence of capitalists prolonged the abstinence theory's life beyond the years in which it retained its phenomenal referent in initial capital formation, and the defence was still used when capitals were yielding volumes of s such that luxury consumption and the fund for accumulation could both increase spectacularly. This shift in the behaviour of capitalists from that described in Weber's 'The Protestant Ethic and the Spirit of Capitalism' to that of Veblen's *The Theory of the Leisure Class* (the latter in fact written before the former) was enough for Marx to dismiss the abstinence theory.[117] Certainly, without the greatest widening of the sense of " abstinence", the fact that large capitalists after a certain point in the history of capital formation did not consume all surplus-value is hardly abstinence, and absolutely not to be compared with the sacrifice of labour as described by Smith, which comparison Senior intended. Such is the volume of s that really the whole language of " savings" was virtually redundant for large capitalists when Marx wrote - virtually unlimited consumption could accompany accumulation. In so far as luxury consumption can still adversely affect a specific capital's expansion by depleting the necessary fund for accumulation, we can say that for any continuing capital, the use of s for luxury consumption will be fitted (hardly, I repeat, curtailed) to allow of accumulation at a competitive level.[118]

I have mentioned that part of Marx's scorn for the abstinence theory stemmed from his displeasure at the lack of consistency of capitalists' rejection of abstinence - except in the very widest possible sense - for themselves when coupled with their enthusiastic advocacy of the salutary effects of privation on the industry of wage-labourers, a privation which they, the capitalists, enforce in a sort of vicarious abstinence.[119] As it is obviously the case that wage rises are a deduction from possible profits,[120] the typical capitalistic attitude to wages must be one of minimisation. I say must be, because wages are a cost open to competitive reduction at least as much as the price of any element of constant capital.[121] Fundamentally, wages will be driven down to the minimum by capital because from the point of view of capitalist *production* the livelihood of the majority of the population is a cost.[122] This is to touch on the vexed issue of the "immiseration thesis" in Marx. I will leave discussion of this for the next chapter as we can allow the tendency to keep wages to a minimum without taking up any position on what that minimum means physiologically and socially.

In a period of significant expansion fundamentally due to an increase in relative surplus value gained by the organic recomposition of an influential amount of total capital, wages may rise due to competition for labour-power. When the new level of productivity is generalised, if not before, the value of labour-power will have fallen. As a result of these compound movements, wages will have risen above the value of labour-power. In the slump, wages will tend to fall. One can imagine a number of possibilities here, but let us first assume that money wages return to their original level. Of course, in this case, though the money wage has not changed, the real wage has risen. Also depending on the reduction in necessary labour-time that has occurred in the raising of relative surplus value, money wages might fall and yet real wages rise.[123] In both of these cases there will have been a rise in profit, surplus value having risen and the money wage not having increased. The money wage can increase and profit still rise either if, because of increased productivity, the number of workers falls to such an extent that wage per worker will not increase v for C, or if v rises but only at a level which still yields a larger profit to capital out of increased s'. There is a maximum level to which wages can rise. It is the level at which accumulation is profitable, and thus the settling of the market value of labour-power after a boom will, we see, also set the new value of labour-power.[124]

There are obviously common themes in all of these possible outcomes of alterations in wages with periods of capital accumulation. Marx, however, left it open as to which specific outcomes would follow because he thought that, although we can say that capital will seek to reduce wages to the minimum possible, what exactly wages would be as a result of changes in the value of labour-power is the unpredictable result of struggle between capital and labour in any period.[125] This element of indeterminacy is regrettable but, when I return to this subject in the next chapter, I hope to show it is in principle remediable. For the present, however, I think it is sufficient to note the limits within which wage rises may vary within a period of capital accumulation and to say that this by no means precludes, in fact it may lead us to expect, some real wage rises with accumulation.

Any such wage rises are the working class' share in the proceeds of accumulation. This being so, the amount of wages cannot tell us everything about them - there is the further consideration of the relative size of this share in the general enrichment. It is very easy indeed to conceive of values of the increase in relative surplus value that will confer to the capitalist a relatively greater share of the increase in social wealth than accrues to the working population even with a wage increase.[126] This can be interpreted in material terms as a vast improvement in the livelihoods of capitalists which the relatively tiny improvement in the working class' living standards very poorly emulates. But I do not think this is principally what Marx had in mind in this idea of relative wages. This was really the working class' production by its labours of the social power of capital that grows ever more relatively strong with accumulation. Many of Marx's comments on wages, including his criticisms of Weston, show that he did not identify struggle over wages with the pursuit of narrow material gain,[127] confirming the impression one receives from his earliest critiques of wage-labour that it is the theme of the self-production of an alien power that is central.

It is the collision of strategies of the expansion of production which can know no internal limit to its cumulative acceleration and of expansions in consumption which are only grudgingly won from that system that Marx regarded as further developing the possibility of crises in the capitalist economy.[128] I have mentioned earlier that Marx saw this possibility, at the most abstract level, as contained in breakdowns in the circulation circuit of capital - money - enlarged capital, and we can now see that dislocation between the production of surplus value and its valorisation for the purpose of further accumulation is subject not merely to chronic disproportionality but to acute contradiction due to the capitalist forms of production and consumption. I will sketch out a form of the actualisation of this possibility in crises shortly, but for now I would like to return to the scheme of expanded reproduction in order to detail the position we have now reached.

Recalling our statement of the condition of exchange between departments for achieving the dynamic equilibrium of expanded reproduction, that is $v_i + s4_i + s1_i + s2_i = c_{ii} + s3_{ii}$, we can pinpoint the contradiction we have found in the capitalist economy. Given rising organic compositions and the inability of capital to offset, through various compensations, the tendency which these give to p' to fall, we will find this tendency manifested in a growing difficulty of the valorisation of the accumulating constant capital of the department ii by the relatively slowly growing variable capital and surplus value of department ii. This means, in essence, an unsaleable mass of consumer goods.[129] We can see two reasons for this.

First, it is now clear that the rates of expansion displayed by the two departmental sectors will be dramatically different, so that $s4_i + s2_i < s3_{ii}$. For $s4_i$ will relatively fall as a result of increases in q, and $s2_i$ will also relatively decline as $s3_i$ takes an increasingly dominant share of s_i. By contrast, $s3_{ii}$ will participate in the general relative rise of c in the entire production process. Second, to develop a point made earlier, the growth of c_{ii} is incremental in a way which the growth of $v_i + s1_i + s2_i$ is not. These revenues, I have assumed, make up the consumption fund (any departure from this assumption can only strengthen the case I am about to make). They may grow, but being consumed in any production cycle, each cycle can contain only a specific revenue sum. However c, given simple reproduction, will always enter into the cycle with an existing value, and the reproduction of that value is the starting point of accumulation. And after a period of accumulation, it is the reproduction of the now increased value of c that is the new starting point of further accumulation.[130] I am not speaking here of the fact that fixed capital will typically yield only part of its value to each turnover period of capital.[131] I am referring to the reproduction of already existing constant capital values that is the starting point of accumulation. This is a crucial issue.

I have argued that Smith was forced to conclude that the labour theory of value did not hold in commercial societies because his idea of the labour involved was defective. He included the costs of the widespread individually owned means of production in the revenue accruing to labour in early societies. When noting that the means of production in commercial societies were the property of a restricted number of owners, he drew the erroneous conclusion that labour no longer accounted for the price of commodities. What happens in his analyses of reproduction is that constant capital in capitalist societies disappears and I have noted that Marx tried to remedy this in his own analysis of reproduction. It is not, however, the narrowly quantitative matters that concern us here, but the description of the form of reproduction under capitalism. In making any new value, the worker, by the very nature of the labour process' utilisation of tools and raw materials, must embody in that new value the value of these means of production. The production of surplus value is a question of the worker being able to produce goods of more value in a working period than he or she requires to support him or herself over that period. But in the production of these goods, the value of the utilised means of production is also transferred.[132] For capital, the labour process will accomplish the reproduction of the existing value of the means of production in the same moment as new values are created. The size of capital is thus increased with every cycle of accumulation. This actualises the cumulative multiplier after the fashion of geometrical growth which we have identified in the law of the tendency of the rate of profit to fall.

The profound contradiction between the infinite urge to expand capital and the minimising attitude to necessary consumption will, given the revolutionary pace of accumulation under *laissez faire* capitalism, quickly manifest itself as the characteristic feature of production really subsumed under capital.[133] By dint of its labour, the working class produces historically relatively vast forces of production. But under the capitalist form of productive relations with nature, those forces are an alien power which stands against its producers. Beyond a certain extent of development, Marx is however arguing, the continued production of this power will involve increasingly severe disruptions in productive relations with nature whilst they remain subsumed to the capitalist form. Let us now turn to Marx's detailing of these disruptions.

We are now able to sum up Marx's analysis of capital through the crucial concept of over-production. The way I would like to do this is to directly address some passages in his economic writings which at once seem replete with very important material but which have been very resistent to interpretation.

The first of these is the following immediately striking[134] section of the *Grundrisse* in which Marx is discussing the inherent limits of capital:

> there is a limit, not inherent to production generally, but to production founded on capital...It is enough here to demonstrate that capital contains a *particular* restriction of production - which contradicts its general tendency to drive beyond every barrier of production - in order to have uncovered the foundation of *overproduction*, the fundamental contradiction of developed capital...The inherent limits have to coincide with the nature of capital, with the essential character of its very concept. These necessary limits are:
>
> 1. *Necessary labour* as limit to the exchange value of living labour capacity or of the wages of the industrial population;
>
> 2. *Surplus value* as limit on surplus labour time; and, in regard to relative surplus labour time, as barrier to the development of the forces of production;
>
> 3. What is the same, the *transformation into money*, exchange value as such, as limit of production; or exchange founded on value, or value founded on exchange, as limit of production. This is:
>
> 4. Again, the same as *restriction of the production of use values by exchange value*; or that real wealth has to take on a *specific* form distinct from itself, a form not absolutely identical with it, in order to become an object of production at all...Hence over-production, the sudden reminder that all these necessary moments of production are founded on capital.[135]

It is, I am sure, correct to read this passage as the initial outline of what we have discussed in its more developed form - Marx's characterisation of capitalism as subject to chronic, incremental crises of over-production.

First, then, necessary labour is, if not the limit of the exchange value of living labour capacity, at least a constant limitation placed upon that value. We have seen that from the point of view of production, capital regards living labour as a cost, as indeed follows from labour-power's position as a commodity like any other. Wages will therefore be restricted as far as possible to the minimum set by necessary labour. Rises in real wages can typically be achieved only through political action to expand the historical and moral content of the minimum standard of the reproduction of labour-power.

Second, surplus value is the limit placed by capital on the amount of surplus labour time that will be worked. For capital will withdraw from production if it cannot valorise the surplus value produced by surplus labour. In so far as the main impetus to the development of the forces of production under capitalism is the pursuit of relative surplus value by the reduction of necessary labour time, the condition of valorising surplus value must stand as a potential barrier to such development.

Third, the possibility of the transformation of capital into money, the possibility of the valorisation of surplus value, will limit production if it is subject to difficulties. There is a double transformation here, of capital into money by the transformation of the use-values produced by capital into the exchange-value which is capital's aim. This latter transformation is ultimately dependent upon the volume of final consumption, and within this on the volume of the consumption of wage-goods. This is to say, the demands of valorisation predicated upon increases in the value of necessary consumption will contradict the essential thrust of capitalist production which is to drive this value down relative to constant capital costs.

Fourth, we are thus fundamentally presented with the restriction of the production of use-values by the form of exchange-value. The form of production in which exchange-value, that is to say commodity production, is generalised, capitalism, will eventually posit the continuation of its own form - of value and surplus value - as a barrier to the expanded production of use-values. Hence over-production; because at certain points in the progress of accumulation the continued expansion of production founded upon this contradictory basis will experience the effects of those contradictions in the breakdown of the accumulation process. The distance between capital and money will widen so far as to be a breach, and this breach will be materially represented in an unsaleable mass of consumer goods, which mass will have an, as it were, reverse multiplier effect on even sectors of the economy producing means of production. Of course, this is not absolute over-production, but it is certainly over-production on the basis of capital. The term "over-production" might be replaced by, for example, under-consumption or over-accumulation, both of which perhaps do more to show the specifically capitalist nature of these episodes. But on reflection over-production brings out this historical peculiarity of these episodes more fully. Crises in the developed capitalist economies are historically unique in that they result from superabundance and not from scarcity (though the latter type can occur exceptionally), and in having this form they declare that human beings have only to consciously dominate their own social life in order to end their domination by nature.

The second rather difficult passage which I would like to try to explain is to be found in what we have as chapter fifteen of volume three, the third chapter on the law of the tendency of the rate of profit to fall entitled 'Exposition of the Law's Internal Contradictions'. Marx here draws his depiction of the immanent contradictions of capitalist production together in order to explain their most obvious manifestation - crises. Having begun to explain his idea that the capital accumulation process contains a contradiction, Marx continues:

> To express this contradiction in the most general terms, it consists in the fact that the capitalist mode of production tends towards an absolute development of the productive forces irrespective of value and surplus value considerations,

and even irrespective of the social relations within which capitalist production takes place; while on the other hand its purpose is to maintain the existing capital value and to valorise it to the utmost extent possible...The methods through which it attains this end involve a decline in the profit rate, the devaluation of the existing capital and the development of the productive forces of labour at the cost of the productive forces already developed. The periodical devaluation of the existing capital, which is a means, immanent to the capitalist mode of production, for delaying the fall in the profit rate and accelerating the accumulation of capital value by the formation of new capital, disturbs the given conditions in which the circulation and reproduction process of capital takes place, and is therefore accompanied by sudden stoppages and crises in the production process.[136]

Capital must, Marx is saying, drive beyond all barriers to production and is able to posit only the absolute development of the productive forces. Though it does this as a result of the competitive enforcement of its own intrinsic nature, capital will find that this development eventually will contradict its nature. Nevertheless, capital will continue to pursue this development even when it threatens capitalist social relations of production - value and surplus value - because each individual capital must do so even at the expense of the interest of capital as a whole. The specific acts through which the development of the productive forces is brought about are cycles of individual capitals' expansion involving the production of surplus value, its valorisation and its subsequent use as a fund for accumulation. The paramount method of the production of surplus value for developed capitalism is the production of relative surplus value, but this is the very process by which capital is brought into conflict with the future expansion of the productive forces. For in creating relative surplus value, capital also creates a tendency of p' to fall and a restricted (by comparison to the growth of the productive forces) market in which that tendency will be actualised in crises.

Crises are in fact periodical devaluations of capital which allow of the cyclical reproduction of the contradiction laden process. After a significant organic recomposition of capital, a certain amount of capital will be producing at above the hitherto existing socially average level of productivity. The volume of output will probably expand because the recomposed capital will attempt to enlarge its market at the expense of its competitors and those competitors will not have altered their behaviours as they are not as yet aware of the challenge. Given the finitude of markets which the capitalist distribution of income affects, any improvement in productivity of real significance will eventually result in unsaleable stocks of consumer goods.

The degree to which this will follow, and to which this glut will affect the whole economy, obviously will depend on numerous factors, but we have seen in the previous chapter that no distinction in principle can be drawn between over-production of specific goods and general over-production. It requires only certain assumptions about the size and range of the increase in productivity in order to generate a model of general crisis. These assumptions are not susceptible to theoretical elaboration here; they are too embedded in specific empirical circumstances. However, it is consonant with the massive disproportion Marx clearly believes develops in capital between the growth of the productive forces and the growth of consumption to postulate that after a certain point in the accumulation of capital further accumulation must tend towards production of general crises. That point is determined by capital's pushing of productivity up to the level where the value of labour power cannot absorb wage goods output. From this point the system is chronically prone to crisis.

Faced with the impossibility of selling all of their commodities, certainly at their prices of production, capitals will compete with one another for market shares. Marx here, we can see, provides some account of the conditions in which competition will lower p', effectively reversing the thrust of Smith's explanation.[137] This competition will reduce the value of commodities towards levels compatible with the new level of productivity. Of course, this will amount to the devaluation of commodities produced by the older methods, commodities which now perhaps simply cannot be sold or can be sold only below their price of production or below even their cost price. All forms of future undertaking calculated on the basis of the old values are thereby thrown into confusion as negotiable instruments which are to be honoured through the proceeds of present production and securities in future production also are devalued. (It is well to note that in so far as the commercial credit apparatus both speeds up the introduction of major new means of production and prolongs the time at which capitals using old methods may continue production, then this apparatus will deepen the extent of the eventual devaluation).[138] Ultimately, the devaluation of capital will be added to by the liquidation of capitals which are unable to succeed in the competitive struggle over the now far too small market (or are unable to speculate, hoard, etc, and thus survive in this way - as good as any other to the capital itself). The assets of these capitals will either simply cease to enter production, or will be radically devalued by being offered to other capitals at well below their value, their market price in the depressed conditions being abnormally low. Even many of the capitals which survive will have to undergo a stagnation if not a devaluation of their capital, because they will be unable to invest all of it in production, and thus will not be expanded during this period.

Such crises certainly involve some physical destruction of means of production and the physical waste of potential labour-power which cannot be productively utilised. But what is of the essence is the destruction of capital values, of which physical waste of capital is just a - not necessary - material expression. For crisis is in fact healthy (though such words slip into absurdity through their use in this connection) for the capitalist economy. Over-production is probably halted by the gross stagnation of the economy in the trough of the crisis, by both variable and constant capital being withdrawn from (by those capitalists who can invest elsewhere) or pushed out of (the capital which is driven out of business) production. However, a fundamental disproportion between the amount of capital invested in production and the market for the product remains and any start up of production would simply bring this to crisis point again. Or rather, whilst this disproportion remained there would be no start up. This is why the forcible destruction of capital values is healthy for the economy. By nullifying a certain amount of capital, the market becomes somewhat unconstricted, and the effect for surviving capitals is rather as if some entirely new market has been opened. For this fundamental reason, as well as because in the crisis the costs of expanding production are abnormally low, the crisis can expect to end. It produces its own conditions for ending when it has proceeded so far with the destruction of existing capitals that it produces viable markets for the remaining capitals. To this basic point, the lowering of capital costs (both variable and constant) is a subordinate point. Crises of over-production tell us that capital needs no help to assault production, only to be released from its own fetters.

Crises are the expression of the capitalist economy's inability to smoothly cope with increases in productivity of anything like the size and range which it continually seeks. The dynamic equilibrium of our model of expanded reproduction can be only a statement of the conditions deviation from which will produce the crises characteristic of the *laissez faire* economy. For instead of the assimilation of the levels of productivity being a smooth process, it is rather an abrupt switch from the old to the new. If we reflect on what we already know of the nature of capitalism as generalised commodity production then we can see why this is so.

New levels of productivity are at first the guarded province of only some capitals. They will typically use these new levels in order to enlarge their market. Given the capitalist, restricted form of consumption, this is tantamount to saying that they will use the new levels to provoke a crisis. The capitals introducing the new methods intend the crisis for other capitals only, but beyond a certain size of change, the reverse multiplier effect of their behaviour must reflect on them, though perhaps to a lesser extent than on others. The market informs capitals with older methods of production, which find their commodities unsaleable at their prices of production, their plant devalued and their business being pushed towards liquidation, that they are now wasting labour. The social average level of productivity has risen above their level of technique. This social judgment on their production is made clear to these capitals in the way in which the social relations of capitalist production must be made clear, after the event of production when they try to valorise their surplus value. Hence the appalling waste of the market system - waste which simply would not arise if the introduction of new methods were planned for the whole economy beforehand. But consciousness of what is going on is specifically what is absent from the capitalist economy.

Though this is so, even this general statement of the causes of crises cannot, let me emphasise, be thought to describe merely a type of disproportionality. There are specific features of the nature of capital which necessarily work in contradictory directions which bring about the realisation of the anarchy of capitalist production in crises as well as in other ways. It is in the nature of individual capitals to seek virtually infinite expansion of their own means of production, to seek to valorise their surplus value and to enter into production only if they feel they will gain what they seek, to increase the value composition of capital, and to restrict the market to the point where the alteration in the level of productivity will provoke a crisis. Hence it is possible to give the above outline of the structural reasons for crises - this would be impossible if crises were simply the outcomes of specifically arbitrary behaviour.

The third and final passage from Marx's economics on which I would like to comment is the following, again from the *Grundrisse*, again when Marx is discussing capital's contradictions:

These contradictions, of course, lead to explosions, crises, in which momentary suspension of all labour and annihilation of a great part of capital violently lead back to the point where it is enabled to go on fully employing its productive powers without committing suicide. Yet, these regularly recurring catastrophes lead to their repetition on a higher scale, and finally to its violent overthrow. [139]

This passage contains two distinct propositions, the first of which follows directly from what we have already seen of Marx's account of capitalism. This is that crises are only merely temporary solutions to capital's contradictions and in fact they leave the situation worse than before. The devaluation of existing capitals will, in its destructively wasteful fashion, be the harbinger of renewed accumulation. And that accumulation will take place with the same intent, for capital can set no limit to its own purely quantitative growth, but in a situation where accumulation faces a more difficult prospect. For now the productive forces have been increased and the lower rate of profit on cumulatively larger investments together with the even more acute relative paucity of consumption which this increase entails set even greater obstacles to further accumulation. We have gone over this before, and I have thought it necessary only to put the point into its proper place here. It leads, of course, to what Marx has in mind in the second of the propositions in the above passage; the eventual violent overthrow of capitalism. This is so large a topic that, after noting how it comes at the end of Marx's analysis, I propose to leave it for treatment separately in the next section of this work.

Notes

1   C2, pp 470-1. On this last point, it will be seen that even the simple reproduction, in value terms, of constant capital must call forth accumulation in other spheres of the economy because of the increased productivity of new machinery over old, even though the former may be entirely charged as depreciation of the latter. TSV2, pp 481-489.

2   C2, p 471.

3   C2(LW), pp 399-402. These passages in C2 are unreliable.

4   EM, vol 28, p 370.

5   C2, ch 20.

6   C2(LW), pp 401-2.

7   Pace Mandel, 'Introduction to Volume 2', sec 3.

8   EM, vol 29, p 34; TSV2, pp 489, 494 and C2, pp 470, 505-9.

9   C3, pp 1012-3.

10   *Ibid*, ch 10.

11   C1, pt 6.

12   C3, pts 5-6.

13   TSV3, addenda and C3, pt 7.

14   EM, vol 29, pp 38-9.

15   C2, ch 20.

16   TSV2, pp 507-13.

17   C2, p 509.

18   *Vide* Sweezy, *The Theory of Capitalist Development*, p 157 n.

19   Marx 'Comments on James Mill', p 211; EPM, pp 270-1 and WLC, pp 77-8.

20   CPE, p 264 and C1, p 16 n 30. Cf Engels, 'Outlines of a Critique of Political Economy', pp 433-4.

21   C3, pp 956-7.

22   C2, ch 20, sec 3.

23   *Ibid*, ch 21.

24   *Ibid*, pp 595-7.

25   C1, ch 4.

26   *Ibid*, pp 645-6. Cf RIPP, pp 1019-23.

27   C1, pt 8. Cf EM, vol 28, pp 426-8.

28   C1, pt 3.

29   *Ibid*, ch 16. Cf RIPP, pp 1023-38.

30   C1, ch 11. Cf EM, vol 28, p 284.

31   C1, pt 4.

32   Or, as Marx sometimes puts it, the degree of exploitation. Eg C3, p 242. This term is too provocative for considered usage and I will not employ it.

33   C1, ch 12.

34   WLC, pp 222-5 and C3, ch 10.

35   C1, ch 6. Cf WLC; *idem*, 'Speech on the Question of Free Trade' and WPP.

36   C1, pp 283-90.

37   *Ibid*, p 762. Cf C3, pp 244-5, 900.

38   *Vide* Sayer, *Marx's Method*. ch 3, n 11.

39   TSV3, pp 364-6; C1, p 774 and C2, ch 5.

40   TSV3, pp 366-7.

41   C3, pp 317-9, 342-3.

42   *Vide*, Sweezy, *The Theory of Capitalist Development*, pp 103-4 and *idem* 'Some Problems in the Theory of Capital Accumulation, pp 11-4.

43   TSV3, pp 382, 385, 386.

44   *Vide* Fine and Harris 'Controversial Issues in Marxist Economic Theory', p 161 and *idem*, *Re-reading 'Capital'*, pp 59-61.

45   *Pace* Okishio, 'Technical Change and the Profit Rate'.

46   *Vide* Steedman, *Marx After Sraffa*, ch 9 appendix.

47   C3, p 420.

48   A number of bourgeois economists, including JB Clark who will be discussed in chapter 10, tried to come to terms with this point by postulating the continuous reproduction of constant capital with no other end than that of reproduction itself. Clark, 'Introduction', p 15. The version of the idea that has been most widely discussed, however, is that of the menshevik M Tugan-Baranovsky, in *Studien zur Theory und Geschichte der Handelkrisen in England*, pp 224-31. The issue with arguments such as Tugan's for indefinite accumulation of means of production is not so much its mathematics but the utter implausibility of its social assumptions in a capitalist context, about which Tugan himself had the strongest reservation. Working within capitalist limits can often turn good ideas into nonsense, for clearly we are running into the same sort of problems that beset Keynes when, after recognising the need for state expenditure to expand aggregate demand, the best thing he could come up with that would not offend vested interests was burying money and digging it up again! Keynes, 'The General Theory of Employment, Interest and Money', p 129. What is interesting is why this idea itself could be thought to be more socially plausible than offending, say, a private food producing company by providing cheap food.

49   C1, ch 25, sec 2. Cf EM, vol 28, p 312-22.

50   C1, p 781.

51   C3, ch 13. Cf EM, vol 29, pp 129-42 and TSV3, ch 23.

52   C3, p 319. Cf EM, vol 29, pp 133-4.

53   I am generally unsympathetic to criticisms of Engels' (or even Kautsky's) editorial work to the extent that they seem to imply that better editorial work would produce a clear text and therefore obscure what, even without sight of all of Marx's scripts, would seem to be a clear fact, that his basic thinking is muddled at many crucial points. I will return to this throughout the rest of this work. However, it would seem that on the specific point of the presentation of the law and the countervailing tendencies, the arrangement which has caused some avoidable misinterpretation was Engels'. *Vide* Seigel, *Marx's Fate*, pp 339-43.

54   *Vide* Robinson, *An Essay on Marxian Economics*, p 36.

55   C1, ch 8.

56   C3, ch 2 nb p 133.

57   *Ibid*, ch 3 nb p 142.

58   EM, vol 28, pp 296-312; TSV2, ch 15 and C3, ch 2 nb p 136.

59   EM, vol 28, p 311, 473-85; TSV2, pp 438-9, 463-4, 467-88, 451-6, TSV3, pp 106-9, 351-2 and C3, pp 349-52.

60 *Ibid,* ch 3. According to Engels' editorial note at the end of this chapter, Marx's as yet unpublished scripts for *Capital* contain graphical plottings of the behaviour of p under the influence of these variables. Whilst it is, of course, to be hoped that the new collected works in English will make these available, the shape of the graphs under various assumptions is obvious enough from the equations.

61 *Ibid,* p 317.

62 *Vide* Robinson, *An Essay on Marxian Economics,* ch 5.

63 C3, pp 339-42.

64 TSV2, p 439; TSV3, pp 240, 302, 311, 369 and C3, ch 3 and p 347.

65 *Vide* Rosdolsky, *The Making of Marx's 'Capital',* pp 399-402.

66 The two most substantial empirical studies in explicit marxist terms are Gillman, *The Falling Rate of Profit* and Mage, *The Law of the Falling Tendency of the Rate of Profit,* and these have been subjected to enormous criticism. It seems clear that the only practicable sources will have to be reworking of statistics collected according to categories derived from other perspectives.

67 C1, ch 10 nb sec 1.

68 *Ibid,* pp 419-20.

69 C3, pp 355-6. The present progress of automation allows of interesting speculations on the basis of what would happen as capital encounters these limiting cases. *Vide* Mandel, *Late Capitalism,* ch 6.

70 EM, vol 28, pp 259-66.

71 C1, pp 774-5.

72 C3, pp 339-42.

73 Eg Grossman, 'Marx, Classical Political Economy and the Problem of Dynamics' and Luxemburg, *The Accumulation of Capital.*

74 *Vide* Mandel, *Marxist Economic Theory,* pp 361-71.

75 *Vide* ibid, p 345.

76 C1, chs 4 and 24.

77 *Ibid,* p 770.

78 *Ibid,* ch 25, sec 2 and C3, ch 27.

79 *Vide* Luxemburg, *The Accumulation of Capital.* ch 7.

80 Chapter 10 will examine this issue again, once Marx's *laissez faire* assumptions have been relaxed.

81 Malthus, *An Essay of the Principle of Population.*

82 Ricardo, 'On the Principles of Political Economy and Taxation', ch 5.

83 Eg the accusation of "baseness" in W, p 428 and TSV2, p 117.

84 Malthus, *Principles of Political Economy.* Marx's fullest discussion of the political economy other than the population principle is in TSV3, ch 19.

85 *Ibid,* ch 19, sec 2

86   CMNABP, pp 194-5.

87   EM, vol 28, p 524; TSV2, ch 6; TSV3, p 61 and C1, p 766 n 6.

88   TSV2, p 121.

89   EM, vol 28, pp 524-9.

90   C1, p 787.

91   *Ibid*, ch 25. Cf W, pp 415-37 nb 428-32 and WLC.

92   C1, p 763.

93   *Ibid*, p 764 n 1.

94   *Ibid*, pp 769-70.

95   WPP.

96   C1, pp 770-2.

97   *Ibid*, ch 25, sec 3.

98   *Ibid*, p 785.

99   *Ibid*, pp 790-1.

100 *Ibid*, ch 25, sec 3.

101 *Ibid*, p 802.

102 *Ibid*, ch 15, sec 6.

103 *Ibid*, ch 25, sec 4

104 *Ibid*, pp 771-2.

105 EM, vol 28, p 527-9.

106 C1, pp 174-5.

107 *Ibid*, p 492. Cf Mill, 'Principles of Political Economy', vol 3, p 756.

108 *Vide* Braverman, *Labour and Monopoly Capital*, ch 17.

109 WLC and WPP.

110 EM, vol 28, p 260.

111 C1, ch 7, sec 2.

112 EM, vol 28, p 335.

113 MCP, pp 485, 486, 487-8.

114 EM, vol 28, pp 336-7.

115 TSV1, p 282 and C1, pp 739-40.

116 Eg Senior, *An Outline of the Science of Political Economy*, pp 58-60, 89.

117 C1, pp 744-6.

118 RIPP, pp 1044-5.

119 C1, p 743.

120 WPP, p 223.

121 C1, ch 10.

122 EPM, pp 235-46; W; WLC; WPP and C1 pt 4.

123 WPP, pp 217-21 and C1, ch 17 nb p 659.

124 WPP, p 223.

125 TSV3, p 312 and WPP, pp 216-26.

126 WLC, pp 216-9; TSV3, p 419 and WPP, p 225.

127 *Ibid*, pp 225-6; C1, p 769 and COGP, p 325.

128 EM, vol 28, pp 341-51; C2 p 391 n and C3, pp 352-3, 367, 419-20, 614-5.

129 C2, pp 595-7.

130 C1, ch 24, sec 1.

131 *Ibid*, ch 8 and C2, pt 2 nb ch 8.

132 *Ibid*, ch 10 nb pp 314-5.

133 MCP, pp 487-90.

134 *Vide* Nicolaus, 'The Unknown Marx,' p 327.

135 EM, vol 28, pp 342-3.

136 C3, pp 357-8.

137 *Ibid*, pp 361-2.

138 *Ibid*, ch 27.

139 EM, vol 29, p 134.

9 The Transition from Capitalism to Socialism

Any sensible comment on Marx's views on the limits to capital accumulation must be preceded by an appreciation of the nature of the text of *Capital* which he left us. The facts are now well enough known[1] to need only a brief statement here. Only volume one, on the revision of which he continued to be occupied at his death,[2] was given in any finished form. Volume two[3] and, even more, volume three[4] were left in a markedly unfinished state and what has so far been made public is the result of very substantial editorial work by Engels. Now, it is necessary to say that Engels' editorial work has its shortcomings,[5] but this is not the main point on which we should focus when we say that volumes two and three are incomplete.

A draft outline of Marx's plans for his economic writings made in 1858[6] gave the skeleton of a huge project in six books which, apart from a first part on capital in general, would cover landed property, wage-labour, the state, international trade and the world market. Whilst there are passages throughout *Capital* reserving topics for anticipated later development[7] which show that Marx had not forgotten this huge plan whilst drafting his scripts, *Capital* itself came to be intended to address, eventually in the three volumes with which we are familiar, a smaller - though in itself enormous - scope, broadly that of the first book,[8] together with briefer treatments of the material on landed property and wage-labour originally intended for other books. A fourth book was to contain the planned history of political economy and, of course, after Kautsky and the Marx-Engels-Lenin Institute, we now have this as *Theories of Surplus Value.*[9]

Now, *Capital* obviously is unfinished even when limited to this relatively restricted scope. But in the sense of having addressed all the necessary points, I would say that *Capital* is complete as we have it. As an account of the developmental tendencies of *laissez faire* capitalism, it has broached the necessary topics by what we have as chapter 15 of volume three. Parts 4-6 of volume three, which describe commercial and financial capital and rent, are necessary for an account of "Capitalist Production as a Whole". But the part on rent is, as I have claimed, clearly anticipated at the beginning of volume one and, as I shall argue, the part on commercial and financial capital adds nothing essentially new. As far as one can judge on the basis of presently available materials, the incompleteness of part 7, which describes the capitalist forms of revenue and thus sociologically sketches bourgeois classes, means that we are missing a section which would have rather beautifully tied up all of *Capital* by linking classes back to the analysis of capitalist production in volume one in two ways. The first is that bourgeois social structure would have been coupled, through an attack on the trinity formula, to the basic critique of fetishism.[10] The second is that the abandoned section on classes would have provided a proper conclusion to the work, describing developing class conflict as the outcome of capital accumulation[11] in the way that is anticipated, for what would seem to be polemical reasons rather than for the sake of clear development,[12] in chapter 32 of volume one. I will argue that much lies behind the failure to complete this chapter, but we can easily construct what Marx would have said *consistent with the original plan* of *Capital* from his voluminous later political writings such as *Wages, Price and Profit*, so there is no insuperable problem of seeing the form of the missing conclusion. The further material in the other originally projected books would, no doubt, have been of the greatest interest. But the organic account of the development of capitalism which Marx was able to give, as it really subsumes production to its nature and as that nature then posits its own limits, is there by chapter 15.

It must be said that *even this* is unfinished, but unfinished in a more serious way. I do not mean that Engels had to carry out his editing work. I mean that what we have of Marx's arguments is not enough for *any* reconstruction because those arguments *cannot* be concluded. We can see that capitalism is going to go and at points in chapter 15, such as the one which I quoted in the last chapter, it is going to go explosively. But how? We are shown appalling factory labour, disgusting living conditions, disproportionality, over-production, surplus population, falling profit, crises, a final collapse, etc, but all lacking a worked coherence in which Marx makes clear claims about how capitalism will go. I cannot improve on Hansen's description of the state of Marx's position:

> When Marx died in 1883, *Capital* remained in its original state, with the end of capitalism posed, at certain points in the text, as the necessary result of a relatively unexplained process and at other points, as the necessary process of a relatively unexplained end.[13]

One could give a very full history of Marxism by describing the consequences of the ways in which various Marxisms have sought to fill in these gaps.[14] Though I put forward the previous chapter as a deliberately faithful account of Marx's views, I can, of course, only set this account against many, many others making a similar claim.

But the particular strength I want to claim for my account is that I do *not* want to show what Marx's "real" account was,[15] either then to affirm it or to reject it. I want to accept that Marx's views are radically unfinished and then to argue that they could not be finished in the way he wanted for the very good reason that the conditions of their applicability were being eroded.

This erosion has taken place in two ways which I shall deal with in this and the next chapter. First, were Marx's critique of classical political economy to be successful, this should mean that the alienated influences of the capitalist economy become less powerful. However, Marx never properly came to terms with this and his account of socialism remains dogged by alienated economic determinations which are unfit to describe it. This has produced enormous confusion in socialist thought since Marx, which will be examined in this chapter. In the next chapter, we shall see that, as the second type of erosion of the applicability of Marx's work, it has actually been *capital* that has been able to more successfully deal with the limits to capital accumulation, by restructuring the form of that accumulation, than labour.

There would seem to have been two main possibilities open to the interpretation of Marx's views on the limits to accumulation as we have seen them in *Capital*. The first is some idea of automatic breakdown in the system, either automatically leading to socialism or creating a non-capitalist space into which the working class will push socialism. The second is some idea that crises will develop and get cumulatively worse and therefore cumulatively less tolerated by the working class, to the point where socialism is established as the better alternative. This divides into many shades in which the relative sizes of the roles of cumulative crises pushing towards socialism or the developing power of the working class pulling towards it are altered. Let us briefly - for the ground has been covered many times - look at the plausibility of these.

A commitment of sorts to automatic breakdown has been a central feature of marxism, particularly during the Second International.[16] Even if we leave aside for the moment the narrowly economic errors sometimes rather comically displayed by attempts to push *Capital* on to this extreme,[17] the political stance which naturally follows, quietism, was reviled by Lenin then[18] and his opinion now is general. It can hardly be doubted that, if actually accepted, breakdown theory has a very deleterious effect on political action, for it produces a belief in the inevitability of socialism which reproduces in the day to day political sphere the abstract conundra which follow from general philosophical determinism.[19] This follows from the extraordinary consequences it has for one's idea of the place of subjectivity in social theory, making the plausible conceptualisation of agency in explanations impossible.[20] But the smugness of many present marxist verdicts on "economism"[21] is both too harsh and not harsh enough.

It is too harsh because, in the effort to separate Marx from breakdown theory, it has to ignore the many indications in *Capital* that support breakdown. I will not direct the reader to those passages in *Capital* and in Marx's other economic and political writings, which provide textual evidence for the breakdown interpretation. I cannot hope to convince anyone who denies their existence as such. But the crucial point is to read such passages in context and, if one is straining to find Marx's context to be a sound one, then these will tend to drop out of focus. I do not see why, necessarily, they should. If one concentrates on discovering "the natural laws of...movement"[22] of capitalism, especially if one looks from the broadly materialist aspect of Marx's "guiding thread" in studying capitalism, "the key to which lies in political economy",[23] one can try to fill up the gaps in Marx's account basically along the lines he provided in *Capital*. These lines are all narrowly economic. As such, breakdown theory arguably is their - these lines in *Capital*'s - most natural development.

On the other hand, relatively recent rejections of "economism" are not harsh enough because they typically fail to point out that "breakdown" is, at root, a nonsensical idea. But the reason for this failure again is, at root, that showing it must, at any other than astounding levels of dogma, implicate Marx. For it just is not fair to look at the absurdities of breakdown theory and, from this, conclude that Marx could not have held to these positions because they are absurd. But this is a common line taken at least since Engels. Engels' own glosses on *Capital* all tend towards some idea of breakdown,[24] and yet, in a number of famous letters on the historical materialist method,[25] we find him criticising the "excesses" and "one-sidedness" of some contemporaneous interpreters. These comments on the nature of "relative autonomy" and "economic determination in the last instance" are now more or less accepted to be the simple saving, by admitting exceptions in an unprincipled way, of the coarse elements of the explanatory strategy which he glossed as historical materialism.[26] It is with the inadequacy of this explanation's corollary in describing Marx's relationship to Hegel that this work began and we are now in a position to reap the fruits of our reconstruction of this relationship.

Engels brought the saving elements of his formulation of historical materialism to bear on the huge range of important political issues on which his distinguished opinion was sought after Marx's death, particularly breakdown. In the instances of their use, we can see that he very badly wants to eat the cake of capitalism collapsing whilst also trying to save the cake of the working class' active commitment to that collapse. Some of these instances amount to no more than a simultaneous approving statement of two valuable but tendentious positions by the simple expedient of holding that someone who held to only one or the other would be in the wrong.[27] Now the claim may be right but this is hardly enough to excuse unproblematic confidence in an antinomy. However, one way in which Engels attempted to save economic determination does have some other than purely historical interest. This was to develop a variant of breakdown theory around his famous remark that we are faced with the alternatives of "revolution or ruin".[28] The idea is clear enough on a cursory glance. Capitalism is collapsing but the collapse does not mean the inevitable victory of socialism. Unless the working class exerts itself, the system may decay into some sort of even worse state, of persistent unresolved crises,[29] chaos,[30] or authoritarian maintenance of an acutely weak economy, etc. Fascism is taken to be the outstanding empirical corroboration of the possibility of this type of system decay.[31]

Now, there is very little that can be said in defence of this idea, which seeks to save a strongly economic determinist argument for socialism by introducing a radical indeterminacy at just the crucial point.[32] However, undoubtedly the most powerful expression of this uncoupling of breakdown and socialism was by Luxemburg and one must immediately acknowledge the gains she thereby made in establishing a drive towards active political participation. Luxemburg's own accounts of the economic tendencies leading to breakdown are surely as mechanical as any ever put forward.[33] But because she was particularly interested in explaining imperialism when it *did* look as if the imperialist powers might eventually destroy each other, she was anxious to stress the reality of the possibility of barbarism and the necessity to work against it.[34] Her political writings are remarkably liberal, wholeheartedly embracing the encouragement of spontaneous working class political actions, the form of which she refused to specify in detail in advance for fear of imposing an outside political will.[35] These writings hold to democracy with a far less quietistic tone than Kautsky[36] and, in so doing, they probably are the furthest expression of just how much political activism in the best sense can be coupled to a quite mechanical idea of economic development.[37]

As a committed politician, however, one can be "spontaneous" in this way only if one is sure that people's spontaneous reaction will be to agree with you. Of course, Luxemburg was. Mechanically working tendencies in the economy eventually would compel this agreement.[38] All goes well until one faces the test of empirical corroboration and when the test is failed one either must retire from the struggle[39] or become rather more, to use the horrid jargon, pro-active.[40] Lenin, who faced a situation in which this type of confidence just could not be sustained and for whom barbarism was represented by the threat of armed reaction and by an economic collapse which would not be represented by the failure of some reproduction tables to add up but in the death of millions for which he was responsible, could hardly conceal his impatience at this naive belief in a sort of invisible hand of socialism.[41] Whilst committed to working class spontaneity when it was the right spontaneity,[42] he put his vast political acumen into a rather more determined effort to supply any want of spontaneously correct political beliefs.[43]

This type of alternative to Luxemburg actually follows from her way of understanding the breakdown of capitalism and cannot be avoided however sophisticatedly one refines the basic position.[44] The outstanding stature of Lukács' *History and Class Consciousness* has already been mentioned in this work and it is in no way a derogation of this to observe that, ultimately, his position on working class consciousness is undercut in the same way as Luxemburg's. Lukács' account of the development of socialist commitment seeks to fill in the simple gap left by Luxemburg's commitment to spontaneity and does so in a way which has left a lasting productive legacy in an enormous range of sophisticated cultural studies. But this is not a wholly productive legacy. The basic tendencies of the capitalist system still are setting up the collapse of capitalism.[45] Lukács' brilliant rejection of economic determinism leaves him the possibility that "ideological inhibitions" may mean that the working class may not work towards the end set out in the tendencies,[46] but the sense of exteriority in the tendencies still is there - Lukács generally refers to this exteriority as the realm of "objective possibility".[47] If the working class sadly does not commit itself properly, this can be only because of "false consciousness".[48] Things of great interest have been developed here,[49] but the basic nature of the explanation is mistaken. In what sense can capitalism be collapsing if it is setting up countervailing factors successfully preventing the collapse? The false consciousness is Lukács' own, for he is committed to saving his account of economic tendencies when the overwhelming evidence is that they are just not working out in the way originally claimed.

All these movements describe the same basic shift in the form of explanation they put forward. An economic tendency is described and corollaries in political developments linked to it in a stronger or weaker way. When spontaneity seems to work in just the wrong way for the purposes of the explanation, the link between economics and politics becomes too weak to really continue to be a link in any other than an unacceptably remote sense. The link, then, has to be restored by strenuous political action - as in Lenin[50] - or, when such work itself seems unlikely to succeed, by cultural explanations, as in Lukács' own work or in much of Western Marxism based on that work. Historical materialism provides a ready framework for this retreat from explanations at the economic "base" to explanations at the "political" or "cultural" "superstructure"[51] and the consequent expansion of the work to be done by "ideology".[52] These explanations may themselves then either show capitalism superstructurally saving itself[53] or ultimately failing to do so,[54] but in either version *all the original claims for the place of the working class in Marx's account of the development of socialism are lost.*

Now, Marx himself did not, indeed, hold to the breakdown position in either its lesser or more deterministic forms and so is not directly responsible for these explanatory outcomes. But this is not really because another and better position predominates in his work but because no position predominates. There are a huge number of interesting statements in Marx which show that he was aware that more sophisticated ideas of explanation were needed than we since have found in the various forms of historical materialism. I personally find it impossible to believe that Marx himself could have written fully considered pieces which would be like those of the later Engels[55] (though this does not necessarily, or indeed at all, preclude approving Engels' work, which has been enormously productive by any reasonable standard), but I do not believe this should alert us to anything other than a problem for Marx. Marx did *not* work these problems out. He did not publish anything after 1859 which attempted carefully to philosophically explicate his ideas of explanation, and this work was left to Engels. On the basis of this record, and given the already discussed absurdity of claiming that Marx let Engels outright distort his (Marx's) work for 24 years, I am bound to say that it is wishful thinking to say that, had Marx undertaken this work of explication, he no doubt would have put things straight.

Certainly, over the specific issue of the working class' involvement in the development of socialism, what Marx has left us is very uneven. There are the basic economic tendencies we have discussed at length and some idea that basically involved in this will be a growing working class commitment to socialism that will deliver the *coup de grace*. This idea can be traced back to the *Critique of Hegel's*

Philosophy of Right and has its most famous expression in the statement in the *Communist Manifesto* that capitalism contains the seeds of its own mortality and, as part of this, produces its own gravediggers.[56] To assess how far can this idea be regarded as part of the statement of the limits to capital accumulation in *Capital*, we must go right back to the analysis of the commodity, particularly to one peculiar commodity - labour-power.

Marx's argument for holding that the working class will put the political impetus behind the development of socialism is that the members of that class can improve their conditions of life in certain fundamental ways only by a general criticism of capitalism. Marx described the conditions of the working class as miserable[57] and its immiseration is so intrinsic to its subordinate class position that it can be overcome only by the abolition of that subordination. But as that subordination is the direct result of the central characteristics of the capitalist economy, it can be abolished only with the abolition of bourgeois society.[58] I have mentioned that understanding "immiseration" is a vexed problem in the interpretation of Marx, as vexed as any other issue. We can clear away some of the problems by seeing that Marx uses this term in at least two different senses which may be distinguished.

The first of these arises in that Marx had some views about the condition of the working class in early stages of factory production which do not necessarily have to apply to established capitalism. Marx would seem to have believed that the material conditions of the initially assembling urban working class were inferior to those which had prevailed in the earlier peasant lifestyle. The production of free wage-labour was accompanied by an absolute decline in the standard of living of those compelled to populate the towns and work in the factories.[59] Whether this was so or not is a question which, though it has generated much impassioned debate, it is difficult to even pose properly[60] on the basis of the available evidence,[61] much less to answer. Marx's view, especially after one realises that it does not preclude an appreciation of the overall gain of being freed from the "universal mediocrity"[62] and "idiocy" of peasant life,[63] is surely at least credible.[64] I do not propose to say anything further upon it, however, as the whole issue relates to primitive accumulation and I would like to discuss the working class within established capitalism.

In turning to this, we come across the second sense in which Marx used immiseration, for his views on the condition of the working class under established capitalism shows that his early moral criticism of the wretchedness of those conditions is scientifically deepened to a very large - if not in the end adequate - degree by being placed within an economic account of the determination of the living standards of the working class as wage-labour.

The theme of absolute immiseration which is to be found in Marx's comments on the initially forming working class is, it has been argued,[65] present in Marx's ideas about what would happen to the living standards of the working class in the course of the development of capitalism. Were this Marx's view, then clearly he is incorrect in a most serious way, but I rather doubt whether we are able to simply dismiss Marx's thought in this area as an unfounded and worthless prediction.[66] Marx certainly does argue that the economic tendency of capitalism is to push wages down to the minimum, for wages are treated as a cost. This is hardly to say that the minimum must absolutely decline or that the tendency for wages to be pushed to this level must have that effect. It no doubt is possible to produce isolated quotations from Marx which seem to show this, but by this sort of method of interpretation anything is possible. An overall look at Marx's ideas on wages shows them to be much more flexible than Ricardo's. Not only are they far more precise about changes during the industrial cycle, but, due to Marx's distinguishing of surplus value and profit, they can very easily allow for a continuing rise in real wages. What Marx does in detail say here is that the value of labour-power will fall and that treating this as the minimum (though obviously it features in competition as the average), money wages will tend to be pushed towards it by certain, competitive pressures generated by developing capitalism.

The falling value of labour-power is central to Marx's account of capitalism. But what does this mean in terms of living standards? Unless wages fall in proportion to the fall in the value of labour-power, this fall will, in fact, mean a rise in real wages and living standards. Let us, however, leave consideration of the size of money wages aside for a moment and briefly expand on the interesting idea of immiseration bound up within the fall in the value of labour-power itself, and the idea which underpins Marx's first empirical illustration in volume one of the general law of capitalist accumulation,[67] the idea of relative immiseration.

The decline in the value of labour-power is part of the enormous growth in the productive power of labour under capitalism. But this historical achievement has a paradoxical form for labour itself. The value of labour-power falls, but this is not meant as a resource for labour but as a resource for capital, for though necessary labour declines, the capitalist will want to use this decline to increase surplus labour. To the extent that the decline in necessary labour is used to produce surplus value, the result will be that the expanded production of capital itself will take place. At any practically conceivable ratio of necessary to surplus labour under capitalism, the labour of the working class will lead to a relatively far greater production of capital than of fruits for labour itself,[68] an affirmation on the basis of the economics of *Capital* of a conviction that the very act of labour under capitalism produces the subordination of labour to an ever deeper extent which Marx had held since 1844.[69]

I have assumed that investment and luxury consumption both can grow until limits on productive re-investment emerge. If we turn away from the problems of re-investment and turn to luxury consumption, the rate of growth in the luxury consumption fund under established capitalism will involve a far greater accumulation of riches by the bourgeoisie than the working class.[70] Relative immiseration in the sense of relatively much faster increase in the riches of the bourgeoisie and the generation of a working class attitude critical of this effect of capitalism may thus be found at the centre of Marx's economics.[71] Relative immiseration does *not* turn on the absolute size of wages.[72] It is a relation and only thus may describe a social comparison.[73] It is no less an account of a philosophically[74] and empirically[75] real source of dissatisfaction with the bourgeois distribution of wealth for all that.

Having seen that Marx is committed to predicting a fall in the value of labour-power and that this involves relative immiseration, let us go on to the other part of what Marx would have to say were this idea to be extended on into any sort of absolute immiseration - that a fall in money wages ultimately greater than the fall in the value of labour-power would overall have to take place. Marx undoubtedly *did* think an economic tendency for this to happen did exist in capitalism[76] and the least that can be said is that at the time there was a great deal of empirical evidence to support him.[77] This tendency is fundamentally composed of the effects on wages of the growth of the industrial reserve army, for this growth will increase the competitive advantage of capital over wage-labour as a whole in the determination of wages.[78] Two types of absolute immiseration can conceivably result from this tendency. One relates to the fate of chronic pauperism which awaits the stagnant element of the growing relative surplus population.[79] This shades - through the other forms of existence of the relative surplus population - into the second conceivable type of absolute immiseration. This is a general pushing down of the money wages of even those in full time work below the value of labour-power.[80]

Marx does set this out as "the absolute general law of capitalist accumulation"[81] but it is not his entire statement on the issue. He locates the main impetus of class struggle at just this point and this struggle specifically moves beyond those laws, positing their abolition. Marx did *not* counsel the working class faced with economic pressures on their money wages to accept the economic inevitability but advised the strongest resistance of those pressures. This is the entire theme of the polemic against Weston in *Wages, Price and Profit*.[82] To be sure, Marx does not say that such actions can consistently hope to counter the economic tendencies of capital, but they can succeed in gradually positing the abolition of those tendencies.

This class struggle is over what Marx calls the historical and moral element in the determination of the value of labour-power. The economic tendency of capitalism is to treat labour-power as a commodity and therefore ultimately to determine wages by determining the value of labour-power as a commodity.[83] However, labour-power is a unique commodity in that the object of valuation is itself an active subject, labour itself. Here we have the nub of the alienating pressures of capital, that human labour be reduced to a commodity, to variable capital and here Marx locates, in the struggle over wage levels, the fundamental class impetus to the rejection of that reduction. Abstract labour is to be challenged in that there is always an element in the settling of the value of labour-power which resists strict economic calculation.[84] This is a social element furnished by the power of human beings - even wage-labourers - to reflect on their situation and to (to various degrees) consciously alter that situation. This is an historical and moral element in that the power of the working class to realise a creative increase in the standards of their life turns, of course, upon social resources such as the traditional standard of life and therefore of legitimate expectation.[85]

The historical and moral element in the determination of the value of labour-power may be relatively large or small. During a period of boom the working class may increase it[86] and conversely during slumps the bourgeoisie may contract it.[87] This of course is a matter of the differing competitive situations in the labour market produced by the cyclical character of accumulation. But, overall, Marx thought the economic tendencies of capitalism - essentially the growth of the industrial reserve army - would increasingly favour the bourgeoisie. The market for labour would ultimately so shrink as to confer an overwhelming competitive advantage on the capitalist. (Of course, we are talking of a most acute social crisis). The point is, however, that the economics of the working class' situation must push it into critique not of a particular competitive situation but into critique of this sort of economic determination of living standards at all. The varying extent of the historical and moral element is, precisely, itself a political issue. The economic tendency of capitalism is to extinguish it altogether. Resistance of this tendency, if it is to be coherent, cannot quibble about the economics, for the economics are internally correct. It must reject such economics. Defence of the historical and moral element is ultimately criticism of the alienation of the capitalist economic calculation of the value of labour-power at all and of the treating of labour as a commodity on which such calculation is based.

It is sometimes argued that Marx did not allow of the possibility of conceiving of a purely physical minimum standard of consumption which would allow of continued bare existence but no more.[88] The evidence for this is constituted of two main points. First, there is a general observation that Marx's materialism so inextricably intertwines historical and natural influences that his conceiving of an ahistorical, physical standard of human existence was impossible. Second, it is noted that Marx was specifically scathing in his criticisms of explicit attempts to formulate such a physical minimum, not only by such as Malthus but even by the leading socialist Lassalle.[89] I would say that the first point is unarguably correct and that consistently Marx would have to rule out the possibility of coherently imagining a purely physically determined minimum standard of existence. From what we have seen of his attitude to Malthus, we can imagine him being rather warm when doing so. Many of his statements on the value of labour power can easily be read as supporting this interpretation.[90] But to say only this is rather to miss the real issue here.

Capital certainly is seeking to push wages down to a purportedly physically ascertained limit and Marx notes a number of attempts to fix this limit.[91] That capital is hereby pursuing an absurd goal which is simply impossible given the historical character of human beings[92] should neither surprise us nor prevent us from recognising the real economic force pushing wages down to this limit in capitalism. The limit is simultaneously absurd and real in the same way as abstract labour. It is pious sentimentality to wish to reject this sort of fixing of living standards given the existence of wage-labour.[93] Only the abolition of wage-labour will abolish this standard, which is intrinsic to it. It is at this point that Marx disagrees with Lassalle. This disagreement arises not because Lassalle argues that there is a pressure towards physically minimum wages, but that his argument follows the population theory in incorrectly identifying this force as an "iron" natural law and not an economic product of capitalism.[94] There is certainly a very real issue bound up in the idea of conceiving of a physically minimum standard of living and that this idea is internally absurd because it stems from the alienated position of labour in capitalism does not detract from the reality of the issue whilst capitalism continues.

Marx's hope would seem to have been that initial struggles over pressures to reduce money wages - which are simply part of the competitive determination of wages and the value of labour-power[95] - would lead, as working class awareness of the fundamental reasons for these obvious pressures develops, into explicit struggles over the preservation and extension of the civilising presence of the historical and moral element of the determination of the value of labour-power and hence into rejection of determining living standards by the value of labour-power. Whilst working class action focuses only on money wage levels it restricts itself to surface phenomena.[96] The only plausible goal of a conscious working class struggle[97] over wage levels can be the abolition of wage-labour, the abolition of the working class itself.[98]

The normal class based competition over wages leads to the working class uniting, first in trades unions (or similar trade combinations), in order to improve their bargaining position as a whole.[99] For Marx, the real fruit of these associations was not the victories in wage competition which they can on occasion bring but the way in which the lesson of such victories becomes ever clearer simply by virtue of the united struggle: that working class unity is a strength which reaches to the heart of modern production.[100] To the extent that trades unions are the immediate product of capitalist wage struggles, trades union aims may tend to be restricted to the illusory goal of continuous success in such struggles.[101] But the evidence of class based power furnished by the trades union experience is invaluable.[102] The real issue here, an issue which can be resolved only by the closest study of the penetrations and limitations bound up in working class political actions,[103] is the formation of a general critical attitude to capitalism and a general conception of the plausibility of socialism.

Marx not only makes the developing struggle over the historical and moral element a reason why the working class should develop a socialist commitment but also tries to describe it as a basic resource allowing the adoption of a strategy of conscious class conflict. Co-operation is the fundamental relation of production in capitalism. It is the extensive division of labour throughout society in generalised commodity production and the intensive division of labour in the factory in the production of particular commodities[104] that allows of the massive development of the productive forces under capitalism.[105] As all social forces are brought under the requirements of production and production is resolved into its component parts on which those forces can be concentrated, an ability to adopt the strategy of increasing productivity by enlarging the scale of the employment of means of production in detailed branches of production is present in capitalism in a sense in which it can be said to be more or less absent from previous modes of production.[106]

Of course, as it is developed within capitalism, co-operation has a capitalist form. This is most obviously so in the coercion exercised in the capitalistic supervision of the labour-process,[107] but more essentially all the powers fostered by co-operation are alienated from the producers as they appear to be a quality, indeed a property, of the capital which brings workers together.[108] Under this circumstance, the marshalling of the power of the co-operative division of labour legitimates the capitalist,[109] for it seems as if the fruits of the division of labour are the fruits of capital itself. However, all this cannot alter that co-operation is a specifically *social* production relation, for it is a relation that makes its sociality its object in that it is precisely by virtue of that sociality that co-operation fosters the development of productive forces. And this sociality expands as the scale of production in all its facets is increased as the means of pursuing relative surplus value.[110] Production is undertaken on what is increasingly a society-wide basis within an interdependent world economy and that interdependence undercuts the atomism of commodity production. Accumulation on the basis of private property in capital thus expands the self-consciously social dimension of production.

It is this inner socialisation of capital that Marx tries to establish as the basis of the positive development of working class consciousness.[111] Class struggle is based on the absurdity of private ownership, and of conducting economic life for the purpose of private accumulation, when the means of production have been developed by, and can only be employed by, the powers of social co-operation. As the bourgeoisie becomes productively redundant, so it falls to the working class to actualise that redundancy. The proper utilisation of the forces of production to fulfil relative and absolute material needs depends on the degree to which the socialisation of the forces of production is pushed through and the necessity of this process faces the working class as a resource and a task.

Particular co-operative developments have an important role. Workers' co-operatives show, Marx claims, the redundancy of the capitalist.[112] Their success can be only limited, however, for as they are particular they are open to localised destructive efforts by the bourgeoisie and, more than this, are simply inadequate to the task of the socialisation of the entire economy which becomes ever more pressing.[113] It is the political organisation of the working class to wrest what is seen as the ever more reactionary residue of bourgeois domination of production that socialisation makes a clear objective.[114]

What Marx has said seems a basically plausible strategy calling both for active political endeavour and yet also showing that conditions are being developed which will allow that endeavour to bear fruit. By saying this, however, I by no means wish to deny that Marx's views on absolute immiseration contain a profound difficulty.[115] The background limits to capitalist accumulation are set out and there is, far less well developed, a class struggle described in the conflict of bourgeoisie and working class over money wage levels linked to those developing limits. Marx has extreme difficulty - so extreme in fact that he does not fully see the problem himself - of running these two elements of his account of capitalist development together. His statement of the laws of motion of capitalism posits the historical obsolescence of exchange-value internally to those laws and carries a very strong explanatory power in doing so. But his statement of the class struggle over wages should *not* have this form.

The struggle initially is internal to capitalism as it is explained as part of a necessary competition arising from the very positing of labour as a commodity. But the laws of motion as Marx describes them do posit absolute immiseration as the general law of capitalist accumulation. As the amount of surplus labour grows, that part that cannot be put to the production of further surplus value is pushed into the reserve army, which pulls the money wage down. The tendency *is* for the money wage to fall towards the value of labour-power and, more than this, for the value of labour power to fall because the historical and moral element will be reduced by competition amongst the growing number of unemployed.[116] Now, Marx obviously had faith in the working class' ability to overcome this law, but this is a *rejection* of the law, *not* its internal working out. His account of the class struggle over wages *must* have a different form to the account of the obsolescence of capitalism.

One of Marx's ways of discussing this issue was to employ Kantian terminology in a distinction between a class "in-itself" and a class "for-itself".[117] The working class as a class of human beings subject to a specific set of most significant social determinations of subordination and exploitation is identified in Marx's political economy of capitalism. We can, at an initial level, social scientifically defend the existence of this class if its existence is posited by explanatory requirements. But so far we are discussing only a class in-itself, for the very powerful reason that its existence may be hypothesised only in social science and may not be recognised by the members of the class themselves. It may be well argued that some shared consciousness and perhaps even some consciousness of shared position are necessary characteristics of any identifiable real social class and I myself would accept this point. Marx, however, was not really interested in mapping out the consequences of working class position for the culture of members of that class except in two respects. One was the basic ideology of fetishism and the second, more peculiar to the working class, was the extent that that culture grasped the fundamental historical determinants of its own production. A culture which did involve such a grasp would constitute a working class for-itself, a working class conscious in the very important sense that it recognised its own class existence and social position.

Marx clearly thought that he had essentially set out the genesis of the working class as a class in-itself in his political economy. From this position, he had then to go on to say that the working class had to develop self-consciousness by bringing to active political fruition the latent strength of its class position.[118] There is a serious difficulty here for Marx. This is that the full development of his account of capitalism must include an explanation of the progressive elements of working class consciousness. I can see no principled ground on which this can be denied. To talk of *Capital* as a purely economic work - as opposed to say *The Class Struggles in France* or *The Eighteenth Brumaire* which study political forms - is just not enough here.[119] There is surely a difference in focus between these works, but not one based on a rigid topographical metaphor but on the generality of the explanations attempted in the different works. Marx was ready enough to bring the general determinations of fetishism within *Capital* and indeed he had to do so was *Capital's* account of capitalism to be adequate. But at this general level, it is equally necessary for Marx to provide an account of the generation of working class consciousness as part of the generation of socialism; but no equivalent explanation of this is really put forward.[120]

What we are forced to recognise is an unacceptable theoretical indeterminateness in the area of working class struggle and the development of socialism out of capitalism. It is surely a fair reading of Marx's principal works to say that the main way in which this indeterminateness is elided is by a recourse to unacceptably mechanical statements in which working class consciousness appears to be a product of alienated economic laws.[121] Though the proletariat is to be self-conscious, Marx's main statements tend to explain socialism more or less along the lines of a necessity derived from his account of capitalism: "capitalist production begets, with the inexorability of a natural process, its own negation".[122] The consequence is that when he turns to the political elements central to working class struggle, these inherently valuable observations appear, against the overall background, to be merely a manoeuvre to save his essentially economic explanations when they are no longer of great value. In this sense, the genesis of indefensible later marxisms, such as breakdown theory,[123] *is* in Marx's works.[124]

It just is not good enough to continue to seek a better Marx within Marx's work which would make those later marxisms bad interpretations.[125] "Interpretation" of this sort is not the issue but rather further development, development from Marx with all this implies of past indebtedness and future direction,[126] and surely the point has come when there is no longer the possibility - there never was the need - of treating Marx as different in principle from other social scientists. Now, saying this does not prevent, indeed it allows, the taking of what one is obliged to take, because it is substantially right, from Marx, the immanent critique of classical political economy and develop it in different ways for which, indeed, there are some hints in Marx. Let me turn to some of those hints before turning to a further major problem.

Marx tries to locate the class struggle over wage levels and, relatedly, over non-wage (welfare) provisions for the relative surplus population within a scheme of the fundamental economic laws of capital and a class based movement to abolish those laws. I presume that it cannot be argued in favour of interpreting Marx as holding to a thesis of *inevitable* absolute immiseration that he thought this struggle would inevitably be resolved against the working class. From what we have seen it is clear that rejection of this inevitability is in a very important way the central theme of Marx's life work. But what is hardly made clear at all is that the statement of the laws of motion of capitalism do not *produce* socialism but socialism must be produced by *abolishing* those laws. It cannot be that, when established, socialism will have abolished capitalist laws, it is that the course of the development of socialism will have to involve the progressive abolition of those laws.

Though Marx's terminology on this issue is by no means always consistent, I think we can identify his idea of full actualised, non-alienated society as "communism"[127] and his idea of the social form which capitalism immediately posits as its own critique as "socialism".[128] Socialism is the initial stage in the actualisation of non-alienated society. It is a society in which the tendencies towards the supercession of alienation generated by capitalism are dominant (whereas in capitalism these tendencies are subordinate to alienating influences) but the alienating residues of capitalist forms are by no means overcome. When they are fully overcome, this is communism.[129]

Let me stress that not all of Marx's uses of "socialism" and "communism" fit in with this rendering of their meaning, for the consistent use of these terms in this way certainly owes more to Lenin than Marx. The rendition is defensible only in terms of the overall fit with Marx's thought which it very arguably possesses, for even when

Marx says "communism" in precisely the fashion that "socialism" should be used given the above distinction, the essential idea of stages in the movement from capitalism to a completely non-alienated society remains.[130] But allowing such a fit does not of course guarantee the coherence of the distinction and its terminological niceness can have a real ground only if it describes a real issue. What does it mean to attempt to demarcate capitalism, socialism and communism? Does this demarcation describe an actual issue?

It has, of course, been widely held that there is an in principle defensible criterion for making this demarcation, which lies in specifying the balance of alienating and non-alienating social influences as this enters into consciousness and is given political effect in the area of class struggle. The predominant historical materialist accounts of Marx's views depict the self-destructive tendencies of capitalist accumulation as a particular form of a general contradiction of forces and relations of production in capitalism. It is possible to use socialism to describe a stage in the development of the contradiction when the relations of production have become reactionary. But I think that initially we might say that this would be a pointless duplication of terminology. (I do not say that Marx was never guilty of this). More than this, however, the most important sense in which it is possible to gauge the way in which the contradiction of forces and relations of production is proceeding under capitalism is precisely through the working class positing of socialism, for class conflict is, according to Marx, supposed to issue from and actualise the liberatory potential of, this contradiction. In this sense, then, the contradiction capitalism-socialism serves as an accompaniment to the contradiction of forces and relations of production in capitalism, the former being the area in which the political ramifications of the latter are developed through the degree of formation of class self-consciousness in the working class.

Marx's reference to socialism as the period of the dictatorship of the working class[131] can be marshalled into this interpretation. The working class seizes political power and uses this to push through the socialisation of capital against bourgeois resistance, in fact to negate the political powers of reaction of the bourgeoisie.[132] Marx's idea was that this particular dictatorship would be qualitatively different to all preceding forms of political domination. The working class comprises the vast majority of people[133] and the forces of production it is trying to free from the restraints of capitalist relations are so intrinsically social that they demand general social control.[134] The implications of this are that the working class dictatorship in fact posits the end of all classes. With the abolition of bourgeoisie, all class partiality will disappear as the working class subsumes all of society, that is to say, it abolishes itself as a class.[135] When this merging of class and society is quite complete, this will be communism.

The issue of the distance between socialism and communism has of course been a most important one in this century. I am quite sure, however, that this was no issue at all for Marx as he addressed the central thesis of *Capital*. The reasons for this are, firstly, the obvious temporal one. More than this, however, though developing from it, is the complete reversal of attitude which addressing the distance of socialism and communism implies by contrast to Marx's project in *Capital*. Socialism is the determinate negation of capitalism - its very plausibility turns on identifying the bases of socialism in capitalism and regarding those bases generously from the point of view of grasping their productive potentials.

From the point of view of the would-be communist, socialism is not a statement of promise but a statement of limitation, for socialism is communism's past as capitalism is socialism's. The necessary presence of capitalist elements in socialism, necessary if socialism is to be developed at all, is a problem of unwelcome survivals for the communist and the issue is the purging of these unwelcome residues.[136] That anyone could claim to take up this communist point of view on other than dogmatic grounds seems to me to be impossible, but I do not want to argue this here. I want only to stress that is obviously the antithesis of the way Marx has to conceive of socialism in *Capital*. Marx could recognise, of course, that socialism is not communism and say this when explaining socialism. But for Marx as he addresses the central problems faced in *Capital* the necessity is not to deride capitalism but to grasp its productive elements. This is essentially a productive rather than a destructive critical attitude, the attitude of immanent critique and celebration rather than denigration of determinate negations. It is an attitude quite absent from purported communist readings of Marx.[137]

With the above ideas we have come, I think, to what is properly the end of Marx's thought on the capitalist mode of production. It is an end in that it postulates the end of capitalism by attempting to postulate the beginning of socialism-communism. The truth of capitalism is revealed by moving on to its future, for that future penetrates the alienated present. Truth, Marx is arguing, is on the scene, is potential in capitalism and socialism begins the process of its actualisation, the full realisation being communism. In saying this we are returned to the essential problem which I attempted to set out in my discussion of Hegel. How can a claim about truth such as Hegel's or Marx's be substantiated? Can Marx claim to have overcome such shortcomings as we found in Hegel? Two things must, I think, be said.

Much of what I first wish to say is merely a summation of the argument advanced throughout this work. Both Hegel and Marx display as probably the foremost characteristic of their writings an intense concern to situate those writings in their intellectual-historical context. The results of this are displayed most clearly in Hegel's histories of aesthetics, religion and philosophy and in Marx's uncompleted history of political economy.[138] More than this, even a cursory reading of Hegel's and Marx's substantive works will reveal how intimately these works are related to their intellectual ancestors. Marx of course included the designation "Critique of Political Economy" in the title of his published economic works. If we are to identify a difference between Hegel's and Marx's ideas of critique, it can hardly be at the initial level of awareness of intellectual context, for the quality of Marx's awareness is inferior to Hegel's, in an extensive if not in an intensive sense. Both awarenesses are also certainly characterised by a sense of their own privilege and of their potential for reflexive reconstruction or re-comprehension of the truth of earlier thought which was but dimly grasped by that thought itself. But there is a difference of the qualities of the senses of privilege here, a difference of principle of critique.

Marx's critique of bourgeois economic thought displays a genuine relationship of learning. It is hermeneutically defensible and if it claims a peculiar privilege, it does so because it sets up a corrigible - and that it is essentially corrigible is more important than any absurd requirement that it be completely correct - understanding of earlier thought as alienated. In the conditions of alienation and consequent distorted communication, the privilege Marx claims is not only defensible but, because it is defensible, it (or something like it) is necessary. I put forward the preceding account of Marx's relationship to bourgeois political economy as justification of this claim.

This is a crucial claim to make for the final sense in which Marx's dialectic of critique is indebted to Hegel's is in claiming an, as it were, circular but non-tautological justification. Marx's account of history and especially of the history of capitalism has led him to posit capitalism's abolition, a point of view obviously non-capitalist in a very important way and is in fact a point of view which in this sense is often described as the point of view of the working class.[139] Marx's given theoretical materials are those of bourgeois political economy, but his conclusions about capitalism disrupt that thought and make it most problematic.[140] There is certainly a sense of the scientific critique of ideological views here. Hegel's absolute truth has a similar distance from alienated views and is just as much the abolition of the "truth" of such views.

Both Hegel and Marx claim, however, to generate their necessary distance from materials furnished by the given and it is in the possibility of doing so that the justification of their critiques - if any - must lie. I have claimed that Hegel fails to secure such justification - his critique cannot in the end be said to be a determinate negation of the given but rather has the distance from the given that attends the presumption of the correctness of one's positions. I hope it is now clear that I do not think that this is true of Marx. Marx generates his socialist comprehension of capitalism from the critique of political economy. When we seek the epistemological justification of the comprehension we are circularly referred back to the critique. However, this is not a tautology but the fundamental circularity of all hermeneutics. That Marx's critique can be thought to be a species of this circularity - notwithstanding in this respect the peculiar criticism that it has to undertake as part of its subject being alienated conditions which distort all dialogue - is, I think, its fundamental intellectual justification.

If all this is accepted, then Marx's account of capitalism must be recognised as the indispensable core of the social scientific understanding of modern society. We can be sure, however, that this intellectual justification is not the one that fundamentally mattered to Marx. The practical justification of his science lies in its informing political critique; and the effectiveness of political work to actualise socialism is the ultimate test of his thought.

It is typical of commentaries on this point that the relationship of science and political action here is left quite open. Marx has presented the science and the work now remains of actualising its conclusions. This is wholly unacceptable. It is to say that the critique of bourgeois political economy has been carried out and yet the formation of working class political power can be left unspecified. But of course the latter is the mechanism of the full accomplishment of the former and we cannot rest with an acceptance of theoretical indeterminacy, an indeterminacy whose disruptive effects within core sections of Marx's thought we have already noted. It is a comic irony that writings which make such a great deal of the unity of theory and practice happily accept disunity at precisely the point where the world is to be revolutionised.[141]

As I have said, it is exactly here that Marx seeks the final productive result of his account of capitalism and there is no ground on which we can leave that result unspecified and yet accept the ultimate adequacy of the account. In so far as it treats of the economic characteristics of capital, this account would seem to be essentially correct and yet though it moves towards the positing of the abolition of capital, it cannot properly specify the way in which this is to be done.

In *Capital* Marx can go so far as to describe the economic laws of motion that internally disrupt capitalist production and create the productive potentials for socialism. He can even go so far as to give economic reasons for the working class' dissatisfaction with capitalism and for its engaging in combinations and struggles against the bourgeoisie over wages. He cannot proceed with explicating the working class' struggle for socialism within a similar framework of economic law, for as the working class actually becomes class conscious and actively takes up socialist aims, it is integral to the whole idea of emancipation that it does so as a conscious decision. This is what is specifically socialist about the working class - it is the first class which carries the banner of social self-consciousness. The working class thereby reduces the area of the operation of the invisible hand, replacing economic necessity by political choice.

This is not to say that the working class's struggle cannot be brought under explanation, but the explanation needs to be of an historically novel form. It cannot be a form reached by the "inversion" of earlier explanations.[142] Classical political economy cannot be inverted to produce an adequate explanation of conscious working class behaviour striving for socialism in the same deterministic way that it formerly could explain alienated behaviour under capitalism. Adequate explanation here has to be fit for social actors who are increasingly aware of what they are doing. It cannot have the form which is needed to account for the actions of those labouring under alienation. The accounts of their own actions which members of the working class themselves put forward must become increasingly self-sufficient as explanations; but this can never be the case for all earlier social actors. Marx very arguably seems to have failed sufficiently to appreciate this crucial point, and it certainly was more or less ignored in later marxisms' stress on law-like, positivistic explanations of the "end of ideology".[143]

One reason for this shortcoming, commonly adduced[144] and no doubt correct, is the influence of the background intellectual climate of scientistic positivism against which Marx wrote. In his aim to, for example, give accounts of economic crises largely in terms of mathematics,[145] Marx gives ample testimony to the effects of this background. Of course, we must be careful over this point. Marx put forward explicit polemics against what he called mechanical materialism and parts of his most directly economic theses contain polemics against the naturalism of, to return to this example, Malthus' population theory. What is more, by extension we can fairly say that appreciation of historical effectivity is central to Marx's work. Recognising all of this, a plausible attitude to take would be to regard what seem to be Marx's confusions of the natural and the social to be marginal to his work. I am sure that this is the best stance on this particular issue, but to treat of Marx's difficulties in this area as turning on the distinction natural/social reflects, I think, more the preoccupations of later social science than Marx's own concerns. Answering objections about Marx's treatment of the actual and the social does not answer the objection I am trying to raise about his conception of socialism, so I shall try to be more precise about his specific concerns.

In the *Dialectics of Nature* Engels tries to situate historical materialism against developments in natural science by subsuming the latter under a dialectic which he claimed already had already generated the former. Historical materialism is to be placed within something of a cosmological context by being placed, along with contemporaneous science, within a purportedly dialectical scheme based on some of Hegel's comments on nature and logic. As we have nothing like a detailed statement by Marx on the point, we cannot say with any confidence how far along this line he would have gone with Engels. As I have mentioned, we have a number of direct statements which show his broad sympathy with a dialectics of nature, but, on the other hand, as I have also mentioned, I personally find it difficult to believe that, should he have undertaken any such dialectics, Marx would not have registered internal difficulties with it that certainly escaped Engels. What I want to argue is that such a project could appear plausible to Marx because he held an aspiration which rather cross cuts the division of natural and social. He works with an idea that he can give an account of the development of socialism that follows essentially the same line as the account which he gives of capitalism; that is to say, he treats of socialism in the same law-like way in which he treats of capitalism. Now, if this is the case, it cannot matter that Marx's laws of capitalism are properly formulated with respect to recognising social determinants, for the determinants they properly describe are those of an alienated society and socialism cannot be subsumed under any such laws.[146] Non-alienated action is its own conscious law and the principles of the explanation of alienated action cannot be extended to cover it. Marx does not seem to have come properly to terms with this, with the result that the working class' class struggle is expressed either in terms that are not apposite or remain intractably vague. Just as Hegel's end of history led not to proper freedom but to acceptance of all that had gone before, so the predominant marxist view of the end of ideology seeks to produce a free, classless society by the automatic working of alienated laws. This is not possible - indeed, it is flatly contradictory. There can be no inversion of the capitalist present to reveal the socialist future, for it is not a given form but a radical openness which the actualisation of socialism posits and not merely for an established socialism but increasingly in all stages of socialism's development.

The task which I would, in effect, assign to Marx is to posit the abolition of his own work;[147] to contemplate the redundancy of *Capital* and incorporate that into its composition. This is an onerous task indeed, one which it seems churlish to accuse Marx of not completing in an orderly fashion.[148] Of course, disorder is to be avoided and the indeterminacy of Marx's accounts of class struggle is unacceptable. But in addressing this problem, we must not underestimate the inner strength of Marx's position which is registered even in this weak area.

Two broad responses to the political failure of Marx's science and to his writings on the class struggle where that failure seems particularly theoretically destructive have, I would say, been made. One is simply to regard later events as overtaking Marx's writings, which are thus regarded as obsolete.[149] The other is to hold to the core of those writings and try to defend them by introducing other variables to take into account the political failure of Marx's programme.[150] An at least conceptual sophistication of the rigid base and superstructure metaphor to allow of a greater independent (or relatively autonomous) effectivity of the political level is one variant of this.[151] Rather more valuable is that variant which takes cognisance of real social changes but claims that Marx's economic[152] or more general social theories[153] are still essentially applicable. One may see both of these broad responses ranged on either side of the debate over whether the post-war western world is post-capitalist.[154]

The latter of these responses clearly is concerned to defend Marx and one may suspect a dogmatism in the way it marginalises very significant social developments in order to do so. But if there is a dogmatism here, it is a very peculiar one, for it is one which willingly surrenders the most defensible elements of its central position in order to support the least defensible ones. The essentials of Marx's class analysis are not lost by admitting change; indeed it is only change that can in the end support that analysis. The defence of Marx has very often been taken up by those who forget this. They continually insist on the undoubted vestiges of narrow capitalist economic necessity which still thwart the socialising thrust of such changes. But it is in the socialist elements of the change that the future lies, as does the spirit, but thereby not the letter, of Marx's thought. Consider the implications of Strachey's argument[155] to the effect that capitalism's life has been extended by those changes wrought by the working class which have made that mode of production more tolerable. Strachey's case for democratic socialism is weakened by the way he puts this, for though he recognises that, of course, these changes are not illusory, he does not grasp their full potential which would be revealed by seeing that a capitalism that embraces them is to that extent no longer capitalism. Of course, this requires the most difficult work of painstaking, detailed critique, but this must be undertaken as these changes *are* the revolution.[156] A failure to recognise this is just the opposite error to taking social improvement to be a direct refutation, or rather, a rendering obsolete, of Marx's work.[157] His analysis does not posit such improvement as being won against capitalism but as an increasingly pressing potential within it. Of course, unless we clearly recognise the necessity of consciously politically working to actualise those potentials, sentiments such as the one I am expressing can lapse into quietism - instead of waiting for the inevitable movement of the working class to abolish capitalism, we wait for capitalism to abolish itself. What happens here is that freedom is even more directly subsumed under the laws of alienated economics.

Though Marx does not specify the peculiar quality of the true politics of self-consciousness, we must now do so. Taking this step allows us to view developments in the capitalist economy in a progressive, rather than a merely negative, light. Those developments within capitalism, such as planning, welfare state provision, the growth of a public sector of employment, etc, which are often taken to be the mark of *Capital's* basic inadequacy, in fact, by their narrowing the area in which capitalism's narrow economic necessity can prevail, do much to confirm Marx's most important theses, which posit just such a narrowing. What Marx is insufficiently clear about is the way that this does entail the increasing obsolescence of *Capital*, for we cannot invert its description of capitalist determinations to produce socialist ones. What presently faces us is the complete rejection of this idea of inversion and the comprehension of self-conscious politics which can politically utilise the resources for socialism that have been - though substantially unself-consciously - produced.

It is just to the extent that socialisation proceeds that the sway of alienated economic forces gives way to that of nascently socially self-conscious planning. Marx suggests that the issues in working class struggle are political ones and this is truer, for the politics involved are actually ones of conscious decision making, than Marx's own work can incorporate, for that work seems tied to the explanation of alienated conditions. The consequence is that Marx either represents these politics in wrong, because basically economic, ways, or leaves them indeterminate. There is no longer any excuse for this. We must radically shift our focus from the realm of alienated necessity to that of self-conscious removal of the present restrictions on free development. We should no longer stand under the thrall of the metaphor of inversion, seeking to find socialism by inversion of alienated determinations, but recognise the limits of the applicability of Marx's, and classical political economy's, economics. For the most important lesson of Marx's dialectic is that the supersession of economic law gives an entirely different set of determinations - those of self-conscious sociality and freedom. Recognising this calls for the essential openness which I have tried to argue must lie at the heart of an in principle corrigible treatment of alienation and the correct point on which to end this chapter is to register this strength. We shall see, however, that in the absence of a socialist command of this strength, this strength has been put to a most paradoxical use.

Notes

1   *Vide* Rosdolsky, *The Making of Marx's 'Capital'*, ch 1; Rubel, 'A History of Marx's "Economics"'; *idem*, 'The Plan and Method of the "Economics"' and Oakley, *The Making of Marx's Critical Theory*, chs 4-6.

2   Engels, 'Preface to the Third German Edition of Volume One', pp 106-7.

3   *Idem*, 'Preface to Volume Two', pp 83-7.

4   *Idem*, ' Preface to Volume Three', pp 90-8.

5   *Vide* Rubel, 'A History of Marx's "Economics"', pp 117-82.

6   Marx 'To Engels, 2 April 1858'. This plan itself is strongly based on an 1857 plan given in EM, vol 28, p 45, but is the first to eliminate the material we now have as the 'Introduction' to the *Grundrisse*. In 1844 Marx had drawn up another outline for an even more huge project, an abandoned work of which we now have only *The Economic and Philosophical Manuscripts*. EPM, p 231. However, the 1857 plan is the first that be related to the eventual shape of *Capital* in any direct way.

7   Eg C3, p 205.

8   *Idem*, 'To Kugelmann, 13 October 1866. Cf *idem*, 'To Engels', 31 July 1865.

9   C1, p 93.

10   That this was Marx's explicit intention is made clear in a letter to Engels of 30 April 1868. Had Marx carried out this intention, this would have done much to allay Eagleton's criticism in *Ideology*, pp 88-9 that the account of fetishism lacks the dynamic edge which would be provided by pointing to ways in which fetishism might be overcome, though the criticism is just enough if one looks only at volume one.

11   Marx also stresses this theme in his letter 'To Engels, 30 April 1868'.

12   Of course, the polemical force is rather lost because volume one ends not with chapter 32 but with the anomolous chapter 33 on colonisation. McLellelan, *Karl Marx*, p 350 n 1 suggests that this was to avoid the attention of the censor. But, as McLellan himself nevertheless hints, the conclusion of volume one is a mess, with RIPP being omitted for no clear reason, and one simply imagines that, under the difficult circumstances, insufficient control was exercised over the production of volume one. The confusion attending the publication of volume one is set out in Oakley, *The Making of Marx's Critical Theory*, pp 94-7.

13   Hansen, *The Breakdown of Capitalism*, p 32. For an evaluation of the unevenness of Marx's background philosophy of history *vide* Tabora, *The Future in the Writings of Karl Marx*.

14   *Vide* Kolakowski, *Main Currents of Marxism*, vol 2.

15   *Pace* eg Molyneux, *What is the Real Marxist Tradition?*, p 65.

16   The most markedly "automatic" tone is found in the accounts of Luxemburg, *The Accumulation of Capital*, sec 1 and Grossman, 'Marx, Classical Political Economy and the Problem of Dynamics'

17   *Vide* Sweezy, *The Theory of Capitalist Development*, ch 11.

18   Lenin, 'The Proletarian Revolution and the Renegade Kautsky'. Of course, as a response to the work he is attacking, Kautsky's 'The Dictatorship of the Proletariat', Lenin's vitriolic comments are extremely unfair. Sec 3 of Kautsky's work in particular contains what seem, with experience of Stalin, to be terribly prophetic analyses.

19 Adler, 'The Sociology of Revolution', pp 137-9 and Bauer, 'Marxism and Ethics', pp 80-2.

20 Exemplified by Plekhanov, 'On the Question of the Individual's Role in History', sec 3.

21 Eg Althusser, 'On the Materialist Dialectic', p 213.

22 Cl, p 92.

23 CPE, p 262.

24 AD, p 263.

25 Engels, 'To Bloch, 21 September 1890'; *idem*, 'To Schmidt, 27 October 1890'; *idem*, 'To Mehring, 14 July 1893' and *idem*, 'To Borgius, 25 January 1894'.

26 AD, pp 254-71.

27 Idem, 'To Bloch, 21 September 1890', p 683.

28 AD, p 153; cf pp 145-6. Luxemburg brought this motif to real prominence by glossing it as " socialism or barbarism" in 'The Junius Pamphlet', p 269.

29 Strachey, *The Nature of Capitalist Crisis*, ch 18.

30 Sorel, *Reflections on Violence*, pp 95-8.

31 Eg Poulantzas, *Fascism and Dictatorship*.

32 *Vide* Parkin , *Marxism and Class Theory*, pp 168-73.

33 *Vide* Bukharin, 'Imperialism and the Accumulation of Capital', sec 5.

34 Luxemburg, 'Speech to the Founding Convention of the German Communist Party', p 412.

35 *Idem*, 'The Russian Revolution', pp 389-90.

36 Cf *idem*, 'The Mass Strike' and Kautsky, 'The Mass Strike'. The quietism of the Second International against which Luxemburg's politics appear even more vividly dynamic emerges very strongly from Nettl, *Rosa Luxemburg*, vol 2.

37 *Vide* Geras, *The Legacy of Rosa Luxemburg*, ch 1.

38 Luxemburg, 'Reform or Revolution?', pp 86-90. An obvious corollary of holding this position is, of course, to deprecate effective social reform as undermining a desirable acuteness in the manifestation of these tendencies. *Ibid*, p 57.

39 As is effectively the position taken up in a rather trivial fashion by eg Shaw, 'The Transition to Social Democracy', pp 42-7.

40 Sorel, *Reflections on Violence*, ch 1.

41 Lenin, 'A Talk With Defenders of Economism'.

42 *Idem*, 'The State and Revolution'.

43 *Idem*, 'Economics and Politics in the Era of the Dictatorship of the Proletariat'.

44 For my good rather than Luxemburg's I must stress that in saying this I do not mean in any way to disparage her indubitable sincerity, for which , of course, she was murdered. I am hardly the first to be troubled by a bad conscience when

obliged to criticise Luxemburg in this way. Cf Bukharin, 'Imperialism and the Accumulation of Capital', ch 5.

45 Lukács, *Lenin,* p 39.

46 *Idem,* 'Spontaneity of the Masses, Activity of the Party', pp 98-102.

47 *Idem,* History and Class Consciousness, p 75.

48 *Ibid,* pp 70-81.

49 *Vide* Meyerson, *False Consciousness.*

50 Hence Lukács' enormous admiration for Lenin as a politician. *Lukács, Lenin,* chs 2-3.

51 *Vide* Hansen, *The Breakdown of Capitalism,* nb ch 8.

52 *Vide* Eagleton, *Ideology,* pp 89-103.

53 Marcuse, *One-dimensional Man,* pp 356-7.

54 Horkheimer, 'Art and Mass Culture', p 290. The desperate weakness of the ritual note of optimism in these passages, which is merely the most pathetic of which I am aware amongst uncounted similar others, surely testifies that the tendency of critical theory is best represented by Marcuse.

55 *Vide* Rubel, 'The "Marx Legend"', p 23.

56 MCP, p 496.

57 C1, p 799.

58 CHPLI, p 186.

59 C1, p 380. Cf Engels, *The Condition of the Working Class in 1844,* p 308.

60 *Vide* Hobsbawm, *Industry and Empire,* ch 4.

61 *Vide* Laslett, *The World We Have Lost,* ch 5.

62 C1, p 928.

63 MCP, p 488.

64 *Vide* Hobsbawm, *Labouring Men,* chs 5-7 and Thompson, *The Making of the English Working Class,* ch 10.

65 Eg Strachey, *Contemporary Capitalism,* p 119.

66 *Pace* eg Vigor, 'Marx and Modern Capitalism' pp 170-2.

67 C1, pp 802-7.

68 WPP, p 255.

69 EPM, pp 271-2.

70 C1, pp 802-8. Cf W. p 422.

71 WLC, p 216.

72 C1, p 799.

73 WLC, p 216.

74 *Vide* Tawney, *Equality.*

75 *Vide* Runciman, *Relative Deprivation and Social Justice,* ch 13.

76   WPP, p 225.

77   *Vide* Eltis, *The Classical Theory of Economic Growth*, pp 303-4.

78   C1, p 792.

79   *Ibid*, p 798.

80   WPP, p 225.

81   C1, p 798. In *Marx's 'Capital' and One Free World*, pp 99-100, Horie claims that the law to the tendency of the rate of profit to fall contains "a fatal error in its logical construction" in that, as the law is built on a diminution of the value of labour power, its working out *must* represent (in Marx's terms, which are quoted) "a progressively increasing mass of use-values and enjoyments". Taking this up in the present context of the interpretation of immiseration, it is clear that Horie is flatly ignoring the effects of labour market competition on the level of real wages. The mistake is to fail to set the reduction in the value of labour power against another part of "the general law of capitalist accumulation", the reduction in the demand for labour power following from rising organic composition. Of course, to say this is not to say that the way Marx himself did do this is correct.

82   WPP, p 225, I have been unable more widely to assess the fairness of Marx's attack on Weston for the British Museum's holding of *The Bee Hive*, the workers' paper in which Weston published a version of his lectures, does not extend back over the relevant years. Marx had arrived at something like the position which founded this criticism of Weston at least as early as 1847. PP, p 210. However, WPP has the profundity which follows from being a lecture worked up from scripts which were to become *Capital*. *Vide* McLellan, *Karl Marx*, pp 369-70 and Oakley, *The Making of Marx's 'Capital'*, p 93.

83   C1, p 274.

84   *Ibid*, p 275.

85   WPP, p 222.

86   C2, p 486.

87   WPP, pp 220-1.

88   *Vide* eg Rosdolsky, *The Making of Marx's 'Capital'*, ch 20 appendix.

89   Malthus, *An Essay on the Principle of Population*, p 304 and Lassalle, *What is Capital?* pp 20-1. I have discussed Marx's attitude to Malthus in chapter 8. His most hurtful attack on Lassalle was made in COGP, sec 2, which was, of course, a circular letter to the leading participants in the formation of the united German workers' party, of whom Lassalle was very arguably the most important. The vitriolic tone of these criticisms seems to owe much to an extreme personal dislike of Lassalle, a dislike which drew much criticism from Marx's earliest biographers as evidence of an inability to tolerate a rival, even one as apparently well intentioned as Lassalle. *Vide* Mehring, *Karl Marx*, pp 270-8 and Ruhle, *Karl Marx*, pp 227-39.

90   Eg C1, p 275.

91   Eg *ibid*, pp 808-11.

92   *Pace* Rowntree, *The Human Needs of Labour*.

93   C1, pp 276-7.

94   COGP, p 325.

95   WPP, p 221-2.

96   *Ibid*, pp 225-6.

97   C1, p 793.

98   WPP, p 226.

99   PP, pp 210-1.

100 MCP, p 493.

101 WPP, p 226.

102 *Idem*, 'On Trade Unions', p 538.

103 PP, p 211.

104 C1, ch 14, sec 4.

105 *Ibid*, ch 13.

106 *Ibid*, ch 15.

107 MCP, p 391.

108 C1, p 453.

109 *Ibid*, pp 449-51.

110 RIPP, p 1024.

111 C1, ch 32.

112 C3, p 571. Cf C1, p 449 n 15.

113 *Idem*, Inaugural Address to the First International Working Men's Association',
     pp 79-80.

114 *Vide* Cole, *Self-government in Industry*, chs 2-4.

115 Nor can it be denied that Marx's account of working class deprivation is far more
     powerful than his account of the positive side of the working class' position. I
     do not, however, agree *pace* Lovell, *Marx's Proletariat*, ch 4, that this constitutes
     an irretrievable weakness in Marx's work, although the imbalance is a most
     serious matter.

116 The tendency amongst those sympathetic to Marx is to deny this for it obviously
     has not been borne out by the empirical evidence of working class incomes. For
     a recent, sophisticated example amongst a very large and often unsophisticated
     literature, *vide* Green, 'The "Reserve Army Hypothesis"'. The point I am trying
     to make, which I hope does justice to *both* the law and Marx's more fundamental
     point about capitalist accumulation, is that the *law* holds good for *laissez faire*
     capitalism, but that the economy is, as Marx's economics require, increasingly
     less capitalist in this sense,

117 PP, p 211.

118 Landor, 'The Curtain Raised' p 395 (this is an interview with Marx).

119 As Gottheil, *Marx's Economic Predictions*, p 169 puts it:

> The nature of the marxian prediction concerning the inevitability of class struggle is essentially political and lies outside the framework of marxian economics.

> Gottheil did much, in this and a number of other connections, to expose the silliness of many of the more blatant attacks on Marx by making us sensitive to what can and cannot come under an "economic law". However, the point is that recognising this *does* cut against Marx himself.

120 In this sense it *is* highly regrettable that volume three finishes as it does, for were it not to have done so, we could see exactly how far Marx's thinking did go on this.

121 *Vide* Castoriadis, 'On the History of the Workers' Movement', p 14 and Thompson, 'The Povery of Theory', p 59.

122 C1, p 929.

123 *Vide* Jocoby, 'The Politics of the Crisis Theory: Towards the Critique of Automatic Marxism II', p 45.

124 *Vide* Hoffman, *Marxism and the Theory of Practice*, p 22.

125 So whilst Lebowitz, *Beyond 'Capital'* contains much of interest and, despite some amazingly silly diagrams, does a great deal to show the lacunae in Marx's account of working class consciousness, it must be doubtful whether this will emerge from the mess that Lebowitz places himself in by his commitment to "orthodox marxism" as a "completely autonomous structure of thought" (p 156) which wholly undermines the thrust of his title. What should be an interesting claim that *Capital* "does not explore...the creation of new social needs for workers" (p 35) is turned into the metaphor of the search for "The Missing Book on Wage-Labour" (ch 2). To the extent that this is a textual claim about the corpus of *Capital* (pp 15-6), it is, of course, just wrong. But this is not really the issue. The point is to criticise the tendentiousness of subsequent "One-sided Marxism" as a failure to explore Marx properly (ch 5). The result of proceeding in this oblique way is that it is impossible to read this book without getting bogged down in fruitless side-issues of interpretation. However, one might expect that Lebowitz was not going to go beyond *Capital* but merely add another book to it when one reads that the features of advanced capitalism which indicate the complete failure of Marx's political programme all "point to a theory *not entirely successful*"! (p 6, my emphasis).

126 *Vide* Lekas, *Marx on Classical Antiquity*, p 150.

127 GI, p 81.

128 *Idem*, 'The Class Struggles in France 1848-50', p 127.

129 COGP, p 320.

130 EPM, p 306.

131 COGP, p 327.

132 *Idem,* 'Conspectus of Bakunin's Statism and Anarchy' p 333.

133 MCP, p 495.

134 GI, p 88.

135 HF, p 36.

136 Althusser, 'Contradiction and Overdetermination', pp 114-6, formalising an idea clearly present in Lenin, eg 'Party Organisation and Party Literature'.

137 I have discussed the issues raised here in 'Rationality, Democracy and Freedom in Marxist Critiques of Hegel's Philosophy of Right'.

138 Rubin can be credited with presenting an, as it were, complete - if abridged - finished version of *Theories of Surplus Value* in his own history based on the *Theories* and meant to be read in conjunction with them, *A History of Economic Thought.*

139 *Vide* Colletti, 'Marxism: Science of Revolution?', p 236. The total relativism of this viewpoint has been alluded to in chapter 1 and I hope to have shown a superior way to ground this broad position (which thereby is substantially changed). The extent that it has held sway previously must really be ascribed to political force. Cf the role of socialist ideologues in Lenin, 'What Is To Be Done?'.

140 *Vide* Pilling *Marx's 'Capital'*, ch 2.

141 *Vide* eg Sanchez Vasquez, *The Philosophy of Praxis*, nb pp 234-8.

142 This, I think, is the kernel of sense in Sorel's criticisms of the influence of Hegel on Marx in the *Illusions of Progress,* pp 207-8.

143 *Vide* Lichtheim, 'The Concept of Ideology' p 21.

144 *Vide* eg Acton, *The Illusion of the Epoch*, pp 107-16.

145 Eg Marx, 'To Engels, 31 May 1873'.

146 *Vide* Lukács, *History and Class Consciousness,* pp 223-55 and Marcuse, 'Freedom and the Historical Imperative'.

147 Cf Unger, *Law in Modern Society,* p 8: "To carry out its own programme social theory must destroy itself".

148 Much less is it justified to go on to say, as does Flew, 'Was Karl Marx a Social Scientist' that Marx was so dogmatic as to hardly deserve being called a scientist. This revival of very tired indeed claims about marxism being a theology shows just what airs contemporary neo-liberalism thinks it can adopt, but as these airs have all been exposed earlier, their re-adoption now is hardly helpful to the proper assessment of *Capital.*

149 Eg Keynes, 'Essays in Persuasion', p 304.

150 I leave aside a common enough, though subsidiary, overall theme which is to delay the time when an assessment of Marx's success or failure can be made. So, writing in 1989(!), Miliband, *Divided Societies,* p 234 tells us:

Class struggle for the creation of democratic, egalitarian, co-operative and classless societies, far from coming to an end, has only just begun.

Well, indeed, but one does wonder whether Miliband fully appreciates just how much this cuts both ways.

151 Eg Jakubowski, *Ideology and Superstructure*, ch 2.

152 Eg Baran And Sweezy, *Monopoly Capital*, ch 1.

153 Eg Bottomore, *Marxist Sociology*.

154 Eg Bell, *The Coming of Post-industrial Society;* Crosland, *The Future of Socialism*, ch 3; Dahrendorf, *Class and Class Conflict in Industrial Society* and Touraine, *The Post-industrial Society*. Representatively defensive critcisms are set out in Frankel, *Capitalist Soceity and Modern Sociology* and Westergaard and Resler, *Class in a Capitalist Society*.

155 Strachey, *What Are We To Do?*, ch 8.

156 *Vide* Stephens, *The Transition from Capitalism to Socialism*, ch 2.

157 Were it right, this interpretation would lead to Marx's being open to cogent right wing criticism, such as is made by Barry, *Welfare*, p 41, as being antagonistic to the welfare state!

10 *Laissez Faire* and Advanced Capitalism

The abolition of economic domination and its replacement by political freedom was, if I may be allowed the necessary grandiloquence, the most important issue facing humanity when Marx died and it has lost none of its significance since. But the broad association between Marx's views and some sort of dramatic collapse of capitalism in the minds of both his sympathisers and his opponents has led to an absurd position in the twentieth century attempt to realise this replacement. Capitalism since 1867 has shown and continues to show determining empirical characteristics which seem to cry out for explanation along the lines Marx indicated, but only in a paradoxical way. The socialising developments within the capitalist economy which confirm the essential thrust of Marx's work do so by making it increasingly inapplicable in detail, most apparently so in respect of working class action. But defences of Marx have often taken the wholly self-defeating line of denying those developments.

It must be recognised that it is not to go against the best way to move on from Marx but to go with it to insist on the overall socialising character of such developments in the capitalist economy. Once one has got unduly mechanistic socialist optimism out of the way, then really this should be appreciated. But the rejection of "reformist" attitudes toward progressive improvements in the capitalist economy is endemic to twentieth century marxism and, though there are many bad reasons for this really based on the apparent success of Bolshevism, the fundamental reason, I will now argue, is that the rejection is based on a substantial truth.

The whole structure of classical political economy's, and thus Marx's, account of the limits to accumulation turns on *laissez faire* capitalism and by 1867, Marx could see that *laissez faire* capitalism indeed was being abolished by its own movements and he coupled this to an (itself not properly worked out) idea that the working class would take advantage of the crises and the socialising developments in *laissez faire* in order to realise socialism. Increasingly after 1867 he effectively relegated his economic writings to second place behind the political activity he thought necessary to bring about socialism on this basis. If we limit our assessment of Marx's views to the assessment of them as an account of the end of *laissez faire* capitalism, they are very powerful indeed. But if they are taken to be an account of the ending of *capitalism* as such, then they have proven to be very seriously wrong, for capitalism has not ended nor shows signs of ending - not signs of appalling waste, anarchy, privation, injustice, etc, but of *ending*. The reason for this is that the socialising developments which Marx identified have *not* been used by the working class to realise socialism as successfully as they have been used by capitalists, in the context of the generalisation of the joint stock form, to save their private ownership of the means of production despite its awful consequences. It is absurd to disregard Marx's views because capitalism has not gone. Advanced capitalism is a very different economy than *laissez faire* and in the explanation of why the former has superceded the latter, views akin to Marx's not only should be regarded but, in fact, as we shall see, have been arrived at by extremely influential bourgeois economists, policy makers, business executives and state officials. But the very success of this use of views substantially in agreement with Marx's views of *laissez faire* capitalism has disrupted his views of socialism.

The key to assessing Marx in the modern world still lies in Hegel. I believe that Marx's account of *laissez faire* is essentially faithful to the requirements of the dialectic and therefore basically is sound; indeed, it is sound in ways that Marx himself did not realise. But the generalisation of joint stock has been the foundation of structural shifts in the capitalist economy away from those tendencies Marx thought would lead to socialism and therefore *the immanent critique of the classical political economy of laissez faire of itself cannot produce socialism*. One cannot immanently develop socialism as a critique of *laissez faire* capitalism when, in so doing, one is setting oneself against the more powerful development of *laissez faire* into advanced capitalism. Marxism after Marx has been very seriously weakened by tending to marginalise or ignore the features which have assumed the greatest importance as capitalism has been restructured into its advanced form. The disastrous consequences which this has had and continues to have are impossible to over-estimate. Whilst socialism failed to adopt the abolition of the independence of the economy as its clear aim, advanced capitalism has - with very little consciousness of doing so - gone a long way towards carrying that abolition out, not with the ultimate aim of social improvement but with the aim of preserving private property. In the space left by confusion in socialist thought, the potential political power released by the end of economic domination has been more fully utilised by capital than by labour.

Advanced capitalism has replaced *laissez faire* and, to the extent that it has done so, it has placed the economic tendencies which were to play a very substantial role in the development of socialism under effective planned controls. Because the planning is capitalist, it is alienated and hardly planning at all in the best sense of the word. But it is debased *planning*,[1] rather than the compulsion of the economic hand, that guides capitalism now and thus the subject of socialist critique has, or at least should have, changed. Though the critique of alienation remains at the core of all hope, it has changed radically since 1867 and not in an overall hopeful fashion. The powers conferred by self-consciousness in the planning of material life have not been taken up not so much by the active working class hoping to use those powers to clear away capitalist limits to the development of wealth and free time but by a bourgeoisie straining - with very great success - to contain that development within those limits.

It seems today that the high point of the success of marxism as a political movement was at the time of the Second International. Putting it this way of course concedes that this was also the time from which the decline of that movement can be identified. That success surely was based on the simple enough point that capitalism at the time seemed quite untenable. This is worth stating quite bluntly. By the last quarter of the nineteenth century, *laissez faire* capitalism had entered into such a state of systemic decay that the future of capitalist property seemed to be called into the most serious question. The market had placed the most serious limits on continued capital accumulation and, in particular, the profound crisis in the international capitalist economy between 1873-96, which Kondratieff identified as the declining phase of a long wave[2] and, whatever one feels about this analysis, about the empirical existence of which there is general agreement,[3] was very widely analysed as signalling the end of capitalism, both by those who hoped for and those who feared this outcome.

When, after Marx's death in 1883, Engels' took on the main burden of efforts to popularise Marx's thought and consolidate the political movement largely based upon it, he had the stimulus of putting his arguments forward in the context of this crisis, which he was able to use to show that the limits to accumulation Marx had identified were becoming ever more pressing.[4] We have seen that the principal line taken by the economists of the Second International, including Engels himself, is to gloss the radical incompleteness of Marx's work at this point as breakdown theory, and present a claim that capitalist accumulation had run against limits that were making its collapse inevitable. That this interpretation now seems very seriously flawed indeed should not detract from the severity of the economic crisis against which it was developed, which gave it an at least plausible contemporary empirical background.

The first "great depression" thus has been given a substantial role in the explanation of the seeming success of marxist political movements at the turn of the century.[5] Nothing more need be said here about this "success". But there *was* a successful development from this crisis, if an even more suspect one, though suspect in a different way. This success is the persistence of capitalism by the abolition of *laissez faire*, and with it competitive limits to capital accumulation, within the framework of capitalist property; that is to say, by the development of advanced capitalism. In order to assess the nature of this "success", it is best *not* to remain within Marx's own work or its developments in the Second International but to turn to those in whose view the quotation marks placed around success above can be removed. These are the influential bourgeois businesspersons and economists who guided the transition from *laissez faire* to advanced capitalism in the wave of centralisation activity that took place in and after the first great depression.

Marx, of course, based his account of capitalism on the leading national economy of the nineteenth century - Britain.[6] This distinction obviously now has passed to the US[7] and it is appropriate that we should focus on US materials, on what recent historiography is describing as the formation of "corporate liberalism" in the US between 1873 and 1916.[8] A generation of American economists, of whom JB Clark, CA Conant, AT Hadley, DA Wells and CD Wright may be taken as representative, held to a view of *laissez faire* as structurally prone to chronic overproduction which has the strongest parallels to that I have identified in Marx. These influential bourgeois economists conceived of the corporation as the principal way of dealing with the problems of *laissez faire* within a broad framework of capitalist property. They did not regard departure from the price mechanism as an unfortunate cost but as an absolutely necessary shift in the nature of capitalist economics if capitalist property was to be sustained. As it was put by perhaps the most interesting of these figures, CA Conant, a leading financier, financial analyst and government advisor:

> The great civilised peoples have today at their command [a] great excess of saved capital which is the result of machine production. It is proposed to point out...how great is this excess, how profoundly it is disturbing economic conditions in the [civilised] countries and how necessary to the salvation of these countries is an outlet for their surplus savings, if the entire fabric of the present economic order is not to be shaken by a social revolution.[9]

Let me set out the thinking behind these remarks.

The First Annual Report in 1886 of the US Commissioner for Labour, Carroll D Wright, was addressed specifically to the causes of "The present industrial depression...the first of its kind",[10] because "No more important and vital question could have been selected for the first work on the Bureau of Labour".[11] In a most comprehensive review of the European[12] and US[13] evidence, Wright concluded:

> the family of manufacturing states, Great Britain, France, Belgium, Germany, and the United States, if not also Austria, Russia and Italy[14] are suffering from an industrial depression novel in its kind, and yet having characteristic features of similarity throughout the whole range of states. It seems to be quite true that in those states considered, the volume of business and of production have not been affected disastrously by the depression,[15] but that prices have been greatly reduced, wages frequently reduced, and margins of profits carried to the minimum range. Over-production seems to prevail in all alike without regard to the system of commerce which exists in either.[16]

Reflection on this crisis was characterised by the remarkable paradox of grandiose celebration of the development of immense economic resources and yet thoroughgoing pessimism about their use. A 1889 review of *Recent Economic*

Changes by DA Wells, one-time US Special Commissioner of Revenue and distinguished academic, began with the following:

> The economic changes that have occurred during the last quarter of a century...have unquestionably been more important and varied than during any former corresponding period of the world's history. It would seem, indeed, as if the world, during all the years since the inception of civilization, has been working up on the line of equipment for industrial effort...that this equipment, having at last been made ready, the work of using it has, for the first time in our day and generation, fairly begun...As an immediate consequence the world...has never been able to accomplish so much.[17]

But when describing the tenor of "The Economic Outlook" occasioned by these developments, one is almost shocked to find Wells saying that:

> The predominant feeling induced by a review and consideration of the numerous economic changes and disturbances that have occurred since 1873...is undoubtedly, in the case of very many persons, discouraging and pessimistic.[18]

The reason is clear enough. The development of productive power has been attended by drastic crises and the improvements in human happiness it has occasioned were equally attended by profound and enormously threatening manifestations of discontent:

> as a necessary sequence of these changes, has come a series of wide-spread and complex disturbances; manifesting themselves in...the discontent of labour and an increasing antagonism of nations...Out of these changes will probably come further disturbances, which to many thoughtful and conservative minds seem full of menace of a mustering of the barbarians from within rather than as before from without, for an attack on the whole present organization of society and even the permanency of civilization itself.[19]

There was, of course, a very great deal of diversity in the detailed explanations of these disturbances but an in fact surprising degree of unanimity in the broad character of these explanations emerges from a review of the contemporaneous works. What first tended to be described was a huge fall in prices, and not merely a fall which is part of the normal swings of supply and demand but a wholly unprecedented and dramatic secular fall:

> the recent fall in the prices of the great staple commodities of the world has been in extent and character without precedent in the world's history...comparing the data for 1885-'86 with those of 1866-'76, the decline...has been extraordinary, and has extended to most countries...the

> estimate of...thirty-one per cent as the average measure or extent of this decline, is not excessive.[20]

The overwhelmingly predominant explanation of this fall was based on an idea of overproduction. As Conant put it in 1901:

> In a practical sense...over-production in respect to effective demand is not only possible but has been the actual history of many leading commodities during the last three decades.[21]

In a first sense, overproduction is merely another way of describing the debilitating fall in prices:

> *overproduction*...describes what, in the time of a crisis, and in the case of many producers, is a reality, the possession of goods they have made and cannot sell, except at a ruinous sacrifice.[22]

But overproduction also captures the essence of what was perceived as the extraordinary novelty of this fall in prices. Wells distinguished between the overproduction that may "occur through lack of progress and enterprise"[23] and others which occur "through what may be termed an excess of progress or enterprise". The former are the disproportionalities that may locally occur simultaneous with demand which because, say, of a lack of transport facilities, cannot be satisfied. But the latter, which now is "intensified to a degree never before experienced"[24] is "industrial over-production"[25] and it:

> is to be found in the results of the improvements of production and distribution which have been made especially effective within the last quarter of a century...as this process is general and, as a rule, involves a steady increase in the improved and constantly improving instrumentalities of production and distribution, the period at length arrives when the industrial and commercial world awakens to the fact that there is a product disproportionate to any current remunerative demand. Here, then, is one and probably the best explanation of the circumstance that the supply of very many of the great articles and instrumentalities of the world's use and commerce has increased, during the last ten or fifteen years, in a far greater ratio than the contemporaneous increase in the world's population, or of its consuming capacity.[26]

The fundamental reason for overproduction and the pessimism it generated was the very increase in productive capacity that gave its unique character to economic life in the last quarter of the nineteenth century. It is the unprecedented growth in productive capacity that typically lowers prices and creates the basic background for overproduction crises by throwing such a huge amount of consumer goods upon the market:

When the historian of the future writes the history of the nineteenth century he will doubtless assign to the period embraced by the life of the generation terminating in 1885, a place of importance, considered in its relations to the interests of humanity, second to but very few, and perhaps to none, of the many similar epochs of time in any of the centuries which have preceded it; inasmuch as all economists who have specially studied the matter are substantially agreed that, within the period named, man in general has attained to such a greater control over the forces of Nature, and has so compressed their use, that he has been able to do far more work in a given time, produce far more product, measured by quantity in ratio to a given amount of labour, and reduce the effort necessary to insure a comfortable subsistence in a far greater measure than it was possible for him to accomplish twenty or thirty years anterior to the time of the present writing (1889)...In a few departments of industrial effort the saving [in time and labour] has certainly amounted to more than seventy or eighty per cent; in not a few to more than fifty per cent [One authority claims] one third as the minimum average [saving] Other authorities are inclined to assign a considerably higher average.[27]

Conant, whose view point was principally financial, added to the appreciation of the cumulative nature of the problem when he drew attention to the pernicious consequences of what he called "the loan fund". By this he meant the huge and rapidly growing supply of savings available for productive investment which were greatly in excess of potential investment for the production of consumption goods:

There was a time when every dollar of available saving was required for productive enterprises in Europe and the United States...But the...employment of labor-saving machinery in farming and manufacturing has promoted saving in almost a geometrical ratio from year to year. The saving has been capitalized into increased producing plant, which has greatly increased the saving of another year, until the amount of capital offered annually for investment in new enterprises has reached several thousands of millions of dollars every year.

The great development in modern society of saving for investment has contributed to increase the tendency to a mis-direction of productive power. Over-production of consumable goods takes place because so large a part of the purchasing power of the community is saved for investment. A better equilibrium would be established between the production of finished goods and the demand for them if the community devoted a larger portion of its purchasing power to obtaining such goods...But so large a part of the earnings of society has been set aside in recent years for investment that the equilibrium between the production of finished goods and the effective demand for them has been broken.[28]

In sum, under these circumstances, production for profit is forestalled and, given that commitments to future production have been made on the basis of expectations of profit, a general crisis ensues:

> The primitive producer, providing directly for his own wants by his own efforts, occupied a very different position from the modern producer, who produces a large quantity of a single article and produces wholly for exchange. If it turns out that he cannot exchange his product for as much of other products as he expected, his calculations of profit are defeated. If he relies for his income upon the margin of profit above cost of production and finds that he cannot sell them for as much, he receives no return for his labor and ceases to be a purchaser of the products of others. If he holds his products for what he considers a fair equivalent in money or in other goods, but the producers of other goods will not pay this equivalent, he finds on his hands a useless stock of goods. When this condition reaches a large number of producers, and effects the mechanism of credit by their inability to fulfil their obligations to the banks, a crisis occurs.[29]

A merely general comparison of this account and that of Marx is sufficient for the point I want to make here. The picture that emerges from these bourgeois economists is in large part that which one gains from Marx, of a geometrically expanding distance between the growth of productive forces as private capital and mass consumption as effective demand. But, of course, in Marx, remedies are considered which contemplate the most radical changes in the economy, indeed in the entire social structure. Growth for reasons other than private accumulation and directly broadening the possibilities of mass consumption are considered as ways of attacking the fundamental causes of overproduction. What, by contrast, is of the essence for understanding of the form of the corporation is that capitalist responses to overproduction were not directed at its root causes but to its superficial representation in destructive competition. Though the critique of Say's law and other variants of the attempt flatly to deny the possibility of overproduction were explored theoretically,[30] the main cause of crisis was, wrongly but understandably from the capitalist point of view,[31] identified as *competition* itself.

All economists of this period acknowledged the simple returns to scale that underpinned the concentration of capital, but WF Willoughby, an economist analysing the concentration of industry for the US Department of Labor, represented the institutional sophistication of the economists I am discussing by not giving them the first importance in his account of concentration:

> The various economies realized by the large establishment are now so generally recognized that it is quite superfluous to comment on them further. We, therefore, turn to a benefit resulting from the concentration of work, which either has been ignored or slighted in all discussions of the question, but which is nevertheless of prime importance.[32]

The factor Willoughby had in mind, and I will return to his analysis, was removing the pernicious effects of competition. Willoughby surely was right in claiming that the avoidance of competition was marginalised in mainstream neo-classical economics, but it certainly was not in the minds of corporate owners and controllers and of the institutionally sensitive economists upon whom I am concentrating. ES Meade of the Wharton School of Finance and Economy of the University of Pennsylvania described manufacturers' attitudes to *laissez faire* thus:

> It is not difficult to understand why the *regime* of free competition was productive of manifold hardships to the manufacturer. Competition might be considered the life of trade, but at the close of the last industrial depression it was regarded as the death of profits. It was highly desirable from the manufacturer's view-point to stop, or at least to abate, this struggle...They desired a larger profit without such an effort to get it...In 1898 and 1899 the time was ripe for a change. Men were weary of competition and the era of combination was gladly welcomed.[33]

The obvious response to these evils of competition is combination. In the 1886 report which we have already mentioned, the US Commissioner for Labor conveyed the following results of his investigators' interviews of manufacturers:

> Many manufacturers have said...in the course of this investigation...that if the employers in any industry would combine under an organization that should have positive coherence there would be no difficulty, so far as that industry is concerned, in regulating the volume of production in accordance with the demand, and that with this regulation of supply on a scientific foundation there would be no opportunity for labour troubles or depressions to occur...The manufacturers, so far as all the facts which can be observed indicate, are correct in their position...Any one great industry, under complete organization, can be regulated by all the forces acting understandingly and together, and it is only through such organization that production can be wisely regulated on the basis of necessity to supply the market.[34]

The testimony of 62 witnesses, chiefly large capitalists, before an Industrial Commission established in 1898[35] was summed up thus, under the heading 'Competition the Chief Cause':

> Among the causes which have led to the formation of industrial combinations, most of the witnesses were of the opinion that competition, so vigorous that profits of nearly all competing establishments were destroyed, is to be given first place.[36]

The first thing that can be remedied by removing competition in this way is the principal characteristic of the *laissez faire* economy, which precisely is its unplanned character, in which sales, or their absence, pass a judgment about investment that is not known in advance:

> Future values have been anticipated; men thought they saw amounts of wealth coming to them that appeared ample. If these had only been real, they would have been justified large expenditures in them. Orders for large amounts of consumers' wealth have been given, and the mills have been set running in order to meet them. The goods come into existence; but the wealth that was seen in a vision of the future has not materialized. The mills have made the cloth, shoes, furniture, etc; and the values that were to have paid themselves have resolved themselves into a mirage.[37]

Against this fundamental potential for crisis, extensive combination offers the theoretically most attractive solution outside of central planning:

> Manufacturers have said...that if the employers in any industry would combine under an organization that should have positive coherence, there would be no difficulty, so far as that industry is concerned, in regulating the volume of production in accordance with the demand and that with this regulation of supply on a scientific foundation, there would be no opportunity for labor troubles or depressions to occur.[38]

If one is apprehensive about the amount of power that this extent of combination would place in a few hands,[39] this does not diminish the power of the basic case for integration through the large corporation:

> Probably the most fundamental benefit resulting to society generally from production on a large scale [after realising economies of scale] is the influence it exerts in steadying production. Ever since the inauguration of the modern industrial regime, industry has been periodically paralyzed, trade injured, and progress brought to a standstill by what are called "industrial depressions"...The injury resulting from this unstable condition of industry cannot be calculated. Any device which will to any degree regulate this intemperance, and steady production, must be welcomed as a great gain to society. This the large industry certainly tends to do. The attempt to control production so as to keep their plants in constant operation has been one of the great motives leading manufacturers to consolidate their enterprises and organize such combinations as trusts.[40]

What has become the central theme of later antitrust policy can be seen to have been given expression right at the beginning of the major centralisation movements. As AT Hadley of Yale put it, "The Good and Evil of Industrial Combinations" had to be weighed and a distinction drawn between necessary and valuable integration through the corporation and unwelcome price distortion through unacceptable levels of combination.[41] The balance predominantly drawn at this time[42] was that public welfare was seen to inhere more in allowing concentration rather than in its prohibition.[43]

The corporations' repertoire of strategies to iron out fluctuations included some which were regarded as quite unobjectionable. These included simple product diversification:

> The large establishment is able to command a larger market; it can offset a falling off in demand in one quarter or in one commodity by the cultivation of trade in another direction or the production of other articles,[44]

and planned purchasing leading through to vertical integration downwards:

> A large concern can purchase supplies upon a more favorable basis. It can...make use of refuse and by-products that are destroyed by the smaller establishments.[45]

Some other strategies, however, occasioned a great deal of disquiet. The major problem of overproduction crises from the capitalists' point of view is the destruction of the value of installed capital because of excess competition. The availability of huge investment funds through the stock market allows of the very quick equipping of plant which may well undercut the competitiveness of earlier installed plant:

> The [securities] markets, especially that for transferable capital, afford a constant menace...to the producer. He knows that if his profits rise above average, the great loan fund of the world is ready to pour into his industry, create new mills and increase to an excessive amount a production which was probably already sufficient to meet effective demand. He knows also, that if a new invention appears upon the market, reducing by 5 per cent. or even a smaller fraction the cost of producing his goods, the loan fund is available for equipping new mills with this invention or enabling his rival to apply it to their old mills.[46]

Corporate owners and controllers simply found it intolerable that huge plant installations could be rendered effectively worthless well within their possible productive lifetimes by this gale of competition. The idea that capital of this size can be moved to other employments by contesting other markets - a sort of "compensation theory" for capital - is simply nonsense:

> Capital once invested in the machinery of production cannot always or easily be withdrawn or converted to other uses. The mobility of capital has greatly increased under the system of banking credits and stock exchange securities, but arguments based upon this mobility refer to the loan fund of floating capital

and are not applicable to capital which has become fixed in mills and machinery.[47]

There can be no doubt that, given restricted markets and the capital stock available through the share, large scale investment was hugely problematic for capitalists.

The response that was made is clear. It was hyper-competitive pricing which cleared out the industry to the point where the remaining corporations, unable to drive each other out of business, agreed on mutually acceptable prices.[48] Andrew Carnegie gives what we can take to be a first hand account of manufacturers' responses to an overproduction crisis:

> prices...continue falling until the article is sold at cost to the less favorably situated or less ably managed factory; and even until the best managed and equipped factory is not able to produce the article at prices at which it can be sold. Political economy says that here the trouble will end. Goods will not be produced at less than cost. This was true when Adam Smith wrote, but it is not quite true to-day. When an article was produced by a small manufacturer, employing, probably at his own home, two or three journey men and an apprentice or two, it was an easy matter for him to limit or even to stop production. As manufacturing is carried on to-day, in enormous establishments with five or ten millions of dollars of capital invested, and with thousands of workers, it costs the manufacturer much less to run at a loss per ton or per yard than to check production. Stoppage would be serious indeed. The condition of cheap manufacture is running full. Twenty sources of expense are *fixed charges*, many of which stoppage would only increase. Therefore the article is produced for months, and in some cases that I have known for years, not only without profit or without interest upon capital, but to the impairment of the capital invested. Manufacturers have balanced their books at the end of the year only to find their capital reduced at each successive balance. Whilst continuing to produce would be costly, the manufacturer knows too well that stoppage would be ruin. His brother manufacturers are of course in the same situation. They see the savings of many years, as well perhaps as the capital they have succeeded in borrowing, becoming less and less, with no hope of a change in the situation. It is in the soil thus prepared that anything promising relief is gladly welcomed...Combinations -syndicates - trusts - they are willing to try anything. A meeting is called, and in the presence of immediate danger they decide to take united action and form a trust. Each factory is rated as worth a certain amount. Officers are chosen, and through these the entire product of the article in question is to be distributed to the public, at remunerative prices.[49]

Of course, the degree of overt collusion Carnegie postulates would now be unusual,[50] but more or less the same outcome is reached, after the clearing out of an industry's price makers down to a few giant corporations, by mutually conscious oligopolistic pricing by the remaining giants, that outcome being "the organization of production":

The tendency to over-production resulting from unrestricted competition has been corrected to some extent during the past decade by the consolidation of industry and the restriction of production. Production has been curtailed in many lines to conform to ascertained or probable demand.[51]

It is clear that towards the end of the nineteenth century, continuing to guide production by the price mechanism was becoming a flat impossibility. Competitive production utilising modern plant required large scale, immobile investment. Such cost advantages as that investment yielded were purely ephemeral given a low elasticity of demand in more or less all markets and the huge powers of ready equipment on the parts of potential rival producers. The time scales for the amortisation of investment needed to be longer because of the disproportion between the size of the investment and the difficulty of opening new markets. But these scales were made unreliable and very often far too short by unrestrained competition. Production for private accumulation *cannot* take place on this basis[52] and another method of organising production seemed, not only, as we have seen, to the socialists of the turn of the century but also to contemporaneous capitalists, to be becoming a necessity. Socialist solutions ultimately tended towards undercutting private property. The capitalist solutions we have discussed put forward corporate organisation as a way of saving that property and, by concentrating on limiting competition, were able to do so. Production for long run profit in markets hugely restricted by inequalities of wealth distribution is made possible by replacing price competition with the oligopolistic pricing which is the principal feature of the corporation. Paradoxically enough, the price mechanism was ousted as the cost of maintaining private property in the means of production.

I want to make my point mainly by reference to the corporation but it is quite absurd to attempt to discuss the advanced capitalist economy by reference to the dominance of corporations alone. One must take into account the other feature that identifies that economy, the huge role in economic management given to the state. Though freed of the price mechanism, corporations still are subject to the fundamental contradiction between their infinite urge to grow and the relatively restricted growth in mass consumption. Of itself, the corporation's ability to make prices actually limits demand in relation to capacity and that capacity grows at exponential rates through the capital concentration powers of the share (and associated debenture financing) and the growth in the productivity of plant. The rescheduling of growth to bring it into line with the longer planning horizons of corporations cannot really alter the overproductive effects of this contradiction in any other than the short term and that state adjustment of aggregate demand was essential became widely accepted by US economists arguably by the turn of the century. A massive expansion in the state's role in regulating the domestic economic environment has proven to be the principal mechanism for the maintenance of advanced capitalist stability. But this policy was developed rather later, strongly intimated under Wilson but rapidly accelerating after the Great Depression,[53] and thus is somewhat outside the period on which I want to concentrate.[54] However, the form in which the necessity of state underpinning of the economy first became manifest was a product of the era upon which we are focusing, to wit, the foreign policy of economic imperialism. The intellectual analysis of imperialism does not have its origins in Hilferding,[55] Luxemburg,[56] Lenin[57] or even Hobson[58] but in earlier, pro-capitalist economic writers,[59] amongst whom let us focus on Conant and PS Reinsch.

Conant's account of imperialism is a perfectly lucid expression of the views one would have (before experience of underdevelopment as a process of net capital *export* from the underdeveloped country) if one organised those views around an inviolable commitment to private ownership. Writing in 1900 he said:

> The United States have actually reached, or are approaching, the economic state where...outlets are required outside their own boundaries in order to prevent business depression, idleness and suffering at home.[60]

Conant described a situation of massive capital saturation in the US and the other capitalist countries:

> It is the excess of saving, with the resulting accumulation of unconsumed goods, in the great industrial countries, which is one of the world maladies of the economic situation today...the conditions which set about in about 1870, when the great capitalist countries first appear to have become fully capitalized to meet all demands which consumers are willing to make out of their earnings. The world's economic history since that time - the intense industrial activity...up to 1873; the long period of stagnation which followed...point to excess of saved capital beyond the effective demand of the community as their underlying cause...under the present social order it is becoming impossible to find at home in the great capitalistic countries employment for all the capital saved which is at once safe and remunerative.[61]

He saw overseas investment as the only means of relieving this saturation and thus relieve the chronic tendency towards declining returns which follows from it:

> The necessity of sending capital abroad is the salient economic lesson of the closing day of the nineteenth century. In recent years interest and discount rates...The real opportunity afforded by colonial possessions is for the development of the new countries by fixed investments, whose slow completion is the only present means of absorbing saved capital without the needless duplication of existing means of production.[62]

Conant had a very clear idea that the US had to turn from being "absorbed for many years in the development of our industries at home" and recognise:

that the United States is rapidly approaching the condition of Great Britain, France, Germany, and Belgium, where she will be compelled to seek free markets and opportunities for investment in the undeveloped countries, if she is not to be crowded to the wall by the efforts of the other great civilized powers.[63]

He also saw that this meant international difficulties:

> outlets might be found without the exercise of political and military power, if commercial freedom was the policy of all nations. As such a policy has not been adopted by more than one important power of western Europe...the United States are compelled, by instinct of self-preservation, to enter, however, reluctantly, upon the field of international politics.[64]

However, it was Reinsch, Professor of Political Science at the University of Wisconsin, who was the principal formulator of the "Open Door" policy, the specific formulation of a formally open world investment system which thus falls into spheres of interest determined by the economic power of any particular imperialist nation rather than a formally closed colonial system based on privileged trade relations within empires. Writing in 1900, just after the end of the US-Spanish war, Reinsch recognised that US isolationism was ended:

> That the United States is to play a leading part in international affairs, - that she is to be one of the five leading world powers, - has been irrevocably decided by the events of the recent past. A nation of our power and resources would be untrue to its vocation if it did not sooner or later realize its duty in this important position to which it has attained.[65]

He coupled this, however, with a fundamental claim that US expansionism should be distinguished from colonial aggrandisement on the European pattern:

> A headlong policy of territorial aggrandizement should be avoided by the United States, as it would entail the danger of burdening our national existence with elements that could not be assimilated and would only weaken the state. It should be the aim of our nation to counteract everywhere, at home and abroad, the ambitions of universal imperialism...Commerce and industry should be developed by establishing trade depots and means of communication, and by upholding the policy of equal opportunity throughout the colonial world, rather than by territorial acquisitions.[66]

This very brief sketch of aspects of the thinking behind the early formation of the advanced capitalist economy has tried to show that its basic structure is formed by an attempt to deal, within the limits of capitalist property, with what was generally accepted to be *laissez faire's* chronic tendency towards overproduction. The abolition of the price mechanism by the principal corporations is regarded as an essential positive step, for it allows such returns to be made as will encourage large scale, efficient investment to take place. Major crises to be overcome by the replacement of market chaos by corporate planning. Alongside this planning, the state will provide the (domestic and) overseas environments in which corporations will be able to expand, for, of themselves, even when oligopolistically organised, they are quite unable to secure a climate of investment opportunity.

Even as brief an analysis as the above of the thinking behind the reconstruction of the American economy from *laissez faire* to what is identifiably advanced capitalism is sufficient to indicate the fundamental undercutting of Marx's account of the limits to capitalist accumulation this reconstruction constitutes. We can recall that those limits are essentially composed of two sets of contradictory multipliers. The first set is that of the cumulative growth in C necessary to produce cumulatively reducing growth in s' that constitutes the law of the tendency of the rate of profit to fall. The second set is that of the growth in $s4_i + s2_i$ which cumulatively outpaces growth in $s3_{ii}$ that constitutes the tendency to overproduction.

The corporate form allows the potential for the indefinite postponement of the effects of these multipliers. Under these circumstances, the laws of the tendency of the rate of profit to fall and of overproduction to increase are not eliminated but they are not degenerative.[67] The price competition which imposes them ever more acutely is absent and so, in *economic* principle, there is no limit to their perpetuation. Now, it should go without saying that holding that advanced capitalism is not subject to the accelerating limits to accumulation to which *laissez faire* is does not mean that advanced capitalism is a defensible mode of production. It is not. It is monstrously irrational and for the vast majority of people living under it it offers, at best, stultification at work and leisure and, at worst, death by starvation or political murder. But the whole point is that criticisms of advanced capitalism must be made in ways which come to terms with the now available *political* choice over ways of organising the economy and not in ways which look for some sort of prop from inevitable economic system deterioration.

It is manifest that - despite some outstanding individual contributions - marxism has dealt overall inadequately with the reconstruction of capitalism on a corporate basis, in some ways hardly better than neo-classicism. What should be said at the outset is that Marx himself is of little use. The joint stock company has but a marginal place in Marx's economic writings. One can readily see why this is so. When *The Wealth of Nations* was published, the joint stock company could be regarded as exceptional.[68] It was exemplified then by the East India Company and Smith's attitude was that, though he could see some limited uses for joint stock,[69] it was a non-competitive organisational form which had to be kept to as narrow a compass as possible.[70] In 1776 this was as justified as contemporary attempts to use Smith's authority to sanction the advanced capitalist economy[71] are ridiculous.

In 1865 when Marx drafted volume three, this was not the case to the same extent.[72] The passage of the Companies Act 1862[73] consolidated what still is the framework of British company law, with limited liability, memoranda and articles, annual general meetings, boards and the necessity of listing particulars and of audit all being given clear recognition in this Act.[74] The remarkable acceleration in the number of incorporations at this time[75] seems, with hindsight, to mark the establishment of the corporation's dominance of the economy. However, in so far as industrial enterprises were concerned, the joint stock form was still dominated by what were clearly unusually huge investments, such as the railways and the canals. The revolution the share introduced into the concentration of industries in which, at that time, less enormous initial investment was necessary had not gathered pace, its full impetus developing, indeed, only under the impact of the first great depression.[76] Marx's observations on the growing size of initial investment seem highly perspicacious[77] and there is more than a little justice in Engels claim, in one of his notes to volume three, that, as he put it, "the second and third degree of joint-stock company" were developed after Marx wrote the fragments on joint stock in volume three.[78] But this does, not, of course, explain why Marx did not use the eighteen years which remained to him after drafting volume three to elaborate these fragments.

The preponderant tone of Marx's comments on joint stock, on the basis of the evidence from those of his economic scripts so far available, was positive and these comments are highly interesting and so very widely known as to require little comment here. What they boil down to is a claim that the joint stock form, in which ownership of capital is distinguished and in a sense separated from control of production, makes the redundancy of the private capitalist manifest.[79] It does so in two ways.

First, under joint stock, the function of supervision resides in a management which must base its claim to manage in competence. The capitalist as a capitalist is merely a money supplier. This undercuts a principal justification for the capitalist based on the alienation of co-operation. When workers are brought together in manufacture, the productive potential of the division of labour is released through their co-operation. However, as has been mentioned, this is not the workers' conscious co-operation but rather, whilst production is capitalist, an alienated co-operation is supplied by the capitalist's organisation of production. Now, the capitalist form of organisation is, of course, exploitative and obstructs economic development. It is the "co-operation" achieved by coordinated domination. But rejecting this form of "co-operation" can follow, however, only from breaking the identification of capital with the very organisation of production at all and allowing the consideration of alternative bases of organisation, and this is just what the separation of ownership and control does:

> since...the mere manager...takes care of all real functions that fall to the...capitalist as such, there remains only the functionary, and the capitalist vanishes from the production process as someone superfluous.[80]

Not only is the capitalist's function thrown into question, so is the basic claim of *private* property to govern production. The management of a joint stock company controls not (only) its own capital but the capital of others. That what is being controlled is a social resource becomes clearer through this general pooling of capital, which undercuts many rationales for the capitalist when he or she disposes of her or his own property:

> all explanatory reasons that were still more or less justified within the capitalist mode of production...now vanish. What the speculating trader risks is social property, not his own. Equally absurd now is saying that the origin of capital is saving, since what the speculator demands is that *others* should save for him.[81]

Now, obviously both of these claims have not worked out in the way Marx intended, and much modern corporate theory would tone them down very considerably. Nevertheless, they form, in my opinion, the kernel of a very interesting claim that, as Marx famously puts it, joint stock represents "the abolition of capital as private property within the confines of the capitalist mode of production itself".[82] It is as if Marx saw joint stock as teaching some of the same lessons as he thought could be drawn from co-operative factories. I do not want to examine this further for I wish to turn to another side of the development of joint stock which Marx mentions but to which he pays lesser attention. It has proven, however, to be more significant.

In volume one, Marx considers the economic consequences of joint stock as if the corporation was merely an accelerated form of private company. Concentration of capital is proceeding through competition, but centralisation speeds the whole process up immeasurably and so should visit the consequences of rising organic composition on capitalism at an accelerated rate:

> accumulation, the gradual increase of capital by reproduction as it passes from the circular to the spiral form, is clearly a very slow procedure compared with centralisation, which needs only to change the quantitative groupings of the constituent parts of social capital. The world would still be without railways if it had to wait until accumulation had got a few individual capitals far enough to be adequate for the construction of a railway. Centralisation, however, accomplished this in the twinkling of an eye, by means of joint stock companies. And while in this way centralisation intensifies and accelerates the effects of accumulation, it simultaneously extends and speeds up those revolutions in the technical composition of capital which raise its constant portion at the expense of its variable portion, thus diminishing the relative demand for labour.[83]

This is the effect, Marx says in volume one, of credit. He clearly has the share in mind as one of the various forms of security, but does not mention the peculiar effects of the share as "credit". When Marx takes up joint stock in what we have of volume three, although the same theme of speeding up accumulation and its corollary developments is present,[84] he also mentions the specific features of the share and, in doing so, hints that joint stock has a potential to disrupt the development of limits to accumulation, but never pursues this at length. Let me attempt to reconstruct what he says from the available fragments.[85]

Marx describes shares as: "titles of ownership to a corporate body, and drafts on the surplus-value that flows in from this each year".[86] This is, of course, right, but only if both parts are understood in a way which is different from their natural meaning on *laissez faire* assumptions.[87] The share owner cannot directly withdraw her or his capital from the corporation,[88] although he or she can sell the interest in the corporation represented by the share.[89] One of the rights making up that interest is the right to receive a dividend in accordance with the corporation's constitution,[90] which Marx refers to as "drafts on surplus-value", but here we must be extremely careful. For, as Marx recognises, these drafts do not take the form of profits but of interest:

> As capitalist production advances...one portion of capital is considered simply to be interest bearing and is invested as such...These capitals, although invested in large productive enterprises, simply yield an interest, great or small, after all costs are deducted - so called "dividends".[91]

Marx lists 'The Increase of Share Capital' as the sixth of the counteracting factors to the law of the tendency of the rate of profit to fall, for he has some inkling of its significance in terms of his overall account of the future of capitalist accumulation:

> The following economically important fact must be noted. Since profit here simply assumes the form of interest, enterprises that merely yield an interest are possible, and this is one of the reasons that hold up the fall in the general rate of profit, since these enterprises, where the constant capital stands in such a tremendous ratio to the variable, do not necessarily go into the equalisation of the general rate of profit.[92]

As dividends from shares are now the predominant form of return to productive investment, we should ask what this means now.

Share investment decisions are *not* based on profitability in any sort of direct way. The corporation's profitability serves only as the normal limit to the fund from which dividends can be paid (without diminishing the working capital of the corporation). By offering dividends, the corporation can attract share capital which, though fictitious in the sense that it is not generated internally in the same way as profits which are reinvested as industrial capital, is just as much capital in the sense of being available for the corporation's next production cycle. The point may best be made through an example of a flotation of a formerly private company. The figures in the example are, of course, purely hypothetical and, indeed, are rounded and exaggerated for clarity. But they do bear internal relationships which are intended to be empirically plausible in an industrial economy with a developed stock exchange. Let us assume:

initial industrial capital of private company = £10m   (1)

average rate of profit = 30%   (2)
∴ private company's profit = (1) x (2) = £3m   (3)
∴ normal dividend fund = (3) = £3m   (4)
average yield of shares in industrial firms = 20%   (5)
∴ share capital = (100 (5)) x (4) = 5 x £3m = £15m   (6)
∴ total capital of public company = (1) + (6) = £10 + £15 = £25m   (7)
extra costs of corporate administration = £2m   (8)
∴ fund for investment = (7) - ((4) + (8)) = £20m   (9)

What is most obvious from this is, of course, the capital concentration powers of the share which through flotation can more or less immediately add £10 to the firm's working capital when the private company would take almost three years to accumulate that amount by means of growth of internal profits.[93] What is more, at the end of the production cycle, the potential yield will be 30% of the enormously increased capital, making the corporations' theoretical potential for growth geometric:

corporation's profit after production cycle = (9) x (2) = £6m   (10)
∴ new normal dividend fund = £6m   (11)
∴ new share capital = (100 (5)) x (11) = 5 x £6 = £30m   (12)

Of course, the redoubling will continue with each cycle.

A further point should be mentioned. Whilst in the long run, internally generated profits are the only source of dividend funds for a sound company, in the short and medium terms any part of an initial capital (or indeed, of debenture or share capital itself) may be used to pay dividends to attract new share capital, in the expectation that the books will be balanced from the growth that follows from use of that capital. Of course, the more one speculates in this way, the more the risk to the investor (and to suppliers and employees, but this is of no account), but these things are possible and have, of course, been done often enough.[94]

Having noted this extraordinary capacity for growth, however, what I want to stress here is just how much flotation relaxes the pressure to accumulate on the firm. On these assumptions, the private company must continue to show a profit of 30% on its total capital or the capitalist will have an incentive to move to another form of investment. This type of compulsion also applies to the payment of interest simply loaned to the private industrial capitalist. The industrial capitalist must be able to use loan capital to realise the average rate of profit or he or she will not be able to pay the average rate of interest to money capitalists, who will invest elsewhere.[95] This sort of compulsion is extremely weakened by the share and does not apply to the corporation in any direct way. The corporation offers a dividend and can set this at whatever level it wishes, including a zero level, subject to certain external or internal pressures on yield. If the corporation wishes to attract share capital, there are pressures on it to offer the average yield and, if it wishes to undertake debenture financing, to offer the average rate of interest. But this presupposes that the corporation wishes to grow and cannot finance practicable growth out of internally generated assets, and the evidence over this overwhelmingly is that the sound corporation aims to finance growth itself.[96] If the corporation does seek investment from capital markets, it does so more or less exclusively from large financial institutions which, to various degrees, adopt a "going concern" attitude to the borrower and are flexible about expected rates of return.[97]

This last point emphasises that what has been said so far has assumed that the only interest the shareholder has in the corporation is in dividends. This is very misleading. The rate of return on shareholdings, generally known as the market capitalisation rate, is a compound of dividend *and* growth in value of the share.[98] Funds may be retained for investment within the corporation so that growth of the corporation, and thus of the value of the share, may well be substituted for the payment of dividends. This is particularly so if the shareholder is also receiving a payment as an employee of the corporation in the form of, say, directors' fees, for then he or she does not need rentier income.[99] The time scales over which the management's dividend policy, allocating earnings between their various uses, tend to be very long term[100] and to strongly subject dividend payments to the availability of funds *after* investment requirements are satisfied.[101]

Furthermore, the dominant shareholders of the advanced capitalist economies should not be seen as purely, or even mainly, as shareholders who regard holdings *only* as alienable investments. When one examines shareholding from the perspective of the ownership of a particular corporation which the shareholding represents, then dividends become even more flexible. The evidence we have is that share ownership is heavily concentrated amongst an economic elite of capitalists (typically with directorships) and top management (typically with a significant equity holding).[102] These dominant shareholders very closely identify with the corporation as an organisation and not with the corporation as a source of income, and obviously subjugate dividend policy to their perspective.[103]

Marx certainly was right to see joint stock as a means of centralisation and a spur to concentration. Capitalism has developed as a system of a limited number[104] of giant corporations working at vast scales[105] to bureaucratic plans[106] administered by professional managers.[107] Accumulation is pursued but in a restrained form[108] compatible with oligopolistic coexistence.[109] In particular, price competition is irrelevant to pricing decisions in the influential sectors of the economy[110] and has been more or less displaced as a form of competition[111] by cost-cutting (whilst holding price constant)[112] and by the sales effort.[113] The smaller firms and consumers in the residual areas of the economy must take the production decisions of the large corporate price makers[114] as the crucially determining boundaries of the relatively unimportant decisions they are left to make.[115] *Laissez faire* no longer exists[116] and the advanced capitalist economy which has replaced it specifically " is not an exchange economy in which the price mechanism regulates all economic activity", and "Thus it follows that the invisible hand theorem of classical theory is not applicable to the capitalist economy".[117]

The planning of growth which follows from oligopolisation of market shares has meant that, as has been mentioned, corporations have typically been able to fund practicable growth from internal funds. To the extent that this has not been the case, it has also meant that *rates* of return to share (or debenture) investment are typically not important.[118] Investment decisions are guided by the opportunity cost of capital.[119] Investors calculate the net present value of their capital if committed to any one (ignoring portfolio investment) of the possible alternatives. They do then, no doubt, invest in the one which yields the greatest rate of return. But it is only if there is some marked strength or weakness amongst the alternatives, and hence a marked difference in rates of return, that significant capital flight is a realistic possibility. The oligopolistic behaviour of the corporations makes such marked disparities exceptional and thus the long-term investor has to be content with an absolute size of return at a rate essentially fixed by the corporations and not by the market.[120]

In sum, in the economic policy space created by the share and by the oligopolisation of the economy based on corporate centralisation, advanced capitalism has developed, as debased planning, a "political" power to put a distance between capitalist private property and the "economic" tendencies which were to abolish it and which Marx hoped would lead to socialism. Through interlocking holdings and directorships[121] and overall financial supervision,[122] a capitalist economic elite now manages a network of interlocked giant financial and industrial institutions[123] which constitute the "strategic command posts"[124] of the advanced capitalist societies.[125] This elite is the core of a continuing ruling class dominating those societies.[126] There are without doubt very significant diversities between the policies and competencies of these elites across nations.[127] However, all wield a power to manipulate inter-institutional relations and macro-economic factors to pursue system stability in the face of incredible disruptions in ways and on a scale simply not foreseen in *Capital*.[128]

When listing the growth of share capital as a counteracting factor to the law of the tendency of the rate of profit to fall, Marx goes on to say:

> From a theoretical point of view, it is possible to include [dividends in the overall calculation of the rate of profit] and we should then obtain a profit rate lower than that which apparently exists and is really decisive for capitalists, since it is precisely in these undertakings that the proportion of constant capital to variable is at its greatest.[129]

Given the position taken in this work, at one general level this must be right on sociological grounds, for dividends must be an aliquot part of surplus value. One can envisage that some such effort as Marx began to undertake of the explanation of what would now principally be treated as debenture financing[130] can be extended to share capital, as indeed it brilliantly was by Hilferding.[131] But how far this can be done in quantitative terms must be an issue, even as a matter of theory. The position one takes will follow from one's opinion of the technical use of value theory, and I am not competent to pursue the matter. What I do want to raise here are some general observations of a qualitative nature about the possibility of reconciling share capital with the law of the tendency of the rate of profit to fall.

With the advantage of one hundred years' hindsight, one can clearly say that the possibilities of this reconciliation are zero. The link to profitability in the corporation is now so tenuous that it makes the law of the tendency of the rate of profit to fall incredibly hard to detect in business behaviour. Leaving aside fundamental questions about the accounting problems of determining accurate profitability figures,[132] the corporation is now so much more able to take longer term views, to reward its shareholders in ways that are far more flexible than profits to industrial capitalists, to schedule production in ways that do as much as possible to smooth out the effects of capitalist organisation, and, because of all these factors, to work with the state over macro-economic planning,[133] that any claim that the law of the tendency of the rate of profit to fall has had anything like the effect on business conduct Marx required it to have must be rejected. If one may take Marx's own observation on joint stock rather out of context, it is: "Private production unchecked by private ownership",[134] and in being so, *it is private production freed of the limits which were to end it represented by the law.*[135]   .

This is not to say that the rising organic composition and overproduction which underlies the law do not have any effect. I take it here that these phenomena are the principal characteristics of the advanced capitalist economy. But the way that these phenomena were to make the redundancy of capitalism manifest to the capitalist (and thence to the rest of society because of resultant crisis) was by operation of the law, and it cannot be said that the law does this. If one accepts this is the case, then most clarity is gained by saying that the law does not obtain. It is hard to do this, for if one does wish to say that the underlying weaknesses of the capitalist economy do obtain, one will be reluctant to give up the law for it seems that the law is necessary to the account of those weaknesses. I am trying to suggest that, though this reluctance is understandable, it should be overcome, for the weaknesses of the capitalist economy are not being visited on capitalists by the law. The law must be rejected in order to seek another means of making sure those weaknesses lead to the socialist restructuring of the economy which will eradicate them.

The tone of interesting subsequent marxist attempts to come to terms with the evidence that the law of the tendency of the rate of profit to fall is seriously wrong has been extremely uncomfortable.[136] The consistent growth of the advanced capitalist economies in the 1950s and 60s, a period which has been called "the golden age" of later capitalism,[137] is obviously *prima facie* counter-evidence to the law, for surely the degree of organic composition should have been acute by this time and, if profitability, investment and growth are at all strongly related, should have prevented this growth.[138] A number of general characteristics of these attempts to defend the law may be noted.

The first is a complaint about the unavailability of the statistical material necessary for empirical testing of the law.[139] Corporate and national accounts are not kept in ways which lead to "real" measures of profitability. To anyone who accepts the criticism of fetishism, this no doubt is highly regrettable. But if the measures by which corporations assess their own performance hide a falling rate of profit over the long-term, then it *is* hidden, that is to say, it has had no effect. Claims such as the following are just wrong:

> The question whether the tendency is *realised* in a declining rate of profit is distinct from whether it is *observable*, present in a phenomenal form in concrete profit rates. It is perfectly possible to argue that the phenomenon of decline is a *real* one but that it is not directly observable in company balance sheets.[140]

The second characteristic is a flat weakening of the empirical claims of the law, so that there is a huge distance between the tendency and actual crisis: "Historical probabilities of crisis are by no means the same as historical "inevitabilities"".[141] The limit to which this can be taken is far more determined by theoretical integrity rather than the actual state of affairs to be described. Sophisticated variants of this impose on the law other determinants of profitability, such as business cyclical movements, and claim that the effect of the law, present in slump, is "neutralised" in boom.[142] What has happened to the clear theme of accelerating crisis in such a treatment? It is reduced to much more woolly statements such as:

> The concrete mechanisms of the economic breakdown of [the] capitalist economy may be open to conjecture. The [import of the] long-term decline of the rate of profit is still far from clear. But a very strong case can be made for the thesis that there are definite limits to the adaptability of capitalist relations of production, and that these limits are being progressively attained in one field after another.[143]

The third characteristic, to some extent endorsed by the form in which the law has been presented by Engels, is a development of the second, to stress the countervailing tendencies and their neutralisation of the law.[144] A development of this is to find new countervailing tendencies, such as armaments spending, which also work against the law: "we should collapse into overproduction and unemployment were it not for some special offsetting factor...Such a mechanism is to be found in a permanent arms budget".[145] Again, one has to ask what is left of the law when it can be "permanently" overcome?

The fourth characteristic is to refashion the law into new forms, forms which escape criticisms which can be levelled at the "rising organic composition *variant*"[146] of the law. It surely should be manifest that this is not a defence of Marx's theory but rather should itself be construed as a criticism. This is acutely obvious from what must be seen as the most indefensible of these variants, the idea of a "profits squeeze".[147] This attributes a falling rate of profit to a growth in real wages claiming an increasing share of surplus value. Whatever its value in explaining supposed falls in the rate of profit, this variant can hardly be a defence of the law, for it cuts against Marx's principal explanatory thrust!

The last characteristic to which I want to draw attention is the hopeful eschatology displayed by much of the writing. Writing as recently as 1988, Perlo was honest enough to emphasise his finding that post-war US corporations had been highly profitable in the title of his book *Superprofits and Crises*. Having stated that this finding was not surprising, he went on to ask in conclusion:

> Will the soaring uptrend in the profits of US capitalism change? Definitely, yes [A] combination of forces is certain to end the rising trend in the rate of gross profits of US big business, and may already have done so.[148]

There seems to be nothing to say, except that Perlo was writing *one hundred and twenty three years* after Marx drafted the law.

I have been rather critical of these contributions in my comments here. It should go without saying that I find much of their *content* highly interesting.[149] What is unhelpful about them is their explanatory *form*.[150] They are unable to relate to the law of the tendency of the rate of profit to fall in a proper fashion, setting themselves the goal of saving this law rather than freely assessing its current plausibility.[151] It would seem to be unarguable, and, as I have said, it is accepted here, that advanced capitalism shows characteristics that make Marx's analysis seem to be of the greatest continuing importance, and these certainly include a fundamental tendency toward overproduction. But one does not have to accept the law of the tendency of the rate of profit to fall, much less other objectionable crisis theories, to show this.[152] Nor does one have to say that the law will eventually triumph in order to criticise the political measures presently taken to offset overproduction. Indeed, of course, the tendency is not to set this criticism on the right foot.[153] By their continuing insistence on a form, however watered down and however much explicitly disavowed, of ultimately "economic" accounts of advanced capitalism, such acceptances are doing the greatest disservice to the analysis of this baneful economy.[154]

It must be insisted that developments based on the joint stock form has made redundant the account of the limits to capital accumulation Marx developed from classical political economy. And one should go further. In hazarding the observation I am about to make, one is only speculating, but I would go on to say that this made it impossible for Marx to finish *Capital*. Volume one can more or less stand as it is and so can much of volume two. But the core of volume three, setting out the limits to accumulation, and, to a lesser extent, those parts dealing with fictitious capital, are called into the most serious question by the share. I have claimed that *Capital* essentially is complete as it is by the end of volume three, chapter 15, and so it is as an account of *laissez faire* capitalism. But volume three could never be complete in the sense required by most marxists subsequent to Marx, because capitalism no longer conformed to the assumptions on which the work was based. I do not know how far it will be possible to assess how far Marx recognised this. For what my own "feeling" is worth, I suspect he had a fairly clear recognition. One awaits the full scripts being made available to pursue the issue.

What can be said is that when Engels did put together volumes two and three, he was able to do so because he did not appreciate the importance of the side of the joint stock form which disrupted Marx's views. In preparing volume three, Engels made brief comments which brought Marx's fragments on joint stock up to date. Noting the growth of the Stock Exchange and associated phenomena,[155] Engels stressed only the ways in which joint stock increased the magnitude of overproduction by the scale of its operations and made easier the socialisation of the means of production by rational concentration.[156] His conclusion in respect of the UK chemical industry could stand as an example of the mistaken optimism to which this one-sided view of joint stock has led, for he claimed that that industry, with the formation of the United Alkali Trust, was "preparing, in the most pleasing fashion, its future expropriation by society as a whole". I am very anxious not to be unfair to Engels when I note that, at the time of drafting this passage, Imperial Chemical Industries, in surviving what was intended to amount to a hostile takeover by Hansen Trust, has narrowly escaped being rendered, in effect, the private property of one man.

Immanent critique seems to have had a paradoxical effect here. The strength of Marx's critique of classical political economy is the closeness of its relationship to its subject, but that subject contained no other than marginal reference to the treatment of joint stock and in this it was seriously mistaken. One can see *now* that the development of the share was an immanent potential in *laissez faire* and that, under the pressures of the limits to accumulation on a competitive basis, this potential could be realised by the development of the corporation as the typical unit of the capitalist economy. It is just this stress on immanence that gives Hilferding's *Finance Capital*, in which investment funds are beautifully presented as a natural development of Marx's account of money, its enormous power. But Hilferding's account was published in 1911 and was dealing, albeit enormously perceptively, with the corporate economy as given fact. (That this fact has not properly been appreciated in the majority of economics since does not alter this). For Marx in 1867, the real task was much more difficult, it was to weigh up the limits classical political economy had shown to apply to *laissez faire* against the potential for avoiding those limits furnished by the still rather nascent joint stock form. It does not really affect Marx's status as an economist to say that, by sticking, at least by default, with classical political economy, he has turned out to be wrong.

We should now be prepared to perfectly openly come to terms with the shunting of the car of marxist economics onto the wrong line by Marx's adherence to an analysis which marginalises joint stock and which thus always gives an account of advanced capitalism in a grudging and ultimately inadequate way. By doing so we are not undercutting Marx's contemporary relevance but providing the ground on which it can be re-established because the core of his work, the critique of economic alienation, is still of the greatest importance. This can readily be shown by returning to the writings of the bourgeois analysts of the corporation I have discussed in this chapter for, in hugely significant ways, these writings are subject to a penetrating critique on the basis of Marx's work.

Notes

1   *Vide* Kidron, *Western Capitalism Since the War*, ch 1.

2   Kondratieff, 'The Long Waves in Economic Life', p 111.

3   *Vide* Rostow, 'Investment and the Great Depression (1873-1896)'. The case against the existence of the depression is summarised by Saul, *The Myth of the Great Depression 1873-96*, but the stridency with which the case is put seems to be at odds with the substance of criticisms raised.

4   Engels, 'Preface to the English Edition of Volume One', p 113.

5   *Vide*, Rosenberg, 'Political and Social Consequences of the Great Depression of 1973-1896 in Central Europe', pp 61-70.

6   C1, p 90.

7   *Vide* Baran and Sweezy, *Monopoly Capital*, p 20.

8   *Vide* Parrini and Sklar, 'New Thinking About the Market, 1896-1904: Some American Economists on Investment and the Theory of Surplus Capital' and Sklar, *The Corporate Reconstruction of Amercian Capitalism 1890-1919*.

9   Conant, 'The Economic Basis of Imperialism', pp 2-3.

10 Wright, *Industrial Depressions*, p 11.

11 *Ibid*, p 13.

12 *Ibid*, ch 1.

13 *Ibid*, ch 2.

14 It is not that the Commissioner is saying that this last group of countries escaped the depression, it is that he is not confident about drawing conclusions about them on the basis of the materials available to him. *Ibid*, p 291.

15 The Commissioner is contrasting his relatively well informed account to "The popular idea of severity of the present depression [which] would lead one to suppose that all branches of business were severely stagnated, and that failures were the order of the day" (*ibid*, p 66). In fact, the popular view, focusing on 8% unemployment in agriculture, trade and transportation and mining and manufacture, had more plausibility than the Commissioner thinks. The other indicators which he thought showed more "gratifying results", such as a relatively low rate of business failure and a relatively slow rate of fall in ouput, show the emergence of the now typical features of the way that the larger corporations schedule their responses to shortfalls in demand according to the availability of credit and the difficulty of defraying various fixed costs. In 1866 labour was a relatively easily defrayed cost. The authoritative account of this period in Conant, *A History of Modern Banks of Issue*, p 661, written with the benefit of ten years of hindsight, concluded that "the multitude of failure caused intense alarm for a while and threatened to bring business to a standstill ".

16 Wright, *Industrial Depression*, p 254.

17 Wells, *Recent Economic Changes*, p v.

18   *Ibid*, p 326,.
19   *Ibid*, p vi.
20   *Ibid*, pp 115, 122.
21   Conant, 'Crises and their Management', p 2.
22   Clarke, 'Introduction', p 2.
23   Wells, *Recent Economic Changes*, p 71.
24   *Ibid*, p 72.
25   *Ibid*, p 74.
26   *Ibid*, pp 72-73.
27   *Ibid*, pp 26-8.
28   Conant, 'Crises and their Management', pp 380-1.
29   *Ibid*, pp 375-6.
30   *Idem*, 'The Economic Basis of Imperialism', pp 5-8.
31   C3, ch 50.
32   Willoughby, 'The Concentration of Industry in the United States', p 85.
33   Meade, *Trust Finance*, p 23.
34   Wright, *Industrial Depressions*, p 287.
35   United States Industrial Commission, *Preliminary Report on Trusts and Industrial Combinations*, p v.
36   *Ibid*, p 8.
37   Clark, 'Introduction, 'pp 4-5.
38   Wright, *Industrial Depressions*, p 287.
39   As Conant was when directly commenting on Wright's suggestion in 'Crises and their Management', p 379.
40   Willoughby 'The Concentration of Industry in the United States', pp 86-7.
41   Hadley, 'The Good and Evil of Industrial Combination', p 377.
42   Set up in this way, as weighing the benefits of industrial concentration against the detriments of loss of competition, reflection on this issue is bound to oscillate and so, caught in this antimony, the history of antitrust law is a history of such oscillations. I have tried to forcibly insist on this and show a way out in 'Why Regulate the Modern Corporation? The Failure of Market Failure'.
43   American Academy of Political and Social Science, *Corporations and the Public Welfare*.
44   Willoughby, 'The Concentration of Industry in the United States', p 86.
45   *Ibid*, p 83.
46   Conant, 'Crises and their Management', p 378.
47   *Ibid*, p 377.

48 *Vide* Bunting, *The Rise of the Large American Corporation 1889-1919* and Lamoreaux, *The Great Merger Movement in American Business 1895-1904*.

49 Carnegie, 'The Bugaboo of the Trust', p 142.

50 The degree of collusion in the initial period of trust formation led, of course, to the passage of the Sherman Act (26 US Stat 206). One can assess the tenor of public opinion somewhat outraged by outright agreements to monopolise which led to the passage of the Act from the illustrative case of *Central Ohio Salt Company* v. *Guthrie* 35 Ohio State 666 (1880), which was discussed at length in the enormously influential post-Sherman decision in *US* v. *EC Knight Co* 156 US 1 (1895) at 27-8 per Marshall Harlan J.

51 Conant, 'Crises and their Management', p 379.

52 *Vide* Robinson 'The Impossibility of Capitalism'.

53 *Vide* Fine, *Laissez Faire and the General Welfare State*.

54 It is, in any case, to a remarkable degree, the history of Keynes and I trust I have made my view on Keynes clear.

55 Hilferding, *Finance Capital*, ch 22.

56 Luxemburg, *The Accumulation of Capital*, sec 3.

57 Lenin, 'Imperialism: The Highest Stage of Capitalism'.

58 Hobson, *Imperialism*.

59 *Vide* Etherington, 'Reconsidering Theories of Imperialism'; *idem* 'The Capitalist Theory of Capitalist Imperialism'; Fieldhouse, 'Imperialism: An Historiographical Revision' and Stokes, 'Late Nineteenth Century Colonial Expansion and the Attack on the Theory of Economic Imperialism: A Case of Mistaken Identity?'.

60 Conant, *The United States in the Orient*, p iii.

61 *Idem*, 'The Economic Basis of "Imperialism"', pp 9-11.

62 *Idem*, 'The Struggle for Commercial Empire'. Cf *idem*, 'Can New Openings Be Found for Capital' and *idem*, 'The United States as a World Power: The Nature of the Economic and Political Problem'.

63 *Idem*, 'The Struggle for Commercial Empire', pp 75, 79. Cf *idem*, 'The United States as a World Power: Their Advantages in the Competition for Commercial Empire'.

64 *Idem*, *The United States in the Orient*, pp iii-iv.

65 Reinsch, *World Politics*, P 311. Cf *Idem*, *Colonial Government*, chs 5-6 and *idem*, *Colonial Administration*.

66 *Idem*, World Politics, p 361.

67 This point just is not sufficiently strongly appreciated by defences of Marx which point to all the obvious enough signs that advanced capitalism is a very seriously malfunctioning economy and say that this shows the continuing plausibility of his views on crisis. Eg Smith, 'Crisis Theory'. Of themselves, these signs cannot

252 The Failure of Marxism

do this work, for whether they are signs of system collapse or signs of system persistence in the face of the pressure of its shortcomings is precisely what is at issue.

In *Capitalism and Crisis*, Gamble and Walton describe the history of the discussion of the law of the tendency of the rate of profit to fall as a history of the emergence of mechanisms by which advanced capitalism has undercut the operation of that law. They nevertheless conclude (p 144) that "The long debate is not over; it has taken a new turn", and this is because they want to conclude that the waste engendered by the operation of these mechanisms now constitutes "the real crisis" (pp 131-7). They do not seem to see that they are using "crisis" in two very different ways, and this wavering over their meaning undermines the very powerful things they do say. I shall return to the explanatory form of crisis statements associated with the law of the tendency of the rate of profit to fall below.

68   Of course, as the joint form came to predominate, this was wrong, and with it, one can say that the whole thrust of classical political economy was wrong. As joint stock was based in *laissez faire,* an adequate theory of *laissez faire* would predict its abolition by joint stock. With the benefit of much hindsight, our view of the nature of the *laissez faire* market is being pushed in this way by contemporary historical scholarship. A particularly bold recent example is Neal, *The Rise of Financial Capitalism,* nb ch 3, which makes very large claims indeed for the role of the joint stock financial institutions of the seventeenth century: "The multinational firms of the United States, Japan, Great Britain and Europe are the inheritors of the East India companies of the English, Dutch and French" (p 230). I regard the pursuing of this inquiry as the largest theme in economic history at present but intend to say nothing about it except in a limited way in respect of Marx here.

69   WN, pp 756-8.

70   *Ibid,* pp 740-58.

71   Eg Friedman and Friedman, *Free to Choose,* pp 19-20.

72   *Vide* Hunt, *The Development of the Business Corporation in England, 1800-1867.*

73   25 and 26 Vict c 89.

74   *Vide* Hadden, *Company Law and Capitalism,* p 22.

75   In 1856, 956 companies had been completely registered under previous company legislation. By 1862, 2,479 additional companies had been registered, with a paid-up capital in 1864 of over £31m. *Vide* Shannon, 'The Coming of General Limited Liability', p 290.

76   In 1885, only 10% at most of important business organisations were limited companies. *Vide* Payne, *British Entrepreneurship in the Nineteenth Century,* p 19.

77   C1, p 777.

78 C3, p 586.

79 *Ibid*, pp 567-8.

80 *Ibid*, p 512.

81 *Ibid*, p 571.

82 *Ibid*, p 567.

83 C1, p 780.

84 C3, p 347.

85 What I want to argue is that the share, in particular, undercuts the role of "credit" per se in Marx's account of the limits to accumulation. Viewed only as a tool of accumulation and a lever of centralisation, "credit" undoubtedly is an accelerator of the tendencies to crisis set out in *Capital*, as is authoritatively argued in Harvey, *Limits to Capital*, pp 324-9. The problem even with as excellent an account as Harvey's is the basic obsolescence of those tendencies,

86 C2, p 423.

87 *Borland's Trustee v. Steel Bros and Co Ltd* [1901] ch 279 at 288 per Farwell J.

88 *Bligh v. Brent* 160 ER 397.

89 *Pinkett v. Wright* 67 ER 50.

90 *Watson v. Sprightly* (1854) 10 Exch 222.

91 C3, p 347.

92 *Ibid*, p 568.

93 £10m initial capital + £3m profits entirely reinvested, compounded at 30% profitability *per annum* over 3 years = £21.97m.

94 Exactly where we stand in terms of the rationality of capitalist finance at the moment emerges perfectly clearly from an analysis of leveraged buyouts by RL Kuhn, editor-in-chief of the *The Library of Investment Banking*. This edifying series is written largely by leading investment analysts and is dedicated to "the investment banking community...the economic catalyst of national and international development". The form of development we can expect based on the self-understanding of this community is as follows:

> How to overpay and get rich?...It's called a "leveraged buyout" (LBO), and what it does is cure the healthy. Take a sound company strong with equity. Sell it. Make it sick, laden heavy with debt. Make it better by rebuilding equity - redeploy assets, cut overhead, pay back debt (not too much), and perhaps improve earnings. Sell it again. Count your money.

Kuhn, 'Leveraged Buyouts I', p 221. One is simply unable to comment when, having seen Kuhn conclude (p 231) that "from a public policy point of view, LBO's can be seen as the refresher of capitalism", one realises that, from his perspective, this is a sensible conclusion.

95 C3, ch 22.

96 *Vide* Donaldon, *Corporate Debt Capacity*, pp 51-6.

97   *Vide* Hodgman, *Commercial Bank Loan and Investment Policy.*

98   *Vide* Williams, *The Theory of Investment Value,* ch 7.

99   *Vide* Gordon, *Business Leadership in the Large Corporation,* p xii. The managerialist conclusions typically drawn from this typically follow from failing to appreciate the degree of overlap between large shareholders and executive salary recipients amongst strategic management.

100 *Vide* Linter, 'Distributions of Incomes of Corporation among Dividends, Retained Earnings and Taxes'.

101 *Vide* Fama and Babiak, 'Dividend Policy: An Empirical Analysis', p 1134.

102 *Vide* Scott, *Corporations, Classes and Capitalism,* ch 9 and Giddens, *The Class Structure of the Advanced Societies,* chs 8-12.

103 *Vide* Scott, *The Upper Classes,* ch 6.

104 *Vide* Aaronovitch and Sawyer, *Big Business* and Hannah and Kay, *Concentration in Modern Industry.*

105 *Vide* Chandler, *Scale and Scope,* pt 1.

106 *Vide* Williamson, *Corporate Control and Business Behaviour.*

107 *Vide* Berle and Means, *The Modern Corporation and Private Property.*

108 *Vide* Simon, *Administrative Behaviour,* pp 37-41.

109 *Vide* Cowling *Monopoly Capital,* ch 2.

110 *Vide* Robinson, *The Economics of Imperfect Competition,* bk 1 and Kalecki, 'Theory of Economic Dynamics', ch 1.

111 *Vide* Chamberlin, *The Theory of Monopolistic Competition,* chs 4-7.

112 *Vide* Steindl, *Maturity and Stagnation in American Capitalism,* ch 4.

113 *Vide* Baran and Sweezy, *Monopoly Capital,* ch 5.

114 *Vide* Scitovsky, *Welfare and Competition,* ch 2.

115 *Vide* Galbraith, *Economics and the Public Purpose.*

116 *Vide* Keynes, 'Essays in Persuasion', pp 272-94.

117 Gerrard, *Theory of the Capitalist Economy,* pp 126.

118 *Pace* Perlo, *Superprofits and Crises,* p 118.

119 *Vide* Hirschliefer, 'On the Theory of the Optimal Investment Decision.'

120 The stock market is the only *market* left with any possibility of controlling corporations after product sales are recognised to be oligopolistic. Eg Manne, 'Mergers and the Market for Corporate Control'. That corporations do not use this market or do so in ways which do not reflect real competition for investment funds is, therefore, highly disturbing to those economists who wish to find some macro-level rationality in the advanced capitalist economy but who do not take advantage of a preoccupation with mathematical technique to blind themselves to the empirical situation. Eg Baumol, *The Stock Market and Economic Efficiency,* p 70. In the light of evidence like this, company law at present is characterised by a desperate attempt to find *something - anything -* controlling

corporate managements. *Vide* Campbell 'Adam Smith, *Farrar on Company Law* and the Economics of the Corporation'.

121 *Vide* Scott, *Corporations, Classes and Capitalism,* ch 3 and *idem, Capitalist Property and Financial Power.*

122 *Vide idem, Corporations, Classes and Capitalism,* ch 4; Coakley and Harris, *The City of Capital* and Scott and Griff, *Directors of Industry,* chs 5-6.

123 And, of course, has a very direct influence on the state. *Vide* Scott, *Corporations, Classes and Capitalism,* ch 5; Jessop, *The Capitalist State;* Miliband, *The State in Capitalist Society* and *idem, Class Power and State Power.*

124 Wright Mills, *The Power Elite,* p 4.

125 *Vide* Scott, *The Upper Classes.*

126 This holds principally for this reason, but also on other indices of social solidarity and exclusivity, this elite remains the core of continuing domination of these societies by a ruling class. *Vide* Scott, 'The British Upper Class'.

127 Britain's particular misfortune in the degree of incompetence of its capitalists is authoritatively described in Chandler, *Scale and Scope,* pt 3.

128 What seems to have been the high point of this to date was the macro-economic pursuit of general incomes policy, aggregate demand management, domestic monetary policy and coordinated international currency and trade relations under Bretton Woods and GATT in the 1950s and 60s. *Vide* Epstein and Schor, 'Macropolicy in the Rise and Fall of the Golden Ages'.

129 C3, p 348.

130 *Ibid,* ch 25.

131 Hilferding, *Finance Capital,* chs 5-8.

132 In an admittedly intentionally provocative formulation, a well respected accounting authority, K Battacharya, has described the situation in this way:

> the major instrument, perhaps the only instrument, we have to diagnose the health of a company, ie the balance sheet, is in the doldrums. You could not have a more meaningless and confused statement holding such a position of great importance with shareholders, analysts...business people in general and the Government. What's more, we are constantly using this instrument to make vital decisions, committing our lives, our jobs, our children's future. An instrument which you can inflate, reduce, change its shape, size, even in our imperfect world...can hardly claim to be a solid platform on which to build our industry and commerce.

Accountancy's Faulty Sums, p 34.

133 *Vide* Cowling, *Monopoly Capital,* ch 2.

134 C3, 569.

135 Hilferding, *Finance Capital,* p 228.

136 Some such attempts are so completely unscrupulous as to be wholly uninteresting, for they boil down to the claim that the law is manifested in any

sort of empirical situation, even including its opposite, that is to say, in a *rising* rate of profit. Eg Balibar, 'On the Basic Concepts of Historical Materialism', pp 283-93. A remarkable irony of many of these discussions is that they are conducted in formalist ways which the discussants ridicule when they attribute them to Hegel. Solutions to the problems which follow from holding on to laws which never seem to have any predictive payoff have been spun out of words - tendency instead of law, underlying rather than phenomenal, etc. As one realises when one understands Hegel, the solutions, if they exist, are not given in the words but in the empirical situation the words purport to describe.

Even amongst accounts which are trying to preserve theoretical integrity, there has been a general rise in the level of complexity and circumlocution which runs wholly counter to the simplification one finds within progressive research programmes. Eg Reuten and Williams, *Value-form and the State*, pt 3.

137 Glyn *et al*, 'The Rise and Fall of the Golden Age',

138 *Vide* Desai, *Marxian Economics*, p 189.

139 Eg Frantzen, *Growth and Crisis in Post-war Capitalism*, pp 115-6.

140 Cutler *et al, Marx's 'Capital' and Capitalism Today*, vol 1, p 157 n. I am happy to be able to say that this statement is not reconcilable with comments elsewhere in this work to the opposite effect, eg vol 2, p 123, which seem exemplary.

141 O'Connor, *Accumulation Crises*, p 60.

142 Eg Mandel, *Late Capitalism*, ch 4.

143 *Idem*, 'Introduction to Volume One' p 86.

144 Eg the main thrust of Gillman, *The Falling Rate of Profit* is to completely shift the significance of selling expenses for definitions of costs and profitability.

145 Kidron, *Western Capitalism Since the War*, pp 48-9.

146 Weisskopf, 'Marxian Crisis Theory and the Rate of Profit in the Post-war US Economy', p 342 (my emphasis).

147 Glyn and Sutcliffe, *British Capitalism and the Profits Squeeze*.

148 Perlo, *Superprofits and Crises*, p 136.

149 To take only two examples which will be utilised later in this work, Kalecki's views on armaments spending and O'Conner's views on the limits of state expenditure under capitalism are indispensable.

150 *Vide* Aaronowitz, *The Crisis in Historical Materialism*, nb ch 7. I press this criticism of form much more strongly than Aaronowitz, however, and feel that some of what he himself says is open to this extended criticism.

151 When put on proper footing, many of these accounts show themselves to be highly productive in detail. Dobb's early version of the profits squeeze idea in *Political Economy and Capitalism*, pp 105-26, for example, is a substantially misleading interpretation of Marx but, when seen as a rival theory in important respects, it is very interesting. *Vide* Shaikh, 'Political Economy and Capitalism: Notes on Dobb's Theory of Crisis'.

152 *Pace* Yaffe, 'The Marxian Theory of Crisis, Capital and the State'.

153 *Vide* Hodgson, 'The Theory of the Falling Rate of Profit', pp 50-4.

154 *Pace* eg Davis and Scase, *Western Capitalism and State Socialism*, p 133.

155 C3, pp 1045-7.

156 *Ibid,* pp 568-9, Cf SUS, p 421.

11 Advanced Capitalism and Socialism

The explanatory shortcomings of the bourgeois economic writings I have discussed in the previous chapter are obvious on even a cursory examination. They are sometimes very great. I have referred to the 1889 paper in which Andrew Carnegie sought to exorcise contemporaneous public fear of 'The Bugaboo of the Trust'. After having, given his own position, modestly put down the creation of trusts to the work of "some of the ablest business men the world has ever seen",[1] he went on to defend those creations by use of a method which represents the application of fetishism to advanced capitalism and which continues to dominate analysis of the corporate economy today. The method is simple enough - one uses free market assumptions to explain away the specific features of the corporation which have made those assumptions untenable and the licence to do this is that those assumptions are taken to be ineluctable features of human life. Thus Carnegie, whose paper heart-rendingly laments the huge size and vulnerable fixity of the capital investments required by modern scales of production, defends oligopoly pricing by imagining that entry into such production is open to all:

> The people of America can smile at the efforts of all her railway magnates and all her manufacturers to defeat the economic laws by Trusts or combinations, or pools, or "differentials", or anything of like character. Only let them hold firmly to the doctrine of free competition. Keep the field open. Freedom for all to engage in railroad building when and where capital desires subject to conditions open to all.[2]

Lines of development like this are, of course, without any real value, other than providing amusement. In particular, the "Freedom for all to engage in railroad building" is priceless, perhaps bettered only by Hadley giving up part of his *magnum opus* to the following:

> Crises have occurred with tolerable regularity ever since the introduction of applied steam power. They have usually come once in ten or eleven years, a fact which led some observers to connect them with sunspots which have a period of the same length.[3]

The reasons these worthless lines are considered is that, though much of this work parallels Marx, the key aspect of Marx's analysis has no parallel. Capitalist property is not considered ineluctable by Marx, indeed that historically specific form of ownership and control of the means of production is what is mainly to be explained. But this property and the form of control of the means of production it represents is simply a given to these writers. All analysis is carried out within limits which are called economic and which are really thought to be of a more or less natural character but which are nothing more than the limits imposed by capitalist property.

Carnegie, for example, makes it explicit that he couples what obviously must have been one of the most acute practical awarenesses of the specific qualities of the trust with a belief that the economy will remain essentially the same after tycoon capitalism because economics will always be the same:

> The great laws of the economic world, like all laws affecting society, being the genuine outgrowth of human nature, alone remain unchanged through all these changes. Whatever consolidations, or watered stocks, or syndicates, or Trusts endeavour to circumvent these...the great laws continue to grind out their irresistible consequences as before.[4]

A particularly picturesque version is given by Conant, who again couples an acute insight into the real reasons for modern economic developments - in this case imperialism - with laughable generalisations:

> The irresistible tendency to expansion, which leads the growing tree to burst, which drove the Goths, the Vandals and finally our Saxon ancestors in successive and irresistible waves over the decadent provinces of Rome, seems again in operation, demanding new outlets for American capital and new opportunities for American enterprise.[5]

The explanatory failures consequent upon this are as manifest as they are still common. I will not further pursue the nature of these explanatory failures, which have, as they generally appear in economic thought, been dealt with at length. For our purposes, a brief indication here on the limits they put on what it might be thought appropriate to do in regard to avoiding the systemic decay of *laissez faire* is required.

What the corporation preserves, in the face of the crisis of *laissez faire*, is capitalist property. Faced with overproduction, there are really two main possibilities which flow particularly clearly from Marx's analysis, which of course is not limited by the constraints of capitalist ownership.

One is to undercut the law of the tendency of the rate of profit to fall by removing profit maximisation as the overweening goal of economic effort. Now, the corporation has done this to some extent, by substituting long term growth for short term profitability, but this is not the real point. However construed, profitability or growth aims at the expansion of private property in either dividends or the growth of the value of stock. The consequences are that rational outcomes from the point of view of the consumer must be subordinated to private wealth. We have seen Meade describe the way that competition came to be seen as an evil by manufacturers and the context in which he puts this is most instructive:

> Invention and improvement are always most active when the lash of competition is applied to the manufacturer, and the consumer profits from the lower values which competition frequently produces and invention confirms. In the interest of public policy, the investment of profits is to be commended; but it should not be forgotten, when the benefits of competition are extolled, that society is a long way from the time when men will labour for the public interest to the relative subordination of their own advantage. Whatever the social and industrial effects of large capital expenditure out of earnings, the manufacturer was not satisfied with the results...It was highly desirable from the manufacturer's point of view to stop, or at least abate, this struggle, which benefitted nobody save the consumer...The producers were tired of working for the public.[6]

Now, what is at issue here is hardly what we need to do to determine what men will or will not labour for, but rather when capitalists will allow others to labour for them, or, if we get away from this way of speaking altogether, when and in what fashion we can employ the means of production. There can be no doubt that the limitation placed by production for private profit on the volume of economic activity is a major distortion of potential rational outcomes - such as planned reduction in the amount of necessary labour time - and it is the continuance of capitalist private property in the corporation which produces it.

The second possibility is a concerted expansion of mass consumption *relative* to the growth of the private wealth contained in the capitalist ownership of the means of production. Again, the corporate economy has, especially since Keynes, embraced this, but crucial residual problems remain. The expansion of mass income was put forward as a solution to unemployment of capital and labour by Wright:

> If...the standard of living for those whose consuming power is...low...can be increased...the problem of the unemployed would pass away. An increase of $1 per week per family of those living under the lower rates of consuming

power...would make a market sufficiently expansive to overcome the margin between actual production and productive capacity.[7]

What is, of course, entirely missing from Wright's advocacy of "All efforts...which have for their purpose the raising of our people to higher levels of living",[8] is any grasp of the necessary political changes that would allow making those efforts central to economic planning. Such efforts require the determination of incomes by means other than competitive wage struggles in the context of a massively skewed distribution of wealth. That is to say, it requires the determination of incomes outside the context of capitalist property, but this is precisely what is precluded by the preservation of that property through the adoption of the corporate form.

I hope that it goes without saying that I do not mean that the outright pursuit of these two strategies would solve overproduction problems, though I would claim it is an essential component of any such solution. For the point is that they *have* been pursued by commitments of resources that are surely enormously in excess of what Marx could reasonably expect in 1867. The very commitment has created its own problems and these problems cannot be solved by merely asking for more commitment. This, as it were, quantitative attitude to the development of socialism is very seriously weak and must be supplemented, indeed subsumed under, a different, qualitative attitude.

The most substantial marxist attempts to demonstrate this have been focused on the misdirections of state expenditure, particularly into armaments spending,[9] which are the corollary of tending to contain the use of that expenditure within bounds set by the maintenance of private property rather than pursue all possibilities of maximising welfare.[10] Especially as I have already indicated my views on these attempts in my remarks on Keynes, I want rather to focus on the nature of the expenses of production under the corporation.[11]

I have already claimed that under advanced capitalism, with price competition highly untypical among the large corporations but the modified urge to accumulate remaining, the predominant forms of competition are cost cutting and the sales effort. Huge budgets are dedicated to the promotion of products, with the consequent subjection of culture to a massively vulgarising influence.[12] How far one should go in representing contemporary culture as degraded[13] need not be taken up here. It is enough to point to what cannot with a good conscience[14] be denied, that massive resources are being committed to that degradation rather than to cultural enhancement.[15] These resources work directly against positive welfare outcomes. The consumer features as the object of a sales effort directed towards expanding the aggregate consumption function[16] and towards altering brand loyalties,[17] and, to the extent that it is successful, the sales effort more or less cuts out consumer choice as a prime determinant of production decisions.[18]

The waste involved in the direct sales effort is, one suspects, hugely exceeded by that involved in pushing that effort back into production, that is to say, manufacturing products in such a way that they will, so far as possible, be saleable under circumstances of chronic demand shortage by artificially stimulating that demand.[19] What happens here is that the pursuit of the reduction of the value of commodities is relaxed in favour of increases of value occasioned by "commodity aesthetics". The commodity itself is produced as an item intended to stimulate sales, not by the lowering of price but by the manipulative stimulation of demand. A degrading pincer movement operates here. On the one hand, pressures to reduce costs, and so increase profit margins, remain central to the capitalist firm, and so the commodities which serve as consumer goods tend to be subjected to the imperatives of large scale production at the expense of their integral quality.[20] Partly to give a competitively saleable appearance in the absence of integral quality[21] and, more importantly, to produce a demand which will utilise available mass consumption power (which itself the corporations in coordination with the state will try to adjust), the commodity passing as a consumer good is designed, and continually redesigned, to incorporate features of spurious novelty. The outstanding example remains the car, in which a potentially liberatory device has been so incredibly wastefully developed that it both represents an immense drain on potential wealth[22] and, increasingly, does not even serve the purpose for which it was developed.[23]

The tendency of this process generally is to produce an identification of happiness with increasing volumes of consumption in the mass of the citizens of the advanced capitalist countries. Only in this way can the pursuit of happiness be identified with the purchase of *commodities* and thus be, so far as possible, subsumed under the system of the capitalist economy. As neo-classical economics centrally recognises, consumption goals as ends in themselves are infinite, and in this way the wanting of commodities is made a potentially infinite boost to the capitalist economy (the potential being, very imperfectly, actualised by aggregate demand management). Of course, this is profoundly contradictory, for it amounts to identifying the means of securing happiness with an unrelievable *lack*, a lack that has,[24] as it must, thwart the actual achievement of happiness by replacing it with a general yearning for more.[25]

The citizen thereby typically features as a consumer, an object to be manipulated. Commodity aesthetics represent the subsumption of the properties of the good to the needs not of the consumer but of the sales effort, and the exercise of rational choice therefore must be minimised, for the commodity tends not to posess rational properties, at least not in a way that would distinguish it from competing products, which are similar at a given level of technique. Information is provided about these commodities in the form of advertising and "advertising becomes information when there is no longer anything to choose from".[26] It is just not enough for advertising practitioners and their apologists to insist how difficult manipulation is because of the obduracy of the target[27] (although appreciation of this is essential for a proper analysis of advertising),[28] for the whole advertising effort aims to penetrate that obduracy and wear the material down. The thrust of the system is towards the debasement of the culture of the great majority of citizens by restricting that culture to forms which are dominated by the sales effort.

The end point of this is the development of a mass society,[29] the principal characteristic of which is the prevention of self-determination by citizens. Working class struggles over wage levels become peripheral as the system, however haltingly and very imperfectly, no longer drives towards the reduction of the value of labour power but is prepared to see growth in real wages, so long as it is directed to the expansion of mass consumption of commodities. This society certainly is, in important senses, "post-capitalist" or "post-industrial", for the system tendency of *laissez faire* capitalism identified by Marx no longer is operative within it. Attempts to show that this mass society is still dominated by capital are no doubt correct, but entirely fail to come to terms with the significance of the novel features exposed by claims about post-industrialism, that the dominance of capital is expressed in an different relationship to labour, one which does not centrally require the driving down of the value of labour power.[30]

The forms of waste[31] occasioned by the sales effort are generally recognised even if, not least because of inadequate commitment of research resources to it, highly imperfectly quantified. What has so far been insufficiently appreciated is just what this waste means for our understanding of capitalism. Clearly, this waste is imposed by the *system*. The corporate managements which produce in this way do not chose to do so - they feel compelled by the market. There is no doubt that the market has a very serious influence on corporate managements - just read the trade press or any former corporate manager's memoirs - and the fetish under which they live certainly is an invisible but effective power over them. But this fetish is closing off the consideration of a vast range of superior alternative allocative arrangements and, whilst to this extent this confirms the enormous continuing importance of Marx's fundamental critique of alienation, it is doing so in a way directly contrary to the way Marx envisaged.

I have argued in the previous chapter that the two multipliers which are to make capitalist accumulation impossible, the law of the tendency of the rate of profit to fall and the tendency to overproduction, are indefinitely postponed by corporate reconstruction. It should be remembered that these two multipliers manifest the historically progressive but self-destructive essential feature of capitalism, the reduction of necessary labour-time. It is this economically imposed reduction, neither willed nor comprehended by the capitalist but enforced by competition under the invisible hand, that Marx claims to be the fundamental impulse to the development of socialism. The cost of the maintenance of capitalism has been that this progressive feature has disappeared from it. The very basis on which capitalism was to produce its own gravediggers, by lowering wage levels, has been undercut, for in its advanced form, capitalism centrally embraces rises in wages, though not reductions in necessary labour time. Working class struggles based on resistance to the economic imposition of privation are misdirected. Undoubtedly it is the case that whilst income provision remains dominated by wage labour, whilst wages continue to be treated as costs by firms, and whilst the distribution of income remains wildly uneven, so poverty will continue amidst any amount of plenty.[32] But recognition of this must be coupled to a recognition that there is no longer a central economic tendency to reduce wages themselves. Labour itself will be debased and there will be enormous resistance to the increase of free time. But corporate capitalism will continue to inflate the value of labour power by the needless supply of the commodities which make up the value of the reproduction of labour, and in co-operation with the state is prepared to adjust aggregate demand in line with this. It must be said that, in the basic sense envisaged by Marx, the wage struggle therefore is fundamentally conceded, though the concession has continually to be refought against structural defects in the capitalist organisation of work and consumption through the labour market,[33] which are often - as at present - exacerbated by persistent *laissez faire* ideological impulses to drive wages down.[34] What should be said is not that advanced capitalism is an economy of privation but that it is an economy of systematic and wholesale waste with no *economic* tendency to be otherwise.

Let us, massively unfairly, leave aside the underdeveloped countries[35] and just look at what has happened overall in the advanced capitalist countries. In the hundred and thirty years since the Ten Hours Bill was introduced, the working day has shrunk by less than a fifth. The nature of the labour process remains subject to an alienating reduction to abstract labour and, to the extent that consumption is installed as the overriding goal of human life, labour becomes merely a pain which must be endured to gain access to the funds necessary for consumption. This negative experience of work must be understood as an essential product of the *success* of the advanced capitalist restructuring of workers' welfare.[36] Were state employment and employment subsidy removed, unemployment would have increased enormously and, as it is, mass unemployment remains endemic. At the same time, technological increases in use value productivity surely have been greater than in all previous human history combined.

That the contradictory multipliers Marx thought facts like these represented have been made less antagonistic is hardly to be celebrated unless one completely identifies welfare with the preservation of capitalist property. These multipliers have *not* been used to diminish the realm of necessity by remorselessly driving down the value of labour power and increasing the margin of free time (and putting this to valuable use) but have been used to artificially inflate that value by cramming mass consumption values into necessary labour. The core feature of advanced capitalism is that the reduction of necessary labour time has been indefinitely postponed in order that production for private profit be maintained. The stultification of citizens reduced to being only consumers would arguably constitute the complete negation of the entire enlightenment project,[37] and with this capitalism's claims to be a civilising force are lost.

One very important consequence of this should not be disparaged to the extent that it represents an enormous growth in private wealth expressed in terms of the use value productivity of necessary labour time. To the extent that the citizen of the advanced capitalist countries is close to continuous employment or to someone in continuous employment, that citizen has participated in an enormous growth of use-value consumption. Claims that Marx's views about immiseration were wrong *must* be conceded in this very important sense.[38] But there is nowhere for this growth to go except in further cramming of use-values into necessary consumption, and the stupefaction through satiation of consumption needs that this implies is destroying the sense of necessary involved in necessary labour. The vast majority of labour is now unnecessary and a system which will allow this to be recognised, and allow the all round development of human beings occasioned by the reduction of necessary labour time envisaged by Marx in 1844, is a prerequisite of significant further development of civilisation.[39]

Laissez faire capitalism would appear to have driven the reduction of necessary labour time down to the point where this economic tendency made further accumulation on a *laissez faire* basis impossible. Instead of the process of production then being taken into socially self-conscious control which may have made the reduction of time spent in labour (or other conceivable collectively agreed goals) the aim of economic development, capitalism has been restructured into an advanced, corporate form, in which the dominance of private property has been retained and production locked within its alienating influence. The very wage struggles which Marx thought central to socialism are given a critical place in the reproduction of corporate capitalism.[40] This is a tyranny of affluence[41] rather than poverty, and it is a tyranny which socialism hitherto has been unable to understand.

It must be made clear that what is at issue is the end of economics, or rather, the recognition that the modern corporation has brought positive economics - the economics of global scarcity and necessity - to an end.[42] Such general, systemic "economic" indicators as now remain relevant to advanced capitalism are the expressions not of productive corporate governance but of our failure properly to bring the corporation under socially self-conscious and generally responsible control.[43] There are no sensible global indicators of scarcity in the present economy,[44] the central feature of which is enormous waste directed by the giant corporations in the interest of their own preservation rather than the satisfaction of properly determined needs. "Economic necessity" is the rubric under which the owners and controllers of corporations pay themselves - so very reluctantly - millions of dollars. The critique of corporate governance is the contemporary form of the critique of alienation. Reflection on the general pattern of criticism of advanced capitalism influenced by the marxist theories discussed in the last two chapters shows it to have been essentially wrong headed. Its focus has been on the "economy" when the economy has ceased to be determinant.[45]

One obvious consequence, the most pointed one, is that "marxism" has signally failed to speak to working class political concerns but has, in what often amounts to a truly pathetic display of petulance, tried to force those concerns into its economistic mould; blamed the working class, which has other concerns, for not being true to itself and, when the blame has produced few penitents, lost all interest in that reprobate class.[46] Another consequence, a highly significant one now if we are to frame policies which address the actually determinant influences on the advanced capitalist economy, is that the public law of corporate regulation, surely the nexus of any meaningful control of the contemporary economy, has had very little socialist attention paid to it and is, in fact, almost non-existent,[47] with its most developed form, anti-trust, quite irrelevant to the fundamental issues.[48] Marxist attempts to criticise the typical exclusion of workers' and consumers' interests from corporate planning typically have been cast at too broad a level of generality and lack a detailed knowledge of the working of the corporation.[49] It is essential that the immanent critique of capitalism be centrally fashioned in a political way dictated not by its *laissez faire*, economic form but by its advanced, political form. We must make political decisisons whether we want our material life to continue to be organised in this degrading and wasteful (and, for many, still poverty stricken) way. The economy carries no tendencies which will push us to the right decisions.[50]

Paradoxically, it is through this critique of the alienated dominance of economics that defensible technical marginalism might hope to be restored.[51] At the moment, neo-classical economics makes a number of claims about the global character of the advanced capitalist economy - which essentially boil down to an absurd misdescription of it as being explicable as the sum of the actions of rational, utility maximising individuals - that lead to its scathing rejection by any self-conscious social theory. But in this sundering of social awareness and technical economics, a very valuable resource is lost.[52] If, utilising Marx's critique of alienation, we might dispose of advanced capitalism's claims about the global character of the economy, then plausible markets set within socially self-conscious boundaries determined by political decisions might be established.[53] On this basis, a properly sympathetic re-evaluation of bourgeois recognitions of the limits of the market, principally aggregate demand management and welfare economics, which can allow of their integration into a thoroughgoingly socialist critique of capitalism, can and should be pursued.[54]

With this recasting of the very idea of the market, not as an alienated dominant social structure but as a technical economic allocative mechanism to be politically employed when this is regarded as proper, we have come to the point where this work can be concluded.

In both Hegel and Marx the critique of alienated beliefs is viewed as an inversion of those beliefs. The power this idea of critique as inversion has had can hardly be denied, but it is important now to realise its limitations. After the inversion, similar influences as those which produced the earlier alienated beliefs are *retained*, though given a new form. In Hegel, this leads to the idea of the end of history, a position in which all fundamental determinations are now known and future progress will be a matter of working within those determinations. Though inimical to the better parts of Hegel's thought, it is clear that this idea of absolute knowledge can lead to a most thoroughgoing dogmatism, and strong hints of this are to be found throughout his work. In Marx's reworking of this, what is inverted is classical political economy in order to produce the economic determinations which are to produce socialism. But in their economic character, these determinations share substantial parts of the fundamentally alienated characteristics of the laws of political economy. Again, it is now clear that this could very seriously misdirect the socialist effort, and this surely is what, overall, has taken place.

Althusser and Coletti, amongst others, have been right to draw attention to the potential weaknesses of a simply "inverted" Hegel. It would seem clear that their own conclusion, that this cannot be a description of Marx's position, was given politically, in the bad sense. They were sure that Marx's positions fundamentally had to be correct and could not come to terms with their own analysis when it showed that his positions might contain a fundamental mistake. Of course, if one looks at the matter other than, in this bad sense, politically, Marx's stature is as little effected as, say, Galileo's by a the somewhat less than astounding discovery that his work contains very serious errors.

Driven into increasingly tendentious interpretations of Marx's work in order to avoid having to come to terms with its basic weaknesses, Althussert and Colletti were unable to discover the real sources of its strength. Those sources very substantially do lie in Hegel. Absolute freedom and socialism have another, far more liberatory, potential, the power to realise social self-consciousness and to show the openness of the choices now available to free humankind. As the grasping of this power is a function of social self-comprehension, and the creation of the organisations which will allow this, this is properly called a political issue, and it is the dominance of politics over economics that now should be grasped as central to socialism. Socialism must be viewed as a process of social reflection (which requires organisation and struggle) which allows us to actualise our now potential freedom and not as a process of the working out of alienated economics.

In an incredible irony, it is, however, advanced capitalism that has made best use of this potential freedom. The corporation and the capitalist state have brought economic imperatives under sufficient control to protect capitalist property by the debased planning of the system. A new horizon for capitalist accumulation has thus been opened, but only at the cost of turning the formerly progressive system into a system of outright waste. The reduction of necessary labour time has been slowed or halted to maintain the commodity economy, at the cost of the systemic production of alienated and appalling outcomes. Socialist critique must not now wait for economic tendencies but must outright politically attack this waste.

This work has been critical of Marx and, as a corollary of combating the absurd status to which his work has been elevated in the majority of discussions of it, an unduly harsh tone may have been adopted. Let me try to finish on the correct note. Marx's attempt to realise the hegelian critique of alienation has been the most progressive force for the extension of freedom since 1789. That its - God knows, inevitable - lacunae have been the ultimate source of events which have rivalled in horror the consequences of persistent capitalism is immensely tragic. But no sensible criticism could claim that these events are faithful to Marx's spirit and to his lifetime of dedicated work. If I now want to recognise the failure of marxism and in that sense move beyond Marx, it is in a way that continues to insist on his enormous achievements and is, I hope, in line with that spirit.

Notes

1   Carnegie, 'The Bugaboo of the Trust', p 143. Carnegie is actually being a little gracious, for he is specifically referring to the founders of Standard Oil and , in particular, to Rockefeller as the " genius at [its] head".

2   *Ibid*, p 149.

3   Hadley, *Economics*, p 295. Amongst the observers was, of course, Jevons, who reported his findings in *The Theory of Political Economy*, p 136. To his credit, Hadley rejects this explanation.

4   Carnegie, 'The Bugaboo of the Trust', p 141.

5   Conant, 'The Economic Basis of "Imperialism", p 326. What should be stressed after reading this passage, written in 1898, is how good it makes Engels look!

6   Meade, *Trust Finance*, pp 22-3.

7   Wright, 'The Relation of Production To Productive Capacity', pp 673-4.

8   *Ibid*, p 674.

9   Eg Kalecki, 'The Impact of Armaments Spending on the Business Cycle After the Second World War'.

10 Eg O'Connor, *The Fiscal Crisis of the State*, Chs 7-9.

11 This leads me to ignore very interesting accounts of the restructuring of the labour process as an advanced capitalist regulatory process grouped around the notion of "neo-fordism". Aglietta, *A Theory of Capitalist Regulation* and Pallioix, 'From Fordism to Neofordism'. Though insufficiently distanced from the predeliction for crisis discussed in the previous chapter and though often expressed in an unnecessary verbiage, these accounts have been, overall, unusually productive.

12 *Vide* Adorno and Horkheimer, *Dialectic of Enlightenment*, pp 120-67 and Adorno, 'Culture Industry Reconsidered'.

13 The high point arguably is represented by cultural studies directly influenced by Althusser's 'Ideology and Ideological State Apparatuses'.

14 Some such denial is essential to the public defence of corporate advertising and things to this effect do appear. It is impossible not to conclude that a lack of integrity is involved in making claims that advertising is a source of information when obviously the issue is the sort of "information" being conveyed. *Vide* Chamberlin, *The Theory of Monopolistic Competition*, ch 4. But even this lack of integrity is eclipsed by defences of advertising based on the claim that it has *no* effect, which are quite disgracefully conducted. Let us leave aside the waste involved in this production of no effect. *Vide* Scherer and Ross, *Industrial Market Structure and Economic Performance*, pp 572-3. The particularly unscrupulous characteristic of these defences is that they set up a concept of manipulation which requires a citizen to be under rather direct control and the claim then follows when this type of control obviously is found not to exist. Eg Hayek, 'The Non-sequitur of the Dependence Effect'. This just is not the way an open mind would approach the issue, but such a mind would wish to explain a puzzling phenomenon and not just explain it away. *Vide* Baran, 'Theses on Advertising', pp 223-35. Faced with the difficulty of denying advertising manipulation, the predominant way in which the issue is taken up in welfare economics is to try to balance the disutility of spending vast sums to manipulate citizens against the

utility of staving off the stagnation of demand. Such are the choices of the modern economy. *Vide* Baran, *The Political Economy of Growth*, pp 19-28.

15   *Vide* Galbraith, *Economics and the Public Purpose*, p 161. Cf *idem*, *The Affluent Society*, ch 11.

16   *Vide* Peel, 'Advertising and Aggregate Consumption',

17   *Vide* Chamberlin, *Theory of Monopolistic Competition*, ch 6, sec 1 and Cowling *et al*, *Advertising and Economic Behaviour*, ch 4.

18   *Vide* Scitovsky, *Welfare and Competition*, ch 28.

19   *Vide* Baran and Sweezy, *Monopoly Capital*, pp 132-44.

20   *Vide* Haug, *Critique of Commodity Aesthetics*, pp 22-4.

21   *Ibid*, pp 24-34.

22   Baran and Sweezy placed great emphasis on the car in *Monopoly Capital*, pp 138-41. They relied on estimates of the cost of automobile changes up to 1960 by Fisher, Griliches and Kaysen ('The Cost of Automobile Model Changes Since 1949'). This work was based on Griliches' calculation of 'Hedonic Price Indexes for Automobiles'. Griliches' subsequent work (*idem*, 'Notes on the Measurement of Price and Quality Changes', and Ohta and Griliches, 'Automobile Prices Revisited') brings the damning evidence up to 1971, with certain subsequent indications of similar trends (*idem* 'Automobile Prices and Quality').

23   Gordon, *The Measurement of Durable Goods Prices* attempts to present a new set of price indexes for durable goods, including automobiles (ch 8), which, in essence, show that price inflation has been lower than official estimates because these estimates systematically understate quality increases' impact on price. Gordon's most impressively extensive argument that "durable goods prices have increased much less" than in official estimates (p 520) does not, however, properly speak to Baran and Sweezy's use of Griliches' hedonic index. Now, it is hard to imagine that Gordon would wish directly to address Baran and Sweezy's argument, but not to do so leaves an acute problem in relation to cars. In earlier work (*idem* 'Measurement Bias in Price Indexes for Capital Goods'), Gordon attempted to give positive values to styling changes as quality improvements. This is simply to assume away the real problem, of whether these changes *are* improvements, and in his published book Gordon largely eschews these "subjective and anecdotal" judgements (*idem*, *The Measurement of Durable Goods Prices*, p 365). He wisely devises his price deflator with a stress on the rational properties of car design, such as environmental quality and fuel economy. The problem with this is obvious. As this stress hardly captures the real motivation of car redesign, it can hardly begin to capture the real cost of innovation. Fuel economy, for example, has been pursued largely as part of an attempt to allow cars to travel at up to three times the legal speed limit in the US! This argument is a highly technical version of the defence of the US space programme that it gave us the non-stick frying pan! Furthermore, at least the

non-stick frying pan is of use, whilst this cannot easily be said of the 150 mph car.

24 *Vide* Wachtel, *The Poverty of Affluence.*

25 *Vide* Leiss, *The Limits to Satisfaction.*

26 Adorno, 'The Schema of Mass Culture', p 73.

27 Eg Wilmshurst, *The Fundamentals of Advertising*, p 16.

28 *Vide* Sinclair, *Images Incorporated*, ch 1.

29 *Vide* Giner, *Mass Society.*

30 *Vide* Gorz, *Farewell to the Working Class*, chs 1-4.

31 I do not want to undertake to argue here that these are wasted. The only way to dispute this is to take up the total agnosticism about the defensibility of revealed preferences that, since Pareto, has been central to general equilibrium theory. Responding to this argument is important but, as it takes us into the plausibility of analysis of the conditions of existence of Pareto optimality when these conditions can never exist, it is rather tangential to my argument here.

32 The extent of poverty in the advanced capitalist countries and the tenacity of its persistence should not, of course, be underestimated. The startling quality of Townsend's massively authoritative *Poverty in the United Kingdom* is, despite the differences over the measurement of poverty, just how readily it invites comparison with Booth and Rowntree. The most acute form of advanced capitalist poverty, the experience of inner city "life" in the United States, should speak for itself, but, of course, it does not. *Vide* Harrington, *The Other America.*

33 *Vide* Hinrichs and Offe, 'The Political Economy of the Labour Market' and Berger and Offe, 'The Future of the Labour Market'. Though I will ignore it here, it seems unarguable that recent increases in the pace of internationalisation of capital investment will increasingly produce a competitive impulse to cut wages in the advanced countries by drawing on the potential labour forces of the underdeveloped and now of the former communist countries. *Vide* Smith, *Uneven Development.* This source of increase in absolute surplus value is a profoundly destabilising impulse which, no doubt, the capitalist countries will handle very badly indeed, with resultant widespread misery. I see no reason, however, to elevate this and related destabilising influences such as the electronic mobility of pure finance, to some qualitative shift in the nature of advanced capitalism, *pace* Lash and Urry, *The End of Organised Capitalism.* What certainly should come to an end, however, are claims to continue to understand capitalism which continue to be organised on classic lines, such as the attempt to discover capitalism's "weakest link" which rather gives away the game in Lash and Urry.

34 *Vide* Block, 'Rethinking the Political Economy of the Welfare State'.

35 As Enzenburger so clearly puts it:

The "wealth" of the over-developed consumer societies of the West...is the result of a wave of plunder and pillage unparalleled in history. It is therefore, a kind of wealth that produces unimaginable want.

The picture emerges clearly enough from World Bank, *World Development Report*, figs 1 and 2 which show that "more than 1 billion people - more that a fifth of the world's population, live on less than a dollar a day - a standard of living that Western Europe and the United States attained two hundred year ago". I do not in any sense mean to disparage the immense suffering of the mass of the population of the underdeveloped countries when I abstract from that suffering. But having to concede the political quietism of the western working classes, it became the central tack of many Marxists to try to find a new proletariat in the poverty stricken of the "third world". Eg Frank, *Capitalism and Underdevelopment in Latin America*. The central feature of this sort of thinking, which really amounted to no more than a terribly unprincipled attempt to hold on to old views by applying them to the poor of the underdeveloped countries when there was overwhelming counter evidence to their continuing application to the working class of the imperialist countries, surely is its own poverty. Of course, the account of underdevelopment was of the greatest value. Eg Baran, *The Political Economy of Growth*, chs 5-7. But, amongst the reasons why the exposure of the baneful effects of imperialism could not be pressed through to effective criticism of that imperialism was the economic cast of the criticism, which set out to identify further immiseration amongst people already so horribly poor as surely not to need to be subjected to his type of analysis. The "third world" has now lost political force and perhaps even its claim to exist as such. *Vide* Harris, *The End of the Third World*. This surely shows how pressingly the economic approaches which set up the third world need to be rethought. *Vide* Menzel, 'The End of the "Third World" and the Failure of Grand Theories'.

36 *Vide* Luke, 'Anti-work?', p 194.

37 *Vide* MacIntyre, *After Virtue*. A great amount of attention has been given to this idea in many works which claim that the rational aspirations of "modernity" themselves are largely eschewed in present day capitalism. Surely something of great interest is being driven at here, but it is often hard to see what, for many of these works seem to feel obliged to give testimony to the eclipse of reason by being written in such a way which is evidence of, and not distanced commentary on, that eclipse. Eg Baudrillard, *For a Critique of the Political Economy of the Sign* and *idem, In the Shadow of Silent Minorities...or the End of the Social*.

38 *Vide* eg Schmookler, *The Illusion of Choice*, pp 21-4.

39 Lane, *The Market Experience*.

40 *Vide* Cawson, *Corporations and Welfare*. The integration of corporatist labour relations into a picture of a relatively smoothly functioning planned capitalism is carried furthest in Shonfield, *Modern Capitalism*. There can be little doubt that corporatist strategies are always precarious because of the persistent clashes between capital and labour. *Vide* Schmitter, 'Still the Century of Corporatism?'

Nevertheless, much marxist criticism of corporatist political theory would appear to be outright reactionary, for it continually stresses that corporatist wage accommodations are in some way peripheral to the advanced capitalist economies, and therefore something of a sham to be penetrated by active labour movements, when, rather, they are absolutely central to those economies and socialism should come to terms with this. It is not enough continually point to the limits of corporatist incomes policies. Eg Strinati, *Corporatism, the State and Industrial Relations*. The task is to develop the policy beyond those limits. Flat rejection of incomes policy is simply an absurd line for a socialism to take. An admittedly exaggerated but instructive example is provided by Cliff, *The Crisis*, which is subtitled *Social Contract or Socialism*. This work advocated militant rejection of "the social contract", the general incomes policy which the Labour Party attempted to establish in co-operation with the Trades Union Congress in 1974, in favour of the development of a "socialist planned economy", the central feature of which would appear to be the *absence* of a plan for income. The degree to which the wrecking of an incomes policy largely drawn up by labour organisations subsequently led to an increase in working class welfare by contributing to the initial electoral success of Thatcherism must be open to a certain degree of doubt.

41 *Vide* Galbraith, *The Affluent Society*.

42 Unger has placed the rejection of arguments from economic necessity within a wider criticism of institutional and structural fetishism based on the exposure of "false necessity". Unger, *Social Theory: Its Situation and Its Task*, ch 8.

43 *Vide* Block, *Postindustrial Possibilities*, nb ch 5. Block's book is of similar status to Beck's *Risk Society* in indicating the proper form of future political determination of basic resource allocation.

44 *Vide ibid*, ch 1.

45 Any amount of waste is central to the advanced capitalist economy and, in this respect, however technically useful marginal analysis remains, it is absurd to see the current economic problem as one of global scarcity. However, unable to give up his line of thinking, many marxists, despairing of seeing anything like Marx's limits to accumulation bring capitalism down, have found another such economic limit. It is the environment! Eg O'Connor 'Capitalism, Nature, Socialism: A Theoretical Introduction'. If we keep going the way we are, we are told, then "it will become apparent that environmental considerations should act as a binding constraint on production". Armstrong *et al*, *Capitalism Since 1945*, p 343. Of course it is a question of the first importance whether we should continue to despoil the natural world in the way advanced capitalist economies tend to do. But this political issue, a criticism of the capitalist economics that produce these outcomes, should not itself be posed in eschatological and economistic terms, for they are at best misleading. Armstrong, Glyn and Sutcliffe, for example, should stress the political implication of their demonstration of the extreme costs of advanced capitalism's persistence. But they do not have the confidence to do this,

so they feel obliged to conclude on a brief economic eschatological note, picking on the environment as a new location for the eschatological tendency, despite all that has preceded this conclusion having been an authoritative account of advanced capitalism's persistence despite its in so many ways abysmal performance. The issue *must* be rethought in the way indicated by Beck's idea of "reflexive modernisation". Beck, *Risk Society*.

46   *Vide* Anderson, *Consideration on Western Marxism*, pp 24-48.

47   *Vide* Campbell, 'Adam Smith, *Farrar on Company Law* and the Economics of the Corporation'.

48   *Idem* 'Why Regulate the Modern Corporation: The Failure of Market Failure'.

49   The best modern exceptions to this would seem to be German analyses of co-determination, eg Streeck, 'Co-determination: After Four Decades'.

50   The conclusion of Baran and Sweez's economic critique in *Monopoly Capital* is moral outrage. This feature has often been criticised but it shows just how much ground they made towards developing a proper basis for the wholesale criticism of advanced capitalism. When Bowles *et al*, *Beyond the Waste Land*, ch 7 brings the exposure of waste more up to date, it also valuably went on to conclude that the continuation of this waste was possible only because of a failure of democracy (pt 3).

51   As I have argued in 'The Social Theory of Relational Contract: Macneil as the Modern Proudhon', p 86; 'The Reform of the Market and Labour's Economic Policies' and 'Why Regulate the Modern Corporation?: The Failure of Market Failure', pp 129-31.

52   As I have argued in 'Ayres Versus Coase: An Attempt to Recover the Issue of Equality in Law and Economics'.

53   *Vide* Elson, 'The Economics of the Socialised Market' and *idem*, 'Market Socialism or Socialisation of the Market'.

54   *Vide* Stephens, *The Transition from Capitalism to Socialism*.

Bibliography

Places of publication are in the UK unless otherwise indicated.

S Aaronovitch and M Sawyer, *Big Business*, London, Macmillan,1975

S Aaronovitch, *The Crisis in Historical Materialism*, 2nd edn, London, Macmillan, 1990

HB Acton, *The Illusion of the Epoch*, London, George Allen and Unwin, 1962

M Adler, 'The Sociology of Revolution', in Bottomore and Goode, eds, *Autro-Marxism*, pp 136-46

TW Adorno, *The Culture Industry*, London, Routledge, 1991

TW Adorno, 'Culture Industry Reconsidered', in *idem, The Culture Industry*, ch 3

TW Adorno, *Negative Dialectics*, London, Routledge and Kegan Paul, 1973

TW Adorno, 'The Schema of Mass Culture', *in idem, The Culture Industry*, ch 2

TW Adorno and M Horkheimer, *Dialectic of Enlightenment*, London, Verso, 1979

M Aglietta, *A Theory of Capitalist Regulation*, London, New Left Books, 1979

L Althusser, 'Contradiction and Overdetermination', in *idem, For Marx*, pp87-128

L Althusser, 'Elements of Self-criticism', in *idem, Essays in Self-criticism*, pp 101-61

L Althusser, *Essays in Self-criticism*, London, New Left Books, 1976

L Althusser, *For Marx*, London, New Left Books, 1977

L Althusser, 'Ideology and Ideology State Apparatuses', in *idem, Lenin and Philosophy and Other Essays*, pp 121-73

L Althusser, 'Introduction: Today', in *idem, For Marx*, pp 21-39

L Althusser, Is It Simple To Be a Marxist In Philosophy?', in *idem, Essays in Self-criticism*, pp 163-207

L Althusser, *Lenin and Philosophy and Other Essays*, 2nd edn, London, New Left Books, 1977

L Althusser, 'On the Materialist Dialectic', in *idem, For Marx*, pp 161-218

L Althusser, 'Philosophy as a Revolutionary Weapon', in *idem, Lenin and Philosophy and Other Essays*, pp 13-25

L Althusser, 'Preface to Capital Volume One', in *idem, Lenin and Philosophy and Other Essays*, pp 69-101

L Althusser and E Balibar, *Reading 'Capital'*, 2nd edn, London, New Left Books, 1977

American Academy of Political and Social Science, *Corporations and the Public Welfare*, New York (USA), McClure, Philips, 1900

S Amin, *Eurocentrism*, London, Zed Books, 1988

P Anderson, *Arguments Within English Marxism*, London, Verso, 1980

P Anderson, *Considerations on Western Marxism*, London, Verso, 1979

Anon, *Observations on Certain Verbal Disputes in Political Economy*, London, R Hunter, 1821

Anon, *Philogelos, or the Laughter- lover*, Amsterdam (Netherlands), JC Gieben, 1983

RP Appelbaum, Karl Marx, Newbury Park (USA), Sage, 1988

A Arato and E Gebhardt, eds, *The Essential Frankfurt School Reader*, Oxford, Basil Blackwell, 1978

Aristotle, *Ethics*, Harmondsworth, Penguin, 1976

P Armstrong *et al, Capitalism Since 1945*, Oxford, Basil Blackwell, 1945

NS Arnold, Marx's *Radical Critique of Capitalist Society*, New York (USA), Oxford University Press, 1990

KJ Arrow, *Collected Papers*, Cambridge (USA), Belknap Press, 1984ff

KJ Arrow, 'Economic Equilibrium', in *idem, Collected Papers*, vol 2, ch 6

KJ Arrow, 'Limited Knowledge and Economic Analysis', in *idem, Collected Papers*, vol 4, ch 12

CJ Arthur, 'Dialectic of the Value-form', in D Elson, ed, *Value*, pp 67-81

J Austin, *The Province of Jurisprudence Determined*, London, Weidenfeld and Nicolson, 1955

F Bacon, 'The New Organon', in *idem, The New Organon and Related Writings*, pp 31-268

F Bacon, *The New Organon and Related Writings*, Indianapolis (USA), The Library of Liberal Arts, 1960

AM Bailey and J Llobera, *The Asiatic Mode of Production*, London, Routledge and Kegan Paul, 1981

S Bailey, *A Critical Dissertation on the Nature, Measure and Causes of Value*, London Hunter, 1825

S Bailey, *A Letter to a Political Economist*, London, R Hunter, 1826

S Bailey, *Money and Its Vicissitudes in Value*, London, E Wilson, 1836

E Balibar, 'On the Basic Concepts of Historical Materialism', in Althusser and Balibar, *Reading 'Capital'*, pp 199-308

J Banaji,' From the Commodity to *Capital'*, in Elson, ed, *Value*, pp 14-45

PA Baran, *The Longer View*, New York (USA), Monthly Review Press, 1969

PA Baran, *The Political Economy of Growth*, Harmondsworth, Penguin, 1973

PA Baran, 'Theses on Advertising', in *idem, The Longer View*, pp 223-35

PA Baran and PM Sweezy, *Monopoly Capital*, Harmondsworth, Penguin, 1966

ZG Baranski and JR Short, eds, *Developing Contemporary Marxism*, London, Macmillan, 1985

JD Barrow, *Theories of Everything*, Oxford, Oxford University Press, 1991

N Barry, *Welfare*, Milton Keynes, Open University Press, 1990

K Battacharya, *Accountancy's Faulty sums*, London, Macmillan, 1992

J Baudrillard, *For a Political Economy of the Sign*, St Louis (USA), Telos Press, 1981

J Baudrillard, *In the Shadow of Silent Minorities...or the End of the Social*, New York (USA), Semiotexte, 1983

O Bauer, 'Marxism and Ethics', in Bottomore and Goode, eds, *Austro-Marxism*, pp 78-84

WG Baumol, *The Stock Market and Economic Efficiency*, New York (USA), Fordham University Press, 1965

U Beck, *Risk Society*, London, Sage, 1992

FC Beiser, *The Cambridge Companion to Hegel*, Cambridge, Cambridge University Press, 1993

D Bell, *The Coming of Post-industrial Society*, London, Heinemann, 1974

J Bentham, *An Introduction to the Principles of Morals and Legislation*, London, Athlone Press, 1970

T Benton, 'Natural Science and Cultural Struggle: Engels and the Philosophy of the Natural Sciences', in Mepham and Ruben, eds, *Issues in Marxist Philosophy*, vol 2, ch 4

T Benton, *Philosophical Foundations of the Three Sociologies*, London, Routledge and Kegan Paul, 1977

T Benton, *The Rise and Fall of Structural Marxism*, London, Macmillan, 1984

J Berger and C Offe, 'The Future of the Labour Market', in Offe, *Disorganised Capitalism*, ch 2

G Berkeley, *Philosophical Works*, London, Dent, 1975

G Berkeley, 'A Treatise Concerning the Principles of Human Knowledge', in *idem, Philosophical Works*, pp 61-127

AA Berle and G Means, *The Modern Corporation and Private Property*, rev edn, New York (USA), Harcourt Brace, 1968

E Bernstein, *Evolutionary Socialism*, New York (USA), Schocken Books, 1961

WH Beveridge, *Full Employment in a Free Society*, London, George Allen and Unwin, 1944

J-M Beyssde, 'The Idea of God and the Proofs of His Existence', in Cottingham, ed, *The Cambridge Companion to Descartes*, ch 6

R Bhaskar, *The Possibility of Naturalism*, 2nd edn, Sussex, Harvester, 1989

R Bhaskar, *A Realist Theory of Science*, Sussex, Harvester, 1978

R Bhaskar, *Scientific Realism and Human Emanicipation*, London, Verso, 1986

G Bird, 'Hegel's Account of the Kant's Epistemology', in Priest, ed, *Hegel's Critique of Kant*, ch 2

J Bird, 'A Giant's Voice from the Past' (8 September 1989) no 879 *Times Higher Education Supplement*, p 17

R Blackburn, ed, *After the Fall*, London, Verso, 1991, ch 19

R Blackburn, ed, *Ideology in Social Science*, Glasgow, Fontana, 1972

M Blaug, 'Another Look at the Labour Reduction Problem in Marx', in Bradley and Howard, *Classical and Marxian Political Economy*, ch 5

F Block, *Postindustrial Possibilities*, Berkeley (USA), University of California Press, 1990

F Block, 'Rethinking the Political Economy of the Welfare State', in Block *et al*, eds, *The Mean Season*, pp 109-60

F Block, *et al*, eds, *The Mean Season*, New York (USA), Pantheon Books, 1987

E von Böhm-Bawerk, *Capital and Interest*, New York (USA), Augustus M Kelley, 1970

E von Böhm-Bawerk, 'Karl Marx and the Close of His System', in Sweezy, ed, *'Karl Marx and the Close of His System' by Eugen von Böhm Bawerk and 'Böhm-Bawerk's Criticism of Marx' by Rudolf Hilferding*, pp 1-118

L von Bortkiewicz, 'On the Correction of Marx's Fundamental Construction in the Third Volume of *Capital*', in Sweezy, ed, *'Karl Marx and the Close of His*

System' by Eugen von Böhm Bawerk and the 'Böhm-Bawerk's Criticism of Marx' by Rudolf Hilferding, pp 199-221

HH Boss, *Theories of Surplus and Transfer*, London, Unwin Hyman, 1990

WH Bossart, 'Hegel on the Inverted World' (1982) vol 13 *The Philosophical Forum*, pp 326-41

J Boswell, *Life of Johnson*, Oxford, Oxford University Press, 1980

T Bottomore and P Goode, eds, *Austro-Marxism*, Oxford, Clarendon Press, 1978

T Bottomore, *Marxist Sociology*, London, Macmillan, 1975

S Bowles *et al*, *Beyond the Waste Land*, Garden City (USA), Anchor Books, 1983

I Bradley and M Howard, *Classical and Marxian Political Economy*, London, Macmillan, 1982

H Braverman, *Labour and Monopoly Capital*, London, Monthly Review Press, 1974

J Broadhurst, *Political Economy*, London, Halebard and Sons, 1842

W Brus and K Laski, *From Marx to the Market*, Oxford, Clarendon Press, 1979

NI Bukharin,*The Economic Theory of the Leisure Class*, London, Monthly Review Press, 1972

NI Bukharin, 'Imperialism and the Accumulation of Capital', in Tarbuck, ed, *'The Accumulation of Capital: An Anti-critique' by Rosa Luxemburg and 'Imperialism and the Accumulation of Capital'* by Nikolai I Bukharin, pp 151-270

NI Bukharin, 'The Policy of Theoretical Conciliation', in *idem, The Economic Theory of the Leisure Class*, appendix

NI Bukharin, *The Politics and Economics of the Transition Period*, London, Routledge and Kegan Paul, 1979

DG Bunting, *The Rise of the Large American Corporations 1889-1919*, New York (USA), Garland, 1986

E Caird, *Hegel*, Edinburgh, William Blackwood, 1883

A Callinicos, *Is There a Future for Marxism?*, London, Macmillan, 1982

D Campbell, 'Adam Smith, *Farrar on Company Law* and the Economics of the Corporation' (1990) vol 19 *Anglo-American Law Review*, pp 185-208

D Campbell, 'Ayres Versus Coase: An Attempt to Recover the Issue of Inequality in Law and Economics' (1994) vol 21 *British Journal of Law and Society*, pp 434-63

D Campbell, 'Individualism, Equality and the Possibility of Rights' (1991) vol 6 *Connecticut Journal of International Law*, pp 507-27

D Campbell, 'Rationality, Democracy and Freedom in Marxism Critiques of Hegel's Philosophy of Right' (1985) vol 28 *Inquiry*. pp 59-74

D Campbell, 'The Social Theory of Relational Contact: Macneil as the Modern Proudhon' (1989) vol 18 *International Journal of the Sociology of Law*, pp 75-95

D Campbell, 'Truth Claims and Value-freedom in the Treatment of Legitimacy: The Case of Weber' (1986) vol 13 *Journal of Law and Society*, pp 207-24

D Campbell,'Why Regulate the Modern Corporation?The Failure of Market Failure', in McCahery *et al*, eds, *Corporate Accountability and Control*, pp 103-31

D Campbell and DR Harris,' Flexibility in Long-term Contractual Relationships: The Role of Co-operation' (1993) vol 20 *Journal of Law and Society*, pp 166-91

GA Caravale, ed, *Marx and Modern Economics*, Aldershot, Edward Elgar, 1991

A Carnegie, 'The Bugaboo of the Trust' (1 889) no 148 *North Amercan Review*, pp 141-50

AB Carter, *Marx: A Radical Critique*, Sussex, Wheatsheaf, 1988

T Carver, *Engels*, Oxford, Oxford University Press, 1981

T Carver, *Friedrich Engels*, London, Macmillan, 1989

T Carver, *Marx and Engels*, Sussex, Wheatsheaf, 1983

T Carver, *Marx's Social Theory*, Oxford, Oxford University Press, 1982

C Castoriadis, 'On the History of the Workers' Movement' (1976-7) no 30 *Telos*, pp 3-42

A Cawson, *Corporatism and Welfare*, London, Heinemann, 1982

Centre for Contemporary Cultural Studies, *On Ideology*, London, Hutchinson, 1978

EH Chamberlin, *The Theory of Monopolistic Competition*, 8th edn, Cambridge (USA), Harvard University Press, 1962

EH Chamberlin, ed, *Monopoly and Competition and their Regulation*, Cambridge, Cambridge University Press, 1955

AD Chandler, *Scale and Scope*, Cambridge (USA), Harvard University Press, 1990

JB Clark, 'Introduction', in Rodbertus, Overproduction and Crises, pp 1- 18

S Clarke, 'Althusserian Marxism', in S Clarke *et al, One-dimensional Marxism*, pp 7-102

S Clarke, *Marx, Marginalism and Modern Sociology*, 2nd edn, London, Macmillan, 1991

S Clarke *et al, One-dimensional Marxism*, London, Alison and Busby, 1980

T Cliff, *The Crisis*, London, Pluto Press, 1975 J Coakley and L Harris, The City of Capital, Oxford, Basil Blackwell, 1983

RH Coase, *The Firm, the Market and the Law*,Chicago (USA), University of Chicago Press, 1988

RH Coase, 'The Firm, the Market and the Law', in *idem, The Firm, the Market and the Law*, ch 1

RH Coase, 'The Lighthouse in Economics', in *idem, The Firm, the Market and the Law*, ch 7

D Coates *et al*, eds, *A Socialist Anatomy of Britain*, Cambridge, Polity Press, 1985

GA Cohen, 'Functional Explanation, Consequence Explanation and Marxism' (1982) vol 25 *Inquiry*, pp 27-56

GA Colien, 'Functional Explanation: Reply to Elster' (1980) vol 28 *Political Studies*, pp 129-35

GA Coben, *History, Labour and Freedom*, Oxford, Clarendon Press, 1988

GA Cohen, *Karl Marx's Theory of History*, Oxford, Oxford University Press, 1978

GA Cohen, 'The Labour Theory of Value and the Concept of Exploitation', in *idem, History, Labour and Freedom*, ch 11

GA Cohen, 'Reply to Elster on 'Marxism, Functionalism and Game Theory' (1982) vol 11 *Theory and Society*, pp 483-96

GDH Cole, 'Introduction', in Marx, Capital, vol 1 (Everyman edn), pp v-xxv

GDH Cole, *Self-government in Industry*, rev edn, London, Hutchinson, 1972

GDH Cole, *What Marx Really Meant*, London, Victor Gollancz, 1934

L Colletti, 'Bernstein and the Marxism of the Second International', in *idem, From Rousseau to Lenin*, pp 45-108

L Colletti, 'From Hecel to Marcuse', in *idem, Front Rousseau to Lenin*, pp 111-40

L Colletti, *From Rousseau to Lenin*, London, Monthly Review Press, 1972

L Colletti, *Marxism and Hegel*, London, Verso, 1979

L Colletti, 'Marxism: Science or Revolution?', in *idem, From Rousseau to Lenin*, pp 229-36

A Collier, *Scientific Realism and Socialist Thought*, London, Harvester Wheatsheaf, 1989

RG Collingwood, *The Idea of Nature*, Oxford, Oxford University Press, 1960

AB Collins, 'Hegel's Redefinition of the Critical Project', in Westphal, ed, *Method and Speculation in Hegel's 'Phenomenology'*, pp 1-13

CA Conant, 'Can New Openings Be Found for Capital?', in *idem, The United States in the Orient*, ch 4

CA Conant, 'Crises and their Management' (1901) vol 9 *Yale Review*, pp 374-98

CA Conant, 'The Economic Basis of "Imperialism"', in *idem, The United States in the Orient*, ch 1

CA Conant, *A History of modern Banks of Issue*, 6th edn, New York (USA), Putnam, 1927

CA Conant, 'The Struggle for Commercial Empire', in *idem, The United States in the Orient*, ch 3

CA Conant, 'The United States as a World Power: Their Advantanes in the Competition for Commercial Empire', in *idem, The United States in the Orient*, ch 7

CA Conant, 'The United States as a World Power: The Nature of the Economic and Political Problem', in *idem, The United States in the Orient*, ch 6

CA Conant, *The United States in the Orient*, Port Washington (USA) Kennikat Press, 1971

FC Copleston, 'Hegel and the Rationalisation of Mysticism', in Steinkraus, ed, *New Studies in Hegel's Philosophy*, pp 187-200

MC Cornforth, *Dialectical Materialism*, London, Lawrence and Wishart, 1953

J Cottingham, *Descartes*, Oxford, Basil Blackwell, 1986

J Cottingham, ed, *The Cambridge Companion to Descartes*, Cambridge, Cambridge University Press, 1992

F Cowley, *A Critique of British Empiricism*, London, Macmillan, 1968

K Cowling *et al, Advertising and Economic Behaviour*, London, Macmillan, 1975

K Cowling, *Monopoly Capital*, London, Macmillan, 1983

CAR Crosland, *The Future of Socialism*, London, Jonathan Cape, 1956

A Cutler *et al, Marx's 'Capital' and Capitalism Today*, vol 1, London, Routledge and Kegan Paul, 1977

A Cutler *et al, Marx's 'Capital' and Capitalism Today*, vol 2, London, Routledge and Kegan Paul, 1978

T Cutler *et al, Keynes, Beveridge and Beyond*, London, Routledge and Kegan Paul, 1986

R Dahrendorf, *Class and Class Conflict in Industrial Society*, London, Routledge and Kegan Paul, 1959

M Dalla Costa and S James, 'Woman and the Subversion of the Community', in idem, eds, *The Power of Women and the Subversion of the Community*, pp 21-56

M Dalla Costa and S James, eds, *The Power of Women and the Subversion of the Community*, rev edn, Bristol, Falliner Wall Press, 1975

H Davis and R Scase, *Western Capitalism and State Socialism*, Oxford, Basil Blackwell, 1985

D Defoe, *Robinson Crusoe*, Harmondsworth, Penguin, 1965

G Della Volpe, 'For a Materialist Methodolocoy of Economics and of the Moral Disciplines in General', in *idem, Rousseau and Marx and Other Writings*, pp 159-204.

G Della Volpe, *Logic as a Positive Science*, London, New Left Books, 1980

G Della Volpe, *Rousseau and Marx and Other Writings*, London, Lawrence and Wishart, 1978

M Desai, *Marxian Economics*, Totowa (USA), Rowman and Littlefield, 1979

M Desai, 'Methodological Problems of Quantitative Marxism, in Dunne, ed, *Quantitative Marxism*, ch 1

M Desai, 'The Transformation Problem', in Caravale, ed, *Marx and Modern Economic's*, vol 1, ch 1

R Descartes, 'Discourse on the Method', in *Philosophical Writings*, vol 1, pp 111-51

R Descartes, 'Meditations', in *Philosophical Writings*, vol 2, pp 3-62

R Descartes, *Philosophical Writings*, Cambridge, Cambridge University Press, 1985ff

W Dilthey, The Construction of the Historical World in the Human Studies', in *idem, Selected Writings*, pp 133-54

W Dilthey, *Selected Writings*, Cambridge, Cambridge University Press, 1976

M Dobb, *Political Economy and Capitalism*, 2nd edn, London, Routledge and Kegan Paul, 1940

G Donaldson, *Corporate Debt Capacity*, Cambridge (USA), Graduate School of Business, Harvard University, 1961

KR Dove, 'Hegel's Phenomenological Method', in Steinkraus, ed, *New Studies in Hegel's Philosophy*, pp 34-56

SP, Dunn, *The Fall and Rise of the Asiatic Mode of Production*, London, Routledge and Kegan Paul, 1982

P Dunne, ed, *Quantitative Marxism*, Cambridge, Polity Press, 1991

T Eagleton, *Ideology*, London, Verso, 1991

R Edgley, 'Dialectic: The Contradictions of Colletti' (1977) vol 7 *Critique*, pp 47-52

D Elson, 'Market Socialism or Socialisation of the Market' (1988) no 172 *New Left Review*, pp 3-44

D Elson, 'The Economics of a Socialised Market', in Blackburn, ed, *After the Fall*, ch 19

D Elson, ed, *Value*, London, CSE Books, 1979

J Elster, 'Cohen on Marx's Theory of History' (1980) vol 28 *Political Studies*, pp 121-8

J Elster, 'Further Thoughts on Marxism, Functionalism and Game Theory', in J Roemer, ed, *Analytical Marxism*, pp 202- 20

J Elster, 'Introduction', in Elster and Moene, eds, *Alternatives to Capitalism*, ch 1

J Elster, *Logic and Society*, Chichester, John Wiley, 1978

J Elster, *Making Sense of Marx*, Cambridge, Cambridge University Press, 1985

J Elster, 'Marxism, Functionalism and Game Theory' (1982) vol 11 *Theory and Society*, pp 453-82

J Elster and KO Moene, eds, *Alternatives to Capitalism*, Cambridge, Cambridge University Press, 1989

W Eltis, *The Classical Theory of Economic Growth London*, Macmillan, 1984

F Engels, 'Anti-Duhring', in Marx and Engels, *Collected Works*, vol 25, pp 1-309

F Engels, 'The Condition of the Working Class in England in 1844', in Marx and Engels, *Collected Works*, vol 4, pp 295-596

F Engels, *Dialectics of Nature*, in Marx and Engels, *Collected Works*, vol 25, pp 311-629

F Engels, 'Ludwig Feuerbach and the End of Classical Gemian Philosophy', in Marx and Engels, *Selected Works in One Volume*, pp 584-622

F Engels, 'Outlines of acritique of political Economy', in Marx and Engels, *Collected Works*, vol 3, pp 418-43

F Engels, 'Preface to the English Edition of Volume One', in Marx, *Capital*, vol 1, pp 109-13

F Engels, 'Preface to the Third German Edition of Volume One', in Marx, *Capital*, vol 1, pp 106-8

F Engels, 'Preface to Volume Two', in Marx, *Capital*, vol 2, pp 83-102

F Engels, 'Preface to Volume Three', in Marx, *Capital*, vol 3, pp 91-111

F Engels, 'Review of Karl Marx, *A Contribution to the Critique of Political Economy*, in K Marx and F Engels, *Collected Works*, vol 16, pp 465-77

F Engels, 'Socialism: Utopian and Scientific', in Marx and Engels, *Selected Works in One Volume*, pp 375-428

F Engels, 'To Bloch, 21 September 1890', in Marx and Engels, *Selected Works in One Volume*, pp 692-3

F Engels, 'To Borgius, 25 January 1894', in Marx and Engels, *Selected Works in One Volume*, pp 704-6

F Engels, 'To Fischer, 15 April 1895', in Engels and Marx, *Letters on 'Capital'*, p 292

F Engels, 'To Marx, 24 May 1876', in Marx and Engels, *Collected Works*, vol 45, pp 117-9

F Engels, 'To Marx, 28 May 1876', in Marx and Engels, *Collected Works*, vol 45, pp 122-4

F Engels, 'To Marx, 6 March 1877', in Marx and Engels, *Collected Works,* vol 45, 206-7

F Engels, 'To Mehring, 14 July 1893', in Marx and Engels, *Selected Works in One Volume,* pp 699-703

F Engels, 'To Schmidt, 27 October 1890', in Marx and Engels, *Selected Works in One Volume,* pp 688-90

HM Enzenberger, 'A Critique of Political Ecology' (1974) no 84 *New Left Review,* pp 3-31

GA Epstein and JB Schor, Macropolicy in the Rise and Fall of the Golden Age', in Marglin and Schor, eds, *The Golden Age of Capitalism,* ch 3

S Estrin and D Winter, 'Planning in a Market Socialist Economy', in Le Grand and Estrin, eds, *Market Socialism,* ch 5

N Etherington, The Capitalist Theory of Capitalist Imperialism' (1983) vol 15 History of Political Economy, pp 38-62

N Etherington, 'Reconsidering Theories of Imperialism' (1982) vol 21 *History and Theory,* pp 1-36

EL Fackenheim, *The Religious Dimension of Hegel's Thought,* Bloomington (USA), Indiana University Press, 1967

EF Fama and H Babiak, 'Dividend Policy: An Empirical Analysis' (1968) vol 63 *Journal of the American Statistical Association,* pp 1132-61

A Ferguson, *An Essay on the History of civil Society,* Edinburgh, Edinburgh University Press, 1966

MJ Ferreira, *Scepticism and Reasonable Doubt,* Oxford, Clarendon Press, 1986

JG Fichte, *Science of Knowledge,* New York (USA), Appleton-Century-Croft, 1970

DK Fieldhouse, 'Imperialism: An Historiographical Revision' (1961) vol 14 *Economic History Review,* pp 187-209

JN Findlay, 'The Contemporary Relevance of Hegel', in MacIntyre, ed, *Hegel,* ch 1

JN Findlay, Hegel: A *Reexamination,* London, George Allen and Unwin, 1958

JN Findlay, 'Reflexive Asymmetry: Hegel's Most Fundamental Methodological Ruse', in Weiss, ed, *Beyond Epistemology,* pp 154-73

B Fine and L Harris, 'Controversial Issues in Marxist Economic Theory' (1976) *Socialist Register,* pp 1-32

B Fine and L Harris, Rereading *'Capital',* London, Macmillan, 1979

S Fine, *Laissez Faire and the General Welfare State,* Ann Arbor (USA), University of Michigan Press, 1967

FM Fisher et al, The Cost of Automobile Chances Since 1949' (1962) vol 70 *Journal of Political Economy,* pp 433-51

JC Flay, 'Hegel's Inverted World' (1970) vol 23 *Review of Metaphysics*, pp 662-78

A Flew, 'Was Karl Marx a Social Scientist?'(1991)vol 11 *Free Inquiry*, pp 37-41

MN Forster, *Hegel and Scepticism*, London, Harvard University Press, 1989

M Foucault, *The Order of Things*, New York (USA), Random House, 1973

AG Frank, *Capitalism and Underdevelopment in Latin Anierica*, New York (USA), Monthly Review Press, 1969

H Frankel, *Capitalist Society and Modern Sociology*, London, Lawrence and Wishart, 1970

DJ Frantzen, *Growth and Crisis in Post-war Capitalism*, Aldershot, Dartmouth, 1990

M Friednlan, *The Counter-revolution in Monetary Theory*, London, Institute of Economic Affairs, 1970

M Friednian and R Friedman, *Free to Choose*, Harmondsworth, Penguin, 1980

HG Gadamer, *Hegel's Dialectic*, New Haven (USA), Yale University Press, 1976

HG Gadamer, 'Hegel's Inverted World', in *idem, Hegel's Dialectic*, ch 2

JK Galbraith, *The Affluent Society*, 4th edn, Harmondsworth, Penguin, 1991

JK Galbraith, *Economics and the Public Purpose*, Harmondsworth, Penguin, 1975

A Gamble and P Walton, *Capitalism and Crisis*, London, Macmillan, 1976

N Geras, *The Legacy of Rosa Luxemburg*, London, New Left Books, 1976

N Geras, 'Marx and the Critique of Political Economy', in R Blackburn, ed, *Ideology in Social Science*, pp 284-305

N Geras, *Marx and Human Nature*, London, Verso, 1983

N Geras, 'Proletarian Self-emancipation' (1973) no 6 *Radical Philosophy*, pp 20-2

B Gerrard, *Theory of the Capitalist Economy*, Oxford, Basil Blackwell, 1989

I Gerstein, 'Production, Circulation and Value' (1976) vol 3 *Economy and Society*, pp 243-91

A Giddens, *Capitalism and Modern Social Theory*, Cambridge, Cambridge University Press, 1971

A Giddens, *Central Problems in Social Theory*, London, Macmillan, 1979

A Giddens, *The Class Structure of the Advanced Societies*, 2nd edn, London, Hutchinson, 1981

A Giddens, 'Commentary on the Debate'(1982) vol 11 *Theory and Society*, pp 527-39

A Giddens, *The Constitution of Society*, Cambridge, Polity Press, 1984

A Giddens, *A Contemporary Critique of Historical Materialism*, vol 1, London, Macmillan, 1981

A Giddens, *A Contemporary Critique of Historical Materialism*, vol 2, Berkeley (USA), University of California Press, 1987

A Giddens, *New Rules of Sociological Method,* 2nd edn, Cambridge, Polity Press, 1993

J Gillman, *The Falling Rate of Profit,* London, Dobson, 1957

S Giner, *Mass Society,* London, Martin Robertson, 1976

A Glyn and B Sutcliffe, *British Capitalism and the Profits Squeeze,* Harmondsworth, Penguin, 1972

A Glyn et al, The Rise and Fall of the Golden Age', in Marglin and Schor, eds, *The Golden Age of Capitalism,* ch 2

JW Goethe, *Faust,* pt 1, Harmondsworth, Penguin, 1949

D Goodway, ed, *For Anarchism,* London, Routledge, 1989

D Gordon, *Resurrecting Marx,* New Brunswick (USA), Transaction Books, 1990

RA Gordon, *Business Leadership in the Large Corporation,* Berkeley (USA), University of California Press, 1961

RJ Gordon, 'Measurement Bias in Price Indexes for Capital Goods' (1971) ser 17, no 2 *Review of Income and Wealth,* pp 121-74

RJ Gordon, *The Measurement of Durable Goods Prices,* Chicago (USA), University of Chicago Press, 1990

A Gorz, *Farewell to the Working Class,* London, Pluto Press, 1982

HH Gossen, *The Laws of Human Relations,* Cambridge (USA), Massachussetts Institute of Technology Press, 1983

FM Gottheil, *Marx's Economic Predictions,* Evanston (USA), Northwestern University Press, 1966

A Gramsci, *Selections from the Prison Notebooks,* London, Lawrence and Wishart, 1971

F Green, 'The "Reserve Army Hypothesis"', in Dunne, ed, *Quantitative Marxism,* ch 7

Z Griliches, 'Hedonic Price Indexes for Automobiles', in National Bureau of Economic Research, ed, *The Price Statistics of the Federal Government,* pp 173-96

Z Griliches, 'Notes on the Measurement of Price and Quality Changes', in National Bureau of Economic Research, ed, *Models of Income Determination,* pp 381-404

S Groll, 'The Active Role of "Use-value" in Marx's Economic Analysis' (1 980) vol 12 *History of Political Economy,* pp 336-71

H Grossman, 'Marx, Classical Political Economy and the Problem of Dynamics' (1 977) vols 2-3 *Capital and Class,* pp 32-55, 67-89

D Guerin, 'Marxism and Anarchism', in Goodway, ed, *For Anarchism,* ch 3

R Guttman and T Puttnam, eds, *The Labour Process and Class Struggle (CSE. Pamphlet 1),* London, Stage 1, 1976

P Guyer, 'Thought and Being', in Beiser, ed, *The Cambridge Companion to Hegel,* ch 6

J Habermas, *Communication and the Evolution of Society,* London, Heinemann, 1979

J Habermas, 'Hegel's Critique of the French Revolution', in *idem, Theory and Practice,* ch 3

J Habermas, *Knowledge and Human Interests,* rev edn, London, Heinemann, 1978

J Habermas, *Theory and Practice,* London, Heinemann, 1974

J Habermas, *The Theory of Communicative Action,* vol 1, London, Heinemann, 1984

J Habermas, *The Theory of Communicative Action,* vol 2, Cambridge, Polity Press, 1987

J Habermas, 'Towards a Reconstruction of Historical Materialism', in J Habernias, *Communication and the Evolution of Society,* ch 4

T Hadden, *Company Law and Capitalism,* 2nd edn, London, Weidenfeld and Nicolson, 1977

AT Hadley, *Economics,* New York (USA), Putnam, 1896

AT Hadley, 'The Good and Evil of Industrial Combination' (1897) 79 *The Atlantic Monthly,* pp 377-85

MB Hamilton, *Democratic Socialism in Britain and Sweden,* London, Macmillan, 1989

L Hannah and J Kay, *Concentration in Modern Industry,* London, Macmillan, 1977

FR Hansen, *The Breakdown of Capitalism,* London, Routledge and Kegan Paul, 1985

M Harrington, *The Other America,* Baltimore (USA), Penguin, 1967

N Harris, *The End of the Third World,* London, Tauris, 1986

J Hartnack, 'Categories and Things-in-themselves', in Priest, ed, *Hegel's Critique of Kant,* ch 3

D Harvey, *The Limits to Capital,* Oxford, Basil Blackwell, 1982

WF Haug, *Critique of Commodity Aesthetics,* Cambridge, Polity Press, 1986

SW Hawkina, *A Brief History of Time,* New York (USA), Bantam Books, 1988

FH Hayek, The Non-sequitur of the Dependence Effect' (1961) vol 27 *Southern Economic Journal,* pp 346-48

GWF Hegel, *The Difference Between Fichte's and Schelling's System of Philosophy,* Albany (USA), State University of New York Press, 1977

GWF Hegel, 'Dissertatio Philosophica de Orbitis Planetarium', in *idem, Sämtliche Werke,* vol 1, pp 3-29

GWF Hegel, *Faith and Knowledge*, Albany (USA), State University of New York Press, 1977

GWF Hegel, *Gesammelte Werke*, Hamburg, Felix Meiner Verlao, 1968ff

GWF Hegel, 'Hegel's Foreword to H Fr W Hinrich's *Die Religion im inneren Verhaltnisse zur Wissenschaft'*, in Weiss, ed, Beyond Epistemology, pp 221-44

GWF Hegel, 'Lectures on the Proofs of the Existence of God', in *idem, Lectures on the Philosophy of Religion*, vol 3, pp 153-367

GWF Hegel, *Lectures on the Philosophy of Religion*, London, Kegan Paul, Trench, Trubner, 1895

GWF Hegel, *Lectures on the History of Philosophy*, vol 1, London, Routledge and Kegan Paul, 1892

GWF Hegel, *Lectures on the History of Philosophy*, vol 2, London, Routledge and Kegan Paul, 1894

GWF Hegel, *Lectures on the History of Philosophy*, vol 3, London, Routledge and Kegan Paul, 1896

GWF Hegel, *Logic*, Oxford, Clarendon Press, 1975

GWF Hegel, 'Phänomenologie des Geistes', in *idem, Gesammelte Werke*, vol 9

GWF Hegel, *Phenomenology of Mind*, 2nd edn, London, Georere Allen and Unwin, 1931

GWF Hegel, *Phenomenology of Spirit*, Oxford, Clarendon Press, 1977

GWF Hegel, *Philosophy of Nature*, Oxford, Oxford University Press, 1970

GWF Hegel, *Philosophy of Right*, Oxford, Oxford University Press, 1967

GWF Hegel, *Philosophy of Mind*, Oxford, Clarendon Press, 1971

GWF Hegel, *Philosophy of History*, New York (USA), Dover Publications, 1956

GWF Hegel, *Sämtliche Werke*, Stuttgart, Ludwig Fromann Verlag, 1927ff

GWF Hegel, *Science of Logic*, London, George Allen and Unwin, 1969

GWF Hegel, 'To Schelling, 1 May 1807', in Kaufmann, *Hegel*, p 319

GWF Hegel, 'Wie der Gemeine Menschenverstand die Philosophic Nehme', in *idem, Gesammelte Werke*, vol 4, pp 197-238

M Heidegger, *Being and Time*, Oxford, Basil Blackwell, 1980

M Heidegger, *Hegel's Concept of Experience*, New York (USA), Harper and Row, 1970

R Hilferding, 'Böhm-Bawerk's Criticism of Marx', in Sweezy, ed, *'Karl Marx and the Close of His System' by Eugen von Bi5hm Bawerk and 'Böhm-Bawerk's Criticism of Marx' by Rudolf Hilferding*, pp 119-96

R Hilferding, *Finance Capital*, London, Routledge and Kegan Paul, 1981

K Hinrichs and C Offe, 'The Political Economy of the Labour Market', in Offe, *Disorganised Capitalism*, ch 1

J Hirschliefer, 'On the Theory of the Optimal Investment Decision' (1 958) vol 66 *Journal of Political Economy*, pp 329-52

PQ Hirst, 'Althusser and the Theory of Ideology', in *idem, On Law, and Ideology*, pp 40-74

PQ Hirst, *Marxism and Historical Writing*, London, Routledge and Kegan Paul, 1985

PQ Hirst, *On Law and Ideology*, London, Macmillan, 1979

T Hobbes, *Leviathan*, Harmondsworth, Penquin, 1968

T Hobbes, *Man and Citizen*, London, Harvester, 1978

T Hobbes, 'On Man', in *idem, Man and Citizen*, pp 33-85

E Hobsbawm, *Industry and Empire*, Harmondsworth, Penquin, 1969

E Hobsbawm, *Labouring Men*, London, Weidenfeld and Nicolson, 1968

JA Hobson, *Imperialism*, 3rd edn, London, Unwin Hyman, 1988

DR Hodgman, *Commercial Bank Loan and Industrial Behaviour*, Champaign (USA), Bureau of Economic and Business Research, University of Illinois, 1963

GM Hodgson, *After Marx and Sraffa*, London, Macmillan, 1991

GM Hodgson, 'The Theory of the Fallincy Rate of Profit', in idem, *After Marx and Sraffa*, ch 2

J Hoffnian, *Marxism and the Theory of Practice*, London, Lawrence and Wishart, 1975

J Holmwood and A Stewart, *Explanantion and Social Theory*, London, Macmillan, 1991

S Hook, *From Hegel to Marx*, Michican (USA), Ann Arbor Paperbacks, 1962

T Horie, *Marx's 'Capital' and One Free World*, London, Macmillan, 1991

M Horkheimer, 'Art and Mass Culture', in *idem, Critical Theory*, pp 273-90

M Horkheimer, *Critical Theory*, New York (USA), Continuum, 1986

D Howard, *From Marx to Kant*, 2nd edn, London, Macmillan, 1993

C Howe and KR Walker, eds, *The Foundations of the Chinese Planned Economy*, New York (USA), St Martin's Press, 1989

RC Hsu, *Economic Theories in China* 1979-88, Cambridge, Cambridge University Press, 1991

D Hume, *A Treatise of Human Nature*, Oxford, Clarendon Press, 1978

BC Hunt, *The Development of the Business Corporation in England, 1800-1867*, Cambridge (USA), Harvard University Press, 1936

E Husserl, *Ideas*, London, George Allen and Unwin, 1931

E Husserl, *Phenomenology and the Crisis of Philosophy*, New York (USA), Harper and Row, 1965

E Husserl, 'Philosophy as Rigorous Science' in *idem, Phenomenology and the Crisis of Philosophy*, pp 71-147

F Hutcheson, *A Short Introduction to Moral Philosophy*, Glasgow, R Foulis, 1747

F Hutcheson, *A System of Moral Philosophy*, London, A Millar, 1755

J Hyppolite, *Genesis and Structure of Hegel's 'Phenomenology of Spirit'*, Evanston (USA), Northwestern University Press, 1974

J Hyppolite, *Studies on Marx and Hegel*, London, Heinemann, 1969

M Itoh, *The Basic Theory of Capitalism*, London, Macmillan, 1988

FH Jacobi, 'David Hume über den Glauben', in *idem, Werke*, vol 1, pp 1-310

FH Jacobi, *Werke*, Leipzig, Gerhard Fleischer, 1815ff

R Jacoby, 'The Politics of Crisis Theory: Towards the Critique of Automatic Marxism' (1975) no 23 *Telos*, pp 3-52

F Jakubowski, *Ideology and Superstructure*, London, Allison and Busby, 1976

M Jay, *Marxism and Totality*, Cambridge, Polity Press, 1984

B Jessop, *The Capitalist State*, Oxford, Basil Blackwell, 1982

WS Jevons, *Theory of Political Economy*, 5th edn, Harmondsworth, Penquin, 1970

ZA Jordan, *The Evolution of Dialectical Materialism*, London, Macmillan, 1967

M Kalecki, *Collected Works*, Oxford, Clarendon Press, 1990ff

M Kalecki, 'Tne Impact of Armaments Spending on the Business Cycle After the Second World War', in *idem, Collected Works*, vol 2, pp 351-73

M Kalecki, 'Theory of Economic Dynamics', in *idem, Collected Works*, vol 2, pp 209-348

I Kant, *Critique of Pure Reason*, London, Macmillan, 1933

I Kant, *Critique of Practical Reason*, New York (USA), The Liberal Arts Press, 1956

I Kant, *Ethical Philosophy*, Indianapolis (USA), Hackett, 1983

I Kant, 'Groundine, for the Metaphysic of Morals', in *idem, Ethical Philosophy*, bk 1

I Kant, 'Idea for a Universal History with a Cosmopolitan Intent', in *idem, Perpetual Peace and Other Essays*, pp 29-40

I Kant, *Latin Writings*, New York (USA), Peter Lang, 1986

I Kant, *The Metaphysical Elements of Justice*, Indianapolis (USA), Bobbs-Merrill, 1965

I Kant, 'Metaphysical Foundations of Natural Science', in *idem, Philosophy of Material Nature*, bk 2

I Kant, 'The Metaphysical Principles of Virtue', in *idem, Ethical Philosophy*, bk 2

I Kant, 'A New Exposition of the First Principles of Metaphysical Knowledge', in *idem, Latin Writings*, pp 58-109

I Kant, *The One Possible Basis for a Demonstration of the Existence of God*, New York (USA), Abaris Books, 1979

I Kant, *Perpetual Peace and Other Essays*, Indianapolis (USA), Hackett, 1983

I Kant, *Philosophical Correspondence* 1759-99, Chicago (USA), University of Chicago Press, 1967

I Kant, *Philosophy of Material Nature*, Indianapolis (USA), Hackett, 1985

I Kant, 'To Herz, 21 February 1772', in *idem, Philosophical Correspondence 1759-99*, pp 70-6

I Kant, 'To Lambert, 2 September 1770', in *idem, Philosophical Correspondence 1759-99*, pp 58-60

I Kant, 'The Use in Natural Philosophy of Metpahysics Combined with Geometry. Part One. Physical Monadolgy', in *idem, Latin Writings*, pp 11 5-34

W Kaufmann, *Hegel*, Notre Dame (USA), University of Notre Dame Press, 1978

W Kaufmann, 'The Hegel Myth and Its Method', in MacIntyre, ed, *Hegel*, ch 2

K Kautsky, 'The Dictatorship of the Proletariat', in *idem, Selected Political Writings*, pp 98-125

K Kautsky, *The Economic Doctrines of Karl Marx*, London, NCLC Publishing Society, 1936

K Kautsky, 'The Mass Strike', in *idem, Selected Political Writings*, pp 54-73

K Kautsky, *Selected Political Writings*, London, Macmillan, 1983

G Kay, *The Economic Theory of the Working Class*, London, Macmillan, 1979

G Kay, 'A Note on Abstract Labour' (1 976) vol 5, no 1 *Bulletin of the Conference of Socialist Economists*

G Kay, 'Why Labour is the Starting Point for *Capital*', in D Elson, ed, *Value*, pp 46-66

R Keat and J Urry, *Social Theory as Science*, London, Routledge and Kegan Paul, 1975

JM Keynes, *Collected Works*, London, Macmillan, 1971ff

JM Keynes, 'Essays in Persuasion', in *idem, Collected Works*, vol 9

JM Keynes, 'General Theory of Employment, Interest and Money', in *idem, Collected Works*, vol 7

M Kidron, *Western Capitalism Since the War*, rev edn, Harmondsworth, Penguin, 1970

S Kierkegaard, *Concluding Unscientific Postscript*, Princeton (USA), Princeton University Press, 1941

S Kierkegaard, *Journals and Papers*, Bloomington (USA), Indiana University Press, 1967ff

A Kojève, *Introduction to the Reading of Hegel*, New York (USA), Basic Books, 1969

L Kolakowski, 'Althusser's Marx' (1971) *Socialist Register*, pp 111-28

L Kolakowski, *Main Currents of Marxism*, Oxford, Clarendon Press, 1978

ND Kondratieff, 'The Long Waves in Economic Life'(1935) 17 *Review, of Economic Statistics*, pp 105-15

K Korsch, 'Marxism and Philosophy', in.*idem, Marxism and Philosophy and Other Essays*, pp 27-85

K Korsch, *Marxism and Philosophy and Other Essays*, London, Monthly Review Press

WT Krug, *Briefe über de Neuesten Idealism*, Leipzig (Germany), Muller, 1801

RL Kuhn, 'Leveraged Buyouts I', in *idem*, ed, *The Library of Investment Banking*, vol 4, ch 11

RL Kuhn, ed, *The Library of Investment Banking*, vol 4, Homewood (USA), Dow Jones-Irwin, 1990

A Labriola, *Essays on the Materialist Conception of History*, Chicago (USA), Charles Kerr, 1908

P Lafargue, The Evolution of Property', in *idem, The 'Evolution of Property' and 'Social and Philosophical Studies'*, pp 1-104

P Lafargue, *'The Evolution of Property' and 'Social and Philosophical Studies'*, London, New Park, 1975

I Lakatos, 'History of Science and Its Rational Reconstructions', in *idem, Philosophical Papers*, vol 1, ch 2

I Lakatos, *Philosophical Papers*, vol I, Cambridge, Cambridge University Press, 1978

I Lakatos, 'Popper on Demarcation and Induction', in *idem, Philosophical Papers*, vol 1, ch 3

D Lamb, *Hegel - From Foundation to System*, The Hague (Netherlands), 1980

JH Lambert, *Neues Organon*, Leipzig (Germany), Gerhard Fleischer, 1764

NR Lamoreaux, *The Great Merger Movement in American Business 1895-1904*, Cambridge, Cambridge University Press, 1985

DS Landes, *The Unbound Prometheus*, Cambridge, Cambridge University Press, 1969

R Landor, 'The Curtain Raised', in Marx, *The First International and After*, pp 393-400

RE Lane, *The Market Experience*, Cambridge, Cambridge University Press, 1991

O Lange, *Political Economy*, vol 1, Oxford, Pergamon Press, 1963

J Larrain, *A Reconstruction of Historical Materialism*, London, Allen and Unwin, 1986

S Lasli and J Urry, *The End of Organised Capitalism*, Madison (USA), University of Wisconsin Press, 1987

E Lask, 'Fichte's Idealismus und die Geschichte', in *idem, Gesammelte Schriften*, vol 1, pp 1-274

E Lask, *Gesammelte Schriften*, Tubingen (Germany), JCB Mohr (Paul Siebeck), 1923ff

H Laski, *A Grammar of Politics*, 5th edn, London, George Allen and Unwin, 1967

P Laslett, *The World We Have Lost*, London, Methuen, 1971

F Lassalle, *What is Capital?* New York (USA), International Publishing Co, 1899

Q Lauer, 'Hegel on Proofs for God's Existence' (1964) vol 55 *Hegel Studien*, pp 443-65

J Le Grand and S Estrin, eds, *Market Socialism*, Oxford, Clarendon Press, 1979

MA Lebowitz, *Beyond 'Capital'*, London, Macmillan, 1992

H Lefebvre, *Dialectical Materialism*, London, Jonathan Cape, 1968

W Leiss, *The Limits to Satisfaction*, Toronto (Canada), Toronto University Press, 1976

P Lekas, *Marx on Classical Antiquity*, Sussex, Wheatsheaf, 1988

VI Lenin, *Collected Works*, London, Lawrence and Wishart, 1963ff

VI Lenin, 'Economics and Politics in the Era of the Dictatorship of the Proletariat', in *idem, Collected Works*, vol 30, pp 107-17

VI Lenin, 'Imperialism: The Highest Stage of Capitalism, in *idem, Collected Works*, vol 22, pp 185-304

VI Lenin, 'Materialism and Empirio-criticism', in *idem, Collected Works*, vol 14, pp 17-361

VI Lenin, 'Party Organisation and Party Literature', in *idem, Collected Works*, vol 10, pp 44-9

VI Lenin, 'Philosophical Notebooks', in *idem, Collected Works*, vol 38

VI Lenin, 'State and Revolution', in *idem, Collected Works*, vol 25, pp 381-492

VI Lenin, 'A Talk with Defenders of Economism', in *idem, Collected Works*, vol 5, pp 313-20

VI Lenin, 'Two Tactics of Social Democracy in the Democratic Revolution', in *idem, Collected Works*, vol 9, pp 15-140

VI Lenin, 'What Is To Be Done?', in *idem, Collected Works*, vol 5, pp 347-529

VI Lenin, The Proletarian Revolution and the Renegade Kautsky', in *idem, Collected Works*, vol 28, pp 227-325

N Levine, *The Tragic Deception*, Santa Barbara (USA), Clio Books, 1975

JLewis, 'The Althusser Case'(1972) vol 16, nos 1-2 *Marxism Today*, pp 23-8, 35, 43-8,

Li Fuchun, 'For the Sake of Socialist Construction Strengthen Planning Work Throughout the Country', Howe and Walker, eds, *The Foundations of the Chinese Planned Economy*, ch 3

G Lichtheim, *The Concept of Ideology and Other Essays*, New York (USA), Vantage Books, 1967

G Lichtheim, The Concept of Ideology', in *idem, The Concept of Ideology and Other Essays*, pp 3-46

J Lintner, 'Distribution of Incomes of Corporations Among Dividends, Retained Earnings and Taxes' (1956) vol 46 *American Economic Review*, pp 97-113

J Locke, *An Essay Concerning Human Understanding*, rev edn, Oxford, Clarendon Press, 1979

J Locke, *Two Treatises of Government*, Cambridge, Cambridge University Press, 1963

LE Loeb 'The Cartesian Circle', in Cottingham, ed, *The Cambridge Companion to Descartes*, ch 6

D Lovell, *Marx's Proletariat*, London, Routledge, 1988

K Löwith, *From Hegel to Nietzsche*, London, Constable, 1965

H Lubasz, 'Marx's Initial Problematic: The Problem of Poverty' (1976) vol 24 *Political Studies*, pp 24-42

G Lukács, *History and Class Consciousness*, London, Merlin, 1971

G Lukács, *Lenin*, London, New Left Books, 1970

G Lukács, *Marx's Basic Ontological Principles*, London, Merlin Press, 1978

G Lukács, 'Spontaneity of the Masses, Activity of the Party, in *idem, Tactics and Ethics*, pp 95-105

G Lukács, *Tactics and Ethics*, London, New Left Books, 1972

G Lukács, *The Young Hegel*, London, Merlin Press, 1975

T Luke, 'Anti-work?' (1981-2) no 50 *Telos*, pp 193 -5

R Luxemburg, *The Accumulation of Capital*, London, Routledge and Kegan Paul, 1951

R Luxemburg, 'The Junius Pamphlet', in *idem, Rosa Luxemburg Speaks*, pp 257-331

R Luxemburg, 'The Mass Strike', in *idem, Rosa Luxemburg Speaks*, pp 153-218

R Luxemburg, 'Reform or Revolution?', in *idem, Rosa Luxemburg Speaks*, pp 33-90

R Luxemburg, *Rosa Luxemburg Speaks*, London, Pathfinder, 1970

R Luxemburg, 'The Russian Revolution', in *idem, Rosa Luxemburg Speaks*, pp 365-95

R Luxemburg, 'Speech to the Founding Convention of the German Communist Party', in *idem, Rosa Luxemburg Speaks*, pp 400-27

D MacGregor, *The Communist Ideal In Hegel and Marx*, London, George Allen and Unwin, 1984

A MacIntyre, *After Virtue*, Gloucester, Duckworth, 1985

A MacIntyre, ed, *Hegel*, London, University of Notre Dame Press, 1976

H Magdoff and PM Sweezy, 'Listen Keynesians', in *idem, Stagnation and the Financial Explosion*, ch 2

H Magdoff and PM Sweezy, *Stagnation and the Financial Explosion*, New York (USA), Monthly Review Press, 1987

SH Mage, *The Law of the Falling Tendency of the Rate of Profit*, Phd thesis, Columbia University (USA), 1963

J Maier, *On Hegel's Critique of Kant*, New York (USA), Columbia University Press, 1939

TR Malthus, *An Essay on the Principle of Population*, Cambridge, Cambridge University Press, 1989

TR Malthus, *Principles of Political Economy*, Cambridge, Cambridge University Press, 1989

E Mandel, *The Formation of the Economic Thought of Karl Marx*, London, New Left Books, 1971

E Mandel, 'Introduction to Volume Two', in Marx, *Capital*, vol, 2, pp 11-79

E Mandel, 'Introduction to Volume One', in Marx, *Capital*, vol, 1, pp 11-86

E Mandel, *Late Capitalism*, London, New Left Books, 1975

E Mandel, *Marxist Economic Theory*, London, Merlin Press, 1968

B de Mandeville, *The Fable of the Bees*, Harmondsworth, Penguin, 1970

HG Manne, 'Mergers and the Market for Corporate Control' (1965) vol 73 *Journal of Political Economy*, pp 110-20

H Marcuse, 'Freedom and the Historical Imperative', in *idem, From Luther to Popper*, pp 209-23

H Marcuse, *From Luther to Popper*, London, New Left Books, 1972

H Marcuse, 'Karl Popper and the Problem of Historical Laws'. in *idem, From Luther to Popper*, pp 191-208

H Marcuse, 'A Note on Dialectic', in Arato and Gebhardt, eds, *The Essential Frankfurt School Reader*, pp 444-51

H Marcuse, *One-dimensional Man*, Boston (USA), Beacon Press, 1964

H Marcuse, *Reason and Revollition,* Henley, Routledge and Kegan Paul, 1955

SA Marglin and JB Schor, eds, *The Golden Age of Capitalism,* Oxford, Clarendon Press, 1990

A Marshall, *Principles o Economics,* 8th edn, London, Macmillan, 1920

K Marx, *Le Capital,* vol 1, Paris, Maurice Lachatre, 1873

K Marx, *Capital,* vol 1 (Everyman Edition), London, Dent, 1957

K Marx, *Capital,* vol 1, Harmondsworth, Penguin, 1976

K Marx, *Capital,* vol 2, London, Lawrence and Wishart, 1956

K Marx, *Capital,* vol 2, Harmondsworth, Penguin, 1978

K Marx, *Capital,* vol 3, Harmondsworth, Penguin, 1981

K Marx, 'The Class Struggles in France 1848-50', in Marx and Engels, *Collected Works,* vol 10, pp 45-239

K Marx, 'Comments on James Mill', in Marx and Engels, *Collected Works,* vol 3, pp 211-28

K Marx, 'The Commodity', in *idem, Value: Studies by Marx,* pp 7-40

K Marx, 'Conspectus of Bakunin's *Statism and Anarchy,* in *idem, The First International and After,* pp 333-8

K Marx, 'A Contribution to the Critique of Political Economy', in Marx and Engels, *Collected Works,* vol 29, pp 257-417

K Marx, 'Contribution to the Critique of Hegel's Philosophy of Law', in Marx and Engels, *Collected Works,* vol 3, pp 3-129

K Marx, 'Contribution to the Critique of Hegel's Philosophy of Law. Introduction', in Marx and Engels, *Collected Works,* vol 3, pp 175-87

K Marx, 'Critical Marginal Notes on the Article 'The King of Prussia and Social Reform'. By A Prussian', in Marx and Engels, *Collected Works,* vol 3, pp 189-206

K Marx, 'Critique of the Gotha Programme', in Marx and Engels, *Selected Works in One Volume,* pp 315-31

K Marx, 'Economic and Philosophical Manuscripts', in Marx and Engels, *Collected Works,* vol 3, pp 229-346

K Marx, 'Economic Manuscripts of 1857-8', in Marx and Engels, *Collected Works,* vol 28 and vol 29, pp 1-255

K Marx, 'The Eighteenth Brumaire of Louis Bonaparte', in Marx and Engels, *Collected Works,* vol 11, pp 99-197

K Marx, *Ethnological Notebooks,* Assen (Netherlands), Van Gorcum, 1972

K Marx, *The First International and After,* Harmondsworth, Penguin, 1974

K Marx, 'Introduction to the French Edition of *Socialism: Utopian and Scientific*', in Marx and Engels, *Collected Works*, vol 24, pp 335-9

K Marx, 'Inaugural Address to the First International Working Men's Association', in *idem, The First International and After*, pp 73-81

K Marx, 'Notes on Adolph Wagner', in *idem, Texts on Method*, pp 179-219

K Marx, 'On Friedrich List's Book', in Marx and Engels, *Collected Works*, vol 4, pp 265-93

K Marx, 'On the Division of Labour', in Marx and Engels, *Collected Works*, vol 16, pp 617-8

K Marx, 'On Trade Unions', in *idem, Selected Writings*, p 538

K Marx, 'The Poverty of Philosophy', in Marx and Engels, *Collected Works*, vol 6, pp 105-212

K Marx, 'Proceedings of the Sixth Rhine Province Assembly: Third Article', in Marx and Engels, *Collected Works*, vol 1, pp 224-63

K Marx, 'Results of the Immediate Process of Production', in *idem, Capital*, vol 1, 941-1084

K Marx, *Selected Writings*, Oxford, Oxford University Press, 1977

K Marx, 'Speech on the Question of Free Trade', in Marx and Engels, *Collected Works*, vol 6, pp 450-65

K Marx, *Texts on Method*, Oxford, Basil Blackwell. 1975

K Marx, *Theories of Surplus Value*, pt 1, London, Lawrence and Wishart, 1963

K Marx, *Theories of Surplus Value*, pt 2, London, Lawrence and Wishart, 1969

K Marx, *Theories of Surplus Value*, pt 3, London, Lawrence and Wishart, 1972

K Marx, 'Theses on Feuerbach', in Marx and Engels, *Collected Works*, vol 5, pp 3-5

K Marx, 'To Engels, 2 April 1858', in Marx and Engels, *Collected Works*, vol 40, pp 296-304

K Marx, 'To Engels, 31 July 1865', in Marx and Engels, *Collected Works*, vol 42, pp 172-4

K Marx, 'To Engels, 24 August 1867', in Marx and Engels, *Collected Works*, vol 42, pp 407-8

K Marx, 'To Engels, 30 April 1868', in Marx and Engels, *Collected Works*, vol 43, pp 20-6

K Marx, 'To Engels, 23 May 1868', in Marx and Engels, *Collected Works*, vol 43, pp 38-40

K Marx, 'To Engels, 31 May 1873', in Marx and Engels, *Collected Works*, vol 44, pp 504-6

K Marx, 'To Engels, 25 May 1876', in Marx and Engels, *Collected Works,* vol 45, pp 119-21

K Marx, 'To Engels, 25 July 1877', in Marx and Engels, *Collected Works,* vol 45, pp 250-3

K Marx, 'To Kugelmann, 13 October 1866', in Marx and Engels, *Collected Works,* vol 42, pp 327-9

K Marx, 'To Kugelmann, I I October 1867', in Marx and Engels, *Collected Works,* vol 42, pp 440-3

K Marx, 'To Kugelmann, 30 November 1867', in Marx and Engels, *Collected Works,* vol 42, pp 489-90

K Marx, 'To Schott, 3 November 1877', in Marx and Engels, *Collected Works,* vol 45, p 287

K Marx, *Value: Studies by Marx,* London, New Park, 1976

K Marx, 'The Value-form' (1978) vol 4 *Capital and Class,* pp 130-50

K Marx, 'Wage-labour and Capital', in Marx and Engels, *Collected Works,* vol 9, pp 197-228

K Marx, 'Wages, Price and Profit', in Marx and Engels, *Selected Works in One Volume,* pp 185-226

K Marx, 'Wages', in Marx and Engels, *Collected Works,* vol 6, pp 415-37

K Marx and F Engels, *Collected Works,* London, Lawrence and Wishart, 1975 ff

K Marx and F Engels, 'The German Ideology', in *idem, Collected Works,* vol 5, pp 19-539

K Marx and F Engels, 'The Holy Family', in *idem, Collected Works,* vol 4, pp 3-211

K Marx and F Engels, Letters on 'Capital', London, New Park Publications, 1983

K Marx and F Engels, 'Manifesto of the Communist Party', in *idem, Collected Works,* vol 6, pp 477-519

K Marx and F Engels, *Selected Works in One Volume,* London, Lawrence and Wishart, 1968

W Marx, Hegel's *'Phenomenology of Spirit',* New York (USA), Harper and Row, 1975

J McCahery *et al,* eds, *Corporate Accountability and Control,* Oxford, Oxford University Press, 1993

D McLellan, *Karl Marx,* St Albans, Granada, 1976

D McLellan, *The Young Hegelians and Karl Marx,* London, Macmillan, 1980

G McLennan *et al,* 'Althusser's Theory of Ideology', in Centre for Contemporary Cultural Studies, *On Ideology,* pp 77-105

JME McTaggart, *Studies in Hegelian Dialectic,* Cambridge, Cambridge University Press, 1922

JME McTaggart, *A Commentary on Hegel's Logic,* Cambridge, Cambridge University Press, 1910

ES Meade, *Trust Finance,* New York (USA), Appleton, 1903

JE Meade, *The Intelligent Radical's Guide to Economic Policy,* London, George Allen and Unwin, 1975

R Medvedev, *Let History Judge,* 2nd edn, Oxford, Oxford University Press, 1989

RL Meek, 'From Values to Prices: Was Marx's Journey Really Necessary?', in *idem, Smith, Marx and After,* pp 120- 33

RL Meek, 'Marginalism and Marxism', in *idem, Smith, Marx and After,* pp 165-75

RL Meek, *Smith, Marx and After,* London, Chapman and Hall, 1977

RL Meek, *Studies in the Labour Theory of Value,* London, Lawrence and Wishart, 1973

F Mehring, *Karl Marx,* Sussex, Harvester, 1981

M Mendelssohn, *Gesammelete Schriften Jubilaumsgabe,* Stuttgart (Germany), Friedrich Fromann Verlag, 1974

M Mendelssohn, 'Morgenstunden', in *idem, Gesammelete Schriften Jubilaumsgaube,* vol 3, pt 2

U Menzel, 'The End of the "Third World" and the Failure of Grand Theories' (1991) vol 44 *Law and State,* pp 44-78

J Mepham and D-H Ruben, eds, *Issues in Marxist Philosophy,* Sussex, Harvester Press, 1979

I Meszaros, *Marx's Theory of Alienation,* London, Merlin Press, 1975

D Meyerson, *False Consciousness,* Oxford, Clarendon Press, 1991

R Miliband, *Class Power and State Power,* Cambridge, Polity Press, 1983

R Miliband, *Divided Societies,* Oxford, Clarendon Press, 1989

R Miliband, *The State in Capitalist Society,* New York (USA), Basic Books, 1969

J Mill, *Commerce Defended,* London, T Grace, 1808

JS Mill, *Collected Works,* Toronto (Canada), University of Toronto Press, 1965ff,

JS Mill, 'On Liberty.', in JS Mill, *Collected Works,* vol 18, pp 213-310

JS Mill, 'Principles of Political Economy', in *idem, Collected Works,* vols 2-3

J Millar, *The Origin and Distinction of Ranks,* Bristol, Thoemmes, 1990

L von Mises, *The Theory of Money and Credit,* 2nd edn, New Haven (USA), Yale University Press, 1953

S Mohun, 'Value Theory', in Baraski and Short, *Developing Contemporary Marxism*, ch 2

J Molyneux, *What is the Real Marxist Tradition?*, London, Bookmarks, 1985

C de Montesquieu, *The Spirit of the Laws*, Cambridge, Cambridge University Press, 1989

GE Moore, 'A Defence of Common Sense', in *idem, Philosophical Papers*, ch 2

GE Moore, *Philosophical Papers*, London, George Allen and Unwin, 1959

G Mueller, 'The Hegel Legend of "Thesis-Antithesis-Synthesis"' (1958) vol 19 *Journal of the History of Ideas*, pp 411-4

GE Mueller, 'The Interdependence of the Phenomenology, Logic and Encyclopaedia', in WE Steinkraus, ed, *New Studies in Hegel's Philosophy*, pp 18-33

GRG Mure, 'Hegel: How and How Far is Philosophy Possible?', in Weiss, ed, *Beyond Epistemology*, pp 1-29

G Myrdal, *The Political Element in the Development of Economic Theory*, London, Routledge and Kegan Paul, 1953

National Bureau of Economic Research, ed, *Models of Income Determination*, Princeton (USA), Princeton University Press, 1964

National Bureau of Economic Research, ed, *The Price Statistics of the Federal Government*, New York (USA), National Bureau of Economic Research, 1961

L Neal, *The Rise of Financial Capitalism*, Cambridge, Cambridge University Press, 1990

P Nettl, *Rosa Luxemburg*, Oxford, Oxford University Press, 1966

M Nicolaus, 'The Unknown Marx', in Blackburn, ed, *Ideology in Social Science*, pp 306-33

R Norman, *Hegel's Phenomenology*, London, Sussex University Press, 1976

C Norris, *Spinoza and the Origins of Modern Critical Theory*, Oxford, Basil Blackwell, 1991

R Nozick, *Anarchy, State and Utopia*, Oxford, Basil Blackwell, 1974

A Oakley, *The Making of Marx's Critical Theory*, London, Routledge and Kegan Paul, 1983

GD O'Brien, *Hegel on Reason and History*, Chicago, University of Chicago Press, 1975

J O'Connor, *Accumulation Crisis*, Oxford, Basil Blackwell, 1984

J O'Connor, 'Capitalism, Nature, Socialism: A Theoretical Introduction' (1988) vol 1 *Capitalism, Nature, Socialism: A Journal of Socialist Ecology*, pp 11-38

J O'Connor, *The Fiscal Crisis of the State*, New York (USA), St Martin's Press, 1973

C Offe, *Disorganised Capitalism*, Cambridge, Polity Press, 1985

M Ohta and Z Griliches, 'Automobile Prices and Quality' (1986) vol 4 *Journal of Business and Economic Statistics,* pp 187-98

M Ohta and Z Griliches, 'Automobile Prices Revisited', in Terleckyj, ed, *Household Production and Consumption,* pp 325-90

N Okishio, 'Technical Change and the Profit Rate' (1961) vol 7 *Kobe University Economic Review,* pp 86-99

B O'Leary, *The Asiatic Mode of Production,* Oxford, Basil Blackwell, 1989

B Ollman, *Alienation,* Cambridge, Cambridge University Press, 1976

JJ O'Malley *et al,* eds, *Hegel and the History of philosophy,* The Hague (Netherlands), Martinus Nijhoff, 1974

J O'Neill, Modes of Individualism and Collectivism, London, Heinemann, 1973

G Orwell, The Road to Wigan Pier, Harmondsworth, Penquin, 1989

R Owen, *'A New View of Society' and 'Report to the County of Lanark',* Harmondsworth, Penquin, 1969

R Owen, 'Report to the County of Lanark', in idem, 'A New View of Society' and *'Report to the County of Lanark',* pp 199-270

C Palloix, 'From Fordism to Neofordism', in Guttman and Puttnam, eds, *The Labour Process and Class Struggle (CSE Pamphlet 1),* pp 44-67

HB Parkes, *Marxism: An Autopsy,* Boston (USA), Houghton Mifflin, 1939

F Parkin, *Marxism and Class Theory,* London, Tavistock, 1979

P Parrini and MJ Sklar, 'New Thinking About the Market, 1896-1904: Some American Economists on Investment and the Theory of Surplus Capital' (1983) vol 43 *Journal of Economic History,* pp 559-78

T Parsons, *The Structure of Social Action,* New York (USA), Free Press, 1968

PL Payne, *British Entrepreneurship in the Nineteenth Century,* 2nd edn, Basingstoke, Macmillan, 1988

D Peel, 'Advertising, and Aggregate Consumption', in Cowling *et al,Advertising and Economic Behaviour,* ch 9

VM Perez-Diaz, *State, Bureaucracy and Civil Society,* London, Macmillan, 1978

V Perlo, *Superprofits and Crises,* New York (USA), International Publishers, 1988

W Petty, *Economic Writings,* New York (USA), Augustus M Kelley, 1986

W Petty, 'Political Arithmetick' in Petty, *Economic Writings,* pp 232-313

P Piccone, 'Lukács' *History and Class Consciousness* Half a Century Later' (1969) no 4 Telos, pp 95-103

AC Pigou, *The Economics of Welfare,* 4th edn, London, Macmillan, 1932

G Pilling, *The Crisis of Keynesian Economics,* London, Croom Helm, 1986

G Pilling, Marx's *'Capital'*, London, Routledge and Kegan Paul, 1980

RB Pippin, *Hegel's Idealism,* Cambridge, Cambridge University Press, 1989

RB Pippin, 'You Can't Get There from Here', in Beiser, ed, The *Cambridge Companion to Hegel,* ch 2

J Plamenatz, *Man and society,* London, Longman, 1963

R Plant, *Hegel,* London, George Allen and Unwin, 1973

GV Plekhanov, 'On the Question of the Individual's Role in History', in *idem, Selected Philosophical Works,* vol 2, pp 283-315

GV Plekhanov, *Selected Philosophical Works,* London, Lawrence and Wishart,1977ff

GV Plekhanov, "'What Should We Thank Him For?" An Open Letter to Karl Kautsky', in *idem, Selected Philosophical Works,* vol 2, pp 340-51

GV Plekhanov. 'The Development of the Monist View of History', in *idem, Selected Philosophical Works,* vol 1, pp 486-7032

KR Popper, 'Back to the Presocraties', in *idem, Conjectures and Refutations,* ch 5

KR Popper, *Conjectures and Refutations,* 4th edn, London, Routledge and Kegan Paul, 1972

KR Popper, *The Logic of Scientific Discovery,* rev edn, London, Hutchinson, 1980

KR Popper, *Objective Knowledge,* rev edn, Oxford, Oxford University Press, 1979

KR Popper, 'On the Status of Science and Metaphysics', in *idem, Conjectures and Refutations,* ch 8

KR Popper, 'On the Sources of Knowledge and Ignorance', in *idem, Conjectures and Refutations,* pp 3-30

KR Popper, *The Open Society and Its Enemies,* 5th edn, London, Routledge and Kegan Paul, 1966

KR Popper, 'Truth, Rationality and the Growth of Scientific Knowledge', in *idem, Conjectures and Refutations,* ch 10

KR Popper, *Unended Quest,* Glasgow, Fontana, 1978

KR Popper, 'What is Dialectic?', in *idem, Conjectures and Refutations,* ch 15

KR Popper, 'Why are the Calculi of Logic and Arithmetic Applicable to Reality?', in *idem, Conjectures and Refutations,* ch 9

N Poulantzas, *Fascism and Dictatorship,* London, New Left Books, 1974

S Priest, ed, *Hegel's Critique of Kant,* Oxford, Oxford University Press, 1987

P-J Proudhon, *The Philosophy of Poverty,* London, Twentieth Century Press, 1900

P-J Proudhon, *What is Property?,* London, William Reeves, 1898

T Reid, *Essays on the Intellectual Powers of Man,* Cambridge (USA), MIT Press, 1969

T Reid, *An Inquiry into the Human Mind*, Chicago (USA), University of Chicago Press, 1970

KL Reinhold, *Beytrage zur Leichtern Uebersicht des Zustandes der Philosophie*, Hamburg (USA), Freidrich Perthes, 1801

PS Reinsch, *Colonial Administration*, New York (USA), Macmillan, 1905

PS Reinsch, *Colonial Government*, Freeport (USA), Books for Libraries Press, 1970

PS Reinsch, *World Politics*, New York (USA), Macmillan, 1900

G Reuten and M Williams, *Value-form and the State*, London, Routledge, pt 3

D Riazanov, *Karl Marx and Friedrich Engels*, London, Monthly Review Press, 1973

D Ricardo, 'On Protection to Agriculture', in *idem, Works and Correspondence*, vol 4, pp 201-71

D Ricardo, 'On the Principles of Political Economy and Taxation', in *idem, Works and Correspondence*, vol 1

D Ricardo, *Works and Correspondence*, Cambridgre, Cambridge University Press, 1951ff

J Richardson, *Existential Epistemology*, Oxford, Clarendon Press, 1986

L Robbins, *The Nature and Significance of Economic Science*, 3rd edn, London, Macmillan, 1984

J Robinson, *The Economics of Imperfect Competition*, 2nd edn, London, Macmillan, 1969

J Robinson, *An Essay on Marxian Economics*, London, Macmillan, 1966

J Robinson, 'The Impossibility of Capitalism', in Chamberlin, ed, *Monopoly and Competition and their Regulation*, ch 3

K Rodbertus, Over-production and Crises, New York (USA), Burt Franklin, 1898

J Roemer, Analytical Foundations of Marxist Economic Theory, Cambridge, Cambridge University Press, 1981

J Roemer, ed, *Analytical Marxism*, Cambridge, Cambridge University Press

J Roemer, *Free To Lose*, Cambridge (USA), Harvard University Press, 1988

J Roemer, 'Introduction', in *idem*, ed, *Analytical Marxism*, pp 1-7

R Rosdolsky, *The Making of Marx's 'Capital'*, London, Pluto Press, 1977

ME Rosen, 'Hegel', in Wintle, ed, *Makers of Nineteenth Century Culture*, pp 282-4

S Rosen, *GWF Hegel*, New Haven, Yale University Press, 1974

H Rosenberg, 'Political and Social Consequences of the Great Depression of 1873-1896 in Central Europe' (1943) nos 1-2 *The Economic History Review*, pp 58-73

WW Rostow, 'Investment and the Great Depression 1873-1896' vol 8 *Economic History Review*, pp 136-58

J-J Rousseau, *Emile*, London, JM Dent, 1911

J-J Rousseau, *The Social Contract and the Discourses*, rev edn, London, Dent, 1973

J-J Rousseau, 'The Social Contract', in J-J Rousseau, *The Social Contract and the Discourses*, pp 163-278

BS Rowntree, *The Human Needs of labour*, rev edn, London, Longmans Green, 1937

B Rowthorn, 'Skilled Labour in the Marxist System' (1974) vol 3, no 8 *Bulletin of the Conference of Socialist Economists*

J Royce, *Lecture on Modern Idealism*, New Haven (USA), Yale University Press, 1919

M Rubel, 'A History of Marx's "Economics"', in Rubel, Rubel on Karl Marx, ch 3

M Rubel, 'The "Marx Legend"', in Rubel, Rubel on Karl Marx, ch 1

M Rubel, 'The Plan and Method of the "Economics"', in Rubel, *Rubel on Karl Marx*, ch 4

M Rubel, *Rubel on Karl Marx*, Cambridge, Cambridge University Press, 1981

D-H Ruben, *Explaining Explanation*, London, Routledge, 1990

D-H Ruben, *Marxism and Materialism*, 2nd edn, Sussex, Harvester, 1979

D-H Ruben, 'Materialism and Professor Colletti' (1975) no 4 *Critique*, pp 61-74

II Rubin, *Essays on Marx's Theory of Value*, Montreal (Canada), Black Rose Books, 1973

II Rubin, *A History of Economic Thought*, London, Ink Links, 1979

0 Ruhle, *Karl Marx*, New York (USA), New Home Library, 1943

WG Runciman, *Relative Deprivation and Social Justice*, Henley, Routledge and Kegan Paul, 1966

B Russell, *History of Western Philosophy*, London, George Allen and Unwin, 1950

A Sanchez-Vasquez, *The Philosophy of Praxis*, London, Merlin Press, 1977

J-P Sartre, *Being and Nothingness*, London, Methuen, 1958

JB Say, *Treatise on Political Economy*, New York (USA), Augustus M Kelley, 1971

SB Saul, *The Myth of the Great Depression 1873-96*, rev edn, London, Papermac, 1972

D Sayer, *Marx,'s Method*, 2nd edn, Sussex, Harvester, 1983

D Sayer, 'Science as Critique: Marx Versus Althusser', in Mepham and Ruben, eds, *Issues in Marxist Philosophy*, vol 3, ch 2

FWJ Schelling, *System of Transcendental Idealism*, Charlottesville (USA), University Press of Virginia, 1978

FWJ Schelling, 'To Hegel, 2 November 1807', in Kaufmann, *Hegel*, pp 324-5

FM Scherer and D Ross, *Industrial Market Structure and Economic Performance*, 3rd edn, Boston, Houghton Mifflin, 1990

PC Schmitter, 'Still the Century of Corporatism' (1974) vol 36 *Review of Politics*, pp 85-131

AB Schmookler, *The Illusion of choice*, Albany (USA), State University of New York Press, 1993

JA Schumpeter, *History of Economic Analysis*, New York (USA), Oxford University Press, 1954

T Scitovsky, *Welfare and Competition*, rev edn, London, Allen and Unwin, 1952

J Scott, 'The British Upper Class', in Coates *et al*, eds, A Socialist Anatomy of Britain, ch2

J Scott, *Corporations, Classes and Capitalism*, 2nd edn, London, Hutchinson, 1985

J Scott, *Capitalist Property and Financial Power*, Sussex, Wheatsheaf, 1986

J Scott, *The Upper Classes*, London, Macmillan, 1982

J Scott and C Griff, *Directors of Industry*, Cambridge, Polity Press, 1984

J Seigel, *Marx's Fate*, Princeton (USA), Princeton University Press, 1987

CNW Senior, *An Outline of the Science of Political Economy*, London, New York (USA), Augustus M Kelley, 1965

NW Senior, *Principes fondamentaux de l'jconofitie politique*, Paris (France), J-P Aillaud, 1836

A Shaikh, 'Political Economy and Capitalism: Notes on Dobb's Theory of Crisis' (1978) vol 2 *Cambridge Journal of Economics*, pp 233-51

A Shaikh, The Poverty of Algebra', in I Steedman ed, *The Value Controversy*, pp 266-300

HA Shannon, The Coming of General Limited Liability' (1931-2) vol 11 *Economic History* pp 267-91

GB Shaw, 'The Economics of Socialism', in *idem, Essays in Fabian Socialism*, pp 1-29

GB Shaw, *Essays in Fabian Socialism*, London, Constable, 1932

GB Shaw, 'The Jevonian Criticism of Marx', in PH Wicksteed, *The Common Sense of Political Economy*, vol 2, pp 724-30

GB Shaw,The Transition to Social Deniocracy', in *idem, Essays in Fabian Socialism*, pp 31-61

A Shonfield, *Modern Capitalism*, rev edn, Oxford, Oxford University Press, 1969

H Simon, *Administrative Behaviour*, 3rd edn, New York (USA), Free Press, 1976

J Sinclair, *Images Incorporated*, London, Croom Helm, 1987

P Singer, *Marx*, Oxford, Oxford University Press, 1980

MJ Sklar, *The Corporate Reconstruction of American Capitalism 1890-1916*, Cambridge, Cambridge University Press, 1988

A Smith, *The Wealth of Nations*, Oxford, Oxford University Press, 1976

JE Smith, 'Hegel's Critique of Kant', in O'Malley *et al*, eds, *Hegel and the History of Philosophy*, pp 109-28

N Smith, *Uneven Development*, Oxford, Basil Blackwell, 1984

R Smith, 'Crisis Theory', in ZG Baranski and JR Short, eds, *Developing Contemporary Marxism*, ch 1

RC Solomon, 'Hegel's Concept of *Geist*', in MacIntyre, ed, *Hegel*, ch 5

RC Solomon, *In the Spirit of Hegel*, Oxford, Oxford University Press, 1983

W Sombart, *The Quintessence of Capitalism*, London, T Fisher Unwin, 1915

G Sorel, *The Illusions of Progress*, Berkeley (USA), University of California Press, 1969

G Sorel, *Reflections on Violence*, London, Collier Macmillan, 1961

H Spencer, *First Principles*, 6th edn, London, Williams and Northgate, 1908

B de Spinoza, *Chief Works*, New York (USA) Dover Publications, 1955

B de Spinoza, 'On the Improvement of the Understanding', in *idem, Chief Works*, vol 2, pp 3-41

P Sraffa, *Production of Commodities by Means of Commodities*, Cambridge, Cambridge University Press, 1960

WT Stace, *The Philosophy of Hegel*, New York (USA), Dover Publications, 1955

JV Stalin, 'Dialectical and Historical Materialism', in *idem, The Essential Stalin*, pp 300-33

JV Stalin, *The Essential Stalin*, London, Croom Helm, 1973

JV Stalin, 'Economic Problems of Socialism in the USSR', in *idem, The Essential Stalin*, pp 445-81

I Steedman, 'The Irrelevance of Marxian Values', in Caravale, ed, *Marx and Modern Economics*, vol 1, ch 9

I Steedman, *Marx After Sraffa*, London, New Left Books, 1977

I Steedman, 'Marx on Ricardo', in Bradley and Howard, *Classical and Marxian Political Economy*, ch 3

I Steedman, 'PH Wicksteed's Jevonian Criticism of Marx', in *idem, From Exploitation to Altruism*, Cambridge, Polity Press, 1989, ch 7

I Steedman, ed, *The Value Controversy*, London, Verso, 1981

J Steindl, *Maturity and Stagnation in American Capitalism*, New York (USA), Monthly Review Press, 1976

WE Steinkraus, ed, *New Studies in Hegel's Philosophy*, New York (USA), Holt, Rinehart and Winston, 1971

JD Stephens, *The Transition from Capitalism to Socialism*, Urbana (USA), University of Illinois Press, 1979

R Stern, *Hegel, Kant and the Structure of the Object*, London, Routledge, 1990

J Steuart, *An Inquiry into the Principles of Political Economy*, etc, London, F Boyd, 1767

E Stokes, 'Late Nineteenth Century Colonial Expansion and the Attack on the Theory of Economic Imperialism: A Case of Mistaken Identity?' (1969) vol 12 *The Historical Journal*, pp 285-301

J Strachey, *Contemporary Capitalism*, London, Victor Gollancz, 1935

J Strachey, *The Nature of Capitalist Crisis*, New York (USA), Covici Friede, 1935

J Strachey, *What Are We To Do?*, New York (USA), Random House, 1938

W Streeck, 'Co-determination: After Four Decades', in *idem, Social Institutions and Economic Performance*, ch 5

W Streeck, *Social Institutions and Economic Performance*, London, Sage, 1992

D Strinati, *Capitalism, the State and Industrial Relations*, London, Croom Helm, 1982

A Swingewood, *Marx and Modern Social Theory*, London, Macmillan, 1975

PM Sweezy, 'Marxian Value Theory and Crises', in I Steednian, ed, *The Value Controversy*, pp 20-35

PM Sweezy, 'Some Problems in the Theory of Capital Accumulation' (1974) vol 24 *Monthly Review*, pp 11-4

PM Sweezy, *The Theory of Capitalist Development*, New York (USA), Monthly Review Press, 1968

PM Sweezy, ed, *'Karl Marx and the Close of His System by Eugen von Böhn-Bawerk and 'Böhm-Bawerk's Criticism of Marx' by Rudolf Hilferding*, London, Monthly Review Press, 1949

J Tabora, *The Future in the Writings of Karl Marx*, Frankfurt (Germany), Peter Lana 1983

KJ Tarbuck, ed, *'The Accumulation of Capital: An Anti-critique' by Rosa Luxemburg and 'Imperialism and the Accumulation of capital' by Nikolai I Bukharin*, New York (USA), Monthly Review Press, 1972

JME Taggart, *A Commentary on Hegel's Logic*, Cambridge, Cambridge University Press, 1910

JME Taggart, *Studies in Hegelian Dialectic*, Cambridge, Cambridge University Press, 1922

RH Tawney, *Equality*, London, George Allen and Unwin, 1952

C Taylor, *Hegel*, Cambridge, Cambridge University Press, 1975

C Taylor, 'The Opening Arguments of the *Phenomenology*', in MacIntyre, ed, *Hegel*, ch 6

NE Terleckyj, ed, *Household Production and Consumption*, New York (USA), National Bureau of Economic Research, 1976

G Therborn, *Science, Class and Society*, London, Verso, 1980

EP Thompson, *The Making of the English Working Class*, Harmondsworth, Penguin, ch 1968

EP Thompson, 'The Poverty of Theory', in *idem, The Poverty of Theory and Other Essays*, pp 193-397

EP Thompson, *The Poverty of Theory and Other Essays*, London, Merlin, 1978

EP Thompson, 'Time, Work Discipline and Industrial Capitalism' (1967) no 38 *Past and Present*, pp 56-97

D Thomson, ed, *Political Ideas*, Harmondsworth, Penquin, 1969

N Thulstrup, *Kierkegaard's Relation to Hegel*, Princeton (USA), Princeton University Press, 1980

S Timpanaro, *On Materialism*, London, Verso, 1980

S Timpanaro, 'The Pessimistic Materialism of Giacomo Leopardi' (1979) no 116 *New Left Review*, pp 29-50

A Touraine, *The Post-industrial Society*, London, Wildwood House, 1974

P Townsend, *Poverty in the United Kingdom*, Harmondsworth, Penguin, 1979

A Trendlenburg, *Logische Untersitchlingen*, Hildesheim (Germany), Reprografischer Nachdruck, 1964

R Triga, *Reality at Risk*, 2nd edn, London, Harvester Wheatsheaf, 1989

M Tugan-Baranowsky, *Studien zur Theorie und Geschichte der Handelkrisen in England*, Jena (Germany), G Fischer, 1901

ARJ Turgot, *On Progress, Sociology and Economics*, Cambridge, Cambridge University Press, 1973

ARJ Turgot, 'On Universal History', in *idem, On Progress, Sociology and Economics*, pp 61-118

H Uchida, *Marx's 'Grundrisse' and Hegel's 'Logic'*, London, Routledge, 1988

RM Unger, *Law in Modern Society*, New York (USA), Free Press, 1976

RM Unger, *Social Theory: Its Situation and Its Task*, Cambridge, Cambridge University Press, 1987

United States Industrial Commission, *Preliminary Report on Trusts and Industrial Combinations*, Washington DC (USA), Government Printing Office, 1900

V Venables, *Human Nature: The Marxian View*, New York (USA), Harper and Row, 1975

DP Verene, *Hegel's Recollection*, Albany (USA), State University of New York Press, 1985

F Vicarelli, *Keynes: The Instability of Capitalism*, London, Macmillan, 1984

G Vico, *The New Science*, Ithaca (USA), Cornell University Press, 1984

PH Vigor, 'Marx and Modern Capitalism', in Thompson, ed, *Political Ideas*, ch 13

P Wachtel, *The Poverty of affluence*, New York. (USA), Free Press, 1983

L Walras, *Elements of Pure Economics*, Homewood (USA), RD Irwin, 1954

P Walton and A Gamble, *From Alienation to Surplus Value*, London, Sheed and Ward, 1976

M Walzer, *Spheres of Justice*, Oxford, Basil Blackwell, 1983

EE Ward, 'Marx and Keynes' *General Theory*' (1939) vol 15 *Economic Record*, pp 152-67

JWN Watkins, 'The Alleged Inadequacy of Methodoloaical Individualism' (1958) vol 55 *Journal of Philosophy*, pp 390-5

JWN Watkins, 'Historical Explanation in the Social Sciences', in O'Neill, ed, *Modes of Individualism and Collectivism*, pp 166-78

JWN Watkins, 'Ideal Types and Historical Explanation', in O'Neill, ed, *Modes of Individualism and Collectivism*, pp 143-65

JWN Watkins, 'Methodoloaical Individualism: A Reply', in O'Neill, ed, *Modes of Individualism and Collectivism*, pp 179-84

JWN Watkins, 'The Principle of Methodolocical Individualism' (1952) vol 3 *British Journal for the Philosophy of Science*, pp 186-9

JWN Watkins, 'Third Reply to Mr Goldstein' (1959) vol 10 *British Journal for the Philosophy of Science*, pp 242-4

S Webb, *Socialism in England*, Aldershot, Gower, 1987

M Weber, *Economy and Society*, London, University of California Press, 1978

M Weber, *General Economic History*, New Brunswick (USA), Transaction Books, 1981

FG Weiss, 'Cartesian Doubt and Hegelian Negation', in O'Malley *et al*, eds, *Hegel and the History of Philosophy*, pp 83-94

FG Weiss, ed, *Beyond Epistemology*, The Hague (Netherlands), Martinus Nijhof, 1974

TE Weisskopf, 'Marxian Crisis Theory and the Rate of Profit in the Postwar US Economy' (1979) vol 3 *Cambridge Journal of Economics* pp 341-78

DA Wells, *Recent Economic Changes*, New York (USA), Appleton, 1889

JH Westergaard and H Resler, *Class in a Capitalist Society,* Harmondsworth, Penguin, 1975

KR Westphal, Hegel's *Epistemological Realism,* London, Kluwer, 1989

M Westphal, 'Hegel's Theory of Religious Knowledge', in Weiss, ed, *Beyond Epistemology,* pp 30-57

M Westphal, *History and Truth in Hegel's 'Phenomenology',* New Jersey (USA), Humanities Press, 1979

M Westphal, ed, *Method and Speculation in Hegel's 'Phenomenology',* New Jersey (USA), Humanities Press, 1982

PH Wicksteed, '*Das Kapital:* A Criticism', in *idem, The Common Sense of Political Economy,* vol 2, pp 705-24

PH Wicksteed, *The Common Sense of Political Economy,* London, Routledge and Kegan Paul, 1933

H Williams, *Hegel, Heraclitus and Mary's Dialectic,* London, Harvester Wheatsheaf, 1989

JB Williams, *The Theory of investment Value,* Cambridge (USA), Harvard University Press, 1938

R Williams, *Problems in Materialism and Culture,* London, Verso, 1980

R Williams, 'Problems of Materialism', in *idem, Problems in Materialism and Culture,* pp 103-22

OE Williamson, *Corporate Control and Business Behaviour,* Englewood Cliffs, New Jersey, Prentice Hall, 1970

P Willis, *Learning to Labour,* Farnborough, Saxon House, 1977

WF Willoughby, 'The Concentration of Industry in the United States' (1898) vol 7 *Yale Review,* pp 72-94

J Wilmshurst, *The Fundamentals of advertising,* London, Heinemann, 1985

HT Wilson, *Marx's Critical Dialectical Procedure,* London, Routledge, 1991

KP Winkler, *Berkeley,* Oxford, Clarendon Press, 1989

D Winter, 'Market Socialism and the Reform of the Capitalist Economy', in Le Grand and Estin, eds, *Market Socialism,* ch 6

J Wintle, *Makers of nineteenth Century Culture,* London, Routledge and Kegan Paul, 1982

World Bank, *World Development Report 1991,* Oxford, Oxford University Press, 1991

C Wright Mills, *The Power Elite,* New York (USA), Oxford University Press, 1956

CD Wright, *Industrial Depressions (First Annual Report of the US Commissioner for Labour),* Washington DC (USA), Government Printing Office, 1886

CD Wright, 'The Relation of Production To Productive Capacity' (1897-8) vol 24 *The Forum,* pp 290-302, 660-75

Xue Muqiao, *China's Socialist Economy,* Beijing (PRC), Foreign Languages Press, 1981

D Yaffe, 'The Marxian Theory of Crisis, Capital and the State' (1973) vol 2 *Economy and Society,* pp 186-232

J Zelený, *The Method of Marx,* Oxford, Basil Blackwell, 1980

R Zimmerman, 'Hegel's "Inverted World"' (1982) vol 13 *The Philosophical Forum* pp 342-70

Name Index

Subject Index